THE
WORLD
OF
GEORGE
JEAN
NATHAN

The World of George Jean Nathan
© 1918,1921,1922,1923,1925,1926,1927,1928,1929,1930,1931,1932, 1935,1940,1941,1942,1943,1944,1946,1947,1948,1949,1950,1951,1952, 1998 by the Estate of George Jean Nathan

ISBN 1-55783-313-3

Library of Congress Cataloging-in-Publication Data

Nathan, George Jean, 1882-1958.
    The world of George Jean Nathan : selected essays and reviews / edited by Charles Angoff ; epilogue by Patricia Angelin.
        p.   cm.
        ISBN 1-55783-313-3   (pbk.)
        I. Angoff, Charles, 1902-   II. Angelin, Patricia, 1954-
    III. Title.
    PS3527.A72A6   1998
    814'.52--dc21   97-28486
                                                                        CIP
British Cataloging-in-Publication Data
A catalogue record of this book is available from the British Library

APPLAUSE BOOKS

211 West 71st Street
New York, NY 10023
Phone (212) 496-7511
Fax: (212) 721-2856

A&C BLACK

Howard Road, Eaton Soccon
Huntingdon, Cambs PE19 3EZ
Phone 0171-242 0946
Fax 0171-831 8478

Distributed in the UK and the European Union by A&C Black

First Applause Printing, 1998

THE WORLD OF GEORGE JEAN NATHAN:

Essays, Reviews, & Commentary

**Edited by
Charles S. Angoff**

**Epilogue by
Patricia Angelin**

APPLAUSE
NEW YORK • LONDON

Sam Friedman

❀ v ❀

PREFACE

THIS anthology, I believe, represents George Jean Nathan in all the various facets of his long writing career. Too many people consider him merely a dramatic critic. He has written on marriage, politics, doctors, metropolitan life, the ballet, love, alcohol—on virtually every major aspect of contemporary life—and he has had something shrewd or amusing to say about them. Indeed, nearly half of his books have nothing to do with the drama, and those which do deal with the drama contain much that has little or no relationship to it.

Most of the present volume is culled from works now out of print. Several of them, though published many years ago, hold up so well that I hope they will be republished. I have especially in mind *The Critic and the Drama,* which first appeared in 1922, *The World in Falseface,* which was published the following year, and *The Autobiography of an Attitude,* which came out two years after that. Nathan's dramatic principles are in *The Critic and the Drama;* he has not stated them so well, with such meticulous logic, and in such detail in any other single book. The other two books introduced a relatively new and stimulating type of essay-writing into America. There is one original piece in this volume, "On Monthly Magazines." It is Nathan's only published statement on the theory and practice of journalism.

In my Introduction I make no effort at any formal evaluation of Nathan's critical ideas or of his basic attitudes toward life; this is hardly the place for it. I only attempt to summarize these ideas and attitudes, and to offer a few sidelights upon his personality.

The year 1952 marks Nathan's seventieth birthday. In some European countries there is a custom, when an important man of letters reaches this age, for other writers, and even for representatives of the government, to commemorate the event in a proper manner. In the United States that is not generally done. I hope that this volume will serve as a sort of commemoration. George Jean Nathan has earned it.

CONTENTS

INTRODUCTION

GEORGE JEAN NATHAN cannot properly be fitted into any critical or philosophical school. On occasion he practices the critical impressionism of Huneker, but he can also be profoundly dialectical, as can readily be seen by examining *The Critic and the Drama,* first published thirty years ago and still one of the most searching works of modern dramatic criticism in English. He has often donned the jester's cap with deliberate intent to bring forth smiles, laughter, and howls, and thus has led the superficial to put him down as little more than a critical vaudevillian, but he has also revealed so thorough a knowledge of dramatic and general cultural affairs that it has won the admiration of the most learned academicians. He has publicly acknowledged himself a hedonist, with personal pleasure as his only guiding principle, yet the day-to-day program of his life makes a mockery of his hedonistic philosophy; in point of fact, few writers work so hard and so conscientiously and with such iron self-discipline as he does. He claims to be indifferent to the generally accepted moral code, yet he lives by a very strict code himself, and that code is really not so different from the generally accepted one as he thinks. He has said some unfriendly things about America and Americans, but deep down in his soul he knows that he would be unhappy in any other country.

Nathan is in a class by himself. He is an American plus. Perhaps the late Ernest Boyd came closest to the truth about him when he said that Nathan was the most European American he had met here. He is Indiana (his birthplace) and Cornell (his college) and Philadelphia (long his mother's residence) and New York (his home for nearly fifty years),[1] but he is also the Vienna woods and Paris and London and Berlin.

---

[1] Nathan's first critical work appeared in the New York *Herald* in 1906.

II

Nathan's influence on the American theatre during the past thirty years has been enormous. He, more than any other critic, was responsible for the emergence of the O'Neill drama, which first brought American dramaturgy to serious world attention. He also did much to bring the better European drama to this country. Bahr, Molnár, the Quinteros, Echegaray, Sierra, Pirandello, Lennox Robinson, Porto-Riche, Sacha Guitry, the Čapeks, Georg Kaiser, and a score of others owe whatever hearing they have had among us largely to Nathan. More recently, he has labored heroically in behalf of Sean O'Casey, of whom he has written with profound understanding.

Nathan's theory of the drama is not something he has created *in vacuo*. It flows naturally from his theory of art, and this, in turn, flows naturally from his basic attitude toward life. He has put it in a nutshell thus: "Life, to me, is artificial; all my criticism of the drama is based on the theory that drama is artificial life. There isn't so very much difference, in my way of looking at things, between life as it factually is and life as it is shown in the theatre." To Nathan, then, the world is a theatre, and the two are subject to the same rules of criticism.

What relationship has art to "truth"? Nathan replies thus: "Art is the haven wherein the disillusioned may find illusion. Truth is no part of it. Nor is the mission of art simple beauty, as the textbooks tell us. The mission of art is the magnification of simple beauty to proportions as heroic as to be almost overpowering. Art is a gross exaggeration of natural beauty: there never was a woman so beautiful as the Venus di Milo, or a man so beautiful as the Apollo Belvedere of the Vatican, or a sky so beautiful as Monet's, or human speech so beautiful as Shakespeare's, or the song of a nightingale so beautiful as Ludwig van Beethoven's." Art, basically, is not logical. "Great art," says Nathan, "is as irrational as great music. It is mad with its own loveliness."

What is the nature of drama as an art? It is "dancing literature; a hybrid art," says Nathan. Thus it is—and has to be—often an inferior art. "Art is an evocation of beautiful emotions; art is art in the degree that it succeeds in the evocation;

drama succeeds in an inferior degree. Whatever emotion drama may succeed brilliantly in evoking, another art succeeds in evoking more brilliantly." Literature, music, even painting and sculpture are greater arts than drama. Yet great drama has a garden—and not so small a one—that it alone can properly cultivate, and that garden has not seldom given forth a beauty unsurpassed by that of any other garden. "The drama is an art with a feather in its cap and an ironic smile upon its lips, sauntering impudently over forbidden lawns and through closed lanes into the hearts of those of us children of the world who have never grown up. Beside literature, it is the Mother Goose of the arts; a gorgeous and empurpled Mother Goose for the fireside of impressible and romantic youth that, looking upward, leans ever hushed and expectant at the knee of life. It is a fairy tale told realistically, a true story told as romance. It is the lullaby of disillusion, the chimes without the cathedral, the fears and hopes, and dreams and passions of those who cannot fully fear and hope and dream and flame themselves."

Art and happiness are not inevitably related. Says Nathan: "Great drama is the rainbow born when the sun of reflection and understanding smiles anew upon an intelligence and emotion which that drama has respectively shot with gleams of brilliant lighting and drenched with the rain of brilliant tears. Great drama, like great men and great women, is always just a little sad. Only idiots may be completely happy. Reflection, sympathy, wisdom, gallant gentleness, experience—the chords upon which great drama is played—these are wistful chords." The aim of great drama? It is "not to make men happy with themselves as they are, but with themselves as they might, yet alas cannot, be."

Nathan, as has been said, does not subscribe to any particular theory of criticism. He believes that "there are as many sound and apt species of criticism as there are works to be criticized." The critic and the artist are, in a sense, collaborators. "Art is a partnership between the artist and the artist-critic. The former creates; the latter re-creates. Without criticism, art would of course still be art, and so with its windows walled in and with its lights extinguished would the Louvre still be the Louvre. Criticism is the windows and the chandeliers of art; it illuminates the enveloping darkness in which art might otherwise rest only vaguely discernible, and perhaps altogether unseen."

Or, to put it differently, "As art is a process of magnification, so criticism is a process of reduction. Its purpose is the reducing of the magnifications of art to the basic classic and aesthetic principles, and the subsequent announcement thereof in terms proportional to the artist's interplay of fundamental skill and overtopping imagination."

Drama, says Nathan, "is a two-souled art: half divine, half clownish. Shakespeare is the greatest dramatist who ever lived because he alone, of all dramatists, most accurately sensed the mongrel nature of his art. Criticism of drama, it follows, is similarly a two-souled art: half sober, half mad. Drama is a deliberate intoxicant; dramatic criticism, aromatic spirits of ammonia; the re-creation is never perfect; there is always a trace of tipsiness left. Even the best dramatic criticism is always just a little dramatic. It indulges, a trifle, in acting. It can never be as impersonal, however much certain of its practitioners may try, as criticism of painting or of sculpture or of literature. This is why the best criticism of the theatre must inevitably be personal criticism. The theatre is itself distinctly personal; its address is directly personal. It holds the mirror, not up to nature, but to the spectator's individual idea of nature."

Nathan maintains that there is no such thing as objective criticism. "Criticism is personal, or it is nothing. Talk to me of impersonal criticism, and I'll talk to you of impersonal sitz-bathing. Impersonal criticism is the dodge of the critic without personality. Some men marry their brother's widow; some earn a livelihood imitating George M. Cohan; some write impersonal criticism."

Nathan's own criticism is most highly personal. It is thoroughly honest in that it is a perfect reflection of his personality. Perhaps the only one at all like him was George Bernard Shaw when he wrote musical and dramatic criticism. But Shaw himself, after he left the critical arena, hailed Nathan as "Intelligent Playgoer Number One." Gordon Craig considered

Nathan even greater than Shaw. He said: "It would be a mistake to say that Mr. Nathan is as clever as Bernard Shaw . . .
as a critic he is twice as clever. . . . To say that Mr. Nathan
possesses a clearness of vision, a breadth of horizon and vigor
of ideas seldom found in present-day dramatic criticism would
be to miss the target. . . . Change the word 'seldom' to 'never'
and you hit the bull's eye. . . . Add to this that Nathan is an
artist and let us all sleep the better for the fact."

Like all good critics, Nathan can be read for himself, with
little or no regard for the work or the writer he is writing
about. His critical work has its own reason for being. Nathan
has especially endeared himself to a host of readers by his
utter lack of respectability, his persistent and wholly unmeas-
ured childlike delight in saying precisely what is in his mind.

Nathan's evangelical labors in behalf of O'Neill are now
historic. It is difficult to imagine what would have become of
O'Neill if Nathan had not taken him in hand, so to speak, at
the very beginning. He blew the trumpets for him season after
season, badgered the Broadway producers to do him, shamed
the Theatre Guild into sponsoring him, and then watched the
momentum of all this tremendous effort win for O'Neill the
Pulitzer Prize and, eventually, the Nobel Prize. While Nathan
may have exaggerated O'Neill's claims to greatness, he has
earned the enduring gratitude of the American people for
tirelessly championing him. It was Nathan more than anybody
else who made America realize what a treasure it had in the
author of *The Moon of the Caribees, Bound East for Cardiff,
Desire under the Elms,* and *Anna Christie.*

Nathan has not often been guilty of what he calls "bloomers"
of blindness or overenthusiasm. It is truly remarkable how well
his judgments, by and large, appear to hold up. Probably no
other critic has been "right" more often than he has. His ability
to give the long-view judgment seems to be almost fabulous.
He hailed good works by Maxwell Anderson, S. N. Behrman,
George Kelly, and Vincent Lawrence, among others, immediately, and for reasons that carry conviction many years later.
And he was equally quick to damn feeble works by the same
authors, and for reasons that also carry conviction to this day.

As the drama, like every other art form, is filled with a far

larger number of inferior than superior claims to serious attention, Nathan has found it necessary very often to be severe in
his criticism. Who can deny the truth of Nathan's oft-repeated
assertion that "dramatic art in America for the greater part
has become a playwriting business, and its practitioners are
largely racketeers with a dramatic sales talk, devoid of anything remotely resembling literary taste, literary ability, and
literary education. Most of them read and act like pulp writers
crossed with telegraph key-men."

One of Nathan's pet dislikes is Noel Coward, who, he has
said, "has nothing to sell but his own vast personal boredom."
What Nathan did to Coward's enormously successful, both
commercially and critically, *Design for Living* will probably
long be a model of critical vituperation. He branded it "a
pansy paraphrase of *Candida,* theatrically sensationalized with
'daring,' gay allusions to hermaphrodites, 'gipsy queens,' men
dressed as women, etc., and with various due references to
'predatory feminine carcases' and to women as bitches." The
celebrated Coward humor? "This vaudeville humor Mr. Coward cleverly brings the less humorously penetrating to accept
as wit by removing its baggy pants and red undershirt and
dressing it up in drawing-room style. But it remains vaudeville
humor just the same."

Another pet dislike of Nathan's is Clifford Odets, all of
whose works (with the exception of *Awake and Sing*) impress
him as little better than merchandise. The opinion he wrote
of Odets' *The Country Girl* may well be taken, in substance,
to represent Nathan's general opinion of Odets' work:

"As the stage director of his own play he again betrays his
conviction that prolonged pauses between speeches will persuade an audience that not only is the dramatic more dramatic
than it essentially is but that the pauses will lend an import to
lines that haven't any and, in addition, will give auditors the
impression that the characters, whom he has not supplied with
any slightest evidence of the fact, are doing a lot of deep
meditating and thinking. . . . He is also fond of another trick,
which seems equally to throw many of his reviewers off the
scent, and that is to gloss over explosions of speech and behavior, which are plainly recognizable as contrived solely for

momentary melodramatic effect, with immediately subsequent apologies for them by the characters involved. His dialogue . . . is furthermore in greater part merely sharp and biting in its directed delivery. He uses his characters as cuspidors at which they in turn spit out their lines. The lines are terse and abrupt and hence have the superficial air of inner bite, but their content is toothless. . . . He is still fetched by the 'strong' episode out of a score of past, dead plays in which a man works himself into a spasm of vituperation, slaps a woman, thrice cries out 'I hate you!' and then suddenly seizes her in his arms, passionately kisses her, and breaks down into a gentle 'I love you.' . . . And he . . . invites us to believe that neuroticism and talent are one and indistinguishable. He writes, in brief, not with cool ink but with ethyl alcohol, out of a papier-mâché prop bottle. He is theatrical not in the sense of true theatre but in the sense of falsified stage."

Another dramatist whom Nathan cannot stomach is T. S. Eliot. *The Cocktail Party* was hailed as a masterpiece of drama, philosophy, and verse by most American and British critics. To Nathan it was, "plainly, bosh sprinkled with mystic cologne," and so "excessively windy" that "it might have profited Eliot if he had heard Joe E. Lewis' song, *Sam, You Made the Pants too Long*." But what troubled Nathan most was Eliot's message: "Eliot's religious philosophy, insofar as one can penetrate its opium smoke, here suggests that of a sophomore Methodist boning up for examinations in Catholicism, and his sexual philosophy is no less that of a man whose dalliance with women seems to have been confined to hand-holding in an ivory tower."

III

One of the pleasures of the theatre, to Nathan, is that "it is one of the best subjects in the world from which to fashion a variegated assortment of predicates. . . . [It] offers to the man who writes about it a hundred convenient opportunities to air his views *con sordini* on nearly everything under the sun."

But before discussing this aspect of Nathan's career, some

remarks about his contribution to journalism. The name of Mencken has loomed so large in the world of quality journalism, and rightly so, that that of Nathan, his editorial colleague for nearly twenty years, has been partly overlooked. Nathan's contribution was also significant. It was Nathan who chiefly engineered most of the deals with which the names of the two of them were associated in the first two decades of the century. Nathan invited Mencken to be his co-editor on the *Smart Set*. This magazine was Nathan's, as the *American Mercury* was Mencken's. As first reader on the *Smart Set*, Nathan "discovered" James Joyce's *Dubliners* for America, and he also selected Somerset Maugham's short story "Miss Thompson," which he saw as wonderful play material—though Maugham himself ridiculed the idea. This is the story that eventually became the play *Rain*. Mencken, of course, contributed enormously to the magic of the *Smart Set*, but the effervescent quality of the magazine, the magnificent abandon, and the Bohemianism (in the best sense) were, it seems, chiefly Nathan's.

When Mencken began to introduce politics into the *Smart Set*, Nathan became alarmed. He had no interest in politics himself, but he also felt that the *Smart Set* was no place for it. Mencken did not agree, and continued to pour in political comment. The disagreement became a rift, and the rift became far more pronounced on the *American Mercury*. As Mencken's interest in politics grew, he wanted more and more to turn the *Mercury* into a political organ. There was a battle between the two editors when Nathan brought in O'Neill's *All God's Chillun Got Wings*. Nathan looked upon this play as an editorial gift from heaven, but Mencken was against printing it altogether on the ground that it did not belong in the *Mercury*. The play was published, but it only highlighted the sharpening divergence between the two. Not long afterward, because of this fundamental difference of opinion, the two men parted forever as editorial collaborators.

Nathan, who had almost never worked on newspapers in any capacity save as a critic, was perhaps more appreciative of the true function of magazines than was Mencken, who had been associated with the Baltimore *Sun* all his adult life and hence was inclined, on occasion, to think of magazines in terms of newspapers.

IV

Nathan has written at great length about the man-woman relationship, in all its forms. "What a man looks for in a woman," says Nathan, "is something, I daresay, like a good piano minus the loud pedal. What he looks for is tone, modulation, essential precision, music that is well composed, soft and lovely." The woman of real life, he feels impelled to say, is nothing but a doll, a toy. "Woman is and always has been primarily a plaything . . . in her heart of hearts she knows the truth of it." She is happy only when she is treated as a plaything and acts like one. In this respect, "all women are, at bottom, much the same." Marriage does not in any way change a woman's desire to be treated as a plaything, to be a beautiful doll. "The man who is married to a woman who is not a plaything is married to a woman who may venerate him and be loyal to him but who doesn't really love him." Nathan cannot understand any man who seeks any serious form of intellectual companionship in a woman, because he finds no evidence that women have real intelligence. They have only "emotional intelligence."

The women Nathan likes most are those "who believe the words in popular songs." The illusory words add a momentary richness to the illusion of the women, and hence make life a trifle pleasanter, which is about all that women of real life have to offer. He sees only misery and futility in the whole modern movement for the "emancipation of women." He points out that woman suffrage has not in the slightest improved politics, since women in love always vote the same way their husbands do, and women not in love have no opinions that merit serious consideration. Woman suffrage, according to him, has only nourished the bad taste in those women born with bad taste, and turned most border-line women, as regards manners, into second-rate men, and in general lowered the position of women as a whole in society. "Good God," he has exclaimed, "isn't it better for a woman to be kissed than

for her to win a vote of confidence from what is euphemistically called the electorate?" Women get all their ideas from
men, he says. They originate nothing. They merely overhear
men, and echo what they hear. Women never echo what other
women say. Instinctively they know better. It is a fact—and
honest women, adds Nathan, do not deny it—that "the best
woman is the inferior of the second-best man."

Nathan's attitude toward love is a compound of youthful
cynicism and impatient despair. He is all for it, so to speak,
but he never forgets that it's a snare and a delusion, as lovely as
the rainbow and no more to be relied upon. In his thirties
Nathan's heart leaped at the sight of a pretty girl, and he sang
tender songs to her as he saw her pass him in the boulevards
of the world, especially in Paris and Berlin. His chapters on
both cities in *Europe after 8:15,* which he wrote in collaboration with H. L. Mencken and Willard Huntington Wright
("S. S. Van Dine"), contain some of his most romantic writing.
He was still in love with girlhood and womanhood a decade
and more later, when he was obsessed with this or that feminine vision. Yet even then one could hear a faint oboe note in
the background of his singing—a consciousness of the vanity
and impermanence and illusion of it all.

In the end, Nathan says, love is a trivial thing. Men do not
fall in love with women. They fall in love with hair-dos, lisps,
perfumes, gaits, smiles, teeth, contours of necks and bosoms,
fit of girdles as imagined through a dress, architecture of
noses, tones of voice, little moles on the face, telephone voices,
silences (wrongly interpreted as charity or politeness or knowledge), whiteness of skin (wrongly interpreted as meticulous
cleanliness), brownness of skin (wrongly interpreted as robust health), the manner of sipping a cocktail. Never with
women, says Nathan, because there is so little about them to
be loved (in which they are unlike men), and because a woman's personality is no more than the amalgam of her hair-do,
tone of voice, mole on the neck, gait, and so on. Love, then, "is
the democrat of the emotions," as "hatred is the aristocrat." As
a matter of fact, almost any woman can instill love in some man
or other, if she puts on the necessary allure—which comes not
from within her, but from a drugstore, a couturier, and other

such merchants in charm. "Love demands infinitely less than
friendship." According to Nathan, men—including some of the
very greatest, God help them—marry women for qualities they
would consider totally insufficient in hiring a butler or a chauffeur or a bank guard.

The tragedy for men, Nathan points out, is that what they
seek in love is totally different from what women seek. Generally men seek comfort, the right to exclusive adoration, or
some sort of spiritual Nirvana. Women, especially those who
still have not felt the frost of advancing years, have other
ideas. "What a young girl seeks in love is a species of discomfort—and this she may find, readily enough, in an alliance with
a man seeking comfort alone. A love that is comfortable is unknown to youth; when love becomes comfortable it is, to
youth, no longer love. . . . Love is the emotion that a woman
feels always for a poodle dog and sometimes for a man."

Love, for a man, perhaps even more than for a woman, is
a variable thing. The type of woman one loves at thirty, says
Nathan, is certainly different from the type of woman one
loves at forty or fifty. Love is about as eternal as a treaty of
perpetual peace signed between two nations. "It is possible a
man may love only one woman in his life. So, for that matter,
is it equally possible that a man get through life with only one
pair of trousers." Women love most intensely in the period before the end of the twenties. Thereafter, most of the time, they
give themselves to whatever man will have them and who is at
all possible. When a woman has begun to add up the advantages and disadvantages of marrying this or that man, passion
has gone out of the way. "When a woman past thirty embraces
the man she loves, she embraces all the dreams that she has
dreamt and lost irrevocably."

Nathan denies that there is any mystery about the unstable
character of marriage. The significant point is not that there
are so many divorces, but that there aren't many more. There
is more misery among married folk than is publicly known.
Marriage and unhappiness become synonymous very quickly.
Besides, the basic impulse behind marriage is wrong. "Marriage is based on the theory that when a man discovers a
particular brand of beer exactly to his taste he should at once

throw up his job and go to work in the brewery." Further, to expect marriage to bring one more happiness than one had before is downright silly, says Nathan. There is nothing more magical about marriage than about ham sandwiches or fine wine. "The great majority of married folk fail to achieve enduring happiness for the same profound reason that the great majority of bachelors and spinsters fail to achieve enduring happiness. Happiness is merely an incident in life, not life itself. To ask of marriage that it perpetuate happiness is therefore to ask of the family doctor that he cure one's cold in the head so magnificently that one will never have a cold in the head again."

V

Nathan's work bristles with epigrams and paradoxes. In this respect he might be called, up to a point, the American Oscar Wilde. But the writer whose general outlook is most like Nathan's is Somerset Maugham. Both have made almost a personal religion of their utter indifference to mankind. Both boast of their concern only for themselves, of their dominating interest in the shimmer and dazzle of living, of their frankly cruel disregard for the miseries that perennially afflict the vast, silent majority of the two and a half billion men and women upon the earth. "What interests me in life," says Nathan, "is the surface of life: life's music and color, its charm and ease, its humor and its loveliness. The great problems of the world —social, political, economic, and theological—do not concern me in the slightest. . . . What concerns me alone is myself, and the interests of a few close friends. For all I care the rest of the world may go to hell at today's sunset." Nathan's motto is "Be Indifferent." He looks upon society as designed solely for the pleasure and comfort of the aristocratic minority. "Life, as I see it, is for the fortunate few—life with all its magic lanterns, and sudden, lovely tunes, and gay sadness."

Nathan admits that the life of the aristocratic minority is subject to the laws of despair and disillusionment. Indeed, this despair and this disillusionment form the only democracy Nathan believes in. The paradise of the late teens and twenties is a fool's paradise. "After thirty, the individual's pleasures fall into the pigeonholes of his set predilections. . . . He finds soon or late they are in themselves very much of a piece and that each is but a recurrent echo of its former self. And presently each quondam pleasure becomes a stereotyped thing, to be undertaken, at best, in the half-light of duty; and, furthermore, the indulgence in each of them becomes more and more irksome and peace-disturbing."

Not long ago I visited Nathan when he had a spell of illness. He has lived in the same hotel since 1906, when he began writing dramatic criticism, and in the very same apartment for the past twenty-eight years. It looks like an ancient and honorable and wonderful second-hand bookstore. Books and pictures are all over—piled high on chairs and on the floor. There are busts of Nathan himself serving as doorstops, there are plaques on the walls, some probably dating back to his fencing days at Cornell, others gifts from cultural and not-so-cultural organizations. There is a huge papier-mâché Indian head, standing on a table, close by a group of wineglasses that he must have got two or three decades ago. Hard by a window is a heavy and wonderfully large writing table, piled with papers and pens and pencilled notes. (Nathan writes all his things in longhand and then has the script typed by a professional typist.)

Not used to illness, Nathan felt talkative and I kept my silence most of the time. He talked about F. Scott Fitzgerald (why in his opinion *The Great Gatsby* was an inferior book), Sean O'Casey ("Did you notice the violinist in his eyes?"), television and particularly the current queens in the field ("They have voices like cash-registers or calliopes—and imagine the romantic appeal of a girl selling an automatic washing-machine!"), radio breakfast-programs ("The husbands should get annual Nobel Prizes for Christian kindness"), what veils do to dancing girls that tights can never do, the very sad state of quality periodical journalism in the United States and the reasons for this, the last letter he received from Bernard Shaw ("That really made me feel good!"), how he met a female author whom he discovered on the *Smart Set* years ago ("She

can't write any more, but she still has ink on her fingers, and
I wonder how it got there"), a practical joke with embarrassing results that he and Mencken had played on one of
their more gullible publishers some twenty years ago, why
freckle-faced girls should be taken more seriously than they
have been, how wonderful some of O'Casey's unproduced
plays are and how sad it is that New York producers have not
yet taken them up, the virtues of both vegetarianism and meat-
eating, the continuing inferiority of the works of Clifford
Odets, the last tragic days of Ernest Boyd ("Remember the
article he wrote for the *American Spectator* in which he
said that adultery is preferable to multiple matrimony?"), a
good nerve tonic, the ravages of neuralgia (which has troubled him for forty years), the prospects for the Yankees next
season (Nathan has just become a convert to the cause of this
American League club), the immeasurable superiority of the
writer's life to that of any other on the globe, the charm of
some of the early short stories of Edith Wharton and Willa
Cather, Somerset Maugham as a writer and as a man, Nathan's
and Mencken's difficulties in escaping the non-literary demands of the illiterate females who vainly yearned to appear
in the *Smart Set* ("With the most insistent ones we used to
make dates at certain trees in Central Park and never show
up"), James Boswell's strange combination of lechery and
piety, Roxy's degrading influence on American entertainment,
how to judge a girl's mind ("Ask her how she would get to the
Grand Central Station; if her answer is fifty per cent correct,
she is intelligent enough"), and several other subjects.

When I left him I felt refreshed. He has the true artist's
magnificent irrepressibility of spirit. He has added an engaging
liveliness to the American scene. He has been a definite force
in our cultural life. He will be remembered and he will be
read, I believe, for a long time.

CHARLES ANGOFF

THE WORLD

OF

GEORGE JEAN NATHAN

CONFESSIONAL

Myself

WHAT manner of organism am I? What are my fundamental habits of thought, my tastes, prejudices, predilections, eccentricities—in short, my pitch and tone? The topic does not at all interest me personally, since the attributes in question have been imbedded in me for too many years and, even were I to wish it, it is now too late for them to undergo any change. But it may possibly interest the customers of my critical performances, who, it seems to me, have a right to know the nature of the creature whose opinions, sometimes perhaps very peculiar, they have been buying, inner-sight unseen, for so unbelievable, if gratifying, a stretch of time.

I am, it may be confided at the outset, in many respects the average man—if I do not unduly flatter myself. What has periodically been written about me to the contrary, though sweet in intention, I do not believe. Though I may have had more experience in various directions than the average brother, it has not much profited or elevated me in any essential way and I remain, for better or worse, largely the original package. That is to say, while my personal philosophy and ideas, such as they are, may differ markedly from the communal norm, their mouthpiece is by habit and in practice at bottom a conventional member of human society. He respects, now and then against his cynical, better judgment, the time-honored and accepted precepts and, though he sometimes slips from grace, does his damnedest to live up to them. He hopes that by and large, whatever his pleasant, happy and contenting departures from what is generally approved, he nevertheless still is what the gods, in their more worldly and rational moments, describe as decent.

Though in no respect sentimentally inclined, your subject

does not subscribe to the theory, so popular with the adolescent Strindbergs, that any degree of sentiment is incompatible with a majestic brain and that the man who goes so far as even to allow that a field flower is a rather pretty thing or that a girl with a straight nose and soft hair merits a look is *ipso facto* one with a mind not to be trusted by simon-pure intellects.

Indignation is as foreign to my system as piety or self-satisfaction. That is, indignation toward others, though when the situation warrants, it would seem that my dander rises over stupidity, incompetence, and vainglory. What indignation there may be in my chemical composition otherwise is directed rather toward myself and is inspired by the consciousness that, despite certain gifts which I feel are in me, I am not a lot better than I factually am. I have, I think, improved in performance as the years have traveled on, but there is, I am fully aware, a heap of room left and, though people are occasionally kind enough to contradict me, I am not so chipper as I once was, for all some seeming external evidence to the contrary. I work as hard as ever I did, or at least I think I do, but I sometimes say to myself that, since I have already done what I consider to be my share, I am foolish to do so and not take life a little easier. But I don't listen to myself and grunt and groan and plod on nevertheless.

The reason, I daresay, is that, being a writer, I cannot, like Trigorin, help myself and, since there does not seem to be much chance in my lifetime of anyone instituting a Writers Anonymous, I despair of a cure. As Osbert Sitwell explains the agonizing malady, "An author can never take a holiday. It is impossible for him to become another sort of person; he must absorb and reflect and observe the whole time . . . Even while he is asleep, the writer's subconscious mind is always busily occupied in preparing various ideas to lay before him when he wakes." I shall not be so hypocritical as to say that it is a bore, but it is pretty close to one. The head buzzes with all kinds of what seem transiently to be ideas; a hundred tosses on the pillow eventually give birth to some word to replace the arid one which has been set down in the daylight chore; the old, unbeatable urge to say one's say on paper hastens the breakfast coffee. And to what end—aside from a momentary stimulation, an evanescent smugness—God alone knows.

Since, in the very nature of the critical profession, one is faced with bad work out of all proportion to good, it is not possible for the practitioner to erase from his reader's mind the impression that he is a chronic grumbler or, worse, one who seeks to lift himself to a bogus eminence by demolishing the performances of others. The impression is understandable, but there is no way to prevent it. That is, there is no way to prevent it save one were willing to indulge in equivoque, in false generosity, or in language tricked to make palatable unpalatable fact. I have never been able to persuade myself that contemptible work merits any such strain and courtesy, and as a consequence there are undoubtedly some, indeed perhaps many, who believe that I take a mean delight in what they choose to call destructive criticism.

Though, of course, it is easier, as every critic comes to learn, to write an interesting detractory review than an interesting favorable one, I would be only too happy to exert myself in the latter direction night after night were the occasions to justify it. But it need hardly be mentioned that the great majority of them unfortunately do no such thing, and detraction is consequently the only honest course left open. There is, however, a saving and salving personal reflection. If, after more than forty years in practice, such a wealth of detraction were not proved by time to have been sound, I would have lost all my readers long before this, and not only all my readers but all the many editors who in that protracted period have bought my opinions for good money. It is this thought that consoles me when frequently those opinions are taken icily to task by others.

I read now and then that I have offended this or that complainant by what he terms my air of infallibility. If ever I have given any such impression I assure you that it has been very far from intentional and must have been the result of a deplorable, slipshod manner of expression. Never for a moment have I ever regarded myself as infallible. I have in my day negotiated some of the handsomest bloomers on record, and in all probability will accomplish more of an even greater beauty. I have also, however, in that same period made some admirable guesses, and I am not loath to admit it. But, though I think that by this time I have learned my job about as well as ever I shall be able to learn it, I no more look upon myself as being always right than I look upon any other man in a like way. My average has not been so bad; in fact, it has been pretty good, if I say so myself; but there nevertheless are on the library shelves some thirty-five or more volumes in which my mistakes are embalmed for posterity.

I have mentioned the subject of my prejudices and predilections. I should like to be able to say that I am completely free from bias on both counts, but I fear that I cannot. I have an open mind, in a manner of speaking, but it has been open for so long now that some bugs have flown in through the doors and windows. Among these insects are, in the first category, a hostility toward the pretentiousness that invests the writings of men who mistake an excessive ambition for high competence; a prejudice against playwrights who seek to palliate their emotional immaturity with anonymous injections of the borrowed mature thought of others; a distaste for the kind of dramatic cynicism born of obviously limited experience; and an acute disrelish of popgun revolutionaries, dewy sentimentalists, one-cake-soapbox philosophers, commercial uplifters, and greasepaint mentalities in general.

But some butterflies have flown in also and in that category are a cordiality toward the daring young fellows who, whether successfully or not, try honestly to express the plays that are in them without regard for the scholastic injunctions of the standpatters; a warm friendliness toward skeptics of the accepted, popular points of view; an affection for men who do not subscribe to the theory that drama is not literature and who do subscribe to the beauty of language and the surge and burst of the poetic line; a hospitality toward the unstrained simplicity that so often is just around the corner from profundity and much nearer to it than the strained complexity which frequently passes in the drama for lofty thought; and a respect for any head that has in it, besides a brain, a little of the wayward music that colors and enlivens life.

There are, as everyone knows, no morals in art, but art and

hack work are two different things and I cannot get steamed up, like many of my colleagues, when censorship, albeit intrinsically imbecile, has at some piece of junk on the score of its alleged immorality. Suppression of such rubbish, whether on one ground or another, seems to me to be a desirable thing and, if there is no other way to get the business done than through its morals, I say go ahead, and with my blessing. The notion that if one gives an inch to censorship it will take a mile is not inevitably true, and those who believe it would do well to look up the records of the last Amercan theatrical century. I am constitutionally opposed to censorship *per se,* but I am not so silly as to believe that if it intermittently descends upon such guano as *Sex, Pleasure Man,* and the like it will in due and bumptious course seek also to outlaw *Oedipus Rex* and *Measure for Measure.* This is not to say that at times it has not gone too far and has made itself ridiculous, but in the whole history of our theatre's last one hundred years I can find no more than two plays out of many thousands which in any critical sense have suffered unjustly and, of the two, one was soon given a clean bill of health by the courts and reproduced. Nor in that same history can I find a single instance where, if one of the censored junkpots had not been interfered with, its continued life would in any degree have profited the stage. Foul claptrap belongs in the garbage can, and I cannot see that it matters who puts it there, whether it be censors, police, critics, or the theatre's customers themselves. The people who make it their profession to boil against any and all censorship on any and all occasions impress me as being more than merely obtuse. They lose the battle by sniping with bean-shooters.

What is hailed in the Broadway theatre as success frequently to my way of looking at things is contemptible failure. A successful play, it seems, is not necessarily one of quality but one, however shabby, that, like chewing gum, hot dogs and Harry Truman, is endorsed by a sufficiently large number of people, many of them of doubtful taste and mentality, to make it a winner. Thus, there is no distinction between a mere box-office success like *Kiss and Tell* and a box-office plus critical and artistic success like *Strange Interlude.* Successes like *Abie's Irish Rose, White Cargo,* and *Junior Miss* are lumped under the same label with successes like *Rain, The Green Pastures,* and *Victoria Regina.* Intrinsic worth does not figure in Broadway's calculations; it is only money that counts— money, money, money, the golden god of tin minds.

It is accordingly often that plays which Broadway sneers at as failures figure among the most reputable and respected plays in the theatre. It is a sorry critic, indeed, who would prefer, for example, a big Broadway success like *Edward, My Son* over a rank box-office failure like *A Highland Fling,* an acclaimed success like *John Loves Mary* over a quick failure like *A Sound of Hunting,* or what Broadway labels a smash hit, like *The Happy Time,* over what it nominates an immediate dud, like *My Heart's in the Highlands, The Beautiful People,* or *Outrageous Fortune.* It has been that way for many years now. The money losers are worthless drama in the Broadway estimate, the money makers are masterpieces. Yet over the years compare, among scores of others, such stark failures as Birmingham's *General John Regan,* Dukes' *The Man with a Load of Mischief,* O'Neill's *Marco Millions* and *The Fountain,* O'Casey's *The Plough and the Stars,* Porto-Riche's *L'Amoureuse,* and Johnston's *The Moon in the Yellow River* with such triumphant and blessed successes, such box-office record breakers, such Broadway endorsed jewels, as *Seventh Heaven, East Is West, Kiki, What a Life!, Room Service, Janie,* and *I Remember Mama.*

I must agree with Marcus Aurelius Antoninus. Said that stoic philosopher, reflecting on what so large a portion of mankind calls success: "Success, it stinks."

[From *The Theatre Book of the Year, 1949–1950,* Foreword.]

Self-Revelation

"A BEAST RISETH OUT OF THE SEA."—In the exposition of what I myself happen to believe, it is certainly not my purpose to argue or even to hint that this personal set of beliefs is either philosophically or emotionally admirable or that its adoption by anyone else is a consummation devoutly wished on my part. I suspect that what other men believe, though it be often objectionable to me, may stand them in quite as sound service as my own beliefs stand me, and that it may contribute equally to their self-esteem, happiness, bank accounts, worldly eminence, and wives' low opinion of them. A man's beliefs, after all, save he be a professional practitioner of letters and hence a racketeer of words, a self-blackmailer and a Judas unto himself, are and should be his private, personal property, as safe from vulgar public scrutiny as his underwear. There is something indelicate, even bounderish, in exposing one's most secret articles of faith, a fact appreciated by the relatively gentlemanly among the professional carpenters of letters mentioned, as may be witnessed by the obvious posturings, evasions and mendacities they indulge in when they engage, for hire, to contribute to the public prints. There is about the "beliefs" they expound on such occasions a considerable air of fraud; it is plain that, while they are ostensibly betraying their confidences, they are withholding much that is true of themselves and of their private philosophies, and much that, being true, would be altogether too embarrassing to set down in print. By way of subterfuge, they accordingly offer to the public a bold, forthright, cocksure and impudent front—but with their fingers carefully crossed behind their backs. If we may put any trust in the gossipy records, there never lived a bigger liar than Rousseau, and if I personally out of long association know anything of a number of writers who are in the habit of undressing their beliefs in public, you have my word for it that the ghost of Rousseau still walks.

While I do not desire to appear in the light of an exceptional truth-teller and while frankly confessing that I entertain certain beliefs that a delicacy inherited from an illegitimate great-uncle, together with a skepticism as to the police, forbids me indiscriminately to merchant, there are certain convictions, deeply imbued in me after forty-odd years on this earth, that seem to me legitimately communicable. The first of these is that, of all philosophies governing life and conduct, that sponsored by the Cyrenaic academy, somewhat qualified, is the only one that is eminently satisfactory, eminently workable and productive of any real happiness. In a hedonism that combines the forthrightly egoistic with a modest measure of the altruistic, that governs its pleasures partly by intellect and partly by emotion—depending upon the vagaries and humors of the occasion—and that foams effervescently in the wake of work seriously and painstakingly done, I believe above all other beliefs. To me, pleasure and my own personal happiness—only infrequently collaborating with that of others—are all I deem worth a hoot. It would make me out a much finer and nobler person, I duly appreciate, to say that the happiness and welfare of all mankind were close to my heart, that nothing gave me more soulful happiness than to make others happy and that I would gladly sacrifice every cent I have in the world, together with maybe a leg, to bring a little joy to the impoverished and impaired survivors of the late Afridi raids in India, but I have difficulty in being a hypocrite. As a matter of fact, the happiness and welfare of mankind are not my profession; I am perfectly willing to leave them to the care of the professional missionaries of one sort or another; I have all that I can do to look out for my own happiness and welfare. And so has any other man, unless he happens to be a multi-millionaire, a failure in life who seeks to conceal his failure from himself in devoting himself to worse failures than himself, a gourmand of publicity, or a devout server of God. I happen to be exactly none of these—though, so far as the second catalogue goes, I surely do not view myself as a stunning success—and I consequently regard myself as a sufficient problem without looking about me for other problems.

That I am selfish and to a very considerable degree possibly offensive is thus more or less regrettably obvious. All that I am able to offer in extenuation is that so are most other men if you dig down into them and, paying no attention to their altruistic pretensions, get at the hearts of them. In all my experience I have yet to find and know intimately a man worth his salt in any direction who did not think of himself first and foremost. He may drop a quarter into the hat of a beggar (when somebody is looking); he may have gracious manners; he may obey the punctilio on every occasion; he may be genial and liberal and hearty; he may buy the drinks when it comes his turn; he may be scrupulously polite, considerate, and superficially lovable. But under it all his first interest, his first consideration and his first admiration are reserved for himself. The man who thinks of others before he thinks of himself may become a Grand Master of the Elks, a Socialist of parts, or the star guest of honor at public banquets, but he will never become a great or successful artist, statesman, or even clergyman.

Happiness is the goal of every normal human being. As it is given to few men to die happy, the best that man can hope and strive and pray for is momentary happiness during life, repeated as frequently as the cards allow. Pleasure, whatever its species, is the drink in the desert. It is the beautiful, transient reward of travail and pain. There is no other reward, except for those still sufficiently aboriginal to believe in an hereafter. The ambrosia of the gods, the lovely angels, eternal blue skies and peace, the music of golden harps are too far off and dubious so far as my own metaphysic goes. I prefer to trust to the more realistic and visible Vouvray Perlier, pretty girls, Mediterranean coast, and symphony orchestras of the here and now.

What makes for pleasure and consequent happiness? Each man to his own poison. In my case, a life devoted, both professionally and in leisure hours, to literature, drama, criticism, music and the arts generally, with due and careful heed paid to a moderate but satisfying alcoholic diet, guaranteed by a constantly replenished wine cellar, to decently prepared foods, to the society of selfish and hence interesting comrades, to the amiable company of amiable women, and to the avoidance of any and everything that might disturb my annoying equanimity. The life of a writer has always seemed to me to be about as good a one as any low human being could hope for. His office is in his hat; his tools are in his pocket; his boss is himself; he is foot-loose, free, clockless, independent. He can say what he wants to, however inexpedient, injudicious and discommodious, and get paid handsomely for what other working men would promptly get sacked for. He can keep his mind alive and kicking with controversy and enjoy himself in putting his inferiors in their places. He can, with relatively little work and with easy hours—if he has any talent at all— earn a very satisfactory livelihood. He moves in a world not of trade but of ideas. He deals in words, for which he doesn't have to lay out a cent and hence takes no financial risk, instead of in commodities that have to be paid for first out of his own funds. He is rewarded for his fun, like most artists, where other men are rewarded more often only for their misery. Serious or gay, he is a playboy in a world that other men run for him with the sweat of their brows.

As a very humble and lowly member of the craft and as one who still has a very considerable distance to go before he may deserve the name of artist, I can yet appreciate the tremendous advantages over other men that a real artist enjoys. In the first place, he has contempt, that most valuable of human self-wrought and self-sustained gifts. In the second place, he has liberty, freedom and autonomy—more than any other man. In the third place, he can be himself at all times and in all places. He can work when he feels like working, loaf when he feels like loafing, keep superiorly aloof from politics and all other such scurvy diversions of the rabble. He is free always to choose his friends as he will, without the usual man's often necessary regard for their business connections and influence; he may be indiscreet without damage to his work; he can tell the world to go to hell and make the world like it. If any man stands a chance for happiness on this earth, it is the artist who has the choicest position at the post.

Although I myself, due doubtless to defective skill, have to work pretty hard, I do not believe in too hard work. The hardest workers are and properly should be the congenital clerks, bookkeepers, millhands, and suchlike pathetic incompetents and slaves. The superior man should be able and privileged to take life with relative ease. A life spent in constant labor is a life wasted, save a man be such a fool as to regard a fulsome obituary notice as ample reward. Show me a man who, as the phrase goes, works himself to death and I'll show you an unimaginative dolt. There is a lot of amusement in this world and a man should get his full share of it. There probably never lived but two men who gained importance and honorable celebrity in this selfsame world who did not take considerable time off in which to have some sport, and of the two exceptions one is suspect because of his peculiar taste for communion with birds, while the other finds at least part of his story still scouted by many millions of people. Alexander the Great, even in the midst of wars, had an eye for the more comely Theban maidens; the whoopee of Caesar and Marc is history; Shakespeare spent as much time with the bottle as with the pen; Frederick and later Bismarck obeyed that impulse on many an occasion; a number of the greatest composers led the lives of movie actors; even the great Warren Gamaliel is reputed to have devoted not all of his time to affairs of state. . . .

"Work," airily observed a character in a play of the late Haddon Chambers', "is for workmen." An Englishman, Chambers once remarked to me that he has written the line as an evangelical text for Americans. I believe about work as I believe about drink: it should be used in moderation.

I believe in a college training but not in a college education. The latter, I have learned from personal experience, is worth very little; the former, which imparts a knowledge of the value and uses of leisure, a somewhat superior ease and serenity, and a humorous view of indignation, whatever form the latter may take, is not without its advantages.

I believe in the state of bachelorhood, at the very least up to the age of fifty. Thereafter, a man may conceivably marry to his benefit, but certainly not before. The arguments in favor of earlier marriage, customarily advanced by the presumptively purer of the species, strike me as being peculiarly obscene and, where they are not obscene, hollow. The superior biological and hence inferentially superior amatory qualifications of the younger in years constitute one of the chief of these arguments. While fully conscious of the importance of sex in any contentful marital relationship, such a *plaidoyer* seems to me to be as illogical as it is indelicate, since it contends that two persons possibly ill-suited to each other in every other way—spiritually, intellectually, socially and economically—are to be recommended, endorsed and applauded as lifelong companions simply on the ground of their virtuosity in anatomical arithmetic. Another favorite contention is that a man should marry while he is still malleable, that is, before he becomes set in his habits—in other words, that the moulding of a man's character, his psyche and his future should be entrusted not to himself but to a woman. Up to the age of fifty, a man should be responsible to himself and to his work alone. A wife, however sympathetic, patient and charming, by very reason of her sympathy, patience and charm, would be a too pleasant and agreeable distraction. At fifty, a man has learned himself more or less completely, and has sounded out fully the possibilities and potentialities of his profession and his career. Then and only then should he consider matrimony. It is a rare marriage, negotiated at or after that age, that does not turn out prosperously and satisfactorily. The great majority of marriages that go on the rocks are those contracted in earlier years.

I am against all reforms and reformers. The world, as I see it, is sufficiently gay, beautiful and happy as it stands. It is defective only to those who are themselves defective, who lack the sagacity, imagination, humor and wit to squeeze out its rich and jocose juices and go swimming in them. With Norman Douglas I agree: "I am not the stuff of which reformers are made; rather than indulge in that variety of meddlesomeness I would sweep a crossing. Nine tenths of the reformers of humanity have been mischiefmakers or humbugs. I have no desire to be added to the list. A man who has reformed himself has contributed his full share towards the reformation of his neighbor."

While I do not care for money and own to the somewhat vainglorious boast of never having consciously written a line with any thought of its marketability in mind, I am neither poseur nor fool enough to affect an air of disdain of it. The man with money in his pocket not only enjoys a power that men without money do not; he is also in a position to do his work in the world more carefully, more independently, more truthfully and more successfully. The best artists living today, the men who are doing their finest work, are without exception men who have no need longer to worry about financial matters. They have looked out for that first. A destitute and miserable man may write a good book, or paint a good picture, or write a good piece of music, but the records hint that he seldom, in these days, contrives to do another.

It seems to me that the writers who are loudest in proclaiming their veneration of truth are most often simply vociferous admirers of their own pet fallacies. As for me, while given to an equal esteem of truth, I freely confess that I do not know what the truth, the final truth, about most things is and—like my colleagues alluded to—conceal my doubts and misgivings in self-persuading and, I hope, occasionally more publicly convincing convolutions of the English language, periodically enriched with more or less showy borrowings from French, German, Italian and Polack. As with most men, I believe most positively in my own ideas, right or wrong. These, to me, constitute the truth, whatever others may think of them. Once I believe a thing head and tail, no one can alter my conviction.

It also seems to me that the current fashionable American literary school of cynicism as to sentiment, love and romance is cheapjack, fraudulent and silly. The American, as I have on more than one occasion observed, being generically the most sentimental of men, is ashamed of his sentiment and, like a man with thinning hair who drops miscellaneous jokes at the expense of baldheads, seeks to conceal or at least to divert uncomfortable attention from the fact by deprecating it in others. The most cynical writers in America today are personally so many honeydew melons, happily and sweetly sentimental husbands and fathers. It is merely that, like uncertain and unconfident men ever, they offer their public protestations of hard-boiled manliness—in the American definition—in order to hide from their womenfolk, laughing up their sleeves, their irresolution, nervousness, weakness and innate childishness. Romantic love is the privilege of emperors, kings, soldiers and artists; it is the butt of democrats, traveling salesmen, magazine poets and the writers of American novels.

My code of life and conduct is simply this: work hard, play to the allowable limit, disregard equally the good or bad opinion of others, never do a friend a dirty trick, eat and drink what you feel like when you feel like, never grow indignant over anything, trust to tobacco for calm and serenity, bathe twice a day, modify the aesthetic philosophy of Croce but slightly with that of Santayana and achieve for one's self a pragmatic sufficiency in the beauty of the aesthetic surface of life, learn to play at least one musical instrument and then play it only in private, never allow one's self even a passing thought of death, never contradict anyone or seek to prove anything to anyone unless one gets paid for it in cold, hard coin, live the moment to the utmost of its possibilities, treat one's enemies with polite inconsideration, avoid persons who are chronically in need, and be satisfied with life always but never with one's self. An infinite belief in the possibilities of one's self with a co-incidental critical assessment and derogation of one's achieve-ments, self-respect combined with a measure of self-surgery, aristocracy of mind combined with democracy of heart, forth-rightness with modesty or at least with good manners, dignity with a quiet laugh, honor and honesty and decency: these are the greatest qualities that men can hope to attain. And as one man, my hope is to attain them.

I am against snobbery in all its lovely American forms. As a born American, I suppose that I am naturally and unpleas-antly infected with some of the bacteria, but I keep about me constantly a large and handy assortment of antitoxins. I am for all religions equally, as all impress me as being equally hollow. The variation is merely one either of external and superficial beauty or hideousness of spectacle. I believe that no man's life is finally complete and rounded—to quote an eminent Hungarian—without a wife, a child, a home, though I have not practiced what I preach and have neither wife nor child and live in that apologetic substitute for a home, a New York apartment. (It looks out on a building given over to shyster lawyers!) I believe, with Nietzsche, though I dislike the banality of dragging him forth on every occasion, that so long as you are praised, believe that you are not yet on your own course but on that of another. And also that it happens sometimes by an exception that a man only reaches the highest when he disclaims his ideal, for this ideal previously drove him onward too violently, so that in the middle of the track he regularly got out of breath and had to rest.

I respect J. Pierpont Morgan but not Rockefeller. Morgan is hard-fisted, hard-punching, ruthless, brave, forthrightly avaricious and lacking in all hypocrisy. Rockefeller, a moral coward, wraps himself in the seven veils of church and charity by way of concealing the true golden-yellow color of his psychical epidermis from the public eye. I admire Clemenceau for his courageous errors and disrelish Wilson for his cowardly exactitudes. I have little patriotism, for patriotism, as I see it, is often an arbitrary veneration of real estate above principles. I believe that one intelligent man is worth ten parcel of beautiful women, but I would rather spend an evening with the beautiful women. I believe that intelligent men should be taken on at lunch. I believe that whiskey and gin are bad for the system and that wine and beer are more beneficial to it than all the drugstore philtres in Christendom. I owe my glowing health to wines and beers, although I occasionally drink whiskey and gin and find that, despite my belief to the contrary, they do not seem to do any particular damage. I believe that Richard Strauss is the only substantial living composer, that Sinclair Lewis is the most significant purely American novelist, though Willa Cather is the best writer, that there is not a living statesman worth serious consideration, that Stephen Phillips is a greater poet than many think, that the only young serious dramatist on the Continent at the moment worth talking about is Franz Werfel, that one of the sharpest humorists that America has produced is W. E. Hill, that the most beautiful spot in the world is a certain little inn hidden away on the bank of a stream in the Black Forest, that Lindbergh, Coste, Byrd and all that crew are absurd futilitarians, that the best place to eat on earth is, first, Madame Génot's in the Rue de la Banque, Paris, and, second, the Vieux Logis in the Rue Lepic of the same town, that Spatenbräu is the most perfect beer, that the faint cinnamon smell of a carnation is the most gratifying of all flower perfumes, that the only completely original playwright since Ibsen is Pirandello, that the only authentic gentlemen left in the world are the Austrians, that athletic sports, save in the case of young boys, are designed for idiots, that money is meant to be spent and not saved, that since we are all now duly and perfectly aware that America has its full share of Rotarians, Kiwanians, and Ku Kluxers, not to mention the Anti-Saloon League, the W.C.T.U., the Y.M.C.A., the D.A.R. and the Methodist Board of Temperance, Prohibition and Public Morals, we may as well stop harping on the subject, that it is occasionally well, by way of making the world more palatable, to indulge one's self luxuriously in a remission of judgment and delude one's self momentarily with illusion, and that, when all is said and done, each and every man's philosophy of life, whatever it may be, is profoundly right so long as it makes him happy.

[From *Testament of a Critic*, 1931, pp. 3–18.]

LITERARY PERSONALITIES

Sinclair Lewis

LATE one afternoon eleven years ago, our mutual friend, T. R. Smith, then managing editor of the *Century Magazine,* telephoned Mencken and myself at our office and bade us come up to his flat that evening for a drink. When we got there, we found with Smith a tall, skinny, paprika-headed stranger to whom we were introduced as one Lewis. The fellow was known to neither of us save as the author of a negligible serial that had appeared in the *Saturday Evening Post* and that had subsequently been gathered between book covers and, to me specifically, as the author of a play called *Hobohemia,* produced the year before down in Greenwich Village and exquisitely—if I may be permitted so critically indelicate a word—epizoötic.

Barely had we taken off our hats and coats and before Smith had an opportunity even to fish out his *luxe* corkscrew from behind his *luxe* sets of the works of the more esoteric Oriental and Polack amorists, when the tall, skinny, paprika-headed stranger simultaneously coiled one long arm around Mencken's neck and the other around mine, well nigh strangling us and putting resistance out of the question, and—yelling at the top of his lungs—began: "So you guys are critics, are you? Well, let me tell you something. I'm the best writer in this here gottdamn country and if you, Georgie, and you, Hank, don't know it now, you'll know it gottdamn soon. Say, I've just finished a book that'll be published in a week or two and it's the gottdamn best book of its kind that this here gottdamn country has had and don't you guys forget it! I worked a year on the gottdamn thing and it's the goods, I'm atelling you! Listen, when it comes to writing a novel, I'm so far ahead of most of the men you two think are good that I'll be gottdamned if it doesn't make me sick to think of it! Just wait till you read the gottdamn thing. You've got a treat coming, Georgie and Hank, and don't you boys make no mistake about *that!*"

Projected from Smith's flat by the self-endorsing uproar—it kept up for fully half an hour longer—Mencken and I jumped into a taxicab, directed the driver to speed us post-haste to a tavern where we might in some peace recover our equilibrium and our ear-drums, and looked at each other. "Of all the idiots I've ever laid eyes on, that fellow is the worst!" groaned Mencken, gasping for breath. Regaining my own breath some moments later, all that I could add was that if any such numskull could ever write anything worth reading, maybe there was something in Christian Science too.

Three days later I got the following letter from Mencken, who had returned to Baltimore:

DEAR GEORGE: Grab hold of the bar-rail, steady yourself, and prepare yourself for a terrible shock! I've just read the advance sheets of the book of that *Lump* we met at Schmidt's and, by God, he has done the job! It's a genuinely excellent piece of work. Get it as soon as you can and take a look. I begin to believe that perhaps there isn't a God after all. There is no justice in the world. Yours in Xt.,

M.

The book was *Main Street.*

As is sufficiently known, it not only became a best-seller over-night, but it promptly established its author as one of the most observant, penetrating and significant writers in America.

It was more than a year before I ran across our friend again. I had dropped in late one night at a beer conference of four or five literary compeers in a mughouse off Union Square, where we were then in the custom of gathering. We were in the midst of a quiet, if somewhat malty, conversazione when the door flew open and our friend entered. Who had bidden him to come or how he had learned of our meeting-place, no one knew. Jamming down his hat on one of the wall-pegs, he yelled for a Seidel, grabbed a chair and pulled it up to the table, bounced himself up and down on it for three minutes as if it were a mechanical gymnasium horse, and began loudly to sing something in pig-German, accompanying his melodic gifts with gestures that swept two glasses, three Schweitzer cheese sandwiches and one sizable order of Bismarck herring off the table. The song concluded and paying not the slightest heed to our grunts and maledictions, he next yelled for a fresh Seidel (fondly embracing the waiter, whom he addressed familiarly and endearingly as leetle Owgoost), complained bitterly of the slowness of the service, demanded of the assemblage if it did not regard him as the best gottdamn writer in this here gottdamn country, got down at one big gulp three-quarters of the contents of his delivered pipkin, pushed his chair from him, mounted to his feet, cleared his throat several times, and launched into the following declamation:

"Ladies und Chentlemens: It is gewiss a great pleasure, gottinhimmel, für me to have been envited to shpeak to you dis eefining. In rising to address mit you, mit my impromptu shpeech in mine vest pocket, I am reminded uff der shtory uff der zwei Irishers, Pat und Mike, who was riding on der choo-choo car. Pat und Mike, I forgot me to tell you, vas sailors in der Navy. It seems Pat had der unter berth und by and by he heard such a noise von der ober berth und he called oop asking warum? Und Mike he answered, 'Shure und begorra how can Oi ivver get a night's shlape at all, at all? Oi've been tryin' to get into this damn hammock ivver since eight bells!'

"Now, ladies und chentlemens, shtanding up here before you great folks, I feel me a whole lot like Mike und maybe after I've sprechen along für a while, I may feel me so darn shmall I'll be able to crawl me into a choo-choo hammock mineself mit no trouble at all, at all."

At this point, he paused just long enough to shout for another Seidel and to drop what he evidently desired us to believe were rich German and Irish dialects. Then—"Gentlemen," he proceeded, aiming an imaginary hunk of chewed plug-cut at a remote corner of the wall, "it strikes me that each year at this annual occasion when friend and foe get together and lay down the battle-ax and let the waves of good-fellowship waft them up the flowery slopes of amity, it behooves us, standing together eye to eye and shoulder to shoulder as fellow-citizens of the greatest city in the world, to consider where we are both as regards ourselves and the common weal. It is true that even with our two hundred and fifty-two or practically two hundred and fifty-three thousand population, there are by the last census almost a score of larger cities in the United States. But, gentlemen, if by the next census we do not stand at least tenth, then I'll be the first to request any knocker to remove my shirt and to eat the same, with the compliments of yours truly! It may be true that New York, Chicago and Philadelphia will continue to keep ahead of us in size. But aside from these three cities, which are so over-grown that no decent white man, nobody who loves his wife and kiddies and God's great out-o'-doors and likes to shake the hand of his neighbor in greeting, would want to live in them—and let me tell you right here and now, I wouldn't trade a corner lot in this fine city of ours for the whole of any one of them—aside from these three, gentlemen, it's evi-dent to anyone with a head for facts that this grand city of ours is the finest example of American life and prosperity to be found anywhere on God's earth! I don't mean to say we're perfect. We've got a lot to do in the way of extending the paving of motor boulevards, for, believe me, it's the fellow with four to ten thousand a year, say, and an automobile and a nice little family in a bungalow on the edge of the town, that makes the wheels of progress go round! That, gentlemen, take it from yours truly, is the type of fellow that's ruling America today; in fact, it's the ideal type to which the entire world must tend if there's to be a decent, well-balanced, Chris-tian, go-ahead future for this little old planet. Once in a while I just naturally sit back and size up this Solid American Citizen with a whale of a lot of satisfaction."

For at least twenty-five minutes more he kept on in this vein, occasionally lapsing for a few seconds into dubious German, Irish or French dialect and interrupting himself only with admonitions to leetle Owgoost. Finally exhausted, he dropped with a bang into his chair, spilling half the contents of his Seidel over himself, and waited for some sign of approval of his great comedic gifts. There bloomed only a grim silence, save for a quiet remark from one end of the table that the lock on the outer door, evidently defective, had better promptly be replaced with a triple-Siegel. Not in the least disconcerted by the captious lull, our visitor pulled himself together, mopped up the hop moisture from his trousers, and—getting to his legs—lifted the remains of his Seidel above his head and clamorously proposed a toast to the novel he was then working on.

Concluding by this time that there was nothing to be done about it, the assembled literati decided to make the best of things. One got up and raised his Seidel "To our distinguished guest, Sinclair Lewisohn." Another "To Upton Sinclair, author of *Main Street*." A third observed that it was an honor to have Alfred Henry Lewis present, while a fourth ventured to inquire if the guest could by any chance be May Sinclair.

"Well, anyway, what did you guys think of my speech?" demanded leetle Owgoost's best customer.

The answer was a volume of inelegant mouth-noises.

A few months later the speech was found to be the keynote of one of the sharpest, most bitingly satirical and best novels ever written by an American. Its name, if you haven't already identified it, was *Babbitt*.

I began to meet our friend more frequently. He would stop in at my apartment in the late afternoon for a Florestan cocktail, sometimes so moody that he didn't speak five words and at other times so excited and voluble that he would stand up and, apropos of nothing at all, make speeches at me for an hour on end. These speeches, generally couched in dialect of one species or another, were invariably on one of two subjects: himself—in terms of a facetious self-appraisal predicated upon critics who did not sufficiently appreciate him, and myself—consisting for the most part in deplorings of the unhappy facts that I didn't drink enough, that I didn't have the sense to recognize *Hobohemia* for a swell play, that Mencken and I were nice enough fellows all right but that we ought to get married. and that something ought to be done about our recognizing Stuart Sherman anyway. At other times I would call on him in whatever hotel room he was occupying that week. He never used a chair in any such room, but always favored a far end of the bed, the rest of the bed usually being taken up by a

varying and various assortment of individuals who gave one
the impression that he had run down into the street and
herded them in indiscriminately a few minutes before. Who
most of them were, I never had the faintest idea. Many of
them looked like a comic-strip artist's idea of anarchists; they
all talked at once about everything under the sun; and they
all drank his liquor very proficiently. He called them all by
diminutives of their Christian names, always duly announced
in introducing each one of them that each was a grand guy,
and confidently and enthusiastically predicted to me on each
and every occasion that no less than six of those present were
virtuosi of one sort or another who one day would take the
critics off their feet. None of them—there were at least eighty
or ninety he thus eulogized in the period of my visits—has yet
been heard of.

He had been living in London for several weeks with Paul
de Kruif, his collaborator, working on *Arrowsmith*—originally
called *Dr. Martin Arrowsmith*—before I got there on my annual Spring trip. The day I arrived I went to a lunch party,
where I found myself seated between John Drinkwater and
Philip Guedalla, neither of whom I had previously met. I had
not sat down before Guedalla said to me, "You are an American and I have a message for you. If your country doesn't recall Sinclair Lewis at once, there will be war between England
and the United States!" It did not take a confidant of the
oracles to imagine what had been happening. Our friend Red,
as his nickname goes, had all too evidently been living up to
his sobriquet, if not its communistic implications, at least in
its taurian. It developed that the moment he had set foot on
the English shore he had begun to make speeches. These
speeches—according to Guedalla amounting up to the hour to
a total of something like two or three hundred and delivered
in dialect on every conceivable occasion at the rate of a dozen
or so daily, or rather nightly—had mainly to do, it appeared,
with the shameful failure of the English critics, excepting only
Hugh Walpole, to take a proper interest in American literature. Our friend, despite the German, French, Italian, Cockney
and Way Down East dialects in which he couched his diatribes, may have minced words but certainly not meanings.

He not only, while calling loudly for 'arf and 'arf or a spot of whiskey old top, named names, but dates, places and weather conditions. Every now and then, by way of prolonging international amity for a little while longer, it had been necessary for De Kruif, a veritable Sandow of a man, to grab hold of his colleague, pull him down into a chair, and sit on him.

On one occasion, I was informed, our genial friend, being entertained by a lady of title and being congratulated by those present on his literary gifts, had indicated his wholehearted concurrence in the wisdom of the encomiums by running around the room and imprinting a very moist buss on the lips of all the female guests. On another, during a gathering of celebrated English men of letters, he had—after, as is his custom, promptly addressing everyone by contractions of their given names—wound his arms around two of the sedate valetudinarians present and insisted that he be allowed to teach them the American jazz dances. On a third, invited to a dinner in his honor by an English woman essayist and novelist, he had brought along with him two strange Germans, a Russian, three Americans whom he had picked up at the American Express Company that afternoon, and two taxicab drivers, both boiled.

With the completion of *Arrowsmith*, which further established him as one of the most important American novelists of his time, our friend returned to his native land and, finding himself in need of some ready money, applied himself to the writing of a deliberately commercial novel, *Mantrap*, that would need only a camera-man standing behind it and a peroxide blonde in front of it to make a popular moving picture. Always forthright and completely honest with himself whatever the effect of the forthrightness and honesty may be on the delicate sensibilities of such as leetle Owgoost, Englishmen, Pulitzer prize committees and suddenly kissed dowagers, he made no bones of what he was doing, but frankly announced to anyone who would listen that he was, to use his own locution, turning out a swell piece of cheese to grab off some easy gravy.

His literary cheese duly manufactured, he disappeared from New York for a number of months, traveling the West to

gather material for his next piece of work. The night that he
got back, he was put to bed with a high temperature, but the
next morning—the temperature having dropped to 102—he
telephoned Mencken and me to come to dinner with him that
night, assuring us that he was in great shape and never felt
better in his life. We arrived at about quarter to seven and
found that he was still in bed, now with a temperature of 103.
No sooner had we entered his bedroom and hardly had we
begun to denounce him for a mule for having asked us to dine
with him when he was obviously a pretty sick man, than he
jumped out of bed, the tails of his short white old-fashioned
nightgown flapping about him, and—striking an attitude—
began:

"Brothers and sisters, don't you listen for one second to
these wishy-washy fellows that carry water on both shoulders,
that love to straddle the fence, that are scared of the sternness
of the good old-time Methodist doctrine and tell you that details don't mean anything, that dogmas and discipline don't
mean anything. They do! Let me tell you, brothers and sisters,
that justification means something! Baptism means something!
It means something that the wicked and worldly—and here I
point to some of our fellow-citizens—stand for this horrible
stinking tobacco and this insane alcohol, which turns men into
murderers, but we Methodists must keep ourselves pure and
clean and undefiled. But tonight, on this first day of getting
acquainted with you, brothers and sisters, I don't want to go
into these details; I want to get right down to the fundamental
thing that details merely carry out—and what is that fundamental thing? What is it? I'll tell you, brothers and sisters.
It is the Lord Jehovah and His love for each and every one
of us, big or small, rich or poor, drunk or sober. Love! Love!
Love! How beauteous the very word! Not carnal love, not
love of the flesh, but the divine presence. Love is the rainbow
that stands out in all its glorious many-colored hues illuminating again the dark clouds of life. It is the bright morning
and the evening star that, in glad refulgence, there on the
awed horizon, call all our hearts—and that goes for yours,
Georgie, and yours, Hank,—to an uplifted rejoicing in God's
marvelous firmament! Round about the cradle of the babe,

sleeping so quietly while o'er him stands in almost agonized adoration his loving mother, shines the miracle of Love, and at the last sad end, comforting the fond hearts that bear its immortal permanence, round even the quiet tomb, shines Love. What is great art—and I am not speaking of ordinary pictures but of those celebrated Old Masters with their great moral lessons—what is the mother of art, the inspiration of the poet, the patriot, the philosopher and the great man of affairs, be he business man or statesman—yes, brothers and sisters and Georgie and Hank, what inspires their every effort? Love! Love! Do you not sometimes hear, stealing o'er the plains at dawn, coming as it were from some far distant secret place, a sound of melody? (Shut up, you two bums, and listen!) When our dear sister here plays the offertory, do you not seem sometimes to catch the distant rustle of the wings of cherubim? And what is music, lovely music, what is sweet melody? 'Tis the voice of Love! 'Tis the magician that makes royal kings and queens out of plain folks like us! 'Tis the perfume of the wondrous rose, 'tis the strength of the athlete, strong and mighty to endure 'mid the heat and dust of the valorous conquest. Ah, Love, Love! Without it, we are less than beasts; with it, earth is heaven and we are as the gods! Yes, brothers and sisters and you two lice, that is what Love—created by the Almighty and conveyed through all the generations by His church, particularly, it seems to me, by the great, broad, wholesome, democratic, liberal brotherhood of the Methodist Church—that is what Love means to us!"

His temperature having now evidently shot up again, he let out a loud whoop, informed us that we were both low infidels bent for Hell, fell back into bed and, exhausted, was sound asleep a few moments later.

At dinner in a nearby restaurant shortly afterward, Mencken contented himself with a single word of comment. It was: "Bughouse!" At dinner in the same restaurant not very much later as time goes, we were congratulatingly buying our friend drinks on the elaboration of the boudoir harangue—where it figured almost word for word—into his novel, *Elmer Gantry*.

One can always tell a new novel coming on when the oratorical mood in any one, single thematic direction assails our friend. *The Man Who Knew Coolidge* was nothing more than a series of such orations gathered together, with not a word changed. They had been delivered in a variety of places and at a variety of times, including the corner of Fifth Avenue and Fifty-sixth Street at high noon, a beer-house in Hoboken at eleven o'clock at night, another beer-house in Union Hill, New Jersey at two in the morning, the bathroom of my apartment, the men's lavatory at the Rennert Hotel in Baltimore, a publisher's tea at the Sherry-Netherland, several taxicabs, two New York theatre lobbies on opening nights, and the steps of St. Ignatius' Church. *Dodsworth,* a year later, was heralded both before and directly after our friend's European material-seeking trip by innumerable vaudeville performances in the British dialect, aided and abetted by a monocle that he had purchased for the further embellishment of his histrionic talents.

One afternoon a year or so ago, our hero called me up and somewhat mysteriously hinted that I had better be at his house in West Tenth Street at seven o'clock that evening if I didn't want to miss something good. Since he is generally about as mysterious as a traffic cop, my curiosity was aroused and at seven promptly I was on the scene. Three other male guests, as mysteriously summoned, they told me, were already there: one a writer, one a labor leader (our friend at the time was planning a labor novel), and one an intermittent producer of theatre plays. After a cocktail or two, we were bidden to sit to dinner. In the middle of the meal, our host arose and excused himself. Returning a few minutes later, he informed us that he had to have a minor operation performed and had just telephoned the surgeon to come over. We had been invited, it appeared, to stand around and be company while the operation was going on. Protests being of no avail, we had to entertain Lewis while the surgical performance was in progress. "Looking at you guys gives me such a pain," he observed, "that the other one in comparison won't seem so bad."

When some months later the news was flashed over the wires that our friend had been awarded the Nobel Prize, the immense gratification that a number of us felt was slightly modified by qualms as to how the fellow would conduct himself in the presence of Swedish royalty. It was our firm conviction, based upon years of close intimacy, that he would in all likelihood run right up to the Queen, call her by her first name and lodge an aqueous smack upon her lips, and that when he was presented to His Majesty he would promptly and affectionately whack him on the back, put his arm around him, and call him "you old son-of-a-gun." Consequently, on the night the award was announced, some of us gathered together with him and solemnly engaged to offer him sage counsel and instruction in the finer shades of the punctilio.

"For example," we asked him, "what are you going to say to the King when you meet him?"

"What am I going to say?" he roared, waving his arms in the air and knocking over two lamps. "What am I going to say? Well, just you guys listen! 'Your Gracious Majesty and Officers of the Coldstream Guards: It is a great pleasure, let me tell you, for a little feller from Sauk Centre to meet you big Swedes. I feel proud and honored, believe me, boys, and when I get back home and tell the folks of the swell reception you've given me, they're going to be not only proud of me but of you too. After all, we're all brothers in Kiwanis, whether we're Swedes, Americans or Bohunks, and our hearts are in the right place. So what do you all say to going out, King, and having a little drink?' "

Yet once again our friend fooled us. Just as his whistle, however wet and riotous it may be when he is not in the grip of literary labor pains, is ever of an unremitting and almost Pythagorean aridity when he really sits himself down to work, so his conduct at Stockholm turned out to be so formal and proper—indeed, so dismayingly formal and proper—that His August Majesty, together with several members of his court, privy to the eccentricities of American comportment, actually inquired of our hero if he was not, at least on one of his parents' side, partly British.

[From *The Intimate Notebooks of George Jean Nathan*, 1932, pp. 8–21.]

Eugene O'Neill

IN all the many years of our friendship, I have heard Eugene
O'Neill laugh aloud once and only once. We were walking,
after dinner one evening in July, up the long, lonely road just
beyond the château he was then living and working in at
Saint Antoine du Rocher in Touraine. In the country, men who
live in cities generally find themselves talking out of character.
If they are sober, sedate fellows in the city, they become
orally frisky in the country; if they are flippant in the city,
they become more or less solemn and even wistful at the smell
of flowers and manure. Their discourse alters with the scene.
O'Neill, who in the city—for he is essentially a man of cities
despite his inability to write save a cow is mooing or a sea
is swishing beneath his window—has the mien and the conversational *élan* of an embalmer, presently proceeded thus:
"When Princeton, after kicking my tail out of place as an
undergraduate because I was too accurate a shot with an
Anheuser-Busch beer-bottle, and hit a window in Woodrow
Wilson's house right where it lived, some years later suddenly
got proud of its old beer-bottle heaver but magnanimously allowed Yale to claim the hoodlum for its own with an honorary
degree, I found myself in New Haven late one night viewing
a number of old boys of the class of 1880 or thereabouts having a hot reunion with themselves. Three of them in particular,
that I ran across on one of the street-corners, were so grandly
stewed that I had to stand still and watch them. One of them,
it appeared, was president of a big bank in New York; another
was vice-president of one of the big railroads; and the third
was a United States Senator. After playing leap-frog for about
ten minutes, during which one of them fell down and rolled
half-way into a sewer, the three, singing barber-shop songs at
the top of their lungs, wobbled across the street to the opposite corner where there was a mail-box. With a lot of grunts
and after much steaming and puffing, the bank president and
the vice-president of the big railroad got down on their knees
and hoisted their old classmate, the Senator, up on their shoul-

ders in a line with the slit in the mail-box. Whereupon the
Senator proceeded to use the mail-box for a purpose generally
reserved for telegraph poles and the sides of barns."

The boisterous roar that followed his recollection of the
scene marked, as I have said, the only time within my knowledge of O'Neill that he has laughed outright at anything. In
all the years I have known him, the most that has ever issued
from him has been a quiet little chuckle and I have only, in
all that time, heard him chuckle twice, once in New York when
he indulged in a reminiscence of the wonderful free-lunch that
he and his brother Jim used to get with a five-cent glass of
beer (and live on) in a saloon opposite the old Madison
Square Garden, and once at Le Plessis, in France, when he
handed me a newspaper article in Spanish, treating of the
time he once spent in Buenos Aires during his sailor days,
asked me to translate it for him, and I inserted several imaginary paragraphs describing in rich detail his great proficiency
as a tango dancer. He is constitutionally the antithesis of
l'homme qui rit. Nothing even faintly amuses him, unless it
be the remembrance of his dead brother's gift for Rabelaisian
monkeyshines, the singing (in a voice capable of just three
notes, all sour) of old barroom ballads, or remembered tales
of his father, the late James O'Neill who, during the years
when he was a matinée idol, used to parade Fourteenth Street
at high noon daily—after at least three hours spent in dolling
himself up—by way of giving the girls a treat, and who always
made it a practise on Sundays to get to church half an hour
late by way of staging an effective entrance for himself.

Contrary to finding amusement in the world, O'Neill finds
endlessly the materials for indignation. The body of his dramatic writing reflects him more closely, I venture to say, than
that of any other playwright in the present-day American
theatre. Let the dramatic critic of some yokel newspaper in
some yokel town that he has never even heard of write that he
isn't all he should be as a dramatist, and he lets out a vituperative blast of such volume that, once done, he finds himself
completely exhausted. Several times I myself have been denounced, if somewhat more politely, for expressed opinions on

his work. Once, he let me read the manuscript of his play, *Welded,* in which he had great faith. When I reported to him that all I could discern in it was some very third-rate Strindberg, he sharply observed that I couldn't conceivably understand any such play as I had never been married, put on his hat, walked out and didn't let me hear from him for two months afterward. When, several years later, he sent me the manuscript of *Lazarus Laughed* and I wrote to him that I didn't care for it, he replied in the next mail that my judgment of it couldn't be taken seriously by him because I was lacking in all religious feeling and was therefore prejudiced against any such play, and that it was really a masterpiece whatever I thought about it. On this occasion, he was so disgusted with my critical gifts that he didn't write to me again for three months. The same thing happened in the case of *Dynamo,* which in a preliminary manuscript reading struck me as being close to caricature. Even after the play was produced and almost unanimously condemned, he stuck to his loyalty toward it and to his conviction that all the critics were dolts. "It maybe wasn't all it should have been," he subsequently admitted to me, "because I was going through a lot of trouble in family matters when I was writing it, but just the same you're dead wrong about it." And—I happened to be visiting him at the time—he sulked for the rest of the day and condescended only to exchange a curt goodnight with me at bed-time. If a newspaper or any other kind of photographer snaps him without his formal permission, he seethes. If he gets a letter with something in it that displeases him, he mutters sourly over it for twenty-four hours. The petty nuisances and annoyances that every man suffers and quickly dismisses from mind and attention cause him something bordering on acute agony.

After many years of being very hard up, his plays gradually began to make him money. But real money came only with the tremendous success, both as a performed play and published book, of *Strange Interlude,* which netted him close to a half-million dollars. Since boyhood, he had had just two wishes: one, to have some shirts tailored by a first-class London shirt-maker and, two, to own a carriage dog such as he had seen loping after the rigs of the rich in his youngster days.

His greatest satisfaction in *Strange Interlude* was that it had made the gratification of the two wishes possible.

He has a dislike of meeting people that amounts almost to a terror. Even with his few close friends he is generally so taciturn that it is sometimes necessary to go over and poke him to make certain that he is neither asleep nor dead. He sits glumly for hours at a time without opening his mouth, brooding deeply over some undecipherable concern which, upon ultimate revelation, turns out to be a worried speculation as to whether his wife has ordered spaghetti, his favorite dish, for dinner for him that night. Having sat at different tables with him countless times, I have, with rare exception, heard him during the course of a meal say more than two words and they have invariably been—in reply to an inquiry as to whether he would care for any more of this or that—"Why sure." The way to lose O'Neill's friendship is to ask him for oral expressions of opinion on anything (if he feels like expressing an opinion, he will write a letter, and a satisfactorily long one), or to introduce him to any man other than one who knows a great deal about professional sports and who will confine his conversation to that subject. The one great admiration that he has temporarily achieved for any man in the last four years was for Sparrow Robertson, the chief sporting writer of the Paris *Herald,* whom he met just once and found to be "a grand bird." He has a greater respect for Sean O'Casey, but beyond that an aversion to most men of his own profession, asserting that the majority of them are not worth the powder to blow them up, and of all those whom he has met in later years only W. S. Maugham and H. R. Lenormand have any interest for him. He goes to a theatre about once in every five years and then only in Europe because he has heard that some play of his is being done there in a language that he cannot understand. I have known him on only one occasion really to admit that he had been in a theatre. That was when the Russian Tairoff did *All God's Chillun* in Russian in Paris several years ago. He professed to have found it the best production of any of his plays that he had ever seen. "But," I protested, "you don't know a word of Russian. How could *you* tell?" He looked at me pityingly.

"You should have seen the way Tairoff's wife, in the rôle of the girl, brushed those books off the table in that scene in the last act!" he replied with grave seriousness.

Displaying outwardly all the glow and effervescence of a magnum of ice water, he is internally given to huge enthusiasms of all sorts and varieties. Whatever piece of work he happens currently to be working on arouses him to such a pitch of incalescence over its virtues that he will go around all day wreathed in broad, mysterious smiles. And when O'Neill thus smiles, it is as if any other man stood gleefully on his head, waved his arms and legs and let out a bellow that shook the heavens. Familiar with all his longer, as well as with a number of his shorter plays, since their manuscript infancy, I recall only one time when doubt over a script that he was writing assailed him. In all the other cases he was as excited over their merits as a child of the wealthy anticipating on Christmas Eve the gifts he was certain to get. The one exception was a trilogy which he had undertaken. "Would to God," he wrote me, "that this damned trilogy of mine were off of my neck! I'm beginning to hate it and curse the day I ever conceived such an idea. The notion haunts me that I've bitten off a good deal more than I can chew. On my return, the first two acts of the first play struck me as not right, so I've started to rewrite them. And so it goes on! It looks as if the rest of my life was doomed to be spent rewriting the damned thing. I honestly feel very low about it and am anxious to get done with it and free my mind from the obsession of it and get on to something else. When these two acts are done, for better or worse, I'm going to call quits. I don't think I can go through the ordeal of typing it myself now. I'm too fed up. Think it wiser to get it typed. It would bore me so that before the end I would probably burn it."

But not so usually. Confidence generally permeates his being, warming him to the very toes. He says nothing, or at best very little, but the mysterious smiles embroider his features. Of *The Straw*, he informed me, "I have complete confidence in my own valuation of it." *Where the Cross Is Made*, was "great fun to write, theatrically very thrilling, an amusing experiment in treating the audience as insane." "I would like to stand or fall"—in each instance—"by *Bound East for Cardiff, The Long Voyage Home, The Moon of the Caribbees, Beyond the Horizon, The Straw* and *Gold*," he wrote me. Each of these plays, he duly announced, was "my sincerest effort and was written purely for its own sake." Of *All God's Chillun Got Wings*— "Well, I've got it done and I'm immensely pleased with it!" Of *Desire Under the Elms*—"Its poetical vision illuminating even the most sordid and mean blind alleys of life—that is my justification as a dramatist!" Of *Marco Millions*—"there's a whole lot of poetical beauty in it and fine writing." *The Great God Brown* was "a devastating, crucifying new one." *Lazarus Laughed* was "far the best play I've ever written." Of *Dynamo* —"I thoroughly disagree with you about the play. It is *not* far, far below me, I'm sure of that! Wait and see! It will come into its own some day when it isn't judged as a symbolical trilogy with a message to good Americans about what's wrong with them and what to do about it. I think you're wrong this time— as wrong as about *Lazarus Laughed*. Not that you're not right about the excessiveness of the stage directions, but then I thought you knew that my scripts get drastically weeded out in that respect when I read proof and that I always let them slide as they first occur to me until then. A slovenly method, perhaps, but the way I've always worked. Then again, I don't think it's fair to take the speeches of a lot of admittedly inarticulate characters in a particular play as expressions of the general underlying theme of a trilogy—which I obviously never intended them to be." Indeed, even in the case of the latest trilogy, *Mourning Becomes Electra*, about which there were the preliminary doubts already recorded, I received, when the play at length was finished, this comment: "It has been one hell of a job! Let's hope the result in some measure justifies the labor I've put in. To get enough of Clytemnestra in Christine, of Electra in Lavinia, of Orestes in Orin, etc., and yet keep them American primarily; to conjure a Greek fate out of the Mannons themselves (without calling in the aid of even a Puritan Old Testament God) that would convince a modern audience without religion or moral ethics; to prevent the surface melodrama of the plot from overwhelming the real drama; to contrive murders that escape cops and courtroom scenes;

and finally to keep myself out of it and shun the many opportunities for effusions of personal writing anent life and fate—
all this has made the going tough and the way long! And even
now it's done I don't know quite what I've got. All I *do* know
is that after reading it all through, in spite of my familiarity
with every page, it leaves me moved and disturbed spiritually,
and I have a feeling of there being real size in it, quite apart
from its length; a sense of having had a valid dramatic experience with intense tortured passions beyond the ambition or
scope of other modern plays. As for the separate parts, each
play, each act, seem better than I hoped. And that's that."

Wherever he happens to be at the moment happens enthusiastically also to be the place of all places for him to be and
forever live in. Provincetown was "ideal, quiet and the only
place where I could ever work." When in Bermuda, he wrote
me, "I didn't start this letter with any view of boring you by
an expounding of inner principles. It was rather to recommend
Bermuda to you as a place to 'take the waters' in case you're
planning a Spring vacation. The climate is grand. The German
bottled beer and English bottled ale are both excellent. And
the swimming is wonderful, if you like such, which I do above
everything. It has proved a profitable Winter resort for me.
I've gotten more work done than in the corresponding season
up North in many years." When at Belgrade Lakes, in Maine,
he sent me a postcard: "There's tranquility here. A place to
think and work if ever there was one! Ideal for me." "Well,
after a week in London," he wrote, "I am strong for it. It
seems to me that if it were possible for me to live contented
in any city this would be the one. There is something so self-
assuredly nerveless about it. Of course, the weather has been
unexpectedly fine—warm and sunny every day—and that helps.
In short, I've been happier here since I left New York than
ever in my life before." While he was living in Guéthary in
the Basque country, I received the following: "The Basque
country and the Basques hit me right where I belong! According to present plans and inclinations it is here that I shall
settle down to make a home for the rest of my days. Europe
has meant a tremendous lot to me, more than I ever hoped
it could. I've felt a deep sense of peace here, a real enjoyment

in just living from day to day, that I've never known before. For more than the obvious financial reasons, I've come to the conclusion that anyone doing creative work is a frightful sap to waste the amount of energy required to beat life in the U.S.A. when over here one can have just that more strength to put into one's job." When he was in Indo-China, this arrived: "This is the place! There is nothing more beautiful and interesting in the world. It is grand!" Settled for several years in Touraine, he wrote: "This is the place for me! The most beautiful part of France. Here is the ideal place to live and work!" During a motor trip through Spain, I received three postcards from him at different times. One, from Madrid, conveyed this message: "I've never seen a more beautiful spot. It would be a great place to work in." One, from Granada, this: "Spain is most interesting and I'm darn glad we picked it out for a vacation. Granada is quiet, peaceful and immensely attractive. What a place to live and work in!" One, from Malaga, this: "This is the best place I have ever struck in Europe—really good stuff! It'd be a swell place to live and work in." Returned to New York again, he said to me, "Why I ever left here, damned if I know. There's life and vitality here. It's the place for ideas! This is the spot for me and my work." His present passion is for a small island off the Georgia coast. "The best place to live and work I've ever found!"

O'Neill and Sinclair Lewis are alike in one respect. Both have naturally a boyish quality, an innocent artlessness in a number of directions, that will doubtless remain with them to their last years. In it lies much of their charm. Lewis is as excited over a party as any débutante, and a trip to Hoboken on the ferry works him up to a degree of delight comparable only to Robert Fulton's first sensation when he saw his steamboat actually working. O'Neill, for all his solemn exterior, gets an unparalleled pleasure from splashing around in a swimming pool and making funny gurgling noises, from putting on the fancily colored dressing gowns he bought several years ago in China, from singing raucous duets with a crony—"Rosie, You Are My Posy" and " 'Twas Christmas in the Harem" are two of his favorites,—from lying on the ground and letting Blemie, his pet dog, crawl over him, the meanwhile tickling him on the bottom, from watches with bells in them, from the idea that one day he may master the accordion and be as proficient a performer as the vaudeville headliner, Phil Baker, and from drinking enormous glasses of Coca-Cola and making everyone believe it is straight whiskey. When his very lovely wife, Carlotta, comes down to dinner in some particularly striking gown, his face lights up like a county fair. She knows well the effect it has on him and quietly lays in a constantly replenished wardrobe for his relish. "Do you like it?" she will delicately ask on each occasion. And, though his infinite satisfaction is clearly to be perceived, like a little boy who doesn't want to give in and admit anything too quickly, he will invariably mumble, "Well, it's pretty, but I like blue better."

Years ago, he was a drinker of parts. In fact, there were times when he went on benders that lasted a whole month and times when he slept next to the bung-hole of a whiskey barrel at Jimmy the Priest's and when Jimmy, the proprietor, coming to work the next morning, found the barrel one-eighth gone. About four or five years ago, however, he hoisted himself onto the water-wagon and has since sat thereon with an almost Puritanical splendor and tenacity. Like many another reformed bibber, he now views the wine-cup with a superior dudgeon and is on occasion not averse to delivering himself of eloquent harangues against it and its evils. It is not easy to forget his pious indignation when Barrett Clark once ventured to mention his old drinking bouts to him. "Altogether too much damned nonsense has been written since the beginning of time about the dissipation of artists!" he exploded. "Why, there are fifty times more real drunkards among the Bohemians who play at art, and probably more than that among the people who never think about art at all. The artist drinks, when he drinks at all [note the whimsy of that *at all*], for relaxation, forgetfulness, excitement, for any purpose except his art!" So today, it is Coca-Cola, followed by Kalak, with a vengeance.

O'Neill is very slow in making friends. He tests a potential friendship much after the technique of a fisherman, trying out various personal and metaphysical lines, flies and worms to determine what kind of fish the stranger is and to what degree, personally or philosophically, he resembles a sucker. Once he has made a friend for himself, that man remains a friend, in his eyes, until Hell freezes. In all the world I suppose that there are not more than five men at the very most whom O'Neill really regards as friends, and at least three of these are relics of his early more or less disreputable days in Greenwich Village and the adjacent gin-mills. I had known him for exactly ten years until we got to the point where we called each other by our first names.

He has done much of his more recent writing in an enormous chair that he had manufactured for himself in England. It is a cross between a dentist's and a barber's chair, with all sorts of pull-in and pull-out contrivances attached to it and with a couple of small shelves for reference books. A board is so arranged that it can be manœuvred in front of him and on it he rests his pad. Stripped to the waist—he never works, if he can help it, with anything on above his navel—and with his legs stretched out to their full length, he writes everything in long hand and his chirography is so minute that it takes a magnifying glass for average eyes comfortably to read it.

I have never known him to tell a smoking-car story and, if someone happens to venture one while he is around, he sits silent and wide-eyed at its conclusion, as if he couldn't possibly understand it and wonders just what the point is. As for himself, he has just one story and will repeat it, to his apparent own infinite amusement, on the slightest provocation. It is the venerable one known as "The Old Bean," and concerns the braggadocio of an old souse who, despite all the dire catastrophes that befall him, imagines that the tremendous shrewdness of his intellect allows him on all occasions to get the best of everyone else. It is a long story, lasting at least an hour if related at top speed, and I have heard it from him regularly twice a year. Once, telling it to me again and embroidering its details, it occupied the entire time it took us to walk the seven miles from Le Plessis to Tours. The sole other occasion for unwonted loquacity on his part is the reminiscence of his vagrant New York days at the dive known as the Hell Hole and at Jimmy the Priest's where, with a pot-companion named Joe Smith, he shared a room—which they always referred to as "the garbage flat"—for the fine sum of three dollars a month. His particular comrades at Jimmy's, in addition to Joe, included a number of odoriferous colored gentlemen, a press-agent for Paine's Fireworks named Jimmy Beith, and one Major Adams, a red-nosed inebriate of sixty-odd who had been cashiered years before from the British army. This fraternity, hardly ever with more than fifty cents at a time in its combined treasury, subsisted on raw whiskey for breakfast and on what free lunch it could cabbage off the end of the bar during the rest of the day. From time to time, other habitués of the place were accepted into the fold, including an old sea captain named Chris Christopherson, whom O'Neill in later years incorporated name and all into his play, *Anna Christie*, a sailor named Driscoll, whose name suggested to him the Driscoll of *Bound East for Cardiff*, *The Moon of the Caribbees* and *In the Zone*, and a septuagenarian miser who had lived in a small, bare room above the saloon for twenty-two years, who never could persuade himself to throw away a newspaper and who could hardly find room enough to sleep on the floor for the enormous stacks of accumulated copies of the New York *Times*. The favorite tipple of the brotherhood, when one or another of the members—usually O'Neill, who at intervals would contrive to cozen a dollar out of his father—managed in some way to get hold of the price, was, aside from the breakfast rye, Benedictine drunk by the tumblerful. But such treats were rare and makeshifts were necessary. Alcohol mixed with camphor was found—after one got used to the taste—to have a pretty effect. Varnish diluted with water was also discovered to have its points. And there were days when even wood alcohol mixed in small doses with sarsaparilla, with just a soupçon of benzine to give it a certain bouquet, was good enough, in the brothers' view, for any man who wasn't a sissy.

For weeks on end, the brotherhood would sit, or lie, in Jimmy's without stirring out for even a moment's breath of air. That is, all save the Major, who had a hobby for collecting old and wholly useless books of all descriptions, which he never read, and for attending funerals. If he came home any evening without at least three frowzy books garnered from God knows where or without having attended at least two

funerals of persons entirely unknown to him, he would mope
for the rest of the night and would regain his cheer only after
he had drunk a half dozen or so toasts to His Majesty, the
King, in beakers of varnish. It was apparently not the royal
toasts, however, that caused the Major's demise, but something
ponderously diagnosed by a hastily summoned neighborhood
medico as "malicious liver complaint." The Major's funeral
was a gala affair, with the remaining brotherhood so melan-
choliously but none the less richly in its cups that no fewer
than three of the mourners lost their balance and tumbled into
the grave on top of their late brother's coffin.

Nor was it the nature of the brotherhood's refreshments that
unwound the mortal coil of Brother Beith. Learning one night,
while full of Pond's extract mixed with one-eighth whiskey
and three-eighths gasoline, that his dear wife, whom he had
forgotten all about in the fifteen years he hadn't laid eyes on
her, had run off with a fellow in South Africa, he committed
suicide by jumping out of one of Jimmy's upper windows.
Beith's suicide, together with certain personal emotional misfortunes in an encounter with Cupid, weighed upon O'Neill's
mind and—now it may be told—a month or so after Beith took
his life the man who was to become the first of American
dramatists attempted, with an overdose of veronal, to follow
suit. When, one afternoon at two o'clock—the conventional
hour for rising and having whiskey breakfast—O'Neill failed
to stir, failed even to respond to the brothers' nudges, pokes
and peremptory kicks, an ambulance was quickly summoned
and our friend was carted off at a gallop to Bellevue. With the
brothers grouped solicitously about his cot, two interns worked
over him for an hour before he again gave signs of life. Three
hours later, the dose of veronal not having been so large as
he believed, O'Neill was back in the world once more and,
with a whoop of joy, the brothers put on their hats and
moved mysteriously toward the door. "We'll be back soon,"
they observed significantly—and were gone. Four hours later,
they reappeared, all beautifully and magnificently drunk. It
developed that they had rushed to O'Neill's father and had
got fifty dollars from him to pay the hospital fee for his son's
resuscitation. "You dirty bums!" groaned O'Neill, with what

vocal strength he could muster. "How much you got left?" Thirty-two dollars, they reluctantly informed him. "All right, divide!" he insisted. And with his sixteen dollars safe in hand, he rolled over, grinned satisfiedly, and went happily and peacefully to sleep.

We were sitting one late Summer afternoon about two years ago in my rooms in the Avenue Maréchal Foch, in Paris, looking out at the merry-go-round of motor cars in the Etoile and at the Arc de Triomphe in the sinking sun. I asked him— his reflective mood seemed to inspire .the question—what he would like more than anything else out of life.

"The Nobel Prize?" I hinted out of the side of my apéritif glass.

"On careful consideration—and no sour grapes about it because I have had no hopes—I think the Nobel Prize, until you become very old and childlike, costs more than it's worth. It's an anchor around one's neck that one would never be able to shake off," he answered, gulping his tea.

"A more intelligent critical appraisal of your work?" I smiled.

His ears, as is their wont when critics and criticism are mentioned, stood setter-like and challenging on end. "I expect denunciation! It's generally sure to come. But I'm getting awfully callous to the braying, for or against. When they knock me, what the devil!, they're really boosting me with their wholesale condemnations, for the reaction against such nonsense will come soon enough. These tea-pot turmoils at least keep me shaken up and convinced I'm on my way to something. I know enough history to realize that no one worth a damn ever escaped them—so it gives me hope. When I'm generally approved of, I begin to look in the mirror very skeptically and contemplate taking up some other career I might succeed at. So it's all tonic."

He finished his tea.

"I'll tell you what I want and it's the God's truth. I want just what I've now at last and for the first time in my life got! Life has certainly changed for me in the last year or so and for the first time in God knows how long I feel as if it had something to give me as a living being quite outside of the life in my work. The last time I saw you I told you I was happy. A rash statement, but I now make it again with a ten-fold emphasis. And, believe me, it has stood tests that would have wrecked it if it wasn't the genuine article. I feel younger and more pepped up with the old zest for living and working than I've ever felt since I started working. I may seem to slop over a bit, but you don't know into what a bog of tedium and life-sickness I was sinking. I was living on my work as a fellow does on his nerves sometimes, and sooner or later my work would certainly have been sapped of its life because you can't keep on that way forever, even if you put up the strongest of bluffs to yourself and the world in general. Now I feel as if I'd tapped a new life and could rush up all the reserves of energy in the world to back up my work. Honestly, it's a sort of miracle to me, I'd become so resigned to the worst. So be a little indulgent and don't mind my unloading a little of the pop-eyed wonder of it at you!"

At this point Carlotta, his wife, came in, put her arm around him and kissed him.

"Where've you been?" he asked, his face suddenly lapsing again into that perverse little-boy expression.

Carlotta gave him another little kiss.

"I've been shopping for dresses, Genie dear," she said. "Blue ones."

[From *The Intimate Notebooks of George Jean Nathan*, 1932, pp. 21–38.]

H. L. Mencken

FROM the afternoon in the May of 1908 when we first met and bought each other a double Tavern cocktail, there have been only two imitations of differences between us and, as we were doubtless both equally wrong, they could amount in the long run to but little. We have argued with each other, of course; and there have been times when we have called each other asses and paid each for his own drinks; yet soon thereafter, reassuringly concluding that there were many profounder asses in the world than we—to our great self-satisfaction always specifying them loudly by name—we have found ourselves in the same hansom cab or, as the years passed, taxi on our joint and mellifluous way home. What preserved our friendship over so long a period was undoubtedly the conviction, mutually shared, that nothing in this world matters very much in the long run and that it is accordingly profitless to get too much worked up over anything. As a result, we weathered storms together that would have wrecked many another friendship; we met with humor many a situation that would have severed men constitutionally more indignant; and we have, if not so much because of any colossal mutual taste for each other—though I may confide that secretly we regard each other very favorably—as because of a colossal mutual distaste for the same kind of persons and groups of persons and institutions, ridden at peace and worked and played happily together through the greater part of a quarter of a century.

What negligible irritations during the long course of our joint editorial concerns we now and again experienced, because of a lapse on the part of one or the other of us, quickly found themselves dissipated in some such sufficiently terse editorial correspondence as: "If you call this copy-reading, I give up in despair!", with the reply: "If you call this spelling, *I* give up in despair!" When magazine financial matters aroused my friend's incertitude, together with a skepticism as to my uncommon virtuosity in that direction, some such telegram as this from Baltimore ended the momentary anxiety: "If X. ever actually hands over the bonds, don't bother to write. Simply cut off one of his ears and send it to me. I'll understand." If, suffering from a selfish conviction that I was doing too great a share of the work, I wrote him somewhat acrimoniously to that effect, instead of making matters worse by replying directly to the idiotic contention all that he would do would be to send me a lengthy list of his ailments, thus breaking my heart, together with some such irrelevant footnote as, "I hope you put aside a case of that Roederer against my birthday, which occurs on September 12th. In general, as you know, I detest birthday presents, but mature reflection has led me to conclude that I should make an exception of wines and liquors of high tone."

I have alluded to his maladies. In the twenty-odd years that

I have known him, I have received thousands upon thousands of letters from him, and in not a single one has he failed affectingly to mention some hypothetical physical agony that was making life intolerable for him. A complete catalogue of these malaises, ranging all the way from *astasia atactica* to *zoster auricularis*, would extend from here to the end of this notebook, so I confine myself to an illuminating few, quoted from his various communications:

1. I have a sore mouth, can't smoke, my hooves hurt, it is eighty-five degrees, and at least twenty pests are in town.

2. I had a hell of a time yesterday. When I got up, after rolling in at 2:30 with a dreadful package, I found my sister alarmingly ill, and the house was full of doctors all day. It turned out to be alarming, but not dangerous, so I went to the St. Agnes Allgemeinekrankenhaus and had my wart cut off my cheek. When you see me I'll have a superb Schläger scar. My new girl objected to the wart. Without it, she said, I would be 100% perfect. A man is a swine not to please them.

3. Hay fever has begun to caress me. It will knock me off on the train Sunday and interfere with a private engagement in your great city Sunday night.

4. As for me, I am enjoying my usual decrepitude. A new disease has developed, hitherto unknown to the faculty: a dermatitis caused by the plates I wear for my arches. No one seems to know how to cure it. I shall thus go limping to the crematory.

5. My ailments this morning come to the following:
   a. A burn on the tongue (healing).
   b. A pimple inside the jaw.
   c. A sour stomach.
   d. Pain in the prostate.
   e. Burning in the gospel-pipe (always a preliminary of the hay-fever season).
   f. A cut finger.
   g. A small pimple inside the nose (going away).
   h. A razor cut, smarting.
   i. Tired eyes.

6. Knopf is here. I went to Raymond Pearl's house with him

last night and disgraced myself by falling asleep. I begin to break up.

7. My sister is making a really extraordinary recovery. She should recover completely. I assume that I'll be the next to be laid up. I pray, but without hope.

8. I am suffering miserably from my perennial malaises. It won't be long now!

9. I have been trying to start my new book but an infernal infection in the sinuses has got into my larynx and I am most uncomfortable. Immer Trubel! I begin to give up hope.

10. I have got the book going at last. And the sinus is quiescent. But something or other is bound to strike me tomorrow.

11. I sprained my back yesterday helping a taxi chauffeur to disentangle my cab from a collision. It is stiff and painful. But it was due, for I had been running along for nearly a week with no ailments.

12. My hemorrhoids have come back after twenty-one years. The opening gun in God's 1930 Spring offensive against me!

13. Hay-fever has me by the ear and I am making the usual rocky weather of it. It seems to be rather more severe than usual. What a world!

14. I am sweating away, but accomplishing nothing. Yesterday I thought I had the flu but now it has passed off.

15. The difficulty about going away during the hay-fever season is that I have it worse when I get back. Eight or nine years ago I went abroad, as you know, returning in October. All the other customers of the pollen were well by that time and had forgot it, but I had a severe bout.

On his birthday last September, I sent him the following telegram: "From the youthful vantage point of forty-nine, I convey my congratulations on the achievement of your fifty-first birthday. Am sending you by parcel post gift-box containing set of false teeth, a toupé, one cork leg, six bottles of liniment and a copy of *What Every Boy Should Know*." A few hours later, I received this wired reply: "Our Heavenly Father will reward you for that last-aid package but why did you omit bottle of asthma medicine? I am hacking and wheezing like Polonius."

If it isn't one thing, it is another. A relative, it appears in one

letter, "has broken all local records in bankruptcy. His assets
consist of a gold-plated Shriner badge and 50,000 shares of
stock in a silver mine in Delaware." In another he reports that
he is exhausted physically and can do no more work for a
while. "We will simply have to make a change in the editorial
conduct of the magazine [the *Smart Set*]. My assignment to
make love to lady novelette writers in order to get decent novelettes for the magazine is proving altogether too strenuous.
Last week, as you know, I took out three different literary
wenches, bought and drank at least fifty dollars worth of alcoholic liquor, made enough love to inflame two dozen Marie
Corellis, didn't get home until dawn, and what will we get?
Not a damned thing worth printing! And my health is gone!
It's your turn, my boy!" Again, "Eight terrible pests have
showed up at the house in the last three days and driven me
crazy. But I am getting in some work. In fact, I am making such
good progress that yesterday I made no less than two notes for
my new book, one of twenty or thirty words." Again, "My troubles never cease. Now that Sara is quite well again, my sister
has taken her turn in the hospital." Still again, "My new book
is giving me hell, as usual. I wish I had stuck to my father's
cigar business." Still again, "Your words in 'Clinical Notes' in
the forthcoming *Mercury* on the motives behind the yearnings
for rural peace are full of sagacity. I wish you would make a
tour through the country as I did. You would come back as I
have come back, thoroughly disillusioned and disheartened. I
got an immense amount of notice but I believe that I could
honestly say that ninety-nine per cent of it was disgusting. It
left me feeling lonely and miserable. What is the use going on
at the high pace we have kept for all these years if the reward
is such banal triviality? I ought to start my new book but I find
it hard to do so. I am constantly asking myself if it is worth-
while to waste so much energy upon an enterprise whose rewards are so unsatisfying. But what else is there to do? The
rural retirement scheme is absolutely nonsensical and I can
think of no satisfactory alternative. You, yourself, at least have
something ahead in the way of a change. But I see no possibility of anything of the sort for me. I'd only be ten times more
miserable." And again, "My *Mercury* book review department

is terrible this month, fit for *Scribner's*. But I've been having so much trouble with one thing and another down here that it's a wonder to me I didn't shoot myself long ago or start writing for the *New Republic*." And again, "Your vainglorious and slightly offensive boast that you are the biggest horse's asterisk in the world must now come to an end. I beat you by at least eighty miles! I have spent something like $500 on quacks in the hope of learning what is wrong with my foot and the latest one I have consulted, at a fee of $35, yesterday soberly informed me that I ought to have it treated by *an osteopath!* Thinking of the good $35 wasted on such an idiot, I kicked myself all the rest of the day in the tail for a damned fool and the exercise seems to have worked a cure. Today my foot feels fine. But probably the other one will go back on me tomorrow."

The manner in which we conducted our earlier joint editorial control of magazines over a long period may perhaps best be suggested by quoting samples of now yellowed billets that passed between us:

I

(Nathan to Mencken)

Dear Menck:—

Pending your return to New York, I suggest that you leave the Dunsany and Max Beerbohm matters in my hands. While I am in full accord with you regarding the Dunsany piece, I consider you, old cock, an utter ass when it comes to Beerbohm. The essay is mere flafla—Max trying to grab some easy money in the gullible American magazine market. Let him sell it to Tom Smith for the *Century*. Tom admires Beerbohm because Beerbohm's brother, Beerbohm Tree, was a celebrated actor-manager and wore silk spats. Moreover, the readers of the *Century* will like the thing. Such stuff always fetches schoolteachers. I doubt that it would interest our customers. They are, in the main, too sinful to be intrigued by literary sinfulness. The mere name of Beerbohm will not land them. They are hep to all the old magazine dodges, and we can never fool them with gaudy names as Hearst does. As you know, I esteem Beerbohm highly, but it seems to me that he hasn't turned out a

decent piece of work for five years. We have printed much
better stuff by youngsters, for example, Stephen Wheeler.

Let us stick to our agreement to print nothing that we are
not both sure of—that is, if we can get enough stuff of that sort.
We surely get very little out of the magazine save the fun that
is in our jobs, so why bother ourselves with questions of "advisability" and the like? More magazines have been wrecked by
this search for advisability than by anything else I can think
of, save it be too much money. What are the two greatest magazine successes of recent years in America? Obviously, the
Saturday Evening Post and the *Atlantic Monthly,* two corpses
revived into tremendous vigor. Well, neither Lorimer of the
Post nor Sedgwick of the *Atlantic* bothers specifically about
what it is advisable to print, nor even about what his public
wants. Each simply prints what he likes himself. Both have
made fortunes for themselves and the entrepreneurs behind
them by assuming that what *they* like will also be liked by
thousands of other right-thinking men. Our opportunity is just
as clear. Let us assume that there are thousands of other Americans who have just as little virtue in them as I have, and just
as little taste as you.

I am against printing any more so-called poetry by K——,
even if it happens to be good, which is not likely. This K——
has cheapened himself by becoming a public character down
in Greenwich Village. An amiable fellow personally, and with
enough talent, perhaps, to save him from the public hangman,
he has yet converted himself into something that surely doesn't
belong in the magazine—something that seems silly to you and
to me, and hence must seem silly to most of our readers. If you
think he ought to be aided, then pay him a pension out of your
privy purse.

I have invented a new cocktail—very fetching. One third
Gordon gin, one third sloe gin, and one third tangerine juice,
well iced. Two fill the heart with confidence in God. Three
make even such piffle as the Beerbohm essay seem good. I shall
limit you to two.

Don't forget to send me the address of R——. My *Popular
Theatre* will greatly mellow and enrich her mind. A very pretty
creature, but slightly too damned intellectual. I sicken of all

the lady Nietzsches. Whenever I am tired and it is raining, I like to hear pretty chatter, not logic and learning.

G.

II

(*Mencken to Nathan*)

Dear George:—

1. I go with you in the Dunsany and Beerbohm matters. You are the Beerbohmista, not I. I think he blew up in the last century.

2. What you say about the lofty principles of magazine editing diverts and instructs me. You have reached such a stage of cunning that you can put my own ideas into such ingratiating phrases that they convince even me.

3. I enclose a memorandum of R.'s address. Late advices from her are to the effect that she regards me as the White Hope of American literature. No doubt she will be polite to you, as a friend of mine. But don't waste any Gordon gin on a woman who reads the *Yale Review*. That synthetic stuff will please her just as well. If she tries to chuck you under the chin, bid her think of her poor first husband, and what love did for him.

4. I am at work on page proofs, and, as usual, cursing God. Needless to say, the proofs are very muddy, and the queries are all idiotic. I often wonder what has become of all the old-time printers. Most of them were drunkards and pickpockets, but they actually knew how to set up type. I hear that many of the current compositors, and even proofreaders, are women. Another great craft debauched!

5. I am against the last Hussey story. It is a capital piece of work, but it would offend the Catholics, and set every priest in the land to whooping against us. I dislike to outrage the Catholics needlessly, not only because they are the only lodge of Christians who never try to get us barred off the news-stands, but also because they are fundamentally very decent, and detest the uplift almost as much as I do myself. The Hussey story, of course, is sound and true. It would be idiotic to argue that priests never do such things. I know more than one who has gone much further. But the public generalizes, and the gen-

eralization would be false. It would be absurd, certainly, to say that such doings are the rule among them, as petty grafting and bootlicking are the rule, say, among the Methodist clergy. Give Hussey a bottle of vermouth, and he will be glad to change the priest into a Presbyterian.

6. I am full of aches and malaises. No doubt the final breakup is beginning. It is astonishing how all my old vigor diminishes. I used to be able to work fifteen hours a day, but now I am floored after eight or ten. There are days when I find it difficult even to read. A man at my age, having worked as hard as I have for twenty-two years, should retire to some pleasant *Rittergut* and devote himself to raising grapes. I begin to feel very old.

7. Too much ale last night.

8. How much did you say you paid for your last suit of clothes? My tailor is trying to stick me for $105. This seems ghastly. I used to pay $45, and was widely admired as a swell dresser.

M.

III

(*Nathan to Mencken*)

Dear Heinie:—

I'll be good and damned if I give Hussey a bottle of vermouth to change the padré into a Presbyterian. I'll offer him a pint of Acker, Merrall and Condit's California No. 2, but that's as far as I'll go to promote literature in America. I appreciate that you had to give Huneker a small witch-hazel bottle full of green Chartreuse to put clothes on his last heroine and that, accordingly, I owe the firm something, but too much is too much. Let me urge you not to forget that it was I—a year ago—whom you burdened with the job of keeping Dreiser sufficiently oiled to write "Sanctuary" for us, and that the old boy put my cellar back six cases of Pol Roger, three of Macdougal and five of Chambertin 1904. Also let me urge you not to forget that all you gave Walpole when he was over here was a bottle of home-made beer. Unless you loosen up on the Englishmen, we shall have to look elsewhere for stuff. (The *Pictorial Review* crowd must have laid in a magnificent stock.)

I am against the Couperus novel: it is drivel. I am also against the Algernon Blackwood were-wolf nonsense. I am also against the Somerset Maugham second baking of *The Moon and Sixpence*. He has merely strung together what he left out of the novel. Let the big-name magazines have this lot. It is not for us. But I am in favor of using Aldous Huxley's play and the Thyra Samter Winslow story. La Winslow overwrites, but, even so, her work continues to be interesting.

K—— replies that she refuses to reimburse you for the damage her pet dog did to your trousers last Wednesday night. She asserts that the dog was *not* trained to, as you allege, and—further—that your trousers, both legs combined, are not worth the seventy-five cents you demand for cleaning and mental anguish.

The office decorations are coming on nobly. The one-sheet of Louis Robie's "Crackerjacks" looks very tasty. Also the Hoover for President poster. I have my scouts out for photographs of Lillian Russell in tights, Archbishop Mannix and the late Czar Nicholas. I shall autograph them.

Your last literary review is very sour, doctor! Almost as bad as my play review. We are getting stale. We have been writing too much lately. I am tired of work, and think I shall marry a rich widow. I shall name the child Henry.

I have written to both Schnitzler and C——. The latter, I am told, is in London with that French baggage he introduced us to at Monte Carlo six years ago. He has given up writing for the time being. An idiot.

I think that there should be a gilt chair in the office. Imagine the pleasure of steering a fat lady-poet to it, and then watching her collapse on her rear. I'll make an effort to dig up the chair at once. I favor one with two cupids at the top. I recall having seen such a one in the *Vanity Fair* office. I'll drop in casually to see Crowninshield at noon, and steal it. John Williams tells me that he has painted all his gilt Ibsen production chairs a rich mahogany and will use them in his new Ibáñez play. He offers us a blue velvet couch, however; but what could we do with a couch? Let me hear your views on this.

Young Sedgwick is a comer. A cultivated fellow. He writes

well. It is too bad about J—— M——. He should never have married. Take heed!

I spent the week-end with the Scott Fitzgeralds at Westport. Their Jap butler's name is Tanna. I informed Mrs. F. confidentially that he had whispered to me that his real name is Tannenbaum, and that he is a German spy. I have sent him a post-card—addressed Lieutenant Emil Otto Tannenbaum—commanding him to investigate the Fitzgerald cellar and report in code cipher 24-B whether the floor is solid enough to hold a two-ton cannon in the event of war. The rube cops will be surrounding the house by Wednesday. Send him some German newspapers with the haberdashery advertisements marked significantly with red ink. Have them mailed from Washington by your brother. Use German stamps. They will agitate the Westport burlesons.

Tom Smith showed up in my house at five yesterday afternoon elaborately boiled and full of mysterious sotto voce newses about English politics, George Moore, Woodrow Wilson, prohibition raids, the French literary situation, Lloyd George's plans, a Canadian plot against the United States, Joseph Conrad, Marshal Foch, Poincaré, Alys Delysia, and what not. I couldn't make head or tail out of his ominous whisperings. He had on a pair of greenish gray spats and carried an ebony stick with a flashlight in the handle. He also tells me that he has recently got fourteen excellent short stories for the *Century*. A liar.

You are drinking too much. This means more work again for me.

Warner showed up this morning in another new creation—sassafras color. I had to pull down the shades before looking at it.

G.

IV

(*Mencken to Nathan*)

Dear Professor:—

1. I know the gilt chair in the *Vanity Fair* office. It will never do at all. What we want is a genuine piece of the vintage of 1885, with pink damask upholstery. When Dutch Sadie sold out

her place down here, there were four or five such chairs at the auction. Ass that I am, I didn't buy them. John Williams is probably lying about his Ibsen chairs. They were made of reed, heavily gilded, and it would be impossible to make them look like mahogany. He has probably got them in his office at this moment, along with the concrete bust of J. Ranken Towse. Probably Joe Williams would steal both the chairs and the bust for you if you offered him a quart of that Union Hill, N.J., pseudo-gin.

2. Parkhurst, after promising eighteen times to do that piece about the American pianist, now makes the excuse that he has moved six times within the past two months. A quiet month in jail would do him good.

3. I have sent Tannenbaum five copies of the *Berliner Tageblatt,* each plastered with German stamps. Let me know if Fitzgerald is killed when the Westport American Legion raids his house.

4. If Tom Smith actually told you that he had bought fourteen first-rate short stories, then he was tight. The truth is that he has printed exactly one sound short story during the past year, and that one I got for him myself, from Hussey. Hussey is a vain fellow and didn't want to stoop to the *Century,* but I gave him a bottle of Angostura Bitters and he gave up. I suspect that Smith has taken to drugs—probably Glauber's salts.

5. The fact that my current literary piece is flabby stuff is not news to me. I go stale about once a year, and write such stuff that I am almost ashamed to print it. But they get their money's worth during the other eleven months. To get eleven such articles for $4 is really a great bargain. We don't charge them enough.

6. More anon. Hay-fever has me by the coccyx.

M.

Those were bumptious and amusing days and Mencken, despite the circumstance that he was always firmly convinced that one of his legs was already in the grave, spent at least two or three hours a day concocting various elaborate tomfooleries by way of distracting himself from meditations on the Reaper and from the daily grind. Those were the days when the oppo-

sition boys and girls sought to ridicule our literary and critical
pretensions and when we in turn concluded that the most
astute practise on our part would be to set a clown to catch a
clown. Hardly a week passed that some travesty or something
in the nature of the now celebrated "Mencken, Nathan and
God" poem was not projected at one or the other, or both, of
us from the newspaper columns. The "Mencken, Nathan and
God" verses, together with countless paraphrases, are too familiar to call for re-quotation, but I offer a sample or two of
other performances perhaps unrecalled by the present reader:

> Dumbbell, yokel, goof and sap,
>   Fathead, simpleton and silly,
> Imbecile and dolt and yap, .
>   Hanswurst, pantaloon, hili-billy,
> Never mine to scorn or flout you—
> What would Mencken be without you?
>
> Pickle-herring, jackass, dope,
>   Idiot, dinkelspiel and noodle,
> Boob, baloney, half-wit, hansdoodle,
> If it were not for your dizziness
> Nathan would be out of business!

And the following by the eminent Don Marquis, entitled,
"Criticism by Our Own H. L. Mencken":

American literature is imbecilic, because all Americans are
imbeciles. The average American man marries one wife at a
time, and usually pretends to be faithful to her, whether he is
or not. Could anything be more disgusting? The truth is, that
the country is not civilized; it is impossible for any one with
imagination to exist here, unless he insulates himself from the
influences which surround him. I have succeeded in insulating
myself by surrounding myself with George Jean Nathan, the
only person in America, besides myself, who is not a congenital idiot.

Nathan is familiar with the works of Goshoffski, Slimeykoff,
Von Sputum, Schnitzel, Wurst, Badorfski, Von Hasenyager,

Polterspielski, Mangelwurzl, Goulasheff, Pzrztchnsxklchznski and Ziggsky and he sits by the hour and quotes them to me, forming a barrage through which the cretinism of America cannot reach me. I wonder, sometimes, how Nathan has managed to keep himself civilized in America; but he assures me that he has retained his Kultur through association with me. "Mencken," he said to me recently, with that sprightly air of him, "you are colossal."

America was settled by persons who were forced to leave Europe because they were too feeble-minded to exist there. How in the name of God my ancestors happened to get here I do not know. I will have Nathan think up the answer and make up an epigram about it and explain the epigram to me. My ancestors who came to America could not have come because they were stupid, because if this were so their stupidity would manifest itself in me. And I am not stupid. Nathan and I are the only two persons in America who are not stupid.

Nathan is very subtle; sometimes I think he is quite as subtle as I am. We often sit down together and discuss by the hour which of us is the more subtle. No one else in America is subtle, and Nathan and I sometimes think that our subtlety is lost upon America. But, in my thorough and conscientious way, I keep right on being subtle and brilliant, whether I am appreciated or not. Some one has to be subtle and brilliant in this country, inhabited almost entirely by pigs, puritans and halfwits. Nathan and I often wonder if we are not subtle and brilliant enough to bring up the average of the country, in spite of the fact that all the other inhabitants are boobs.

Even if there were any one in America who had anything to say, he would not know how to say it. There is no such one in America who has the faintest conception of what is known in civilized countries as literary style, except Nathan and myself. As an indication of the almost incredible ignorance of Americans, it has been said of me that I have a heavy touch, and that my English is clumsy. The contrary is true; I am perhaps the only person in America whose touch is light, and who is able to write page after page of brilliant causerie in the European manner. I would present many arguments in support of my statement that I have a light touch, and a manner anything but clumsy, did I not know that my audience is incapable of estimating the evidence at its true value. I am never hackneyed, there is nothing stereotyped in my words, there is never any suggestion of cliché.

I have never seen any writing produced in America that is worth my serious consideration; it is all worth nothing more than the raspberry of contempt. So my best criticism is reserved for the authors whose works are quoted to me by Nathan. Nathan quotes all of them in the original languages. In this unlettered country there are very few persons, besides myself and Nathan, capable of doing that; Americans are not only uneducated, but they are inclined to deride education. I have met with a great deal of derision when I was engaged in showing how well educated I am.

Our answer to these pleasantries was forthwith publicly to announce our candidacy for President and Vice-President of the United States and to publish our platform in the pages of the magazine. That platform, embracing one hundred and twenty-two planks—including such items as "We promise to dress exactly as we dressed before election to office and not suddenly affect a note of dignified grandeur by putting on cutaway coats and plug hats"; "We stipulate that we will, immediately after taking office, turn the Philippines over to Japan and that, further, we will coincidentally send Japan a cablegram, prepaid, expressing condolence"; "Since we are writing men by profession, we promise that our public documents and messages will be expressed in language that our constituents can understand"; "We solemnly promise to keep what liquor we need and want in the White House and not in the nearby houses of rich and friendly bounders"; "Believing, as we do, that the influence of the so-called Y.M.C.A. is destructive to the natural instincts and virtues of normal young men, we engage to establish public sanitoria, under competent psychiatrists, for the treatment and cure (if possible) of youths who have been exposed to this pernicious miasma"; and "We agree to kiss no babies, that is, under the age of seventeen"—that platform, in addition to the published planks, was subsequently amplified for our private amusement with various unpublished guarantees, of which the following were examples:

1. We promise to support the spoils system to the utmost and to see to it that the intelligent minority gets all the soft jobs.

2. We promise to hold sacred the obligation to amuse the public and to this end will see to it that enormous arenas are erected all over the country in which, on holidays, the reverend clergy will be turned loose with fire and tongs. The more savage sects, such as Methodists and Presbyterians of Scottish extraction, together with the Rev. W. Sunday, will enter the ring with one arm tied behind them and one eye blindfolded.

3. We promise that all members of the diplomatic corps will be compelled to have their clothes made in England and will be limited in their activities to the nicer amenities of fashionable life. For the purpose of instructing them, one gentleman will be imported each year from Europe.

4. We promise that any legislator introducing a bill to suspend the laws of nature and freedom of conduct shall be immediately re-initiated as a thirty-third degree Elk, with this difference: that for the goat there shall be substituted a fully adult rhinoceros.

5. We promise to place qualifications on all elective and appointive offices as to honor, integrity and mentality, thus automatically disqualifying ninety-eight per cent of the present incumbents.

Never have I known a man who has had so much fun out of life as Mencken had in those years. If, as occasionally happened, one of our business associates in the magazines over which we presided in an editorial capacity found his patriotism offended by an article or an editorial we had published, Mencken had ready for instant use a gang of chain-letter writers, carefully assembled over a period of six years in various parts of the country, who—in response to telegrams—would promptly bombard the office with letters and wires saying that the article or editorial was a masterpiece, the finest thing that the magazine had ever printed, in fact, a wonderful contribution to American literature, and that the communicators warmly congratulated the business heads of the magazine for their courage and integrity in not interfering with the independence of two such very remarkable editors. Whereupon, our associates, flattered, convinced of their great open-mindedness and liberality of viewpoint, and immensely proud of the fact, would take us out and buy us a costly and magnificent lunch, the meanwhile condescending to introduce us, with ill-concealed vanity at being seen in our company, to various bankers, advertising sages and other such dignitaries of their acquaintance. It was at this time, too, that Mencken secretly inaugurated "The American Institute of Arts and Letters (Colored), the Rev. Hannibal S. Jackson, A.B., A.M., Ph.D., LL.D., D.D., Chancellor and Financial Secretary," with head office and chancery at the mythical Sons of Beulah Hall (second floor), Washington, D.C., and—on vivid yellow stationery embellished with a wood-cut of a slightly Ethiopian George Washington—duly informed various eminent Negro-hating politicians and littérateurs in the Southern States that they had been honored with an election to membership and that the inaugural banquet, to which the wives, sisters and sweethearts of the initiates and members were bidden, would be held on a specified date. Other such diversions that entertained our colleague were the mailing broadcast of picture postcards with a photograph of the Emperor Franz Josef's palace at Schönbrunn thereon, together with the caption, "Mr. H. L. Mencken's Summer estates on the Chesapeake," along with stationery prepared for him by a noted Portuguese, engraved with the name of a fictitious legal firm known as Fishbein, Spritzwasser, Garfunkel and Fishbein and conveying to various male friends of a philandering disposition the news that a suit for breach of promise in the sum of one hundred thousand dollars had been instituted against them.

All his letters in that period, to whomever they were addressed, never failed to contain enclosures of tracts on modern dress reform headed "As It Was in the Days of Sodom," urging the recipients to see II Cor. 13:5 and to beseech their womenfolk to abstain from all appearance of immodest dress which exposed the back and chest and limbs—"May every Christian woman take a firm stand against these modern fads, for we feel certain that the devil himself is the direct instigator of every form of immodest dress," or of circulars of the Anti-Tobacco League with the Rev. Frank W. Gunsaulus, D.D., exhorting therein as follows: "I do not believe there is an agency more destructive of soul, mind and body, or more subversive of good morals than the cigarette. The fight against the cigarette is a fight for civilization!" There were also regular accounts of gay parties in his daily correspondence as, for example: "At 7 p.m. today I sit down to a stag but bawdy dinner. X—— is giving it at the House of Mirth I told you of. His gal will be present to see that the imported waiters do not steal anything, and he has made every guest promise on his honor not to sneak upstairs and attempt her. He realizes that he himself will be too drunk to protect her. I shall stick to red wine, with maybe a couple of dozen cocktails to start off"; or "The other night I dropped in at Hermann Oelrichs' atelier and encountered Charlie Chaplin. He had seen Ralph Barton's movie and told me that he believed I had a great deal of acting talent. This resolves my difficulty. I shall take to the film art. If you ever meet Louis B. Mayer, tell him to bear me in mind. I am not unreasonable: I don't want a leading part all at once, but only a chance to prove my gift. Chaplin will coach me in the necessary grimaces." There were, as well, such letters as these to Tom Smith, dictated solemnly by him to our office secretary at the busiest hour in the day and sent off within ten minutes of each other:

I

T. R. Smith, Esq.,
   Editor, the *Century Magazine*, New York City.

Dear Wolfgang:
   We have received your letter and shall be glad to have had the pleasure of having had a chance of having been at the party of which you speak in the letter which we received today. I have just got to town and Mr. Nathan tells me that he has so arranged our engagements that we will be able to be present at the party to which you refer in your letter. I am glad to say that Mr. Nathan has received your invitation and will be present if he arrives in time which he did this morning. Both Mr.

Nathan and Mr. Mencken will be present at the party mentioned in your letter of the 17th inst. which was received this morning.

Very respectfully yours,
H. L. Mencken

II

T. R. Smith, Esq.
Editor, the *Century Magazine,*
New York City.

Dear Llewellyn:

We have not heard as yet if you have obtained the two cuties for us for your party tomorrow night about which you wrote us yesterday in the letter which we received today. Yesterday we wrote you to obtain two such cuties for us for your party, as we told you on that date that we did not like great big girls. You doubtless received this letter yesterday, on which date it was written.

Sincerely yours,
H. L. Mencken

P.S. When we say we do not like big girls, as per our letter of yesterday, we do not mean to say that we like them so small so that you can hardly see them when you look at them. Let them be of fair or medium size, not too large or yet too big.

Coming into the office one morning, he deposited his hat alongside the large brass spittoon which he had bought in Baltimore and installed for his own comfort, and shouted at me: "Chorch, I've got a great idea! John Roach Straton, who is now preaching at the Calvary Baptist Church and who used to be a Baltimorean, is making a lot of raids on the wet places here in New York. Let's invite him to dinner and try to horn in on an invitation to go along. We might get track of some nobby beer-houses that'll be open again for business the day after they're raided." Whereupon, he dictated a letter to the Rev. Dr., duly suggesting that the latter honor us at the meal table with his presence, pulchritude and rich conversational gifts. The next day, came this reply:

One Mencken:

You start your note to me by saying, "If you have forgotten me, then I shall instantly cut my throat." This is a sore temptation to reply by asking, "Who are you?" But I will spare you, Mencken, for old time's sake! I would regret to cut off your fair young life prematurely. Besides which I know it would be embarrassing for you to have to meet Sunday School Field in the nether regions. Besides which, further, I don't know what Pluto would be able to do with both of you on his hands at once!

As for meeting George Jean Nathan, I will be glad to do this, because I know he sorely needs a counter-irritant and an antidote after having associated with you.

I notice your statement that "Down in Baltimore sin is once more triumphant." It was certainly a hard blow to the old town, Mencken, when you and I both had to leave it.

Tell me, honestly now, did Brother S. S. keep a jug behind the door? If there was a jug in the town, I know that your trusty nose would have discovered it, and I always had a sneaking suspicion that you and Brother S. S. had a secret understanding with each other.

I am going away next week for some engagements in the South, but when I come back, I will certainly get into touch with you and Nathan. Of course I understand, Mencken, that the probable object of your letter is to make you and Nathan solid with the pastor of Calvary Baptist Church, so that you can get in on the next vice raid! There are certain conditional limitations, however, to that which I will take up with both of you, confidentially and more in detail, when we meet face to face.

In the meantime, accept assurances of appreciation for your thoughtfulness in writing and please do not allow this letter to fall into the hands of the police, as I would not want any incriminating evidence discovered of a connection between my study and the underworld in the event of a raid on the office of your magazine.

Firmly, but affectionately yours,
John Roach Straton

As Straton had shrewdly detected our invidious purpose, we refrained from further pursuit of the matter, but some time later this second letter, addressed to both of us, arrived:

Gentlemen:—

I am writing to call your attention to the fact that sometime ago we were in correspondence; or, rather, to be more exact, I received a letter from one H. L. Mencken. I do not know whether this character is still running under that name or not. If he has a new alias, I have not been advised of it. I only know that there was a tentative agreement to furnish a dinner, and that said agreement has never been lived up to, nor has the dinner been delivered.

I am writing, therefore, to inquire the thusness of this matter. Was it true that the overtures, which were made to me as above stated, were inspired by the fact that, at the time of that correspondence, New York was excessively arid, and that it was the desire on the part of your firm, with surreptitious purpose, to secure an invitation to accompany me on any further raids that I might be led to make, in the hope that my knowledge of the damp spots in New York might relieve for you two the effects of the aridity hereinbefore mentioned? And is it further true that the matter of the dinner, etc., has been dropped because the aridity in question has been so largely overcome that the wayfaring man, even though he may be a prohibitionist, can get all of the home brew that he desires, and, therefore, that you are not under the painful necessity of looking to this parson and his raids for liquid refreshment?

You will understand, of course, that this letter is written entirely upon the basis of the scientific method. I merely am in search of the truth concerning this situation, and the consideration of the dinner is in no wise material. Hoping, therefore, gentlemen, to receive, at an early date, an acknowledgment of this communication, and any further light which you may care to shed upon the questions considered herein, I am, with all good wishes,

Fraternally yours,
John Roach Straton

I suggested to Mencken that, as Straton had turned the tables on us, we buy him a dinner anyway. "A dinner!" he yelled.
"What do you mean, oaf? The best he'd have got in any case
would have been a Blutwurst sandwich."

In addition to his duties as cavalier to lady novelette writers
in that era, it was part of Mencken's editorial assignment to
write sweet verse for the magazine under a variety of pseudo-
nyms. (There were months when we wrote at least half the
magazine.) Some of the poetry he manufactured was very fair
stuff, while some, upon his becoming duly sober again and
reading it, was voted even by him as being hardly up to the
colossal standard of his richer flights.

Making up the magazine one month, we found that that part
of it which did not consist of our own stuff would have to be
made up in the main of short stories by Ben Hecht, who used
to write available ones at the apparent rate of five or six a week.
"We can't print his name more than twice or three times," argued Mencken. "Tell him to send us some other signatures right
away." I wired Hecht and got this reply: "Herewith, aliases.
1. Barel Barelvitch; 2. Adam Chowsky; 3. Hillaire d'Of; 4. Ivan
Schlivovitch; 5. Moïsse; 6. Irving Reinwein; 7. Pierre Vopika;
8. Feodor Yquem; 9. Alcott Martini; 10. Dri Bere. If you don't
like these, suggest you compose some yourself." So five of the
eight Hecht stories in that issue appeared as the work of such
literary brahmins of Mencken's imagination as John Henslowe
Saltonstall, Elijah Powys Burlingame, the Rev. Dr. Peter Cabot-
Cabot, Ethan Allen Lowell and Jefferson Carter Adams.

Such excursions into jocosity have now become infinitely less
frequent than they used to be. He who once upon a time wrote
topical verses for Lew Dockstader, who composed an article
soberly announcing that the first bathtub ever used in the
United States was one in Cincinnati, Ohio, in 1876—a statement
swallowed whole by the editor of a standard encyclopædia and
duly incorporated by him as fact into the aforementioned
encyclopædia, and who once traveled all the way to France to
have his susceptible friend, Moffatt, threatened with arrest and
a year's imprisonment by a bribed gendarme for beating a
Montmartre peepshow guide out of six francs, causing the
alarmed Moffatt to board the first steamer back to the United

States; he who once sat on Rabelais' lap and assisted in the agreeable low levity of the world, has grown—as have most of us—somewhat more *triste* with the passing of the years. Now and again, however, flashes of the old Mencken still continue to illuminate the new, for no man like Mencken could ever conceivably die with a perfectly straight face. No dinner table at which he sits, accordingly, remains yet entirely undisturbed by one of his habitual lengthy and very intimate disquisitions on the morals and peculiar social habits of the cockroach. His correspondence is still occasionally enlivened with such old-time up-bow flying staccati as "Old X. [an English lady literary critic] naturally hates everything American with a deep and bitter hatred. The last time she was here she came with the definite intention of finding a rich husband and, having failed in that enterprise, she returned home and had to marry an Englishman. No wonder she is indignant"—along with such facetiæ as, "No one seems to have heard of your secret trip to California—that is, no one save Tom Smith, the Associated Press, the Department of Justice, and the various radio announcers"; "You will never see a copy of the telegram. I refuse to show it to you myself and I am warning X—— that if she does so I shall spread the report that she is a colored woman. It was a sweet piece of literature and very discreetly composed. Its effect seems to have been excellent"; and "In the clipping of the Charlton Yarnell society affair I notice a curious thing. First there is a paragraph of 'invited guests.' Then comes one beginning 'Also.' And finally there is one beginning 'Others were.' I observe that Hergy is in No. 2. This is a gross affront to American literature!" Although still loud in his contention that the theatre is a dull institution—a critical philosophy based upon the incompetence of a Baltimore stock company whose production of *East Lynne* he reviewed for a home-town newspaper back in 1905—, he now condescends to enter one occasionally and invariably comes away having had the time of his life, although he will stoutly deny it the next morning. From London, while he was covering the Naval Conference, I got this word: "I went to the theatre last night and a clown, Bobbie Hawes, damn nigh doubled me up. I am bringing him to America to entertain visitors to my estates. Let us match him against that other big wow, Bobby Clark." Yet when, upon his return, I observed to him that this Hawes must be a very funny comedian, "Lousy!" he replied. On a malty cruise to the Caribbean early this year, he alleviated the ship's routine with various contributions to the ship's daily paper, including a confidential description of a contemplated new 1,500-foot super-ship planned by the North German Lloyd. "This Doppelschraubenpostexpressluxuskolossalriesendampfer will have a half-mile cinder track, a stadium seating 2,000 and a fourth class for professors. In the first class accommodations, there will be no cabins, but only apartments. There will also be twenty penthouses. The ship's doctor will have twenty assistants and there will be a hospital equipped to extract fifty appendices and 500 tonsils a day. There will be Catholic and Protestant churches on the top deck, and space for communists, single-taxers, birth controllers and other reformers will be provided on the boat decks, with free soap boxes. There will also be half a dozen speakeasies." Another contribution, published in the paper on the final day of the cruise, gave the passengers landing in New York instructions as to where to find speakeasies, noting that all of them might be visited in a span of sixty years. "Visitors are cautioned," he wrote, "that at the following places in New York no alcoholic refreshments are served: Grant's Tomb (well spoken of), the Cathedral of St. John the Divine, Carnegie Hall, the Hall of Fame at New York University, the Metropolitan Museum of Art, and the Public Library."

In the main, however, the four-handed scherzo that we used to play vivacissimo together on the barroom piano of life has become for him—as, I suspect, for me as well—rather more suggestive of a Ländler waltz.

[From *The Intimate Notebooks of George Jean Nathan*, 1932, pp. 94–121.]

Theodore Dreiser

IT was seventeen years ago that a morning's mail brought to me the brief note from Theodore Dreiser that led that same evening to what was really, save for a casual word some seven years earlier, my first meeting with him. "I urge you please to come down to my place at eight o'clock tonight. I have asked a dozen or so others as well. I want to present to you a significant and very important idea that I have in mind." My curiosity aroused by the cryptical subpœna, I appeared at the little flat in West Tenth Street in which he was then living and ushered by him into a tiny room packed like soda crackers with at least twenty men, all of them talking at once and nine-tenths of them smoking the smelliest cigars that my nose in all its wide experience had engaged. In the group there was only one man whom I had ever seen before, George Luks, the painter. Who the rest were, I had not the faintest idea and haven't to this day, as Dreiser made no gesture toward an introduction further than to announce "Nathan" upon my entrance and as the great news seemed to be completely lost in the enveloping din.

"The others will be in any minute now," he informed me. "Then we can get down to business. In the meantime, find yourself a seat on the floor."

Shortly thereafter four or five more men came in. They, too, were strangers to me, as they seemed to be to one another. As Luks, whom Huneker had once introduced me to, was occupied elsewhere and, as I say, I didn't know anyone else, I duly found myself a place on the floor, sat myself simultaneously on it and a small sticky piece of cake that had evidently been lying there for a couple of days, and awaited the significant and very important Dreiserian evangel. After numerous injunctions praying the assemblage to shut up and listen to what he had to say, Dreiser took his position in the centre of the mob, blew violently for several minutes at the thick cloud of smoke that hid the congress from his view, took out his handkerchief and, catching two ends of it with his fingers, began slowly to roll and unroll it, and proceeded:

"I've asked you all here to tell you of a plan I've thought of and to get your views on it. It's this. There are a lot of writing geniuses in America who are so poor that they can't go ahead with what they've got in them and who need help. Unless they get help, these geniuses, so far undiscovered, will never be heard of. It's my idea that what we all ought to do is to go around and try to interest rich men in these geniuses and get them to subsidize them. Let me hear your opinions."

He had hardly got the word *opinions* out of his mouth than Luks, a low fellow given, it was whispered, to an occasional indulgence in alcoholic liquor, let out such a loud and derisory hoot that poor Dreiser was a full minute in regaining his equilibrium. Fixing the offender with his characteristic cold one-eyed stare, he bade the reason for the unseemly interruption.

"Who are these neglected great geniuses?" Luks demanded. "Just you name me *one!*"

"That's not the point," returned Dreiser.

"Well, if that isn't the point," shouted Luks, "for God's sake what is? Name *one* neglected genius, old boy, and hurry up about it, as this floor is damned hard and my backside is getting sore."

"There are a lot of them," Dreiser insisted, but his confidence began perceptibly to show signs of weakening.

"All right," hammered Luks, taking a swig out of a pocket-flask that he had thoughtfully brought with him. "All right, old boy, but just you go ahead and relieve our minds by naming *one* of them!"

Dreiser continued slowly to roll and unroll the handkerchief, the meanwhile still fixing Luks with that cold left eye.

"I'm waiting, old boy," chuckled Luks, wiping off his mouth with the back of his hand. "Just you name *one!*"

We waited, but Dreiser made no move.

"Well, I guess the meeting's over," said Luks. "Let's get the hell out of here!"

And the meeting was over.

As some men's hobby is collecting postage stamps or Buxbeutel and others' discovering out-of-the-way little restaurants or recondite cocktail mixtures, Dreiser's—like Lewis'—is discovering and collecting geniuses. Since the days of my early acquaintance with him, he has discovered and collected about him more geniuses than ever were heard of in the world before. The only trouble with Dreiser's geniuses is that, for some strange reason, no one ever considers them geniuses but himself, conceivably due to the fact, among other things, that they never seem to have done or to do anything. But though they never produce anything to suggest their dower of genius, Dreiser is in each instance sure that they are geniuses. Who they are or where they hail from, none of Dreiser's friends has ever been able to learn. What is more, their names are for the most part and remain for the most part meaningless. They do not write books or poems or plays; they do not paint or carve out marble; they do not compose music or play the piano, violin or xylophone. At least, if they do, only Dreiser seems to be privy to the news. But that they all are blessed with the divine fire to an incalculable degree, he will confidently assure anyone who will lend him an ear. I myself have met no less than two or three hundred of these great geniuses either in Dreiser's company or upon receipt of letters of introduction from him. But just what direction their genius took or what masterpieces they were responsible for I have never quite been able to make out, although I have listened patiently and politely to their voluble and enthusiastic tributes to their own talents. Looking back over all the theoretical Flauberts, Beethovens, Sardous and Raphaels of Dreiser's faith, there is only one, in point of fact, whose name appears even faintly to have ever been heard of outside of Dreiser's rooms. That one is the recently deceased Charles Fort, a writer happy in the conviction that all science was simply so much blather, and in whose enormous metaphysical and literary prowess Dreiser had fervently and steadfastly believed for all of fifteen years. What has become of his other many pets, I do not, as recorded, know.

When first I met him, Dreiser, as I have said, was living in a couple of two-by-four rooms in West Tenth Street. He was miserably hard up and was existing, he told me, on something like ten dollars a week. But he never whined, never grumbled. In all that time, indeed, I heard him complain only once and that was because whoever lived in the cellar under him—his rooms were on the first floor of a seedy and dilapidated three-story house—made so much noise at night that he couldn't work. He subsequently learned that the cellar was occupied by two Italians engaged in the august profession of counterfeiting. The police some time afterward backed up a patrol-wagon late one night to apprehend the knaves, but the latter, while the police were gumshoeing around the front of the house, quietly departed out of the rear entrance. Thereafter, Dreiser was able to pursue belles lettres in peace.

Although his rooms looked like a brace of dry-goods boxes that had been left on a wharf during several months of severe storms, he had exercised himself to give them a tone. The aforesaid tone was accomplished by covering the two windows with red hangings which excluded all light, illuminating the *mise en scène* with candles, and maintaining a small phonograph in constant operation upon three mournful Russian musical records. There, for hours on end, he would sit in the dim candlelight, rolling and unrolling his handkerchief, and listening in rapt taciturnity and open-eyed wonder to the dolesome emanations from the wax—at intervals of every five or ten minutes opening his mouth only to ejaculate, "Beautiful, beautiful!"

Now and again in those days, Mencken and I would seek to lighten our friend's obstinate moodiness with facetiæ of one species or another, but never with the faintest degree of success. It was one of our juvenile monkeyshines to fill the mailbox outside his door with a variety of objects, including small American flags accompanied by scrawls issuing Black Hand threats, letters ostensibly written by the President urging him to come at once to the White House for a confidential talk, menus of Armenian restaurants affectionately inscribed to him by Robert W. Chambers, Elinor Glyn and Harold Bell Wright, frankfurters tied with red, white and blue ribbons, beer-bottle labels, photographs of the Czar bearing the inscription, "To Theodore, gentleman and scholar—well, anyway, scholar," and other such nonsense. Dreiser's invariable retort was to go out, buy a ten-cent Street and Smith paper-back by Bertha M. Clay and present it to us with the sour remark that it was the only kind of literature either of us could understand. This was his single form of humorous repartee. I still have, among the works of Mlle. Clay that he presented to us, such masterpieces as *Redeemed by Love, or Love Works Wonders, For a Woman's Honor, The Gipsy's Daughter, A Heart's Idol, Another Man's Wife, Gladys Greye* and *His Perfect Trust.*

On one occasion, knowing how badly he needed money, Mencken and I consulted an acquaintance connected with the moving pictures in an effort to get him some kind of offer that might bring him easy funds and permit him to pursue in comfort the novel that he was then working on. We finally got an offer for him of two thousand dollars. All that he would have to do was to pose before the camera in his own person, seated at a desk writing. The picture dealt with a novelist and it was the idea to show a well-known novelist at work by way of an introduction. He was not to figure in the story; after the short series of shots his job would be done and the two thousand dollars would be his. Not without a feeling of satisfaction over our achievement, since it involved no invasion of Dreiser's dignity, we hurried down to tell him of it. Firmly convinced, despite our protestations, that we were up to another joke at his expense, he grew excessively indignant, cursed us out roundly, and refused us the honor of personal contact with him until further notice.

It was fully six months before I saw him again. We found ourselves seated next to each other at a small stag dinner given by T. R. Smith in a private room at the Beaux Arts restaurant. Dreiser, who had succumbed to the geniality of the wassail bowl, was in high spirits, roaring with laughter over any and everything, pulling chairs out from under the guests, offering toasts to the glory of Jehovah, and making loud Swiss music on the table glasses with his knife. "So here you are again, by God!" he bellowed, clapping me lustily on the back and mussing up my hair. "So here you are again. Well, well, well! Look who's here, fellows! It certainly is an awful sight. Yes sir, it certainly is! Take a look, all of you. My God, what a face! So here you are again! It certainly is a great thrill; yes sir, it certainly is! Ho, ho, ho, so here you are again!" And so on for fully fifteen minutes, all to the accompaniment of reverberating yowls of pleasure and chuckles of self-satisfaction over his great sardonic humor. So tickled was he, indeed, over his imagined complete retaliation for the moving picture episode that we became friends again in his eyes and have so remained, without further interruption, until this day.

Only once was that friendship even mildly threatened and that was when Mencken and I, then editing the *Smart Set,* after publishing a number of his manuscripts of the usual more or less despondent nature, suggested to him that he do a story for us of a somewhat different character. "What kind of story?" he wanted to know. "Why not a society story," suggested

Mencken, swallowing a grin. "Something very swell and tony. Get out of the tenements and dirty undershirt atmosphere for a change. It'll do you good." Oblivious of Mencken's jocosity, Dreiser allowed that he might try his hand at some such story and, lo and behold, about two days later the result arrived. The scene was laid in Cincinnati and the occasion was a great ball given by the leader of the élite in that city. The very air quivered with *ton*. There were "no less than dozens of butlers" and the heroine, "an heiress of the *beau monde,* swept down the great staircase attired in very trig green satin." Other ladies present were also attired in "trig green satin" and the climax of the "trig affair" came when the hostess confronted the "fashionable multimillionaire, Mr. Diamondberg" and accused him, in the middle of the ballroom, of having swindled her husband out of a street-railway franchise. When we sent the story back to him, he was surly over our failure to appreciate its elegances and held me equally responsible with Mencken for having wasted his time and energy.

As, gradually, money came to him from his writings and life became easier for him, his nature expanded in many directions. His attitude toward his work did not change, for nothing, I believe, could ever change that. If he had ten dollars in his pocket or ten hundred thousand, nothing or no one could influence him once he took pen in hand. Even in the poor days when at times he was forced by necessity to write on order, he wrote with complete honesty, the best he knew how, and—whether it was liked and accepted or not—with a sincerity that was not to be mistaken. If he has ever done hack work, he at least did not regard it as such. Even the story about the heiress of the *beau monde* attired in trig green satin was an honest job so far as he himself viewed it. But, if affluence altered his attitude toward his work no whit, it altered—and why not?—his manner of living. The first large round sum of money that came to him, the proceeds of the sale of *An American Tragedy* to the moving pictures, resulted in the installing of himself in an elaborate duplex studio apartment, with a brace of colored girls in white capes and aprons to add a note to the scene, with monthly soirées and receptions involving the activities of Hungarian violinists, Russian coloratura sopranos and an interna-

tional and marvelous assortment of dubious pianistic professors, and with a cut-glass punch bowl, banked with lettuce
sandwiches, caviar sandwiches and *petits fours,* glistening in
splendor on the dining-room table. There also followed the purchase of an estate up the Hudson, with a remodeled house
large enough to hold a good part of the Authors' League of
America, and with a swimming pool, a small lodge house for
visiting bachelors, and a set of very dégagé after-dinner coffee
cups. There appeared on the scene, as well, what is known as
"a man," a colored gentleman whose profession embraced the
taking of cards at the door, the pressing of trousers, the service
of beverages and a close scrutiny of the behavior of any visiting poets. "Is it possible that that host of ours was Dreiser,
Theodore Dreiser?" Fannie Hurst once demanded of me in
ironic perplexity upon leaving one of the studio gatherings.
"Say what you will, I won't believe it!"

Dreiser's simplicity, however, for all the great change in his
external surroundings, is still his simplicity of the days when
he hadn't a cent. His friends are still the friends of those days;
his cast of mind is still exactly the same; his diversions are still
composed of such innocent adventures as going to the movies,
having an occasional dinner in some side-street Italian or Chinese speakeasy, or taking a trip to Coney Island, Asbury Park
or Atlantic City. "What I am still looking for," he has told me,
"in the midst of all this success that seems to have come to me,
is some little, greasy one-horse publisher who wouldn't know a
mahogany desk if he saw one but who has a high and very real
love for literature and who, though he may be poor in money,
will have time to talk sincerely with me about my work, and understand the kind of man I am, and let me talk with him
through the nights of all that is in my mind and heart. I am sick
of these business-men publishers with their offices that look
like the *Ile de France* and with their minds that look on books
as if they were so many boxes of merchandise."

A Socialist—"Equitist" he calls it—in philosophy, and a very
indignant one to boot, with a passion for writing letters to
newspapers and magazines inveighing against the rank injus-
tices of the capitalistic system, he is so absolutely earnest in his
convictions that I honestly believe that if the issue were

brought to a head he would be the first to give every cent he owned in the world into the common fund. "I really don't need or want money," he has said to me, "though under the existing order of things you may be damned sure I want and get every dollar that is coming to me. But I could still live on ten dollars a week and probably be just as happy on it." The trip to Russia that he undertook several years ago made a tremendous impression upon him. Among the things other than economic, governmental and the like that moved him deeply and set him to a profound ponderation was Russian art. Immediately upon his return, he sought me out and bade my help in introducing one of the greatest phenomena of this art to America. "It's wonderful!" he proclaimed. "There's nothing in the whole world like it! It will be a revelation to this country!" I asked him what it was. "The Russian ballet," he gravely informed me. "But," I protested, "Americans already know almost as much about the Russian ballet as the Russians. It has been shown here time and again." Dreiser looked at me, disbelief all over him. "You don't say so!" he remarked. "Well, isn't that odd now." He was very much disappointed.

One always finds Dreiser surprised and amazed at what has long been familiar to most persons. When he sees something for the first time, it is discovered to the world so far as he is concerned. Once, returning from a trip through the West, he hotly demanded why no one had ever remarked on the majesty of the Grand Canyon. "It's gorgeous, beautiful, that's what it is!" he announced. "People should be told about it." Going to Europe for the first time at forty, he subsequently delivered himself of a book full of wide-eyed marvelings at various Continental cities, peoples and customs that had already been written about by hundreds of men before him and that were subjects of long-standing knowledge to almost everybody else.

Even more greatly so than O'Neill is Dreiser fundamentally a lugubrious fellow. Despite his fitful excursions into a swollen humor, his nature is cast o'er with melancholy and even his occasional search for diversion of one kind or another has implicit in it a tendency toward and taste for the glum, the depressing and the morbid. While I will not go so far as to say that his favorite form of melody is the requiem, it is pretty safe to say that nothing really appeals to him in the way of music save that which, in the bumpkin expression, is described as "sad." In the movies, to which he often goes, only the more drab and despairful Russian films make any impression upon him, although there is a single qualification here in the instance of the comedy films of Laurel and Hardy, which he peculiarly delights in. He cannot stand high lights and, wherever he lives, his rooms have the aspect of an undertaker's boudoir. When he goes to a restaurant, he prefers one that is so dimly illuminated that he can hardly make out whether he is eating spaghetti or chop suey. He spends many hours in drugstores examining the stocks of pills, medicaments, embrocations and tinctures, which he lays in by the wholesale, never traveling out of reach of a pharmacy without carrying with him a suitcase chock full of his grim purchases. Any man with whiskers is immediately accepted by him as a distinguished and very learned person. His taste in reading is for novels in which everyone dies a horrible death and in which the groans fill at least one hundred and fifty of the book's pages.

Of all the writers whom I know intimately, Dreiser is the only one who actually enjoys the physical business of writing. Whereas the rest of these men hate the actual business of putting their thoughts and inspirations upon paper, complain bitterly of the dreadful chore that literary composition is, and do all sorts of things to try to divert themselves from the misery that envelops them when they sit down to their desks, Dreiser would rather write than do anything else. He looks forward to the day's job as another writer looks impatiently ahead to the hour when it will be finished. "I am a writer; I like to write; and I am wretched when I don't write," he has told me. "If I don't produce three thousand words a day, I'm unhappy." He writes, writes, writes. Commonly regarded as being mainly devoted to the novel form, he has written in more various literary forms than any other American of repute. Aside from novels, he has turned out poetry, long plays, short plays, short stories, travel books, special articles on all kinds of subjects, political and economic feuilletons, special newspaper assignments, Sunday supplement feature stories, pamphlets, essays, personality sketches, magazine articles, newspaper editorials, dramatic criticism, fashion articles, autobiography, novelettes and magazine fillers. He has written on women violinists, interior decoration, carrier pigeons in war time—"Their Use on Warships and Capabilities in Carrying Swift Information," life stories of successful men, electricity in the household, American portrait painters, Japanese home life, the horseless age, American women playwrights, American female harp players, the Society for the Prevention of Cruelty to Animals, the food problem, the subway, the history of the horse, the rural free mail delivery, Hollywood, Ty Cobb, movie actors, antique furniture, American foreign relations, chicken ranches, baseball, railroad wrecks, street-car strikes, insects, matrimonial problems, Marshall Field, Thomas A. Edison, Philip Armour, Chauncey Depew, Mrs. Clara Shortridge Foltz—"A Modern Portia,"—cats and dogs, babies, metal workers, photography, "Artistic and Literary People in the Picturesque Bronx," the cash register business, sweat shops, the right to kill, applied religion, the Authors' League of America, and diseases. . . .

Almost any kind of movement or cause finds in him a ready-made and excitedly eager sympathizer. Ever since he helped to organize something known as the National Child Rescue Campaign back in 1907, he has either been helping to organize or serving on committees to rectify one or another national, political, economic, social or literary ill. His name has figured on more letterheads proposing crusades for or against any and everything than even Mr. Lincoln Steffens' or Mrs. Charles Sabin's. He has been on anti-censorship committees, Sacco-Vanzetti committees, Mooney committees, assistance for starving Armenians committees, baby milk committees, free library committees, committees for a better understanding of the Soviet, bread-line committees, committees for a better understanding of Socialism, committees for a truer understanding of Communism, committees to raise funds for monuments, tenement investigation committees, committees for better movies, committees to reopen wrongful convictions of alleged criminals, literary committees, committees to protest against the sewage conditions at Far Rockaway, anti-noise committees, committees to beautify Greenwich Village, civil liberties committees, committees to look after the welfare of poets' widows, Indiana state anthem committees, committees to erect statues to his late brother, tree-saving committees, sailors' aid committees, committees in protest against the deportation of alleged radicals, committees to investigate the white slave traffic, committees to investigate the condition of mine workers and millhands, committees protesting the lynching of Negro Lotharios, committees against child labor, committees against the high cost of living, pro-Ben Lindsey committees, pro-Jurgen committees, anti-Prohibition committees, and scores of others. If he has ever turned down anyone who asked him to serve on a committee, provided only that it did not involve him in the necessity of attending a banquet, there is no record of the fact.

As to criticism of his writings, favorable or unfavorable, he has for the last twenty years displayed a sublime and complete indifference. Indignant over many things, what is said against him personally or professionally is of not the slightest concern to him. When some friend of his wrathfully brings to his notice some particularly ignorant, prejudiced and nasty critical comment on his work, he quietly rolls and unrolls his handkerchief, chuckles softly and says, "Oh, yes?" That is his invariable rejoinder, amplified only on rare occasions with an adagio ejaculation of the *mot de Cambronne*. In all the long time that I have known him, I recall only three instances when anything printed about him invaded his composure in the remotest degree. On each of these occasions what was said about his writings did not interest him in the least; it was the reflection on him personally that mildly tried his temper. The first instance was when James L. Ford asserted in the New York *Herald* that any man who wrote the kind of stuff that Dreiser wrote should be shot, and that it was impossible for any person in decent society longer to speak to him. The second instance was when the New York *Times*, in an article on Zola's death, pointed out that Zola "had died falling in his own vomit" and that "it would be well for an American writer named Dreiser, a disciple of Zola, to take note." The third instance was when a reviewer on a Montreal paper—I believe it was the *Star*—observed that only a man who had plumbed the depths of perversion could write such a novel as *The Genius*.

One night about a year ago, on the eve of his sixtieth birthday, we sat together over the rosy waters contemplating the literary scene. I telescope a few snatches from his conversation: "Take Shaw. The old fellow makes a sad idiot of himself trying to convince himself through other people that he's still young and spry. I had lunch with him in his flat when I was last in London and guess what the bug did! After each course, he jumped up from the table, grabbed hold of two chairs, placed them some five and a half feet apart, adjusted his chin on one and his feet on the other, and then—in a horizontal position—chinned himself up and down on them for a couple of minutes. When lunch was over and I was safely out of the place, he probably had to go to bed and rest up for twelve hours from the exertion of having impressed me, as he believed, with his remarkable youthful vitality. . . . Take Wells. A notable man, but so persistently damned British in his point of view that I can no longer carry on any correspondence with him. We corresponded for quite a time, but it got so not long ago that his unyielding British prejudices made it impossible for me to get any satisfaction out of trying to exchange opinions with him. . . . Take George Moore. I had a visit with him several years ago and hoped to have a long chat on literature with the old fellow. And what do you imagine he spent the whole three hours talking about? About his prostate gland! . . . The trouble with literary men is that they leave widows. When you once wrote that a widow is the financial remains of a love affair, you said a mouthful, my boy! I tried lately to get together a collection of short stories by poor So-and-So, who died some ten years ago, write an introduction to them, and so not only help perpetuate his reputation but get a little money for his widow. And what did the old girl do? She accused me of a plan to make money for myself, together with a reputation, at her dead husband's expense. A fact! All widows of literary men ought to be buried with them. They're generally all the same. I've run up against any number of them in my time and they always imagine that any friend of their late lamenteds is some kind of ghoul. . . . Andreyev is the world's greatest dramatist. His *Devil in the Mind* is a tremendous play. I know it is, because I happen to know a man who's exactly like his central character. . . . David Graham Phillips was as overestimated as hell. But Harold Frederick and Will Payne were two real geniuses of Phillips' day who were never properly appreciated. . . . Don't talk to me of current American literature. The profound amours of amateur emotions—that's what the bulk of it is. . . . I don't believe in saints, but there's one man on this earth who strikes me as being one, and he's Abraham Cahan. . . . Plagiarism? The hell with it! Take Gross, the Chicago merchant who was a friend of mine, and Rostand who stole his play and made it into *Cyrano de Bergerac*. I thoroughly believe Rostand swiped my friend's play and I helped my friend out in his lawsuit. But Rostand made it into a beautiful thing, didn't he, so what's the odds? . . . Critics are getting too rich. More of them ought to starve to death. Every time I hear of a critic who is hardly getting enough to eat I laugh until I bust my galluses. Nothing personal, however, nothing personal, mind you. Ha-ha-ha. . . ."

[From *The Intimate Notebooks of George Jean Nathan*, 1932, pp. 38–53.]

Ferenc Molnár

WE were sitting one morning two Summers ago, Ferenc Molnár, Dr. Rudolf Kommer and I, in the little garden of a coffeehouse in the Austrian Tyrol. "Your writing?" we asked him. "How do you regard it?" Languidly he readjusted the inevitable monocle to his eye. "Like a whore," he blandly ventured. "First, I did it for my own pleasure. Then I did it for the pleasure of my friends. And now—I do it for money."

[From *The Intimate Notebooks of George Jean Nathan*, 1932, pp. 63–4.]

ON NOVELISTS AND POETS

The American Novelist

WITH a few immediately recognizable exceptions, the novel in America suffers from the fact that it is written by men and women who, for all their pretence to the contrary, are in the matter of mind, life, attitude and environment essentially and actually country-jakes. This imbued yokel grain shows itself whenever they engage themes and characters not themselves intrinsically yokel—and not only then, but also on occasion even when they concern themselves with such very themes and characters. Conning at such times many an otherwise meritorious novel, the more culturally experienced and cosmopolitan reader is periodically alienated from complete concord and respect by the author's unconscious betrayal of himself as cousin at least to the characters he dissects and as a more or less comfortable habitué of the sorry landscape he describes. The American novel in the aggregate has straw in its hair and a trace of cow on its boot even when its hair has been deceptively polished to a tony gloss and when the mark on its boot is English. Written in the main by provincials, worthy though they are, one misses in it that silent and hidden yet pervasively articulate metropolitan and world-balanced note that one finds in the novels of even the lesser Europeans.

[From *Monks Are Monks*, 1929, pp. 62–3.]

Love in American Fiction

WHY is it that none of our later American writers has ever written a good novel dealing with love? Very simply, because none of them knows anything about love, or at best, very little. That is the reason why the only good straight love stories produced in America are very short stories—things like Lee Pape's *Little Girl* or Ruth Suckow's *Just Him and Her* or Edwin Lefevre's *Without End*. All that the American knows about love may readily be put into twenty-five hundred or even fewer words. We have had some pretty fair sex novels, but almost anybody can write a pretty fair sex novel. I have read some good ones by men who had never before lifted a pen—Steele's *One Man*, for example. But it takes a lover to write a novel of love, even before it takes a writer. How many exceptions to that rule can you think of in the great literature of love? Our American novelists who try to write of love haven't anything of the lover in them. They can write convincingly enough of the love of farmhands, mill superintendents, mining engineers, cowboys, yokels and tradesmen, but there they are brought by natural personal limitations to a halt. Their love is simply a theme song for a moving picture, interrupted periodically by forced ironic toots. What American novelist can you remotely imagine as being loved by a Ninon de l'Enclos or de Maintenon—or even a George Sand or Countess d'Agoult?

[From *Monks Are Monks*, 1929, pp. 158–9.]

Poet

A POET, any real poet, is simply an alchemist who transmutes his cynicism regarding human beings into an optimism regarding the moon, the stars, the heavens, and the flowers, to say nothing of Spring, love, and dogs. Was Leopardi less a writer of deathless verse because he was one of the darkest pessimists who ever lived? Show me an optimist and, almost without exception, I'll show you a bad poet.

[From *Monks Are Monks*, 1929, pp. 163–4.]

Ambrose Bierce

WHENEVER I meet a man with a pretense to critical sagacity in the matter of American *belles lettres*, I have an annoying habit of asking him his opinion of the late lost, strayed or stolen Mr. Ambrose Bierce. If, upon the question, he imparts to me a crisp wink, I put him down in my mental files as a fellow worth cultivating. If, on the other hand, he goes into an encomiastic clog, I dismiss him as one whose critical faculties have still not outgrown their adolescence. For I believe that an admiration of Bierce, among men of my generation, is invariably an unconscious hangover from the enthusiasm of their youth, when an epigram—provided only it were sufficiently cynical—was the last word in worldly wisdom and when any story of the occult in which the tall grass was mysteriously agitated by something (spelled with a capital S) was a dark-shudderful masterpiece.

Bierce's persistent reputation as an eminento of letters is undoubtedly due to these long-pants laudators with an unrevoked short-pants rapture. Certainly a sedulous scrutiny of his collected works reveals little adult basis for it. He was, at his best, little more—in *The Monk and the Hangman's Daughter* (a paraphrase of a translation by Danziger of Richard Voss)—than a prelusive George Sylvester Viereck; little more—in *Can Such Things Be?* and *Tales of Soldiers and Civilians* (*In the Midst of Life*)—than a somewhat superior *Black Cat* magazine writer. His fables in *Cobwebs from an Empty Skull* and in *Fantastic Fables* are second-rate Alfred Polgar and fifth-rate Dunsany. And as for his *Write It Right*, the title itself provides abundantly illuminating criticism. As editor of the *Argonaut* and the *Wasp*, Bierce had his points, but his so-called Prattle columns, which he contributed for years to the San Francisco *Examiner*, when re-read today seem pitiably weak and empty beside the columns of such men as Heywood Broun, Westbrook Pegler, *et al*.

It is the consistent custom of Bierce's champions, however, to meet any such derogatory appraisal of his literary performances with the proud exclamation, "Ah, but what of *The Devil's Dictionary!*" This *Devil's Dictionary* is not only one of their powerful legends, but one of literary America's at large. It is held out as the paragon of true and devastating wit, the trump of polished, crystallized acid. Well, take a look at it. I open it and quote a few samples from under the A's alone; they sufficiently suggest the flavor of what is under the B's, C's, D's and on to the Z's:

ABASEMENT, *n.* A decent and customary mental attitude in the presence of wealth or power. Peculiarly appropriate in an employee when addressing an employer.

ABDICATION, *n.* An act whereby a sovereign attests his sense of the high temperature of the throne.

ABSCOND, *v.i.* To "move in a mysterious way," commonly with the property of another.

ACADEME, *n.* An ancient school where morality and philosophy were taught. Academy, *n.* (from academe). A modern school where football is taught.

ADMIRAL, *n.* That part of a war-ship which does the talking while the figure-head does the thinking.

ADMONITION, *n.* Gentle reproof, as with a meat-axe.

AFFIANCED, *pp.* Fitted with an ankle-ring for the ball-and-chain.

AMBIDEXTROUS, *adj.* Able to pick with equal skill a right-hand pocket or a left.

ANOINT, *v.t.* To grease a king or other great functionary already sufficiently slippery.

APOTHECARY, *n.* The physician's accomplice, undertaker's benefactor and grave worm's provider.

APPEAL, *v.t.* In law, to put the dice into the box for another throw.

APRIL FOOL, *n.* The March fool with another month added to his folly.

ARCHITECT, *n.* One who drafts a plan of your house, and plans a draft of your money.

ARMOR, *n.* The kind of clothing worn by a man whose tailor is a blacksmith.

ARSENIC, *n.* A kind of cosmetic greatly affected by the ladies, whom it greatly affects in turn.

Gentlemen, I ask you!

One speculates as to the origins of the notion that Bierce was a considerable somebody. Like the late Richard Harding Davis, he had a superficially impressive front and a superficially impressive manner; these, as they often do, may have contrived to make certain impressionable men confound the big brass sign outside the bank for the amount of gold in its vault.

He had, in addition, a romantic Civil War record, and a romantic war record isn't a bad asset to any writer, particularly in the minds of his contemporary critics who have served in the commissary department, or as pot-bearers in field hospitals and butlers to the General's horse. And there were a number of such in the Civil War. Further, in the San Francisco of his day, Bierce—with his large manner and small competence—was a big toad in a little hole. He looked important; he comported himself importantly; he spouted importantly. He possessed the faculty of investing himself with a certain degree of awesomeness, like a movie actor in the city to the south today who has a Picasso in his bathroom and has once had a Duke stay overnight in his house. What was more, he had that most precious of all speciously impressive gifts: the air of a man who always seemed superior and independent and, even when without a sou in the world, at perfect and lofty ease among those with ample funds.

In every smaller city, there is and always has been some writer or newspaper man who is singled out for matinée-idolizing by his cronies and certain of the town folk. It is a matter partly of local pride and partly of the average man's insistent need to number among his friends and acquaintances someone, however essentially dubious, to talk about, brag about, and in a degree look up to. In every newspaper office in every such city there is one such great hero. Bierce was the selection in the San Francisco of his time. And it was not long thereafter that he was advertised broadcast by his loving friends in the same ecstatic breath with the California climate, the size of the redwood trees, the sunset on the Golden Gate, and the one-dollar girls in Chinatown.

The first and biggest fall-guy was that charming fellow, the late Percival Pollard. Percy—God rest his good soul—was the greatest discoverer of his critical period. Hardly a week passed that he didn't discover a tremendous genius in one corner of the globe or another. In his day, Percy discovered geniuses by the wholesale and by the freight carload. The only trouble with the great majority of his geniuses was that they didn't seem to have much noticeable talent. But that never deterred Percy, as a glance through his critical manifestoes will attest.

Percy's geniuses ranged all the way from *Schuhplättler* in Munich cabarets to female Polish mystics and from mural-painter graduates of comic weeklies to the more comely French young girl aphrodisiacal poets. And in due time and in the natural course of events, Bierce took his place in the Pollard Hall of Fame. That was the send-off, and it was not very long afterward that the younger critics, now grown to more or less venerable manhood, who—along with their still small and enthusiastic Bierce-reading sons—continue to foster the Bierce legend.

[From *Passing Judgments*, 1935, pp. 74–9.]

David Graham Phillips

I HAVE made bold to ascribe the legend of the genius of Ambrose Bierce to the persistent sentimentality (and ignorance) of present-day adults still in their 1890–5 literary diapers. It is my point that it is these uncritical and unwitting throwbacks of youngsterdom who, not taking the trouble to reappraise the enthusiasms of their youth, are largely responsible for perpetuating the doctrine that Bierce, a third-rater if ever there lived one, was a piercing wit, a devastating iconoclastic mind, and a very high-toned literary artist. In the same way I should like to call attention to another great literary hero of the critics and public of twenty-five years ago, and make equally bold to analyze him in the light of a current rereading.

This second hero is David Graham Phillips who, during his lifetime and for some years thereafter, was widely hailed as one of the greatest of American realists and as one of the finest of American novelists. In this last year I have undertaken, in the service of truth and the national honor, to read again every book that he wrote, and I emerge from the grand plunge with the conviction that, if here was an important realistic mind and an important novelist, I am either the poorest judge of intellectual and literary values this side of Columbia University or one whom the wholesale reading in question has paralyzed out of all possibly nascent critical talent.

Although Phillips impressed the infrallectuals of his time as a gratifyingly well-barbered and well-tailored Dreiser, he was essentially little more than a Robert W. Chambers out of an Upton Sinclair. In even the best of his realistic writing a kind of pretty-pretty quality refractorily permeated the scene. And always one had the feeling—as one still has on re-reading him —that his realism was the residuum of suckled indignation rather than of actual experience. He was, as the more modern psychologists would quickly have observed, a snob who envied and even loved the things he professed to hate. He could write, but the blood in his eye blinded him to himself. He was, sub-consciously, the squire of his worst villains.

These villains were (1) women, (2) money, and (3) the world of fashionable society. In one way or another, the bulk of his writing concerned one or the other or all of them. His three earliest works, *The Great God Success, Her Serene Highness* and *A Woman Ventures,* consisted in a savage attack upon the American *haut monde* and the women who were part of it. *The Master Rogue* was a savage attack upon million-aires, as *The Social Secretary* was an attemptedly sardonic one. *Light-Fingered Gentry* again attacked the plutocratic *haut monde. Old Wives for New,* his best work, paid the author's usual compliments to the millionaire, and to woman. *The Fashionable Adventures of Joshua Craig* again touched upon money and ladies of high social standing, as *The Hungry Heart* had to do with a Southern mazuma magnifico and his disconsolate spouse. *The Husband's Story* hammered yet again at the rich American snob, chiefly female. And, *Susan Lenox: Her Fall and Rise,* written for one of the Hearst magazines, underneath its tin-pot movie melodrama plied the same old artillery against social and economic snobberies.

Whatever the variance of approach, the animus at the bot-tom of almost all these novels was generally the same: the animus of a somewhat bedraggled bird longing for a golden cage that was not open to it. Even when allowing, in a mag-nanimous gesture of fairness, glints of virtue to such rich and lofty personages as otherwise he literarily goosed, Phillips could barely conceal his disrelish in betraying even for a moment his own ingrained admiration of them. He performed constantly a

vasectomy on his own secret personal ambitions, and the resulting pain became his sterile literary diatribes. That he could
write, it must be repeated; but to strike a balance between
what he passionately believed and what he passionately tried
personally for his own obsequious comfort to forget, was
within neither his power nor his talent. The self-depuratory
faculty that is the gift of the true artist was denied him.

Phillips was, above all else, first and foremost simply an indignant melodramatist. In his attempted excursions into
humor, traces of the indignant melodramatist still stubbornly
reveal themselves. He was a blood-and-thunder show at five
dollars a seat, doubling psychologically as the hero and villain,
and sometimes even as Little Nell. It was natural, therefore,
that in the turmoil his crusader self often confusedly presented
itself in fierce black moustachios, the while his darker rôle
surprised everyone with a beautiful curly blond wig. He was
a realist self-manufactured in a stage dressing-room. The moment he emerged into the light of day, his make-up was disconcertingly evident.

[From *Passing Judgments,* 1935, pp. 79–82.]

Oscar Wilde and the Epigram

I WISH that some appropriate person would investigate and
report to me why the epigram is so generally viewed as the
arch-criminal of literature. For a reason that I have never been
able to make out, even the best and most intelligent epigram
is looked down on as being frivolous, flippant, and all too easy.
Though it may be quoted for years on end ánd be as wise as
it is witty, it is still regarded as a black sheep, unworthy of the
respect of any mentality duly appreciative of such more copious literary forms as the *Congressional Record* and the cerebral ensembles of Walter B. Pitkin.

The revival of *Lady Windermere's Fan* brings up the matter anew. As Shaw observed in his review of another of
Wilde's plays, "He has the property of making his critics dull.
They laugh angrily at his epigrams, like a child who is coaxed
into being amused in the very act of setting up a yell of rage

and agony. They protest that the trick is obvious, and that such epigrams can be turned out by the score by anyone light-minded enough to condescend to such frivolity. As far as I can ascertain, I am the only person in London who cannot sit down and write an Oscar Wilde play at will. The fact that his plays, though apparently lucrative, remain unique under these circumstances says much for the self-denial of our scribes." That was written more than fifty years ago and it is even truer today than it was then. Nor is it familiarity with the epigrams that has bred contempt; the contempt would be there even were they fresh out of the bottle. Nor, furthermore, is the contempt longer confined to the critics, who usually are blamed for everything; often justly. The attitude is pretty general, like that toward the epigram's illegitimate cousin, the pun, which, however amusing, is similarly always good for a lofty and disgusted grunt.

Again, one speculates, why? Take at random a few Wilde samples:

"The truths of metaphysics are the truths of masks." It took Brieux a whole two and a half hour play (*La Foi*) to say much the same thing, and not half so sharply.

"The history of woman is the history of the worst form of tyranny the world has ever known: the tyranny of the weak over the strong. It is the only tyranny that lasts." The major part of the great Strindberg's dramatic canon is devoted to proving just that.

"Cynicism is merely the art of seeing things as they are instead of as they ought to be." Here, in little, is, among other things, a critical appraisal of much of the classic Russian drama.

"The tragedy of old age is not that one is old but that one is young." Bataille consumed almost three hours to say the same thing in his admired *L'Homme à la Rose*.

"Ideals are dangerous things. Realities are better. They wound, but they are better." Yet Ibsen's *Brand*, Echegaray's *Folly or Saintliness*, Hartleben's *Rose Monday*, and many other such dramas enunciating the idea at great length are highly esteemed.

Along with the epigram, Wilde's sincerity, or rather alleged lack of it, is another favorite disparagement on the part of his critics. When they speak of sincerity, they obviously speak of it according to their own personal standards, not Oscar's. Oscar, for all his occasional self-mockery, was perfectly sincere in following his own lights, peculiarly colored though they were. When at odd times he was guilty of what seemed to be insincerity, it was only obliquely to ridicule the dull sincerity of others. The man's whole life, save in one or two instances, was a testimonial to his sincerity, such as it was. But since wit is so often regarded by the witless as a mark of insincerity— as Shaw, whose sincerity has been raised to a point of obstreperousness, has also discovered to his amusement—Oscar has been tagged with the label.

In what he said, Wilde was for the most part absolutely honest, even though his honesty was difficult of appreciation by men philosophically and emotionally alien to his point of view. In what he did, except in a couple of theatrical instances, he was equally honest; and one of the exceptions concerns *Lady Windermere's Fan*. In that case he dishonestly allowed himself to be influenced commercially in changing his play, though the meritorious critic, P. P. Howe, thinks otherwise and allows it was Wilde's utter disinterest in so-called "good" women that made it all a matter of indifference to him. This, however, seems to be straining a point for the defense. As originally written the important scene read as follows: Windermere (*calling after Lady W.*) "Margaret! Margaret! (*A pause*) My God! What shall I do? I dare not tell her who this woman really is. The shame would kill her. . . ." To make things safer at the box-office, the line was altered to "My God! What shall I do? I dare not tell her that this woman is—her *Mother!*" The change was a concession to cautiously cheap, popular playwriting, and Wilde should have been ashamed of himself. (The present revival properly goes back to the line as first written.) His critics are further in the habit of waxing sarcastic over the fabricated nature of his plots. But, as Howe points out, Wilde is at one with Mr. Bayes of *The Rehearsal* in saying, "What the devil is a plot good for but to bring in fine things?" The plot of *Lady Windermere's Fan*, for just one example, is little more than Bertha M. Clay dressed in silk. But what matter? The plots of some of the best plays in dramatic history are even worse.

It was not plot that interested Wilde, or that should interest any critic not given to an admiration of detective fiction and other such juvenile diversions. It was style, and at style, as at decoration, he excelled. "In all the unimportant matters," he declared without paradox, "sincerity, not style, is the essential." And his style in his dramatic time was as unrivaled as it is in ours. His sense of word and phrase and sentence is almost perfect. "Words," he said, "have not merely music as sweet as that of viol and lute, color as rich and vivid as any that makes lovely for us the canvas of the Venetian or the Spaniard, and plastic form no less sure and certain than that which reveals itself in marble or in bronze, but thought and passion and spirituality are theirs also—are theirs, indeed, alone."

In short, go listen to *Lady Windermere*. Creak sometimes in its rococo tracks as it may, it is still a toothsome play of escape—escape from the flat, humdrum, untutored and inanimate writing of so many of the plays we encounter today.

[From *The Theatre Book of the Year, 1946–1947*, pp. 115–18.]

Style

THE COMMON statement that a writer's style is a true reflection of the man, that his style is an outgrowth of his personality, is often absurd. The truth is that, in the case of many a writer, the personality is an outgrowth of the style. The writer creates a fictitious picture of himself as man in his style and then takes color from his style by way of living up to the popular conception of him. Shaw is an excellent example. His style is of telegraphic dynamite all compact: mentally aphrodisiac adjectives, meat-eating verbs, sequences that are tipsy with the wine of gaiety. The man himself is intrinsically exactly the opposite. Shaw, the man, is no more the blood-brother of the Shaw style than Cabell, the man, is the blood-brother of the Cabell style. Shaw's style is less a true reflection of Shaw as man than, let us say, of John Maynard Keynes as man. Shaw, however, wise showman that he is, has simply created himself in its own image. He has carefully evolved a completely alien and artificial style, set it up as a dummy, and then appropriated the dummy's trousers for himself.

Dreiser's style is Dreiser; Lewis' style is Lewis; Harold Bell Wright's style is Wright. But Lardner's style is no more Lardner, *Homo sapiens* and Great Neck householder, than Dunsany's style is Dunsany, *Homo sapiens* and Gargantuan oyster eater. The ivory elephant that the estimable and realistic Lord wears on a black ribbon around his neck is a concession to his style, just as the open-collar shirt and tousled hair of Jack London were a concession to his. Style is less often the man than the concept of him he wishes his readers to have. The sentence structure, the sequences, the juxtapositions and the verbal trickeries and cadences of many men of letters are no more reflections of their inner beings than the rôles most actors play are reflections of theirs.

[From the *American Mercury,* December 1925, p. 492.]

ON BRITISH CONDESCENSION
TOWARD AMERICAN LETTERS

Entente Cordiale

THE CONDESCENSION of British criticism toward America and
its letters seems to increase as the days go on. While there is
one small wing of that criticism that remains soundly judicial
and even charmingly hospitable in the case of America and
American efforts in the arts, the bulk of critical practise in
England ill conceals its personal feeling and seldom loses an
opportunity to display its dislike of anything American. Some
of these American-baiters are sagacious penmen and know
how to screen, at least in a measure, their actual distaste, but
that distaste eventually comes to the surface none the less, and
it takes no experienced American eye to detect it even while
it is still squirming about under the apparently rippleless
waters. Personally as well as professionally this general branch
of British criticism often has a time trying to hide its sneers
for those Americans who have achieved eminence in the arts
and, in the achieving, have robbed British writers of certain
desirable plums. The attitude encountered in London by
Sinclair Lewis, after he had been awarded the Nobel Prize,
is typical of a frame of mind that has for some years now
been clearly observable.

More candid and more outspoken than many English critics,
the personally most agreeable and inoffensive Miss Rebecca
West has lately betrayed fully the feeling toward this country
as a country that such other critics write between the lines. In
an article in the London *Daily Telegraph*, she states the view
pretty clearly: "Americans will not thank us [she says] for
reading Mr. Edward D. Sullivan's *Chicago Surrenders,* since
it deals with one of their problems, and those it is their habit
to meet with a conspiracy of silence. Were we Americans we

should never talk of the unrest in India, and if any visiting foreigner mentioned Gandhi we should indignantly ask if he came to our country just to insult his hosts. But, in spite of this abnormal sensitiveness, we had better read *Chicago Surrenders*, because it shows that America . . . is the victim of something more than its own incompetence; that it is the martyr of historic forces, and behaving as well as a martyr can."

So far as the arts are directly concerned, the British critical attitude toward Eugene O'Neill nicely suggests the situation. The endorsement as one of the world's leading dramatists that O'Neill has received in many other countries has seemingly offended the patriotic English, and detraction of him is consequently the English critical fashion. With a few exceptions, O'Neill is dismissed as little more than a dramatic charlatan and an impostor. "Intolerable," "a bore," "chooses to organize what he no doubt *supposes* to be Freudian revelations," "humorless conviction," "amateur profundity," "pretentious," "indecently devoid of all æsthetic economy," "handicapped by the native verbosity of the American," "an atrocious prose style," "a completely negligible figure"—these are samples of the tributes paid to him. The point is not that O'Neill's plays may honestly not be to the British critical taste. The point is rather that O'Neill himself, being an American, is not to that taste. The English reserve their praise of Americans for dancing girls, cabaret blues singers and second-rate playwrights who offer British playwrights no serious competition. Let a genuine American artist challenge their artist, and then read what happens to him!

The late Mr. Arnold Bennett, peace be upon his highly talented soul, despite his constant and suspicious insistence that he was hospitable to American writers, never for a moment contrived successfully to conceal his condescension toward the great majority of them. It is true that he praised the work of a half dozen or so of them during his quarter of a century of critical activity, but for every one he praised there were at least a dozen whose work, whatever its quality, ran up against his fundamental aversion to anything American. A very shrewd and enormously touchy fellow, he resented any impli-

cation that this was the case and on occasion, by way of safeguarding his income from American readers of his books,
would go to the extent of charging his critics with being prejudiced against him personally because they had not received
praise from him, when, as a matter of record, he had praised
them but still did not throw them off the scent. I trust I may
not be thought guilty of very poor manners when I point to
a case involving myself. When I published an article several
years ago pointing out the growing anti-American attitude of
British criticism and mentioning Mr. Bennett as among those
who were parties to it, he rushed to print a reply in his reviewing columns in the London *Evening Standard*, wherein he alleged against me that I thus criticized him because he had
never once spoken well of me or of my work and that "in all
likelihood, if I had ever praised him, his attitude would be
found to be quite different." Mr. Bennett, in point of fact, had
been very generous toward me. In the very same journal, in
January, 1927, he had spoken nicely enough of my efforts in certain critical directions—"These illustrious warriors [Mencken
and myself] are very readable. . . . They have done good by
their remarkable castigations of the public attitude towards
literature . . . I read them with gusto." And, some months
after the founding of the *American Mercury*, which he admitted he read with pleasure, he gave out an interview—in
the early months of 1925—in which he observed that Mencken
and I had done "an excellent job." Certainly my charges
against Mr. Bennett could not, therefore, have been based
upon any personal prejudice, as he tried to make out.

The truth about the English critics is that, with a few notable exceptions, they are extremely sensitive to any American
criticism of themselves, however insensitive they may be when
it comes to delivering their criticisms of American critics. Most
of them write books that must rely upon American sales for
any substantial royalties, and they naturally do not like to take
chances on having themselves shown up to their possible customers and readers as being anti-American. But, while seques-
tered in England, they privilege themselves a veritable Roman
slaughter. They mock American literature, American drama,
American criticism, America. Down in their hearts, the most

of them hate us. And there is no good, it seems to me, in their making any further bones about the fact.

* * *

Encore.—If the gentlemen in Downing Street were determined deliberately to spread subtle propaganda in America working toward unpleasant relations between England and the United States, they could do no better, indeed, than to instruct English practitioners and critics of the arts to continue to conduct themselves as they have been doing during the past five or six years. Being myself a humble laborer in the field of the arts and hence more or less naturally inclined to exaggerate the possible effect of such conduct, I nevertheless have difficulty in persuading my less prejudiced other self that the critics, writers and public press of this country are not gradually becoming surfeited with the contemptuous and insulting attitude of the English and will not be long in gagging at it openly.

As for myself, in my capacity as writer and critic, I have, as I have said, little to complain of, for the English in many quarters have been more than bountiful to me, both as regards my critical opinions and my many books that have been published in England. What is more, many of my very closest and dearest friends are Englishmen; some of the happiest times of my life have been spent in England; and it is a not remote possibility that at least part of my later years may be lived out in the quiet of that engaging land. But when I look at the situation without selfishness, I cannot resist the impression that the English—if they wish to retain the friendship of the rank and file of American writers, who have in their power as strong a propaganda weapon for or against as may well be imagined—had better ponder their ways and carefully consider the consequences of the obvious and violent prejudice in which they are currently indulging themselves.

That, to repeat what I have already set down, the majority of English men of letters and English critics dislike America, resent its artists and do not trouble themselves to cloak their antipathy is pretty plain to anyone who makes it a business closely to follow their activities. And not only English men of letters and critics, but Englishmen in the aggregate, save only cosmopolitan members of the aristocracy, a few generously minded publishers, one or two theatrical impresarios and several of the liberal-minded editors, managing editors and literary editors of the London newspapers and weeklies. But that the Englishman in general, whether he be a worker in the arts or in any other field, has a sneer for America ever ready for instant use is a fact not lost upon a nation that only recently, while talking peace out of one corner of its mouth, appropriated out of the other corner another 840 millions of dollars for the upkeep of soldiers, sailors, guns and battleships.

It is a rare book published by an American in England that, whatever its quality, does not suffer critical disparagement, ridicule or an obnoxious condescension. It is a rare American play of any quality that, produced in England, does not suffer the same critical condescension. O'Neill, as noted, has save in four instances—and then with qualification—been patronizingly waved aside in favor of the actors who play him. Only American writers of gangster and crook melodramas have been fully accepted—as freaks and curiosities. It is a rare Englishman who comes to America to lecture who does not delight himself in taking pot-shots at America, and it is a rare Englishman who, on his return home, does not convert the pot-shots into a veritable artillery bombardment. Mr. G. K. Chesterton has done his bit over here as a member of the British Literary Secret Service; Mr. J. B. Priestley—though I hate to mention the fact, for he has been most kind to my literary and critical efforts—has earned the brevet of major-general; Mr. Bernard Shaw, despite his tonic leaven of Irish blood, has given out several statements loftily allowing that he has never even heard of most of our leading novelists; the late Mr. Bennett only once in his entire journalistic critical career condescended to review a book published by an American publishing house that sought to establish itself in England; the award of the Nobel Prize to an American was greeted with derisory catcalls; and Mr. Oliver Baldwin, Labor member of Parliament and son of the Conservative leader, Stanley Baldwin, last year fashioned a fine dunce's cap for himself by demanding idiotically that Foreign Secretary Arthur Henderson determine at once whether there were any British subjects "among the persons who have died from starvation in the United States." Mr. Henderson, it may parenthetically be observed, might have informed him that, if there were, they certainly were not English lecturers and novelists.

To Mr. Chesterton, American writers who do not adhere to Mr. Chesterton's British doctrines are simply, in Mr. Chesterton's disdainful phrase, either "bright young things" or men " who compliment each other by saying 'naughty, naughty!' " Mr. Priestley has said, "I have crossed the ocean before on a 5,000-ton steamer to the West Indies and Central America and from there I turned in the direction of the United States and thumbed my nose." "I am terrifically proud of my popularity in England," he has gone on, "because it is so much harder to get started there, whereas here you run after something without very much provocation and in three months you've forgotten all about it." (In other words, Americans have run without very much provocation after such gimcrack novelists as Dreiser, Cather and Lewis and have forgotten all about them in three months.) Mr. Bennett, writing with his charming British modesty, observed just before his death, after dismissing Willa Cather and Sherwood Anderson as worthless, that a single book review of his laid the foundation of Dreiser's fame in America when nobody here had heard of Dreiser, that he was told that Thornton Wilder's immense success in America was due to his own verdict, etc., etc., and that "the truth is that time after time the vogue for American authors has been started by . . . English critics. I have said in the past, and I say again, that English critics are on the whole better than American critics, just as English short-story writers are on the whole better than American. They have a keener flair and far more courage." Mr. Sydney W. Carroll, president of the London Critics' Circle, has stated that New York critics "are lacking in conscience, sensibility and ordinary decent feelings," that they "have, apparently, not enjoyed the best of education or, if they have, give small evidence of it," that "just as their buildings, the skyscrapers, run to extreme heights, in the same way as their plays run to extreme in vulgarity, excessive sexuality, abnormality of all kinds . . . so do the New

York critics enjoy the work of playwrights and players who 'go the limit'; the moderate, the harmonious, the sane, the temperate, the thing of good taste is not for them; they prefer the freakish, the outrageous, the abominable, the product of Satan"; that "to look at, these critics are the weirdest sort of fellows"; and, finally, that "I often wonder what the English managerial fraternity would think if they substituted the New York critics for the London critics; they would take up pig-breeding within a fortnight!" The illustrious critic of the *Evening Standard* has written, in a review of Matthew Joseph-son's life of Rousseau, that "Mr. Josephson writes badly even for an American biographer, and American biographers seem to have a passion for bad writing." And, to return briefly to O'Neill, a critic in the same journal, who confessed that he had neither seen nor read the particular play, not long ago scoffed thus: "An account of the plot has precipitated me into disrespectful laughter. Here it is, or as much of it as I can find room for. There are a son and daughter who hate their father and mother respectively. The mother takes a lover, and he and she murder the father. The son and daughter then murder the father, whereupon the mother commits suicide. So does the son, and the only blot on the play that I can see consists in the fact that the last curtain appears to leave the daughter still alive." A plot, incidentally, derived directly from the Greek classic drama.

Some time ago, by way of appraising the critical situation more thoroughly, I ordered a London clipping bureau to send me cuttings of all the leading English reviews of American books and plays. A careful survey of hundreds of these reviews has revealed an almost unbroken succession of such qualifica-tions as "For an American, So-and-So writes fairly well," "While such writing can be of no possible interest to English-men," "Although inferior to the same kind of writing done in England," "It is amusing, however, to study the American mind in such matters," "Though Americans write a language we do not and do not greatly desire to understand," "Despite an obvious effort to pattern after English models," "A curiosity in the way of what Americans call literature is," "For those who do not take letters too seriously," and so on. Surely, this sort of thing must in time disgust American writers and the American reading public. If American critics and the American public are as generously honest as they are with British writers, the least they can ask in return is a similar honesty and fairness toward American writers. But while British authors are getting fat with money from the American sales of their books, a reciprocal courtesy and hearing are being designedly denied American authors in England by men perhaps fearful of the inroads they might conceivably make. Such open and above-board British writers and critics as Galsworthy, Nevinson, St. John Ervine, Hugh Walpole, E. V. Lucas, Desmond McCarthy and a few others like them are doing their very best to see to it that American novelists, dramatists, essayists, critics and writers generally get a fair and decent deal, but the writers and critics to the left and right of them are making things very difficult for them. It has remained for Frederick Lonsdale, the British playwright, to come partly to their assistance and to a feeling of potential good will all around by saying, "This derision of America and American writers is a lot of bloody nonsense and shouldn't be tolerated! If I had my way, every time an Englishman came over here and shot off his head, I'd have him deported. We don't stand it in England from foreigners and why should America take it in the cheek from English writers?"

[From *The Intimate Notebooks of George Jean Nathan*, 1932, pp. 125–34.]

ON LANGUAGE

LANGUAGE appears gradually to be divesting itself of its boiled shirt and spats and to be lounging into négligé and pantoufles. In the United States, as Polichinelle knows, slang has usurped so great a part of the King's tongue that the use of the latter is today confined chiefly to justices of the Supreme Court, headwaiters, the reverend clergy and professors in those colleges that can't afford good football teams. In England, slang, some of it of American derivation and much more of it homebrew, has worked its wicked will upon high and low, until presently about the only Englishmen who employ scrupulously meticulous discourse are the pushing ex-tradesmen and war profiteers recently elevated to knighthood. Germany, too, has come under the spell, to such an extent, indeed, that the visiting Berlitz graduate who so much as tries to order a simple *Eisbein mit Erbsenpurée und Sauerkohl* or even a *Rehkeule in Sahne mit Apfelmus* has something of a time about it. But even more than England and Germany does France show signs of the new linguistic dispensation, so many signs, in point of fact, that the French currently find it necessary to get out numerous handbooks explaining the meanings of the countless new incursions into the language, that the nation as a whole may keep abreast of them.

The only thing that keeps slang from becoming an international language, the authentic Esperanto, is its periodic autochthonism. Its occasional purely indigenous and inelastic quality lies largely in its evocation of visual images that are peculiar to its own land and people. The slang of America is thus sometimes as strange and unintelligible on the whole to England as that of England is to Germany or as that of the latter is to America. While there are some words and phrases in each that are readily caught and assimilated by aliens, much of the argot remains cold and dark to them. When an American uses such a word, for example, as *bleachers,* there is evoked a very definite picture of open sunbaked stands which is completely lost to an Englishman or a German. When a German, in turn, employs such a word as, say, *Maultasch,* there is evoked a picture that an American fails to conjure up. When an Englishman uses such a phrase, for instance, as *Black country,* it brings to his mind the picture of mining regions where, to the mind of an American or German, it brings the picture of Negro districts. There are, as I have said, some slang words and phrases that can induce the same visual images in different peoples, among them, for example, the American *cutie* or *bonehead,* the English *topper,* the German *Lausbub'*, and the French *lovelace* (for a seducer) or *lucarne* (garret-window) for a monocle. But in general each country's slang is peculiar to its own collateral image which has inspired it and which it inspires reciprocally.

[From *Monks Are Monks,* 1929, pp. 77–9.]

THE AMERICAN

FROM time to time I have commented upon the more lamentable characteristics of our fellow Americans, to the loud and, I regret to report, sometimes vituperative displeasure of certain of the more recently naturalized patriots. So loud and vituperative has lately this displeasure been, indeed, that its volume has not been matched since the day that I published a treatise pointing out the unexcelled preëminence of Americans and America in a number of obvious directions. I therefore often conclude that perhaps the most effectual way to go about criticizing our co-citizens and the idiosyncrasies of their conduct may be to set forth their good points, so get them angry and then arrive at the truth about them through their own irritated denials and automatic self-analyses. The moment you flatter a man, he psychically pulls off his boots and shows his bare Achilles heel. Denounce him and he keeps his boots on with a view to a reciprocatory kick.

Here, however, I fear that I am concerned less with one of our brother's good points than with one of his dubious ones. I allude to his encompassing veneration of practicability and to his complete subservience to the doctrine of does-it-work? and is-there-any-real-use-to-it? It is this veneration and this subservience that have undoubtedly made the American what he is: the world's money-bags, the financial field-general, but it is this same veneration and subservience that have also undoubtedly made him the most prosaic and least appealing of fellows. Of all men, the American as an individual is most greatly lacking in glamour and romance, and for the simple reason that he is himself skittish of glamour and romance. He is shy of them to the point of downright fear; they and all that they imply and represent are excessively questionable in his eyes and are to be avoided. In this attitude we have, of course, the obvious mark of a *nouveau* and uncertain people.

The worship of practicability and atheism as to the beauty of the impracticable are always attributes of men still psychically in the peasant stage. The charm of the relatively useless is the prerogative of an aristocracy.

Distrust, contempt and even hatred of the arts, distrust, contempt, and even ribaldry for the frolicsome fireworks of romantic passion, impatience running to indignation over Continental ease and irony and the gentlemanly leisureliness of life—these are familiar enough American phenomena. The emotions must be flogged into routine channels; the heart must be kept strictly in place underneath its two-dollar shirt; the eye must be kept straight ahead that it may not be diverted from Success, Respectability, Duty and all the other stereotyped, capitalized goals of prosperity, security and public esteem. There must be censors alert to press the lid on bold and vagrant and beautiful letters, and a voracious yellow press to hold up to ridicule and obloquy any citizen who permits his emotions to step out of line for even a moment, and policemen to collar scoundrels who flirt with pretty women on the streets, and hysterical evangelists to warn against life's agreeable little follies, and the howling of psalm singers to drown out the hurdy-gurdies of homesick Italians and the dancing of little alien tenement girls, and motorcycle police to spy on parked Chryslers after dark, and Sunday laws, Monday laws and Tuesday laws, and God knows what else to make life humdrum in the holy name of what is called Respectability. If England is a nation of shopkeepers, we in turn are a nation of keepers of our neighbor's soul. He may, if we don't watch him, have too good a time and be happy. He must be kept, at all costs, a routine member of the community, a fellow his employer can trust not to steal an extra five minutes at lunch time, a decent citizen—in short, a Success.

[From *Monks Are Monks,* 1929, pp. 130–2.]

ON LIFE AND ITS PLEASURES

Happiness

HAPPINESS, as I have encountered it in this world, consists chiefly in getting no more than one wants and wanting no more than one can get. There is an obvious corollary: *un*happiness consists (*a*) in wanting something that one can't get, or (*b*) in getting something that one doesn't want. The second form is probably the more distressing. The man who goes to a party, drinks too much gin, and, on reaching his office the next day, finds a note indicating that he is engaged to a girl with beer-keg ankles—such a man is obviously far more unhappy than the fellow who, mistaking a transient inebriety for love, offers himself and is rejected. The latter, of course, may suffer. His vanity has been affronted; even his dignity is compromised. But he has not suffered any serious and permanent damage. He can recover. So all through life. The thought that I haven't a million dollars seldom makes me unhappy, though I could use the money judiciously. But if I were informed tomorrow that I had become a grandfather or been awarded the Pulitzer Prize I'd be very much distressed, and my distress would continue, at least in restrospect, all the rest of my life.

The prudent man tries to mold his desires to the probabilities, or, at all events, to the possibilities. He puts away from him all thought of things that are clearly beyond him. Privately, I'd like to be the Shah of Persia, with the right to kill True Believers at so much indemnity a head, but the yearning never makes me really unhappy, for I realize that my theology is a bar. It would be scarcely more absurd for me to want to be one of the Twelve Apostles—a longing which broke the heart of the late Woodrow. But Woodrow was not alone: most politicians, I believe, are intensively unhappy men. The reason therefor lies in the fact that it is a sheer physical impossibility for any one of them to amass all the honors he craves. If he is an assemblyman he longs to be a congressman; if he is a congressman his eye is on the Senate; if he is in the Senate he is ridden all night by dreams of the White House.

Even in the White House there is no peace for a man so bewitched. The case of Woodrow I have mentioned. All the rest are just as unhappy. Think of Roosevelt. His last days were downright tragic. He wanted a third term, a fourth term, an *n*th term. The news that Woodrow was being cheered in the movie parlors cut him like a knife. Were he alive today, he would be envious of Coolidge. It seems incredible, but I believe it to be a fact. Coolidge is walled in by hordes of politicians who envy and hate him. What his own ambition is I don't know—probably to be a Wall Street lawyer. Whatever it is, it makes him unhappy.

That is, unless he is one of the rare men who know how to hold their desires in check. Perhaps he is, though his laugh is rather too sour to make it probable. Dr. Taft, I believe, belongs to the sublime and fortunate company. His laugh is magnificently hearty and innocent. All his life, even while he was in the White House, he was consumed by a desire to sit upon the bench of the Supreme Court. Today he is safely anchored there, in the very best seat, directly on the aisle. His notion of pleasure, I confess, is not mine. If I had to listen to lawyers five hours a day, it would cause me intense suffering; not even listening to bishops would be worse. But every man to his own poison!

[From the *American Mercury*, July 1925, pp. 352–3.]

Toujours Perdrix

"LIFE would be endurable," observed Lord Palmerston, "if it were not for its pleasures." Like many another profound saying, this one has suffered because of its epigrammatic air and has been dismissed as being merely an amusing bit of smart-aleckry. Yet what reflective man of mature years does not appreciate its truth? The so-called pleasures of life, in the instance of each individual, are largely repetitive; they cuckoo one another more or less exactly from year to year, since a man's taste changes little after he has crossed the line of thirty. In his younger years, these pleasures are still fresh and new to him; they have a kick that is infinitely agreeable; but, as time goes on, they lose their erstwhile appeal and gradually become transformed into bores. After thirty, the individual's pleasures fall into the pigeonholes of his set predilections. Some of them are left-overs from his earlier years; others are of a relatively new contour. But, whatever their nature, he finds soon or late that they are in themselves very much of a piece and that each is but a recurrent echo of its former self. And presently each quondam pleasure becomes a stereotyped thing, to be undertaken, at best, in the half-light of duty; and, furthermore, the indulgence in each of them becomes more and more irksome and peace-disturbing.

What are known by less experienced creatures as pleasures, become, when the civilized man has reached forty, for the most part nuisances. Consider such hypothetical pleasures as dinner parties, banquets, receptions, teas, balls, weddings (of other persons), camping, athletic sports, flirtations, all-night drinking bouts, card games, musicales, excursions, three-day motor trips, picnics, college reunions, marching in parades, fighting policemen, and the like. What intelligent, or even half-way intelligent man, can extract amusement out of such things when he has reached his middle years? The answer is: no such man. But, nonetheless, his life of necessity often includes the need of participating in one or more of these pseudo-pleasures, and he does so, obediently, politely and despairingly; and each participation makes him more and more miserable. Each invades his cherished privacy, his serious work in the world, his self-esteem. He is compelled to mingle with idiots and listen to the talk of idiots. He is compelled to kiss brides whom he doesn't want to kiss, to drink more than he wants to drink, to go to places he doesn't want to go to, to speak soft nothings to women who he devoutly wishes were in Hell, to eat badly cooked dishes at badly peopled dinner tables, to hold leaking teacups on his lap and ruin his trousers, in short, to do countless things that seemed agreeable to him once upon a time but that long since have become mildly obnoxious. Yet, such is the lamentable absurdity of human society, he must nevertheless keep going on and on.

[From the *American Mercury*, January 1927, p. 119.]

Discovery and Surprise

ONE of man's profoundest satisfactions comes with the periodic surprising discovery in himself of virtues as to which he was secretly skeptical. Under every man's surface pride in himself there are certain inner misgivings regarding facets of his character. Pretending to honor, is he really so honorable as he thinks himself? Professing integrity, courage, loyalty, honesty, decency, is he actually given to these qualities? Provided with an opportunity safely to profit from the momentary remission of one or another of them, just how far will he go? It is a rare man who can foretell, for there is inevitably in every man a trace of moral mountebank. It is thus that, when occasionally he discovers that what he has believed about himself is strangely authentic, he is, in his secret heart, just a shade electrified.

[From *The Intimate Notebooks of George Jean Nathan*, 1932, p. 279.]

Man's Pleasures

CONSIDER man's pleasures. Soon after coming into the world he gleefully shakes a little tin ball with birdshot in it. A little later on he pulls a string which makes a small wooden figure kick up its legs and wiggle its arms. A bit later he takes a small round clay ball in his thumb and forefinger and shoots it at several other small round clay balls. Presently he sits on a wooden horse and rides around rapidly in a circle to the tune of a barrel-organ until he is dizzy. A few years later he begins to hit at a round leather ball with a stick and, when successful in hitting it, drops the stick and starts running around the lot, touching several sacks of cornmeal on the way. Then, night falling, he puts a stiff piece of white linen against his chest, props up his neck with another piece of stiff white linen, stands face to face with a girl and synchronously shakes his hips and feet with her while several men blow horns and beat upon tightly stretched membrane. Growing older he sits at a table with several other men and spends hours passing around small pieces of cardboard with red and black spots on them. Occasionally he will go out to a converted cow-pasture and hit a little white ball with several different kinds of sticks, uttering happy cries when the little ball falls into a hole in the ground. Coming into old age and preparing to leave the world, he sits at a table with another old man and moves small round pieces of wood across a board marked with little squares. . . .

[From *Monks Are Monks*, 1929, pp. 18–19.]

Experience

IN the common acceptance of the term, a man's experience, for a reason I can't quite make out, is generally associated in the popular mind with trouble. Thus, when we hear that a man has profited by experience, we are asked to believe that his experience has consisted in trials and tribulations. Yet the experience from which a man profits most is vastly less that which has been related to his miseries and woes than that which has been related to his successes and happiness. A man learns little from his defeats; it is his triumphs—in business, in sport, in artistic effort, or in amour—that give him his most valuable tips and teach him his most valuable lessons.

[From the *American Mercury*, December 1925, p. 493.]

ON MARRIAGE

Attitude toward Love and Marriage

LOVE is always a tragedy for the woman. That tragedy she never succeeds entirely in escaping. It is sometimes the tragedy of a broken heart, sometimes the greater tragedy of fulfilment. A broken heart is a monument to a love that will never die; fulfilment is a monument to a love that is already on its deathbed.

2

Of the two loves—that which is felt deeply and that which is simulated—the second becomes the stronger with the passing of time. A woman, for example, forgets the grand passion of her life in the paraphrased and substitute love that has brought her a husband, a home and, with the flood of the years, peace and ease and a remote tranquility.

3

Perhaps the happiest time in the average hansdoodle's life is three weeks before his marriage. It is then that the lady of his knightly yen is just far enough from his reach to enravish and englamor him and yet not near enough to give him that moment of dubiety and pause that comes, in such cases, to even the humblest of God's boobs. The altar is still remote enough to gain enchantment from the loan of distance and not close enough to frighten him. The hansdoodle thus stands momentarily in that most beautiful of all lands, the no-man's land of romantic love. But as the three weeks draw nearer and nearer to the amorous electric chair, his happiness grows correspondingly less and less. For the hansdoodle, no less than the rest of us professors, gradually begins to be besieged by doubts, soever small, that he actually wants what he wants when he wants it. Three weeks ago, he gave up nothing—nothing of freedom, nothing of irresponsibility, nothing of tzigane fancy. But now, at the altar, he sees in a flash what he is leaving behind him—all those things that he has convinced himself he no longer cares for but which yet, as he climbs the church steps, begin to seem never so slightly desirable. His pulse beats with happiness, but his mind ticks with a faint homesickness for the security of the day before, and the day before that, and the days and days before them. And then the honeymoon. And then the hundred and one inevitable little nuisances and concerns that take just a bit of the edge off an erstwhile inviolate romantic dream. And then the days ahead. Often happy, these days, doubtless, but days that miss something—that all important and forever vanished something—of those glad and trembling days three weeks before his anticipation, his illusion and his love were duly checked and labeled.

4

To say that nine-tenths of marriages are unhappy is doubtless untrue. But, looking about me, I venture, and not without a reasonable amount of confidence, the opinion that the marriages that are happy are chiefly those in the period of the twenties and those of the early fifties and beyond. Marriage in these groups of years is apparently pleasant and agreeable to the parties concerned; during these spaces of time there seems to be little or no disagreement or unhappiness. But marriage during the period of the thirties and forties is apparently fraught with trials and tribulations. The couple that hangs together in perfect accord during its thirties and forties is as rare as the ducatoon of Priuli.

5

A man's wife is his compromise with the illusion of his first sweetheart.

6

It is a popular belief, largely cultivated by men themselves, that man is a rooster who would achieve grand delight and satisfaction if, like his Turkish brother, he were permitted to have a harem. While it is perhaps true that here and there one might find a barber, or a jewelry drummer or a movie actor who would actually enjoy such an arrangement, it is far from true that the average man would relish it in the slightest. The average man would care for a plurality of women no more than he cares for a plurality of pairs of patent leather shoes. His taste is pretty uniformly for one woman, one toothbrush, one flag. That taste may undergo a change, of course; it often does. But he would have no more use for six or seven wives—spiritually, emotionally or physically—than he would have for six or seven back collar buttons. To argue that, because of his biological nature, he would have use for a dozen bathrooms.

7

Marriage is the reward that women graciously withhold from the men they have truly loved.

8

A close student of matrimony of many years' standing, it seems to me that the average male candidate for the honor is as greatly in need of professional advice as any other ailing man and that, neglecting to seek this advice, he lays himself open to quite unnecessary risks and hazards. When a man plans to get married—and many a man plans to enter the matrimonial state, whether by instinct, hereditary impulses, tradition, or in the interests of what he believes to be his future well-being and happiness, long before he has picked out the woman who is to be his wife—when, as I say, such a man plans to engage nuptial bliss he seldom if ever seriously considers what type of woman would be the best and safest, and not only the best and safest but the most beneficent, to take unto his bosom. Love, beauty, character, position—such things he meditates upon, but he gives no thought to subjects of much bulkier importance and, giving them no thought, often learns of them, much to his sorrow, when it is too late.

It is my belief, and I pass on the suggestion to young men contemplating holy wedlock, that an orphan is perhaps of all women the one best fitted to be a desirable wife. The fact that she is an orphan automatically gets rid of the father-in-law and mother-in-law nuisance. She is alone in the world and grateful to the man who marries her. Having no one who is very close to her, her husband will seem closer to her than he would to a wife whose parents, or at least one of whose parents, were still living. Furthermore, the orphan is always the more tractable, wistful and tender woman. She has known sorrow, and sorrow, as the old saw wisely hath it, maketh a woman beautiful in the heart. But if the young man open to the lures and splendors of matrimony does not happen to love an orphan, but loves instead, shall we say, a widow, what advice then? My advice then—and I may be forgiven for observing that it is grounded upon a study of the problem ranging over a period of thirty-five years—my advice is to marry only a widow whose first husband either beat her or who died disgracefully, as by having been hanged or being shot in a bawdy house or getting ptomaine poisoning from a free-lunch kippered herring. If the widow's first husband is *in absentia* for other reasons or by virtue of a dignified demise, she will begin to think of him and brag about him a few years after her second marriage, and that marriage will then quickly begin heading for the rocks. Only the widow who hates the memory of Spouse I can make a happy mate for Candidate II. But, yet again, if it is neither orphan nor widow that our ambitious young man has his passion set upon, what then? Well, let us assume that the creature of our young friend's choice is a pea-chick possessed of a considerable wealth, and who is neither orphan nor widow. In this event my long years of investigation and research impel me to discharge the advice that our young friend consider marrying such a petitioner only if he himself be a very poor man. The marriage of a rich young woman and a very poor young man is revealed by the statistics to be generally a happy one, and for a simple reason, whereas the marriage of a rich young woman and a rich young man all too often turns out badly. The rich young man who marries a rich young woman gains nothing from the marriage, or at best little, in comparison with the poor young man. The latter's improved position and comfort operate to make his wife more desirable in his eyes and a marriage that might otherwise end in disaster is thus often perpetuated and made happy until death. There have been cases where a rich woman has kicked her poor husband out of the house, but so far as I know there has never been a case where a poor husband has kicked his rich wife out of the house.

I further always urge my protégés to marry pretty women. The best of women get homely all too soon, and it is well to have a pretty wife at least for a beginning. A pretty wife for five or six years is something: it makes, in memory and retrospect, romantic amends for the damaged wife one must live with in the many years that loom ahead of and beyond these first five or six years. The additional advantage of marrying a pretty girl as opposed to a homely one is obvious. The pretty girl will take out all her spoiled nature, whims and outside flirtations on her husband at the very outset, and thus get them over with. After a few years, when she loses her looks, she will settle down and behave herself, and give her husband no trouble. The homely girl, to the contrary, having no looks to fall back on or bother about, will begin by being twice as sweet and attentive to her husband as the pretty girl, but will end up by taking revenge on him for all the early outside flirtations that she never could enter into and enjoy and that, unlike in the instance of the pretty girl, thus never provided her with an opportunity to let off the steam of her vanity.

I need not pursue the subject farther, at least today. If I have so much as suggested that there is some truth in my prefatory assumptions, I shall be content. I desire merely to add, in conclusion, that all the young men who have thus far followed my advice are happy husbands and fathers. Their wives never fail to remember me, with excellent cigars, at the Yuletide.

9

Women begin to think of marriage on the day that they first feel old; men on the day that they first think old. The thought of marriage enters a woman's head when the past and all its gay and crowded uncertainties seem about to slip from hands that may no longer grasp and toy with them; the thought of marriage enters a man's head when the future and all its grim and lonely uncertainties seem about to slip from hands that, save they grasp them now, may never have the opportunity to convert them into peace and comfort and certainty. No woman, in the highest moment of her happiness, thinks of marriage. She begins to think of it in her moments of misgiving, self-doubt and misery. Marriage, with her, is generally a craft that backs quickly out to sea from a shaky and partly condemned dock.

10

Love is the democrat of the emotions; hatred the aristocrat.

11

The institution known to civilized society as the husband vouchsafes to the student-connoisseur of the *comédie humaine* a source of profitless but none the less diverting speculation. Why, for example, should this husband, as he is called, in nine cases out of ten be to the woman whom he has taken unto his bosom a comic figure, one to snicker at silently or to razz more or less openly after the second cocktail has got in its fine Italian vermouth hand? This husband's wife is certainly not a comic figure, as he himself is, nor does he even for an instant so regard her, yet there he stands a target for her internal derisions and for the derisions, perhaps more charitable, of persons removed from his own hearth and home. My pondering of the problem in behalf of this unfortunate fellow creature has brought me to various conclusions, some of which I have the honor here to divulge.

Courtship, as everyone, including the parties thereto, knows, is a show, a spectacle. This show devolves largely upon the man, for, while it is not a new business for the woman—since woman is in the show business from the cradle to the grave—it is a comparatively new business for the man. Finding himself in love, as the phrase is, he synchronously finds it necessary for himself to take on the emotional and mental attributes of an actor, and to conduct himself much after the manner of a mime cast for the leading rôle in a romantic drama. In the degree that he succeeds in this is he successful in impressing, captivating and winning the heart and hand of his lady love. For it is customarily this actorial projection of her suitor that the lady becomes enamored of and, enveloped in the purple haze it gives out, capitulates to. But no man not an actor by profession can keep up, or feels like keeping up, the performance once the show is over. Some husbands, true enough, go bravely on with the greasepaint comportment and proscenium behavior for a variable number of years after the wedding bells have rung, but soon or late they lapse back into the *status quo,* into the plain, unromantic fellows they were before the divine passion, as the phrase also is, beset them. The moment the husband thus goes back to normal, that moment does his wife, with the wisdom of safely married women ever, translate her disillusion, usually calmly anticipated, into comfortable comedy. The lover's mask is off and he is revealed as simply a poor clown who is often still lovable but who, for all that, is yet a poor clown: a human being who is half a Rudolph Rassendyl with a two-day's growth of beard and half a shaved mealticket.

But while this process of actorial disintegration is going on in the husband, the actorial talents of the wife increase in proportionate ratio. As if realizing that the two of them are cast for a single rôle in the tragi-comedy of the matrimonial relation and that one of them has, so to speak, forgotten his lines, the wife appreciates that it is her duty to carry on the show alone, singlehanded. In this, her long and natural training in romantic artifice stands her in good stead. And thus, while her husband appears to her as a once handsome cuspidor from which all the enamel has been chipped, she continues to appear to the old spittoon a relatively theatrical and effective figure. The average husband is approximately as romantic to his wife as a cow. But despite all the published cynicism to the contrary, the average wife, I fully believe, is a more or less romantic figure to her husband. By romantic I do not, obviously, necessarily mean the creature of starshine and wild white clover that she was before, during and directly after the woo period, but romantic as a man's close possessions remain ever romantic in his eyes, as the scrapbook of his university days, or his old meerschaum pipe, or his dog. It is for the reason that everyone outside of himself is privy to him that the husband is viewed more or less generally as the pitiable figure in an extravaganza: an actor who once played the leading rôle in romantic "Old Heidelberg" condemned now by ironic nature and by homely fate to the permanent rôle of butler in a hinterland stock company.

12

A man sometimes enters upon a new love affair only to protect himself from the irritatingly enduring sentiment of the previous one.

13

In the many learned and eloquent treatises on divorce that have appeared in the various public prints, it seems to me that I and my colleagues in secular philosophy have at times laid too much stress on important things and too little on trivial. The adjectives are used, of course, in their generally accepted sense; hence there is no paradox. What I mean to say, specifically, is this: that the causes of divorce are doubtless infinitely more insignificant, as such things go, than the majority of investigators and examiners believe. The real causes, that is. The reasons that appear in court are generally as far from these real causes as the human eye can reach. Long before a husband has committed adultery, for instance, the divorce germ has entered his consciousness; long before a wife actually runs away from her husband, the seed of divorce has begun to take root in her mind. A hundred little things preface a husband's beating his wife, and so giving her grounds for divorce in certain states, as a hundred little things, which the investigators dismiss as negligible, preface a wife's running off to Paris with the first available chauffeur. What are these little things? Let me guess at a few.

Perhaps one of the chief causes of divorce, or, more exactly, leading up to the act or acts legally recognized as grounds for divorce, is a trivial physical blemish in one or the other of the parties to the marriage. This defect, in the husband's or the wife's person, may be comparatively insignificant, yet no matter. Such a blemish, when lived with for a period of time, has a cruel and devastating habit of burning itself into the eye and consciousness of the other person; it gradually becomes almost a visual phobia; its image will not out. It colors the one person's entire picture of the other; it grows to dominate that picture completely. In time, if the other person is at all sensitive—and four out of five persons are extremely sensitive in this respect—it becomes unbearable. The husband, if it be the husband, begins, almost unconsciously, to look around him at other and theoretically more immaculate women. The look grows steadier . . . Miami . . . the divorce court. Or he deserts his wife, or treats her with cruelty. The wife, on the other hand, if it be the wife, simply gets to the point where she cannot endure the marriage relation any longer, and leaves her husband's bed and board. And the newspapers, in due course, print the ground for divorce, but fail to print the reason. Another reason for the act or acts leading to divorce may be found in the inability of the married parties to stand the æsthetic jars that propinquity forces more or less upon them. This is particularly true of men and women who marry after the twenties have passed into the thirties. Such men and such women have grown so accustomed to physical and emotional independence that the habit is not easy to break. It is much more difficult for them to endure the invasions upon privacy that marriage brings with it than it is for younger persons. For every couple that have been put asunder by adultery, or lack of support, or a carpet-beater, there are two that have split by being compelled to use the same bathroom, or by a bathroom that was too disquietingly close to their bedchamber. There are dozens of other such reasons, each and all overpowering in their superficial triviality. The two that have been set down are perhaps sufficient to suggest many of the rest. A marriage that has weathered stormy seas all too often goes to smash on a pebble.

14

It takes, as they say, all kinds of men to make a world. Toward most of these, although there are many I may not accurately know or understand, I am sympathetic. I at least try to know them and understand them. But there is one kind that passes my comprehension altogether. This kind, try as I will, I cannot filter through my noodle. It is made up of the men who, though they are in love with no one woman and though they are comfortably off in health and in the world's goods, yet view marriage as something they should presently and duly embrace.

15

Love demands infinitely less than friendship.

16

That marriage mellows and civilizes the average man, I do not gainsay. But that is precisely my objection to it so far as I personally am concerned. I am already too highly civilized. Were it not for the overdose of civilization that has been inculcated in me, and that works so often to my economic and spiritual disadvantage, I should doubtless have been married long ago. To ask a man already civilized to get civilized all over again is like asking him to wear two undershirts. I dispute, further, that marriage would benefit my spirit, as certain of my friends and other enemies argue. It would make me too happy, and I could not do my work if I were too happy. A persistent touch of melancholy is essential to artistic enterprise. A happy man may be a successful bishop, dog-catcher, movie actor or sausage-monger, but no happy man ever produced a single firstrate piece of painting, sculpture, music or literature. And I, humble as I am, have aspirations.

Again, it is inconceivable that any woman, once she penetrated my superficial charms, could be devoted to me in the rôle of husband. Never was there such an ignoble crank! If, after ten mellifluous years of marriage and after giving birth to our fourteenth beautiful child, my loving wife were one day to so much as snitch a favorite lead-pencil off my writing-table, I should probably proceed forthwith to the big scene from *The Chinatown Trunk Mystery*. I am not designed for marriage any more than a longshoreman is designed for Christian Science. I have no gift for it. I admire women and I like children, but is it necessary for a man who admires baseball, for example, to play baseball? It is not. I elect to view marriage from a seat in the bleachers.

Still again, we have the theory that marriage is insurance against the evils of romance; that it makes a man safe, and secure, and comfortable. The average bachelor, it is contended by way of proof, is never in as good health as the average benedick. This may be true; but it proves nothing. So far as that goes, I have never known a bachelor who was in as good health as the average mule.

17

Love, Dr. Mencken once argued in the course of a conversation which happened to be engaging us at Muldoon's Health Farm at 5 a.m., is a casual matter, a chance infection, a thing not unlike a cold in the head. "The process of falling in love," he observed, "is as fortuitous and trivial as the process of missing a train. Some fair one, hearing that one has recently received an LL.D. from Yale or made a killing at some swindle, goes to a beauty parlor, has her eyebrows gummed, puts on her best frock, and then leers at one across a dinner-table. The result, by a well-known psychological route, is the genesis of the idea that she has lovely eyes and a beautiful character, and that it would be charming to give her a hug. Or maybe the thing is pure accident. Perhaps she goes to the party without the slightest thought of serious professional business—and one is floored by the perfume she happens to wear, or by her anecdote of her little nephew, Lafcadio, or by the pretty way she takes it when the Colonel upsets his *potage Arlesienne* down her leg, or by the peculiar manner in which her hair is banged, or by the striking combination of cerise and pea-green in her fourth-best party dress. Such is love, a madness worse than hydrophobia. To say that a man should be in love when he marries is to say that a ship-captain should be doubled up with cramps when he steers down the Ambrose Channel. It is a folly."

Although I am not the authority on love that my friend, the affable professor, is—as I politely confided to him at the time while four low Irishmen were running a cold squirt-hose up and down our backs—I permit myself to disagree with him. If falling in love is as easy as he says it is—and has personally demonstrated it to be on at least eleven occasions during the last fiscal year—I have the honor to set myself down as a duffer. No less than one thousand times in my life have I assiduously tried to fall in love, but to be baffled. All the time that I have been eloquently trying to convince myself that the girl eating dinner at my expense was a divine mélange of Debussy, apricots and chiffon, some irrepressible bogle within me has confounded me with the hypothesis that she was merely another Patou gown that hadn't had enough lunch. My imagination and my intelligence meet, to my sorrow, at an eternal Château-Thierry. I have thus far fallen in love, during the forty-odd years of my life, with twenty-seven lace and linen baby collars, eighteen bobbed hairs, forty-three blue dresses, ten lisps, thirty-six pairs of hands on my forehead when I was down with neuralgia, and eleven dozen initialed handkerchiefs and laundry bags, but with not a single girl. What, therefore, am I to do about it? I am helpless. And to ask me to marry a girl I don't love is to ask me to go to Buffalo when I have business in Chattanooga.

18

No marriage can be a successful and happy one which calls upon the man to change his ideas of what constitutes amusement after his day's work is done. If a man whose idea of pleasure after working hours is strip poker or playing a snare drum loves a woman passionately and marries her only to learn that her idea of pleasure in the same hours is Old Maid or Kelly pool, a timetable to Reno, if the man is a gentleman, or one to Atlantic City, if he is not, will be found on the drawing-room table before the year is over.

19

To ask a man to marry on the ground that it will safeguard and comfort him in his later years is to ask him to cut his throat on the ground that he may be down with Bright's disease in 1950.

20

The happiest marriage is not that which defers disillusion, but that which admits it at the outset. Few marriages between completely adult men and women turn out unhappily. Age is happy; youth, unhappy. Illusion is the happiness of the heart; disillusion is the merriment of the mind.

21

I long ago wrote a note to the effect that the man a young woman marries is almost always her second choice. I now beg leave to revise that note. The man a young woman marries is almost always her third choice, if that. Is there, by way of proof, a single young woman in America who would not kick out the man she is to marry, whatever his position in her affections, if the Prince of Wales wanted her for his wife?

22

It is the belief of most persons that a bachelor has a much happier time of it in this world than his married brother. Nothing could be farther from the truth. The married man's misery is confined to one woman. The bachelor's emotional aches spread over a dozen or more.

23

Back of all the romance blather about Uhuhu, Ahahaha, Umhumha and the other South Sea island maidens in whose amiable embraces the Anglo-Saxon heroes of current fictional *opera* find at length the peace and solace and comfort that have been denied them in paler embraces nearer home, there is, I have a notion, a soupçon of disconcerting truth. A man, as I have observed before, is always happiest with a woman who is deferentially his inferior. It is the equality of woman to man in the Anglo-Saxon countries—and not only the equality, but often actually the superiority—that is the cause of man's frequent dissatisfaction with his married lot and of the consequent alarming increase in the divorce rate. A marriage in which the wife knows the difference between a sonata and a *Geburtslied,* the distinction between second growth Pichon-

Longueville and fifth growth Mouton d'Armailhacq, the relative eminence of George Eliot and George Barr McCutcheon, and the batting average of Babe Ruth, is always on its way to consult a shyster lawyer. The most successful marriage is ever the one in which the wife believes the husband to be a compendium of all the refinements of wisdom and understanding, however depressing an ass the husband may really be. And as in marriage, so in love. Since the discovery of ink, there is no record of an Anglo-Saxon's having divorced, for example, a Japanese wife.

24

What a man beyond the years of forty seeks in the woman he marries is less an instrument of future happiness than a bulwark and haven against future unhappiness and disappointments. He chooses his wife not for the better in the years to come, but for the worse. He sees in her not so much a companion for his days of joys as a sympathetic companion for his days of sorrow. He sees her not in terms of music, moonlight and roses but in terms of mother-woman, heart-nurse and guarantee against the loneliness of unromantic old age.

25

I have a theory that no intelligent man ever loves a woman truly until he knows her so well that he doesn't really see her when he talks to her—that is, until she ceases to arrest his actual attention. What he talks to thereafter is an artificiality created by his own imagination. If the woman is clever, she quickly converts herself into this artificiality, or, at all events, tries to do so. If she succeeds, the man is lost. His ideal has him by the ear.

26

Love is an emotion experienced by the many and enjoyed by the few.

27

The bravery of women! How hard they strive to love the men they marry!

[From *The Autobiography of an Attitude*, 1925, pp. 268–92.]

Why Men Marry

A FEW nights ago, there were gathered together in one of the esoteric *salles à boire* of New York, a dozen middle-aged men. All save two were benedicks. As the mineral water began to work its magic on those at the board, the two bachelors bade of their fellows to tell them honestly the reasons that had prompted them to marry the women they had married. What, in other words, precisely had it been about these women that had fetched the men and converted them into husbands. The ten husbands pondered the question gravely and then, in turn, gave out the underlying provocative causes, which I set down seriatim:

1. Because the woman had shared a taste for F. W. Bain's translations of the Hindu *Digit of the Moon* and *Bubbles of the Foam*, could play the piano, and had Japanese eyes.

2. Because the woman disliked public restaurants and jazz music, and liked to stay home nights.

3. Because the woman had a beautiful, soft speaking voice and hated golf and all golf players.

4. Because the man had been thrown over by the woman he really loved.

5. Because the woman had $50,000 in the bank which the man needed to buy a partnership in the firm for which he was working.

6. Because the woman dressed in the way the man admired; because she hadn't bobbed her hair; and because she shared the man's wish to make a trip to Cairo.

7. Because the man was tired of living at his club and because he felt that he was getting old.

8. Because the woman had been attentive to him during an illness of two months' duration.

9. Because the woman had an even temper; because she spoke three languages fluently; and because she was the only woman the man had ever met who didn't wear her fingernails sharply pointed like a Chinaman's.

10. Because she was the best-looking girl at the resort where the man spent his summers.

Although these may at first glance seem to be excessively superficial reasons for the men's marrying the respective women, I thoroughly believe that they represent accurately the basic reasons that often shove men into the state of hymeneal blessedness. It is upon such a profound philosophical basis that the great institution of marriage is frequently founded; it is upon such a basis that the lions and unicorns of genealogy proudly prance and lift their heads to heaven.

[From the *American Mercury*, December 1925, p. 492.]

Men marry for a variety of reasons, few of them self-appreciated and self-apprehended. The reasons they believe they marry for are seldom the real ones. Men, even quite young men, often marry for no other reason than that they are lonely and seek a consoling companionship. Older men frequently marry not because they are immediately lonely or seek companionship but because they fear loneliness in their later years. This is particularly—almost inevitably—true in cases where the man is alone in the world, without living parents or close relatives. He is, like a child, afraid of the dark that lies ahead. Love, money, all the other usual theoretical considerations, have nothing to do with his marrying or with the woman he marries. He just wants to get married, and that is that.

"Love at first sight—there is no other kind of love, for all men's analysis," an eminent Viennese psychologist has lately observed. Although the illustrioso's remark has been widely ridiculed, there is a deal of truth in it. If it isn't love, or at least something quickly leading to love, at first sight, it isn't love. It may be respect, or admiration, or understanding, or camaraderie, or animal magnetism, or anything else of the sort, but it is not love. And it is this first sight, impromptu emotional galvanism that often draws men into marriage without the slightest sober reflection on such matters as have occupied the Viennese Professor Baber's solemn inquiry. A man's eye has much oftener propelled him into wedlock than his heart, and both combined have sucked him into matrimony twenty thousand times oftener than his cerebrum.

Men also marry out of disappointment. The beaten man, the

humiliated man, the disappointed man, the man who has taken
it on the chin in one way or another, is a veritable gull for almost any woman gunning for a mate. And this is even more
true in the case of women. The woman who has been hurt, the
woman who has been disappointed, is ready to take on the first
even faintly eligible man who comes her way.

.   .   .   .

News Item—John Edwards, husband of Maria Sanborn Hotchkiss, writer and prominent figure in public life, committed suicide by shooting himself through the brain early last evening in
his apartment on upper Madison Avenue, where he lived with
his wife. They had been married ten years. Mr. Edwards was
forty-five years old and was connected with the Hercules
Cement Company, 302 West Thirteenth Street.

A maid, Martha Jones, discovered the suicide. She found
Mr. Edwards' body lying on the floor of the bedroom, a bullet
hole in his right temple. He was clad in pajamas. He left no
note. The head office manager of the company which employed
him said that he appeared to be in excellent health when he
showed up for work yesterday morning, that he had never
missed a day at the office, and that his accounts were in perfect
order.

His wife, Miss Hotchkiss, is, in addition to her literary and
lecturing work, active in local political and civic—as well as in
national—affairs. She was recently appointed chairman of the
women's division of the local Unemployment Relief Committee, is chairman of the women's branch of the Civil Liberties
Union, vice-president of the Association for the Betterment of
Foreign Relations, Secretary of the Ohio Society, and has
served on the O. Henry Annual Short Story Award Committee.
She was elected to the State Assembly in 1934, and is at present chairman of the Manhattan Women's Democratic Club and
women's Democratic leader in her district. She is head of the
Women's Amalgamated Charities, vice-president of the Order
of Bookfellows, a trustee of the Girls' Service League of America, recording secretary of the Good Roads Association, Inc., of
the United States, an active worker for the Home Mission
Council, the Humane Association of America, the American

Library Association and the United Chapters of Phi Beta Kappa, a member of the Presbyterian Board of Christian Education, vice-president of the Pan-American Society, secretary and treasurer of the Society for the Prevention of Cruelty to Animals, and assistant secretary of the National Committee on Prisons and Prison Labor. She is also vice-president of the Women's Peace Society and the National Recreation Association, a director of the Roerich Museum and the Sociological Society of America, and a member of the National Council of the Sons and Daughters of Liberty, the American Vocational Association, and the National League of Women Voters.

The police were at a loss to assign a motive for the suicide.

[From *The Bachelor Life*, 1941, pp. 189–201.]

The Endurance of Marriage

THOSE persons who hold against marriage the circumstance that, under the changes which have come about in modern civilization, it doesn't last, that is, that the parties to it tire of the relationship and break up, seem to overlook the fact that the same thing happens between men and women where there is no marriage. I venture to guess that statistics would show that the average marriage lasts just as long and just as comfortably as the average free-love affair. The trouble with all these commentators on marriage lies in their faulty premiss that it logically should and ought to last indefinitely. The premiss is a charming one, but unfortunately it is also an imperfect one. It is corrupted by sentimentality. If the average marriage of sensitive and imaginative persons is a failure because it lasts only five or six years, all that I can say is that the average unsanctified love affair of equally sensitive and imaginative persons is a much greater failure, because it usually blows up long before that time.

[From *Monks Are Monks*, 1929, pp. 34–5.]

ON WOMEN

General Conclusions about the Coarse Sex

WOMAN is of much coarser fibre, of much less delicate sensibility and romantic sensitiveness, than man. A woman of refinement may without shame conceivably love a wholesale cheese merchant, for instance, and marry him, and live with him happily, and be faithful to him, and bear him numerous future wholesale cheese merchants. But it is difficult to think of a man of like comparative refinement loving, without at least a flicker of shame, a woman who confessed to having loved—if only for a day of her life—such a virtuoso of cheeses, however handsome, however noble of spirit, however intelligent.

* * *

That women are of a much cruder æsthetic, spiritual and emotional grain than men is attested to by the few women who, as compared with men, marry for love. It is perhaps not unfair to say that where four men out of five marry for love, not more than two women out of five marry for the same reason. A woman will marry a man for comfort, for money, for spite, for fear of coming age, because she has been jilted by some other man, for social reasons—for a score of reasons other than those prompted by the heart. And what is more, she will be happy with this man who is not the choice of her heart. And what is still more, as time goes on, she will convince herself that she *is* in love with him. A man may do these things, but never with the same self-respect that a woman can do them.

* * *

A woman declined by the man she loves and seeking sanctuary and solace in the embraces of her second choice is rarely the unhappy creature that common delusion insists she is. It is not the woman, but the second choice, for whom Tragi-Comedy, enwrapt in deceptive satins, waits open-armed in the wings.

* * *

The popular theory that danger adds zest to amour is perfumed with absurdity. While it may be true in the case of barbers, it is anything but true in the case of other men. I know. I've tried it.

Amour is only pleasant, only charming, when it is leisurely and comfortable. To scent it with danger is to delete it of its very sub-structure. The man who finds pleasure in making love to a woman with a vigilant husband or to a girl with a father who hides behind a drawing-room portière armed with a baseball bat is the kind of idiot who finds pleasure in seeing how near to the edge of the Grand Canyon he can balance himself without falling over. The most enjoyable love affair in the world would be one in which the woman was at once a widow and an orphan, and the man a Philip Nolan.

* * *

One of the strangest of the many common beliefs concerned with amour is that which maintains it an impossible thing for a man to be equally in love with two women at one and the same time. Doubtless originated by woman's own eternally assiduous Wilhelmstrasse and shrewdly disseminated for her own sly ends, the belief—for all its popularity with the ever-sentimental, ballad-singing male of the species—wears a sour motley. The majority of men are in love with one woman, and one woman only, simply because their acquaintanceship with women is so meagre, so bounded and confined, that they have not had the opportunity nor the good fortune to meet coincidentally another woman of equal charm and equal appeal. Since it is a matter of not infrequent occurrence for a man to fall in love with another woman after he has engaged himself to the one woman with whom he has believed himself singly in love, is it not perfectly reasonable to assume that had he initially met both women simultaneously he would have been taken with each of them equally?

The bachelor is a monument to women's charm. Unlike the

married man, he offers up constant proof of the charm of several women as opposed, in the bigoted instance of the former agnostic, to the charm of one. The heart of a bachelor is a mirror in which every love, peering, sees the image of a love equally beautiful and equally bewitching. The heart of a married man is a mirror upon which lack of adventure and laziness have breathed their obscuring fogs.

❖   ❖   ❖

Every woman, when she marries, fondly believes that she has married but one man: her lover-husband. It is only after a few years, upon looking one day wistfully out of the window, that she suddenly realizes that she committed bigamy.

❖   ❖   ❖

A thing is charming in the degree that it is not true. The truth, nine times in ten, is ugly: but a lie, nine times in ten, is beautiful—or, at least, the flower of a beautiful gesture. The charming woman is not the woman who tells the truth beautifully, yet unconvincingly, but the one who tells a lie prettily and impressively. The charming man is the man who believes that she is lying when she is telling the truth and that she is telling the truth when she is lying. . . . What in all the world could be at once more charming, and less true, than Der Rosenkavalier, or the Paris of Mürger, or the landscapes of Corot, or the memory of one's first sweetheart?

❖   ❖   ❖

That woman who begins saying to a man, "I don't think you love me any more," and who reiterates it from time to time, is already beginning to fall out of love with him.

❖   ❖   ❖

Love is never absolute, entire. In it, though it be as deep as the deepest sea, there is always elbowroom for a bit of a glance at some other man or woman.

❖   ❖   ❖

A man is charming to women in the degree that he does not appeal to men. A woman is charming to men in the degree that she does not appeal to women.

✿   ✿   ✿

The ideal marriage is one contracted by a man and woman who have been jilted by their first loves. It is a marriage securely based upon defeat and disillusion, the only sound ground from which marriage may flower into mutual understanding, into the love that is comradeship, and into the sweet and lasting peace that is ever the child of rosemary.

✿   ✿   ✿

Love, as the word has it, is impossible between an old man and a young girl not, as is commonly held, because youth seeks youth but more precisely because age seeks age. What a man over forty seeks in love is comfort—and this he may find only in one similarly seeking it. What a young girl seeks in love is a species of discomfort—and this she may find, readily enough, in an alliance with a man seeking comfort alone. A love that is comfortable is unknown to youth: when love becomes comfortable it is, to youth, no longer love. A young girl's love is of a piece with riding on a shoot-the-chutes, having a small fishbone lodge in the windpipe, and stepping suddenly from a warm room onto a snow-covered balcony.

(a) Love is the emotion that a woman feels always for a poodle dog and sometimes for a man. (b) Marriage is based on the theory that when a man discovers a particular brand of beer exactly to his taste he should at once throw up his job and go to work in the brewery.

✿   ✿   ✿

What passes for woman's intuition is more often intrinsically nothing more than man's transparency. To argue that there is something almost occult in a woman's instinctive divination of the fact that a man likes her is to argue that there is something almost occult in a rat's instinctive divination of the fact that, close at hand, there is a piece of cheese.

✿   ✿   ✿

No woman has ever loved a man so truly and deeply that she has not at some time permitted herself the thought of the pleasurable heartache his death would bring to her.

*   *   *

To a man, the least interesting of women is the successful woman, whether successful in work, or in love, or on the mere general gaudy playground of life. A man wants a woman whose success is touched, however faintly, with failure. The woman who is sure, resolute and successful, he may want for an associate in business, a friend and a confidante, a nurse or a housekeeper, but never for a sweetheart.

*   *   *

The most gracious heroine of life, as of drama, is the poor girl —and for a simple reason. Money gives a woman confidence, and confidence is the deadliest enemy of a woman's attractiveness and allure. Money gives a woman a sense of security; it steals from her all of her charming little Cinderella wishes; it envelops her with a pampered air; it makes her, if however vaguely, self-conscious. Such a woman no man can take into his arms without some slight, undefined feeling of restraint. When a man embraces for the first time the woman he loves, he first embraces the child in her and then the woman herself. The poor girl is always a child before the great world, with its surprises and hopes and treasures. The rich girl, however young, is always a woman.

*   *   *

The notion that as man grows older his illusions leave him is not quite true. What is true is that his early illusions are supplanted by new and, to him, equally convincing illusions. The man of forty-five has just as many illusions as the boy of eighteen, but they are different illusions. The man of ninety, dying, carries with him to the grave, if not the boyhood illusion of one woman's love, the senescent illusion of all women's faithlessness, and if not the boyhood illusion of the goodness of Santa Claus, the senescent illusion of the goodness of God.

*   *   *

Marriage defeats and humbles the man since it soon or late robs him of his greatest bulwark, *viz.*, vanity. The man who is no longer vain is a man already beaten. The man who is no longer proud of himself, who is no longer possessed of a pretty, healthy conceit, is a man slipping into the living grave. The vanity so essential to his happiness and well being, marriage takes from him. However great his success in material things, marriage, like the steady dropping of water, gradually wears down his antecedent self-pride and self-glory. The married man is the man whom romance has vanquished. He is a Cornwallis at Yorktown. He is the corpse of a bachelor.

※   ※   ※

The common theory that a woman who marries her second choice is more or less a creature for pity is as hollow as most theories cherished by the great yokelry. Not only is the woman not to be pitied; she is rather to be envied and congratulated. A woman's first choice—the man closest to her heart and the one who, had the Fates been kind, she would have gained for mate—is generally a man much less suited to the profession of husband than the temporarily spurned fellow in whom—as second choice—she eventually seeks solace. The first choice is more often than not a gaudy Romeo, good-looking, fun-loving, engaging, witty—but without the substantial qualities possessed by the second choice. These substantial qualities, in the youthful game of romance and amour, do not appeal to the woman: they seem commonplace and unattractive to her as against the easy flash and graceful glitter of her other love. But they are the qualities that make a husband if not a lover. And, having married them, as the years pass by and romance dies out of the world, the woman achieves a peace, a contentment and a happiness that her first choice, had she married it, would never have given her. A woman's first choice belongs not to her maturer years; it belongs to that green and sunlit period of her life when all the world sings a wonderful music, and the clouds are made of cotton. It is for youth, and passion, and gay colors, and the moon. The second choice, the sounder choice, is for the later years when the rain begins to fall. It is the choice for home, for comfort, and for grateful peace.

※   ※   ※

The young woman most attractive to men is not, as is claimed, the completely innocent young woman, but the young woman who, though anything but completely innocent, still looks as if she were completely innocent. The completely innocent young woman—granting that there still exists such an animal—is approximately as interesting to a man as a Sunday school. It is the *Encyclopedia Britannica* dressed in baby blue with eyes downcast and a hurt mouth who grabs us as sure as there's a hell!

❄   ❄   ❄

The theory that a woman loves most the kind of man she can mother vouchsafes, like the majority of blanket amorous assumptions, a number of glaring holes, and one glarer in particular. A woman does not love a man because she can mother him; she mothers him because she can love him. The man-mothering instinct is predicated wholly upon the sweetheart-mistress instinct. A woman no more cares about mothering a man whom she does not love (whether that love is complete or perhaps yet only in an incipient stage) than she cares about kissing the first street-car conductor she meets. Even the woman who takes up the profession of nursing—the professional mother—nurses most carefully, most solicitously and most eagerly that man in the ward whose hair is the smoothest and whose eyes, felt in hers, are most nearly the shade of William Faversham's.

❄   ❄   ❄

Whatever the proficiency of the American in other and lesser fields of enterprise, it is an acknowledged fact that in the art of writing the love letter he is a lugubrious doodle. The love letter written by the Don Juan of the United States—and I speak not of the amateur, but of the comparative crack shot—is as inefficient as a trombone player with tuberculosis. It may succeed—as it does succeed—in snaring a quarry of shop-girls, upper West Side widows, Vassar leftovers, pie-faced débutantes and other such already eager, willing and easily grabable sparrows, but it is seldom, if ever, that it contrives to wing a genuine canary. Nine-tenths of the most desirable young American women marry foreigners—Englishmen, Frenchmen, Italians, etc.—not because the latter are more handsome bipeds than the American (they are generally not so pulchritudinous), nor because they are wealthier (they seldom have nearly so much money), but because they excel the American in the arts of amour, and, more particularly, in the important technical art of the love letter. The American girl who can resist the drive of the love letter of an Englishman can resist the drive of a magnum of champagne. The American girl who can resist that of the love letter of a Frenchman can resist a gallon of whiskey. The American girl who can politely retain her balance after reading the love letter of an Italian can walk a chalk line after inhaling a keg or two.

The Latin understands the great secret of the *billet doux*. Where the American—and not infrequently the Englishman—writes his love letter from the point of view of the time when he composes it, the Latin always writes his from the point of view of the time when his inamorata will receive it. Thus, the Anglo-Saxon writing his beloved at eleven in the morning, writes an eleven a.m. point of view letter. And, thus, the beloved in due time receiving the letter at twilight or eventide or late night, and finding herself in the twilight or eventide or late-night mood, coincidentally finds the eleven a.m. point of view letter as jarring as a 1904 model Peerless and approximately as persuasive as a locomotive whistle.

The Latin never commits this mistake. His love letter is ever devised and composed, not from the time of its mailing, but from the time of its receipt. He figures as closely as he can the hour at which his girl will get the letter, and he writes the letter with that hour, and the girl's associated mood, in mind. It is a strategical technique that no woman, black or white, can withstand. In every such letter there is mailed synchronously, for the convenient use of the girl addressed, a white flag.

❖   ❖   ❖

The most loyal and faithful woman indulges her imagination in a hypothetical liaison whenever she dons a new street frock for the first time.

❖   ❖   ❖

A girl should go to church regularly. To a ritualistic, not an evangelical church, however. The adventure softens her, makes her lovelier, makes her more charming. A girl leaving St. Patrick's is twice as lovely as when she enters. There is a charming wonder in her eyes, a new sweetness and music in her soul. The ritualistic church takes the hardness out of a girl's eyes and heart; it perfumes her with a touch of spirituality that is pleasing to men. The evangelical church, to the contrary, turns her into a sour-ball, a woman with the flash of acid in her eyes and the set of a bear-trap to her teeth. But the other church! What man can resist the allure of a woman who has knelt before high, candlelit altars with the rays of dying suns falling upon her from stained-glass? What man can fail to love a woman who has listened, hushed, for many years to great organs and to soft and rhythmical Latin prayers, and has knelt at vespers in great, dim, majestic cathedrals? Let the dog step up!

❖   ❖   ❖

There are two times in a man's life when he particularly needs the ear of a friend: (1) when he has just lost his old girl, and (2) when he has just got a new one.

❖   ❖   ❖

The beauty of even the most beautiful woman is a comically insecure and fragile thing. The beauty of Helen herself could not have survived so absurdly simple a trial as a combination of red and pink, or wet hair, or circular striped stockings, or a mosquito bite on the eyelid.

❖   ❖   ❖

Woman, with exception so rare that it is negligible, admires intelligence in man only in so far as this intelligence is confined to his dealings and enterprises with other men in the world of men. She has a disrelish for the man who is intelligent in her own presence, in his relations with her. She likes to know that he is intelligent, but indirectly, at secondhand. The man who exercises his intelligence in the presence of a woman may gain a friend or a wife, but never a sweetheart.

❖   ❖   ❖

The chief rock upon which a lasting friendship rests is a strong mutual belief in the same general fallacies and falsehoods.

*   *   *

Woman's function in social and cardiac enterprise is, primarily, as an audience. A man admires a woman not for what she says, but for what she listens to. The more attentively and sympathetically she remains silent before his oracular nonsenses, the more beautiful she seems to him, and the more he loves her, and the sooner he marries her. The girl with the patient eardrum is the girl who first nabs a husband.

*   *   *

There are, as women quickly sense, two distinct types of men. All men may be set down as of the one type or the other. Men are either cheap men or they are not cheap men. The classification has little to do with birth, with family, with education or social position or wealth. But each man nonetheless wears a tag conspicuous, revelatory and unmistakable. A man is either an essential gentleman or an essential bounder. I know a man born of one of the blueblood American families, educated at a great university, rich and conspicuous in the smart metropolitan life, whose soul is the soul of a bounder. I know a cigar-dealer in Broadway, an old man born God knows where and without education or fortune, who has the soul of a gentleman. I know men high in affairs, high in society, high in the estimation of the country, who are muckers; I know a seedy middle-aged man who makes keys to fit my doors, my humidor and my icebox for fifty cents apiece, who has something of the purple in his heart.

A man may be red or yellow or black or white, he may be high or low or rich or poor, but he bears the one brand or the other. Pause a moment and consider the men you know intimately. They drop, one by one, into the one groove or the other as surely, and as relentlessly, as the balls in so many Japanese rolling games.

*   *   *

One of the most fecund and persistent myths of amour is that which maintains that a man, once he is taken with a woman, is intrigued in the degree that she affects indifference toward him. The truth, of course, is that while such indifference, whether honest or assumed, may actually contrive to keep him stepping lively for a short spurt, it very soon thereafter causes him suddenly to halt and get out of the race altogether. The clever woman, desiring to ensnare a man, realizes that the best way to get him is to throw away all the traditional feminine weapons and subterfuges and frankly and openly, yet charmingly, tell him that she likes him. The man thus handled, all folklore to the contrary, is won—and absolutely. The indifference tactic may in the end achieve some vagrom boob, but it has never yet in the history of the world gained for a woman a single desirable, firstrate man.

❀　　❀　　❀

However charming the American woman, there is about her always one thing that keeps that charm from true perfection. Unlike the French woman, she is unable to flirt with two men at the same time without causing one of the men to regard her as being just a trifle vulgar.

❀　　❀　　❀

The flapper of today differs from the young girl of yesterday not in that, unlike her sister of yesterday, she is hep to all the esoteric subjects, but in that, unlike her sister of yesterday, she is hep to all the maidenly artifices which successfully conceal from men her hepness to those subjects.

❀　　❀　　❀

The notion that the dog is an ever-faithful animal and will plough twenty miles through a driving snowstorm with a keg of schnapps tied to his neck in order to rescue his master, no matter how ill the latter may on a forgiven occasion have treated him, is perhaps somewhat sweeter than true. A dog loves a master who treats him kindly, gives him plenty to eat, pets him, warms him with comfortable blankets and tricks him out with pretty collars. But a dog will turn from that master if the latter neglects for a space of time to coddle him, to look out for his well-being, and to pat him occasionally on the head. So, in each instance, will a woman. The American notion that a dog is in this respect superior to a woman is perhaps an exaggerated one.

*   *   *

Woman is most lovable when there has just occurred in her life something that saddens her. No man has ever loved a woman passionately at that moment in her life when she was happiest.

*   *   *

A man, looking back over the bridge of the years, always sentimentalizes his first love affair. A woman always gives hers the laugh.

*   *   *

The greatest happiness is that of the imminent, but not yet quite realized, achievement. To be about to succeed—that is true happiness. To have succeeded—that is to be in the Pschorr brewery, with diabetes.

*   *   *

What makes a man fall in love with a girl? A noble character? A tender disposition? An alert mind? Womanly sympathy? A fine integrity? Dependability? Gentleness, kindness, charitableness? The fact that she is a fit potential mother for his children? Perhaps, but I doubt it. I doubt that a man fell in love with a girl for any of such more or less sound, accepted reasons. What generally gets him is something much less granted, something entirely superficial, something—when viewed after the years—that seems almost absurd. Looking back over the girls I have been in love with, I recall that I fell in love, as the phrase goes, with one because I was fetched by the smooth quality of her speaking voice, with three others because they wore lace or linen baby collars, with one because she stole up behind me one night at a rather formal dance and tickled my ear, with still another because, when drinking a glass of water, she had a habit of holding the glass with both palms, with still another because she had the knack of keeping her pretty hair up without hairpins, and with another still because she had a trick of saying the most unimportant and innocent things to me in a very low voice, as if dangerous spies were lurking all about us. I am an idiot, you say? Undoubtedly. But, unlike you, I am an *honest* idiot.

* * *

Most alluring to man is that woman whose wickedness has to it a touch of the angelic and whose virtue a touch of the devil.

* * *

The instinct of the married man to dally with a woman other than his wife or of a married woman to flirt with some man other than her husband is not in the least the vicious instinct we are sometimes asked to believe. It is natural and, above natural, innocent. When one grows used to a person, or to a thing, the human impulse is ever toward experiment in some other and fresher direction. The man who has been married to a woman for a number of years, who has lived with her, has played upon all her whims and moods, knows her every response to every act, recognizes in advance her every gesture and every tone, is like the man who has owned a piano and has played upon it for the same long length of time. The moment he enters a house with another piano in it, he feels like trying the new one. There isn't a man or woman living who hasn't experienced the innocent wish to try someone's else piano. And there are few married men or women who haven't in a similar way experienced the innocent wish to try someone's else kiss.

* * *

A woman dislikes sentiment in a man in the degree that she is pretty.

* * *

The sweetest memory is that which involves something which one should not have done; the bitterest, that which involves something which one should not have done, and which one did not do.

* * *

The man with a bald head, however eminent his position, always feels slightly ill at ease in the presence of a man whose dome is still well thatched. He feels, however much he may try not to, just a trifle handicapped and inferior. In the presence of a pretty woman, he feels himself called upon to exercise twice the pains of the fellow with hair. The man whose head looks like a freshly laid egg is, in woman's society, ever either Malvolio or Yorick.

❋   ❋   ❋

The girl subsequently alleges with tears that the man had given her hope in the matter of marriage. The man subsequently recalls to himself, by way of supporting his self-respect, that the girl in turn had given *him* hope in that she professed elaborately not to desire, but even to disdain, that hope for marriage.

❋   ❋   ❋

A woman is charming in the degree of her reaction to a charming man.

❋   ❋   ❋

The greatest burden of Prohibition will fall upon amour. Without the friendly cooperation of alcohol, love-making—to the only kind of man that interests a woman—will be a difficult and awkward business. Without a few cocktails cavorting in his middle, a man embarking upon the preliminaries of amour feels too idiotic to continue. His mind is too clear for a business that, however delightful, is intrinsically always banal and silly. His amorous words fall upon his own ears in all their stenciled gauntness. They lack the carelessness, the ardor, the thoughtlessness essential to them and to the great game, qualities that—save in the case of a professional actor, a clergyman or a Frenchman—only a touch of alcohol can bequeath to them. Love-making is a sort of boozy human music, and it can be played only, in the instance of an adult man, upon a keyboard of mellifluous beverages.

❋   ❋   ❋

The contention that women are more intelligent than men (a favorite hokum of such amateurs of the sex as Mencken) has never succeeded in exciting me. That the contention sells books, gains for its sponsor many free deviled-ham sandwiches and pots of tea flavored with rum, and achieves for him a fine reputation for sagacity, open-mindedness and chivalry, I— privy to the enviable facts—am not one to deny. But that it is grounded in truth—that seems to me another matter. The truth is that while women as a class are not so intelligent as men, they are, by virtue of their superior histrionic faculties, able with extraordinary success to make themselves appear so. It is this histrionism that deceives the amateurs. When a male blockhead and a female blockhead get together, the male blockhead keeps his mouth wide open and permits it to betray the news of his blockheadedness. The female blockhead keeps hers closed, winks sagaciously about nothing, droops a lovely blue eye with an empty, but vastly effective, dubiety, negotiates an impressively inscrutable smile, and thus leads the eavesdropping menckens to believe that she is fully privy to the lewd asininity of the fellow.

The platitude that all the good dressmakers and cooks are men, not women, doesn't interest me. That men should succeed over women in such professions as these, which are customarily held to be the especial province of women, has nothing to do with the question of relative intelligence: it assuredly takes no Socrates or Gladstone to make a pretty Peter Thomson or a fine cheese pie: the circumstance that men are better in these fields than women would, indeed, seem to prove that the argument of the amateurs is sound. But, for all the agreeable paradoxes, the fact remains that, save in the single instance of the conflict of sex, the best woman is the inferior of the secondbest man. Women's intelligence is emotional intelligence: it is showy, appealing, moving, and generally gains its ends: but if this is sound intelligence then every highball is a Bismarck, every hypnotist a Huxley. The woman does not argue with a man's mind, but with his eye and his heart—as an actress, playing a colorful and sympathetic rôle, argues. No woman in the history of the world has yet substituted, in her arguments with the male, facts for nose varnish or sharp philosophy for talc and perfume. Woman is the Jap of the sexes: she is shrewd, clever, wily and, nine times in ten, gets what she goes after. Man is the German.

❊   ❊   ❊

The secret of dressing in such wise that the picture shall subtly appeal to men, few young women understand. The true secret— as any man who stops momentarily to reflect and analyze will agree—is for the young woman to dress like a poor country girl expensively.

        ✿   ✿   ✿

A man, weary of the chill and commonplace of his surroundings, seeks the Riviera for pretty new scenery, warmth and quiet. A man thus also seeks woman.

        ✿   ✿   ✿

The trouble with girls is not that one gets tired of them, but that one doesn't. This is the true cause of a man's unhappiness. The popular view is that a man is chronically unable to love a girl long, that he tires of her in due time, and that he is then eager to get rid of her as soon as he can. This is sometimes the case. But more often the opposite is true. He does not get tired of the girl; he continues to like her; he doesn't want to lose her; and his troubles begin.

        ✿   ✿   ✿

The effect of cocktails—or any other alcoholic beverage—upon women is curiously unlike the effect of such tonics upon men. Take, for example, the relation of the effect of alcoholic indulgence to amour. A man and a woman, mutually intrigued, are seated at the table. The man drinks a cocktail, then another, then another, then another. With each successive tipple he becomes more and more excited over the charms of his fair companion, more and more eloquent, more and more eager to imprint a smack behind her little pink seashell of an ear. As one cocktail follows its predecessor down his alimentary canal, he waxes amorous *crescendo, fortissimo.* But consider now the woman.

After her first cocktail, she is in a mood precisely like the mood of the man after *his* first cocktail. After the second, she is in a mood precisely like the man after *his* second. But comes now the curious change. Though his third cocktail increases the man's ardor, her third cocktail almost instantaneously decreases the woman's. As if struck by a ghostly streak of lightning, as if touched by some occult hand, the woman's mood suddenly achieves a certain restraint, a peculiar rigidity, a trace of coolness. The man's third cocktail has sent his acumen packing; the woman's third has brought her acumen back with a rush. She is lit, true enough—as lit as the man—but she is yet, by some esoteric phenomenon, again master of him and of the situation.

All of which is respectfully submitted to such teetotaler moralists as believe that when a woman has had three cocktails she is completely in the villain's power and ripe for the Italianos.

* * *

The most successful technique that a man may employ with a woman is to show interest in her but appear not to care.

* * *

It takes very, very little to make a woman snicker at a worthy man. Let a man be soever noble, soever upright, profound, charming and eloquent, if he happens to have on a collar a size too large for him, he is lost.

* * *

The notion that a pretty girl is prettier if she doesn't know that she is pretty is a sour chestnut. If a pretty girl doesn't know that she is pretty, she ruins her prettiness with carelessly selected colors and with snap-judgment hats and frocks. If she appreciates her prettiness, she commits no such mistake, but carefully—even painstakingly—heightens her prettiness with colors, hats and frocks that melt harmoniously into her prettiness. The pretty girl who is unaware of her prettiness may be a charming girl, but she is never one-half so pretty as the equally pretty girl who knows that she is pretty.

* * *

When the estimable Bell conceived the idea for the telephone, little did the good old soul reckon that it would turn out, in time, to be an innocent and unwitting agent in the dealing of the deuce to the young female of the species. That, more than any other thing, the telephone has been instrumental in bring-

ing the young woman of today to a point where her grandmother wouldn't recognize her, that it is in no little degree responsible for her increasingly loose manners and looser habits,
any mother who takes the time to analyze the situation will
doubtless agree.

Before the introduction of the telephone into general family
use, the young girl of the house, meeting her young man in the
paternal parlor, was naturally subject to the nervousness, shyness, bashfulness, etc. common on such occasions to nine well-
bred young women out of every ten. After weeks of such conferences the friendship of the twain would progress so far as
the hand-holding stage; after months, so far as the first kiss;
after a year or two, probably so far as the proposal of marriage.
The great barriers to intimacy that modesty, awkwardness and
personal idiosyncrasy and reserve always throw up operated
here; and our mothers thus took so long to bring our fathers
around with the ring that we children, as yet unborn and so
comprehending the drollery of love, almost gave up in despair
our chances of ever seeing the Ziegfeld "Follies" and Ernest
Poole initiated into an American Institute of Arts and Letters.

These barriers the telephone gradually did away with, broke
down. It is not so easy—nor so safe—to look a man in the eye
and tell him to go to hell as it is to drop a nickel in a slot at
206th Street, call up Rector ten miles away, and then do it.
Similarly, it is not so easy for a flapper to sit next to a man on
a sofa and, without blushing, tell him to press his ruby lips to
hers. The telephone gives the flapper courage—and more. It
conceals blushes; it gives the strength that is always afforded
by remoteness; it removes, in a sense, the personal equation. It
permits a girl to lie in her bed and talk with a man lying in *his*
bed; it permits her, half-clothed, to talk with him a moment
after its ring has made him hop nude out of his bathtub. Its
delicate suggestiveness is not lost in these instances. Its whisper is the whisper of the clandestine note of the 1870's hidden
in the hole of the old oak; its voice is the voice of the chaperon
asleep. The most modest girl in America, the girl who blushes
even at a man's allusions to his chilblains, once she gets her
nose in a telephone mouthpiece acquires a sudden and surprising self-assurance and aptitude at wheeze. Every time a young

girl calls up a man for the first time, the devil instructs Tyson to
lay aside for him, a year hence, a seat in the first row.

*   *   *

How little it takes to make the beautiful ridiculous: two flies
engaged in amour on the nose of the finest Rembrandt . . .
Washington's farewell to his men read aloud by a veteran of
the Home Guard of 1917–18 . . . a lovely woman engaging an
asparagus.

[From *The Theatre, the Drama, the Girls*, 1921, pp. 218–47.]

Women as Playthings

ALTHOUGH so great a philosopher as Nietzsche defined woman
as a plaything—"the reward of the warrior" was his phrase—any
lesser man who would repeat the definition today would be set
down as an impresario of gibberish. Now that old Friedrich is
dead, it is apparently permitted to Frenchmen alone to write
of women with any degree of honesty. The Anglo-Saxon and
certain others deem it proper to speak of the ladies only in
tones customarily reserved for the Deity; to be a trifle realistic
in the philosophic contemplation of them, they regard as not
quite nice. Yet, unless I am submerged in error, woman is and
always has been primarily a plaything. She herself may at times
and in certain instances try to blink the fact—particularly when
she happens to be so unprepossessing that no man wants her
for a plaything—but in her heart of hearts she knows the truth
of it. Of this truth, a certain increasingly prevalent sexual phenomenon among women offers illuminating evidence. This phenomenon is, in essence, nothing but a challenge and a resentment.

The by this time already irritated reader will have observed
that I generalize about women. He will object to this generalization. But, since it is I and not he who is writing this,
the generalization must stand. Generalizations are not always
faulty. One may generalize with a fair degree of accuracy on
numerous subjects. War is one of them. Hygiene is another.
Sculpture and bock beer are still others. And woman is, I be-

lieve, another still. The men who group women under certain different classifications marry them. And, as Omnipotence has willed it, I happen to be a bachelor. I am not unduly swollen over the fact; I offer it to the jury, indeed, as evidence against myself. I simply remain still to be convinced. Toward the aforesaid conviction, I have at times drifted, but the old tugboat has somehow ever remained in midstream. And there, for the time being, it remains rolling *a cappella* at anchor.

It is, to get back on the key, foolish to group women under various headings. Only men may be so grouped. Men differ, in many essentials. But all women are, at bottom, much the same. The O'Grady and the Colonel's lady, up to the age of thirty-five at least, are sisters under their skins. But do not mistake me, please. I do not pose as a Ph.D. of the fair sex. I simply set down the results of my own observation. If these results collide with your own, then one of us is wrong. It may be I; but it may too, on the other hand, be you. Woman, it seems to me, was wrought primarily by an all-wise Creator for man's entertainment and bemusement. That she is the mother of the race hardly invalidates the point. The moment a man's wife no longer amuses him—I use the word "amuse," obviously enough, in its broadest sense—he grows sick of her and she too, by the act of droll and ironic fate, grows tired of him. The best mother is she who seems to her little son his father's delicate and beautiful sweetheart. No son of a raucous suffragette admires his mother as the son of a sweet and amiable woman does his. A boy in his youngsterhood plays with girls. And, save he be an absurd sentimentalist and an out-and-out emotional Babbitt when he grows up, he continues to do so until he dies. That he may marry offers no argument against this point of view. Ninety-nine men out of a hundred look on their wives as playthings when they marry them, for love is a music written for playthings. When they stop regarding their wives as playthings, they no longer love them with the quality of love that launched their marriage. The woman then loses much of her femininity in the husband's eyes and gains a touch of quasi-masculinity. She becomes, in a word, his partner in the dull business routine of life. He admires her; he respects her; but he no longer loves her in the sense that he originally loved her

—and it is that original love that every wife pines for. The heart of a woman, whatever her age and however wrinkled her face, remains always the heart of a girl.

I have known many women in this life of mine and, among them all, I have never known one who did not, in the lovely heart of her, wish to be, above all the more serious things of the world, a pretty and desirable toy. A woman is always a plaything for the man she truly loves. It is only when she does not truly love him that she takes on a coat of another color. The man who is married to a woman who is not a plaything is married to a woman who may venerate him and be loyal to him but who doesn't really love him. . . . Almost every woman is a plaything on her honeymoon. It is in the years that follow—years often disillusionizing to her—that she changes and ceases to be. She perhaps wishes still to be a plaything, but she no longer has the right playmate. For one can't be a playmate when illusion has gone its way. It is thus that married women so frequently seek innocent unction to their vanity in the company of men other than their husbands. The old longing to be regarded as a plaything tugs at their bosoms; they want to hear the lighthearted old phrases and see the lighthearted old smiles, long since forgotten by the men to whom they are wedded. . . . Every time a woman buys a new dress or puts on a new hat, it is of herself as a plaything that she is thinking. Thinking—but never under any circumstance so analyzing herself. For once she tries to define it, the plaything spirit is already, so far as she is concerned, on its deathbed calling weakly for the hot-water bottle. The moment a woman begins to analyze herself as a plaything, she ceases to be one. A toy doesn't think.

Why is it that the women of the stage are generally more alluring than the women in private life? Because they have about them the plaything air. Has it been woman as woman or woman as plaything that has ruled kings and emperors and the great generals of the world? Is the library of romance full of the stories of women who haven't been playthings or of women who have been? For one woman who wins a man by other means, there are a score who win by their toy quality. . . . I have said that, in her heart, every woman wishes to be a plaything. There are interludes in this wish, of course. There are times when doubt and unhappiness and thoughts of to-morrow turn the light melody into a graver key. But, so long as a woman is immediately happy, so long does she enthusiasti-cally concur in the plaything estimate of her.

I have, in the last two or three years, read no less than one hundred male-made articles in magazines and newspapers en-titled "Why I Have Never Married." The gentlemen who have thus taken the public into their confidence are doubtless en-tirely honest and sincere, but the reasons they assign for never having married would be just as convincing if the articles were written by women. These reasons are generally found to be purely sentimental ones. This man has never married either because, so he says, he has never been able to find a girl like his mother or because the lady on whom he was excessively mashed was drowned five days before the wedding. And that man has never married, he confesses, because he deemed the building up of a shoe factory more important than the building up of a home or because the one girl in the whole world whom he would have married gave him the gate. There are doubtless men who have never married for such reasons, but they are, I believe, few and far between. Though they are, as I have ob-served, sincere and honest in setting down their personal rec-ords, they are, it seems to me, the exception to the rule rather than the rule itself. For one man who hasn't married because he couldn't find a girl with the qualities of his mother or be-cause his first sweetmeat was run over by a Ford, there are a half-dozen like myself who haven't married simply because marriage doesn't strike their realistic minds as being one-half so attractive as bachelorhood.

These so-called cynical fellows are not, however, wholly un-sentimental. The only difference between them and the other fellows is that, while they are perfectly willing occasionally to sentimentalize women, they cannot find it in themselves to sen-timentalize matrimony. At least, not so long as they are still relatively young and comfortable and happy. To particularize, I have never married because, very simply, in the language of a current music-show ditty, I am having too much fun. I can think of nothing that marriage could give me, but I can think

of many things it could take away from me. It could, for example, take away from me the freedom I currently enjoy in unloading into print any view on any subject that comes into my
head. If I were married—this being America—I should have to
stop periodically and deliberate as to the tact of writing and
printing certain ideas which presently I may freely deliver myself of. A married man must ever be more or less conscious of
what people will think of him; there is his wife to be thought
of in her relation to him and to his position in their immediate
community. A bachelor knows no such hindrances. The married man who would write and publish such a treatise as this
would find a rolling-pin waiting for him when he got home.

Marriage could take away my precious privacy, my present
ability to go where I wish to whenever I wish to, my present
agreeable habit of making even more agreeable engagements
at the last moment and breaking less agreeable ones at the same
time, my perfect equanimity of mind, my intense dislike of life-
insurance agents, and my freely voiced credo that there is always a slightly more charming young woman just around the
corner. It could give me nothing otherwise that I, with the
aid of six head of clairvoyants, am able to deduce. It is not
that I shirk responsibility; it is that I shirk what I do not especially regard as responsibility. And connubial bliss is one of the
responsibilities that I do not consider my own. The theory that
it is the duty of every man to marry strikes me as somewhat ridiculous. It may be the duty of every man of a certain kind to
marry, but that is another matter. I personally have the misfortune to be unfitted temperamentally for hymeneal blessedness.
I do not possess the required peculiar technic. That technic demands that a man spend the rest of his life with one woman and
never look at another. Of this technic I am too much of an amateur. It is beyond me. And I am possessed of a strange and uncontrollable feeling that it is similarly beyond the majority of
men who engage it. The manifold diversions that society
devises for itself—dancing, drinking, racing, golf, European
jaunts, charities, mah jong, and so on—are simply proofs of the
constant failure of the technic in question and of the effort to
forget that failure in opiates. These divertissements constitute,
in essence, but a heroic resolve to make the well-mannered best

of a bad bargain. I know many married men; I even know a few happily married men; but I don't know one who wouldn't fall down the first open coal-hole running after the first pretty girl who gave him a wink.

I appreciate that there are some fetching arguments in opposition to the general point of view herein exhibited, but none the less there seem to me to be some equally fetching arguments in support of it. The mere circumstance that a point of view is an unpopular one does not confute it. Although the Anglo-Saxon places woman on a pedestal and the Latin does not, a French or Italian child loves its mother just as much as an English or American child does his. I have always believed that, in fact, real and honest love flourishes best and most beautifully among such peoples as do not foolishly idealize women.

When I say that women are essentially playthings, I use the word not derogatorily but in terms of the highest compliment. My mother was ever a charming and lovely pastime in my father's eyes. My brother and I knew it, and we admired his attitude and loved her the more for it. For we knew other fathers who looked on our boy friends' mothers with harder and prosier eyes, and we saw that these mothers of our boy friends showed it. They scolded their sons, we noticed, a lot more and a lot oftener than our mother did us; and their smiles, we noticed, were sometimes sort of cold smiles where those of our mother seemed not to be. We noticed these differences and many others, and if we then, as youngsters, didn't know the reason for them, that reason we began to know in our more mature and reflective years. . . . There is something infinitely alluring about a plaything. The men who marry women who are not playthings marry for money, for position, for peace and comfort, for a multiplicity of reasons. But these have nothing to do with love. Where a man loves a woman really, you will generally find that the woman is, to him, above everything else the symbol of a boyhood toy. And so too will you frequently find that when a man hasn't married, it is simply because, while he may often have found the right kind of woman, he hasn't yet found the right kind of plaything.

[From *The Autobiography of an Attitude*, 1925, pp. 70–80.]

Enjoying Women

I DECLINE to be a realist where women are concerned. To enjoy women at all one must manufacture an illusion and envelop them with it, otherwise they would not be endurable. To that extent, at least, I am sufficiently realistic. Without this deceptive illusory chicane woman is found to be simply a third-rate man; with it, she is found to be charming, amusing, desirable, lovely. Why spoil a good time? Why be content with anything third-rate when you can so easily—in certain cases—metamorphose it into the first-rate? But, you ask, why fool yourself with women? I ask, in turn, why fool yourself with the whiskey you drink or the God you believe in? The temporary effect is good enough, and it all will not matter a damn after you are dead.

[From *Monks Are Monks*, 1929, pp. 120–1.]

Mens Nana in Corpore Sano

THAT, taking one with another, women's minds are less clean than men's is a fact which, while sufficiently recognized by men in the mass, has yet strangely, so far as I know, not found its commentator and analyst on paper. We have had a few general epigrams on the subject, and we have thought, now and again, that we were about to read some sharp and penetrating affidavit on the matter, but in both cases delicate evasion and polite half-statement have been the only reward of our curiosity. In the interests of lovely truth, therefore, let us make bold to pursue the inquiry a bit further.

Any man who moves about in feminine society and who is not deaf in both ears can testify to the fact that women's conversation, whatever the specific nature of its initial impulse, sooner or later is inevitably bound to get around to sex. The manœuvre may be contrived indirectly and with a certain spurious show of neo-Victorian modesty—in some instances; but once it gains a measure of confidence it stalks into the topic like a bouncer into a barroom. Whereas men, when they enter into the subject, customarily enter into it, often somewhat disconcertingly, with what may metaphorically be described as both feet, women begin by skirting around its edges, by tossing out innuendo, and by playing ping-pong with suggestiveness before getting to the main business of the conversational meeting. A man will say, frankly, openly, and plainly, what is in his mind; a woman will by verbal by-play and insinuation convert what would otherwise be forthrightly clean into something that is vaguely dirty. Women seldom, in sex matters, use the straight-forward, clean-cut, appropriate terms. They rely upon circumlocutions and synonyms which, like burlesque-show strippers, are twice as suggestive as the naked words. They drape their colloquies in gauze veils and, slowly and with deliberately timed oral movements and gestures, remove them, to their twofold—or sevenfold—eroticism.

For this, the still remaining double standard of sex—it still remains for all the vociferous verbal and physical promiscuity of a relative handful of females and for all the editorial fulminations in liberal publications edited by unwanted old maids or fed-up married men who have eyes for their stenographers and obliquely wish to give their wives the gate—the still operative double standard, as I say, is doubtless responsible. Women, under its terms, are denied the privilege of directness and honesty and must perforce take refuge in an arsenal of allusive hints and winks. Their thoughts may be the same as men's thoughts, but the forbidden direct articulation of them serves by repression to make them gradually stagnant and fungus-covered. A man, as the saying is, gets them off his chest and is done with them; a woman is not equally permitted to get them off her mind, and there they remain to crawl about with their increasingly slimy worminess.

This enforced repression seeking vicarious outlet is indicated, among other things, by the stuff that women read. Who are the chief consumers of cheap sex novels and magazines of so-called snappy fiction? The sales statistics show, and emphatically, that they are women—young, medium, and pretty old. The phrase, "shop-girl fiction," tells its own story. On the higher literary but equally sexy level, who have been and are the chief worshippers of D. H. Lawrence, particularly in his *Lady Chatterley's Lover* mood? The answer is too obvious to be recorded.

Women think of sex in the daytime as well as at night, whereas men in general seldom find their thoughts hovering about the topic when the sun is shining. Even Frenchmen and the Viennese hardly begin before twilight. And speculation is inflammation. I have known many men in my lifetime, but I have yet to encounter one who talked or thought about sex at lunch. The majority of women, on the other hand, even those who have to work for a living, allow their imaginations and conversation to play around it from the first application of the morning lipstick to the last dab of cold cream at night. Like hatred, sex must be articulated or, like hatred, it will produce a disturbing internal malaise. The edicts of polite society are responsible to no small degree for women's dirty minds.

Any psychoanalyst or practitioner of psychopathology will tell you that, out of every ten customers and patients, nine are women. And out of the nine, at least eight will be found to be troubled with sex complexes. These sex complexes, the aforesaid professors need hardly tell you, are the result of repressions, and the aforesaid repressions are responsible for all kinds of mental quirks. The injunction, "Get it out of your mind," suggests the nature of the mind and its thoughts. These thoughts are not healthy, but diseased. Concentration on sex, though sometimes unsuspected, has brought with it a species of mental corruption.

Plays dealing with abnormality always find their chief customers among women. When *The Captive* was, previous to its enforced withdrawal by the police, shown in New York, the box-office statistics revealed that five women to every man attended it, and the matinées were patronized almost exclusively by women.

Such pornographic literary trash as Elinor Glyn's *Three Weeks,* the Mlle. Hull's *The Sheik,* and Arlen's *The Green Hat* finds itself in the best-seller class solely because of women.

The sex moving pictures, with Mae West's alone excepted (and they are humorous rather than erotically stimulating), are patronized overwhelmingly, the exhibitors' records assure us, by women.

The heroines of men are Joan of Arc, Florence Nightingale

and Edith Cavell. The heroines of women are Du Barry, Pompadour and Gabriele d'Annunzio.

I have lately had the privilege of scrutinizing the account books of the four leading purveyors of so-called erotica in New York City. Not the cheap dispensers of contemptible pink-backs, but the sellers of books that, for one reason or another, are not supposed to be read by the moral element in the community. The account books of the first, covering the period from January 1, 1934, to July 1, 1934, showed that his customers number 1,810 women as against 254 men. The books of the second, covering a like period, showed 927 women as against forty-six men. Those of the third, covering the time from January 1, 1934, to September 1, 1934, showed 737 women and only thirty-four men. And those of the fourth, covering the period from February 1, 1934, to August 1, 1934, disclosed 462 women as against just fourteen men. I am not acquainted with the sellers of pink-backs, and so, unfortunately, cannot offer statistics in that quarter. But the story on the somewhat higher sex level is sufficiently illuminating. Men usually outgrow their taste for pornography after they have completed, at an early age, the prescribed course of *Only a Boy*, *Fanny Hill* and *Green Girls in Paris*. But women's taste for pornography seems seldom to abate.

Perhaps in no clearer way may we appreciate the dubious quality of the feminine mind than by referring to the question of motion picture censorship and observing the peculiar aberrations of that mind when it serves on the various state censorship committees whose business it is to pass on the morality of the films. Through various esoteric channels, I have managed to glean certain facts and certain information in this direction that offer tasty reading. I herewith present my findings:

1. The male members of three of these censorship boards—there are state boards at the present time in New York, Maryland, Virginia, Ohio, Kansas, Pennsylvania, and for Sunday films, in Massachusetts—found nothing particularly dirty in such words and phrases as "naked," "twin beds," "mistress," "birth control" and "long, lonely nights," but were compelled to demand their deletion upon the insistence of women members of the boards.

2. It was the women on the boards of two state censorship bodies who, against the male members' indifference, forced the elimination from certain films of such innocent spectacles as women's underclothing hanging on a clothes line and a husband appearing in his wife's presence clad in his undershirt and B.V.D.'s.

3. The deletion of such childishly harmless lines as "I wonder if Molly's mother has told her everything" (spoken by the husband on his wedding night), as "You made her so dizzy she had to go in and lie down" (spoken after a kiss), as "I'm from America"— "What part?"— "All of me," as "If you think Americans are good at the Black Bottom, just watch those Africans," and as "Come in, young man, don't be frightened. It's much warmer here than on the balcony," was ordered not by male committee members but by female.

4. Although the male censors could not discern anything excessively foul in a view of a nude little baby, of a girl sitting on a couch with a man's head in her lap, of a man in pajamas, of a girl drawing her feet up on a bench, of nightgowns arranged on a bed, of a nude figure carved on a pipe, and of table bookends showing a female figure's single nude breast, the women censors apparently could.

5. The censorship ladies also saw something extremely filthy in the following lines: "Corinne thinks a mistress is something you read about in a French novel"; "You know, experience should have taught you, my dear, that the name Smith is always suspicious on the hotel register"; "You mustn't think of the man in me, only the artist"; "It wasn't love"; "What's your name?"— "Eve"— "Mine's Adam"; "Is friend husband out of town again?"; and "This girl, painted as a harlot, met death with a smile."

Under beautiful rose-beds, it would seem, there are often sewers.

[From *Passing Judgments,* 1935, pp. 89–96.]

Love in Youth—and Later

IT is possible that a man may love only one woman in his life. So, for that matter, is it equally possible that a man may get through life with only one pair of trousers. The possibility is hardly open to question, but the probability one fears, particularly in the case of an artist like myself, is remote. It is quite possible that a man may remain physically loyal to one woman throughout his life, but it is extremely improbable that he can remain always mentally and emotionally loyal to her. A man's taste in women changes with the passing of time as inevitably as does his taste in literature and neckties. The man who whispers into the ear of a sweet one that she is the only woman he will ever have a penchant for is, accordingly, one of three sorts: a deliberate fraud and liar; an unconscious fraud and liar; or, finally, a man over sixty who, at once deliberately and unconsciously, is telling the melancholy truth.

There are perhaps young men in the twenties who fall in love, as the phrase is, marry the refreshment of their choice, and live with her in peace and comfort until the embalmer enters upon the scene. And so, too, are there perhaps older men who negotiate the same feat. But the mere fact that they spend their lives with one woman and are biologically faithful to her and are relatively content with their lot does not mean—as anyone knows whose eye is gifted in the penetration of externals— that their taste does not occasionally and refractorily wander to some other woman. The wandering of fancy—I will have to admit this much—may be perfectly innocent and eminently moral, but it is there in the backs of their heads none the less and, being there, it offers proof of the theory that though a man may conceivably be a saint in the matter of monogamous uprightness, his taste often resides in a harem.

A man's taste in the fair sex nine times out of ten changes every so often with what is sometimes, even to him, an alarming suddenness. The girl a man of twenty-one admires usually seems to him, in the retrospect of forty, to have been a gimcrack of pretty low grade. If he has married her at twenty-one, true enough, he often doesn't so regard her as the years chase each other down the corridor of the late thirties and middle forties, but that proves nothing. It simply proves that marriage has warped his honest critical talents, has caused him to suspend judgment for the sake of his own vanity and self-esteem, and has made him bury his head in the sand in order to deceive himself that no brilliant caravan ever crosses the desert. But I doubt that one can find a single unmarried man—or, for that matter, married man, provided he has married the girl in question and will tell the truth—who would confess that the girl he fancied in his younger years is exactly the sort of pea-chick he would fancy today, that she is his ideal in every respect, and that it is inconceivable that he could have eyes, ears and æsthetic taste for any other.

A man is not a single, definite, fixed creature all his life: he is a dozen different creatures. He is no more the same man at forty that he was at twenty or thirty than he is the same at sixty he was at forty or fifty. I will admit exceptions, of course; there are a few men who punch the emotional time-clock relatively early in life and stick obediently to the same job until they are carted away to the glueworks. But the average man—and the artist much more so—changes periodically as certainly as the weather changes, even in California. He may always vote the straight Republican ticket; he may always eat an apple before he goes to bed; he may always smoke just so many cigars a day and no more; but his views of women alter every so often. The man who marries in his forties, let us say, thus marries that woman in whom he finds less to laugh at derisorily than in any of the women he has previously known. This diminution of objections to her is what captivates and hamstrings him, and is what our friends, the poets, call love. It is actually less love, in the commonly accepted sense of the word, than it is the man's respect for his improved intelligence in taste. The lad of twenty who jumps to the nearest minister and gets himself married offers his wife the dubious tribute of an amateur taste. He is like a small boy who has learned how to turn a somersault and who confidently offers himself as a professional partner to a star circus acrobat. But the man of maturer years who takes unto his bosom a wife offers her the high compliment of a post-graduate taste and emotion.

Although a suspicion of superficiality, smartiness and lack of sound sense always hovers over epigrammatic expression—for what good reason I have never been able to make out—it seems to me (I recall that I once encountered the idea in some book or other) that the woman an adult man marries is generally a compromise with the illusion of his first sweetheart. That is to say that while the man would not have married his first sweetheart on a wager and while he knows full well that she had as many faults as a second-hand toothbrush, he yet hocus-pocuses her into a romantic legend to fill the actual lack of romance in his life and embodies that legend, in so far as he is able to, in the person of the woman he marries in later years. There is no contradiction here. For though a man's taste in women changes, he often likes to flatter his romantic donkeyishness that it doesn't change—that, in other words, his ideal in women is still the young, wide-eyed girl in gingham who used to throw her broad straw bonnet with the sunflower on it over her shoulder and swing on the garden gate.

For every man who succumbs to the charms of a girl early in life and devotes the rest of his life to admiring her charms and those of no other girl, there are a thousand whose eyes rove hither and thither during their days on earth. In this polygamy of taste lies, indeed, man's, and particularly the artist's, tribute to the fair sex.

[From *Monks Are Monks,* 1929, pp. 20–4.]

The Matter of Faithlessness

THE REASON for woman's greater emotional faithlessness than man's lies very simply in the circumstance that, while man is the more sentimental, woman is the more romantic. The sentimental person's fancy fastens upon a single individual; the romantic person's upon the world at large.

[From *The Intimate Notebooks of George Jean Nathan,* 1932, p. 290.]

The Ultimately Desirable Woman

SINCE it may strike some that my reflections on the heroines of many plays are injudicious, not to say objectionable, I digress as to what may be said to constitute the ultimately desirable woman, the point of view, let it be conceded, being merely that of one long established for better or worse in bachelorhood, though still of open mind.

The very first necessary attribute of such a bonanza is lack of contentiousness, which is to say, the habit of so many women of supporting their egos by arguing with and contradicting a man's opinions on one subject or another. Since only a bore employs a woman as an audience for his profounder convictions and since any man with an ounce of experience and humor knows better than to waste a woman's time in any such manner and indulges in it, if at all, merely by way of slyly determining if he can stand seeing her again, the argumentative female is beaten both ways. This, of course, is far from saying that a woman should not exercise her intelligence at suitable times. The point is that, if she is intelligent, she will quickly recognize the bore for what he is and will not waste her intelligence on him and in the case of the worthier male will recognize just as quickly that he is up to tricks and will effectively keep her mouth shut.

Moodiness is another poison. A man seeks out a woman for pleasant companionship, for something, as Napoleon remarked, in the nature of a holiday; for, in brief, an escape—whether temporary or more permanent—from his work and worry and from the exertion imposed upon him by those males with whom he is brought into daily contact. What he looks for in the woman is surely not the kind of gaiety that can be as depressing as morning-after confetti nor the false exhilaration that wears off as soon as a Swedish massage; but what he looks for is equally and surely not the woman who, whether cheerful or the opposite, has a repertoire of ever changing moods that make an evening spent with her the equivalent of suffering an emotional vaudeville show acted on a rapidly revolving turntable.

The chief characteristic of such a female is the natural possession or affectation of what may be described as the mood wistful, which is enough to drive any man not a nitwit out of his head. The mood, which is offered or practised by some members of the female sex with the pertinacity of a stock company bulldog, is generally purveyed under the impression that the male will mistake it for a first-rate brand of soulfulness.

That some of my brothers may so swallow it, I do not for a moment doubt. I have, indeed, known several, by no means otherwise complete idiots, who have been so deeply impressed and wobbled by it that they have taken the soulful ones to wife, only to learn subsequently that the wistfulness, where inherent, was an incipient melancholia that made life with the lady indistinguishable from squirting a lemon continuously into one's eye or, where simulated, had been studiously utilized as a protective measure against any possibly too early, bumptious overtures.

There are inevitably in the essence of things women whom a man regards lightly and women whom he regards seriously. Take, for example, the witty woman. A man of any education, experience and worldly sagacity may find an intermittent, casual amusement in such a one's company, but he would not consider marriage to her for so much as a split-second, that is, unless he put love out of mind and married her to hard, practical ends for her money or for her abilities as a parlor entertainer of prospective business customers. There is a large difference between a witty woman and one with humor, and woe to the man who confuses the two. A woman without humor is like a man without sense; a witty woman belongs not in a home but on a stage, for wit in a woman often betokens a minimum of gentleness, good-will, quiet understanding and what, for want of a better word, is feminineness. Most often, too, it is not really wit so much as it is meanness.

Composure is another asset in a man's appraisal of a candidate for his serious affections. Not the artificial composure practised by some women, which suggests nothing so much as an overiced soft drink, but an innate serenity of person and character. It is next to impossible for a man to entertain permanent thoughts about a woman who, whether in her serious or lighter moments, indicates a mental and physical nervousness that betrays a lack of easy confidence in herself. The woman who does not possess an artfully concealed but persuasive faith in herself and who substitutes for it either a superficial assertiveness or a manufactured poise fools no man, or at least no man with any experience beyond chorus girls, social climbers, and coloratura sopranos.

What a man looks for in a woman, in short, is something, I daresay, like a good piano minus the loud pedal. What he looks for is tone, modulation, essential precision, music that is well composed, soft and lovely. It may be that some men peculiarly prefer noise in women, but they will be found to be the sort who admire be-bop and jazz above Schubert and Chopin, the sort who believe that good-fellowship in a woman is predicated on the loudness of her laughter, the sort who imagine a good time is to be measured by the amount of din that figures in it. But even such, I venture, seldom think of marriage in the company of the boiler-factory belles. When it comes to any more sensitive male, they affect him like steam drills.

Too many women believe that to interest a man they have to be ever on conversational tiptoes, that they must exercise themselves assiduously to impress him with their stimulative qualities, and that he will not be fetched by them unless they are able to keep his attention popping. They may conceivably interest, even fascinate, him for a spell—that is, if no other kind of woman happens at the time to be available—but it remains that a man reserves his true and deepest love not for the species of woman in whose company he finds himself electrified and enkindled, but for that one in whose company he may feel tenderly drowsy. There is, of course, no way of determining definitely, but it is my guess that so-called "interesting" women are responsible for more husbands seeking divorces than court testimony appears to make out.

The whole question of what is termed love, indeed, calls for some scrutiny. What passes for love in careless definition is frequently not love at all but something analytically of a piece with the effect of alcoholic liquor on one not used to the wassail bowl. In the beginning, what a woman likes to imagine she inspires in a man is less spontaneous love than largely something of his own independent fancy and creation. The man already has his picture of the type of woman he might respond to and, if a woman chances to come along who does not too greatly miss the type, his so-called love is automatically ready to develop. In such circumstances, it is necessary for the woman, if she sets her cap for him, to sustain the picture of her in his mind, however dubious, with every wile at her command.

The more expert in this she is, the more the man's imagination will apply itself to make the picture real, and in the end self-delusion will give birth to what both victims will be pleased to regard as true love.

One of the most disturbing habits a woman may possess is that of emphasis. The female who is given to emphatic likes and dislikes and whose remarks are couched in italics cannot hold the interest of a man for long. That is, any man who by nature is not of the milk-toast variety or any one not a helpless invalid. Emphasis plays so great a part in a man's working life that, when his day's work is done, he cannot stand an extra dose of it, and that woman who indulges herself in it is lost.

Another thing any woman who wishes to make an impression on a man must rid herself of, and quickly, is a tendency to affect an air of superiority over other women. Most men are at bottom chivalrous, though they may not be altogether aware of the fact, and they not only disrelish seeing a woman unnecessarily embarrassed and hurt but disrelish equally the woman responsible for the discourtesy. An inborn air of superiority is accompanied by a natural graciousness; it is never inconsiderate. It is the fabricated air which gives itself away in incivility.

Though it may be bait for amateurs, a woman's flattery of a man, if even slightly overdone, is likely to heighten his suspicion of the dispenser's sincerity. Any man a cut above the kind who carries a painstakingly folded handkerchief in his breast pocket but treats his nose instead to the less immaculate one secreted in a rear section of his garment knows perfectly well what, if anything, there is about him personally or professionally that perhaps merits some commendation. He knows, in other words, just how far flattery of him may go without becoming bogus and silly. If the woman's flattery remains within bounds, he is, of course, pleased. But if, in order to ingratiate herself with him, the woman spreads herself, he says to himself, here is a ninny who doesn't fool me for a minute, who probably does the same thing with every other man she meets, and who wouldn't appreciate any really good points about me if I had them. The woman, accordingly, who confuses a miscellaneous, senseless flattery with amiability soon becomes a trial and a nuisance

I end this treatise of one man's prejudice in respect to the ultimately desirable woman with a few general observations.

However old and wise a man may become, the Cinderella story somehow remains in his fabric and the humble girl consequently never loses her appeal to him. This is not an entirely romantic notion; it has its basis in good sense, since the modest girl often in the end triumphs by virtue of her humility and patience.

It is seldom that the beauty of a woman's face can survive her laughter. A smile is the only visible symptom of amusement that a woman may venture with impunity.

A man will tolerate any criticism of himself from a woman and pay small attention to it. What he will not stand is criticism of his friends.

It is possible for a woman during her lifetime to love a number of men and each for a different and often diametrically opposed quality. A man, on the other hand, however many women he may have loved, has loved each and all of them for the same quality.

In conclusion it may not always be true, yet it has been my experience to find it common, that love and a precisely conducted household do not often go together. When I see a home too scrupulously managed, I generally feel, and learn subsequently, that the love of the man for the woman and vice versa has been chilled in the degree that their ménage has been brought to a point of machinelike operation. Laughing love and the happiness that comes of it are given to carelessness and disarray, at least in some measure. No woman who loves a man deeply and passionately has ever, alas, been a perfect housekeeper.

[From *The Theatre Book of the Year, 1949–1950*, pp. 84–9.]

Cosmetics vs. Humor

WOMEN, as they grow older, rely more and more on cosmetics. Men, as they grow older, rely more and more on a sense of humor.

[From the *American Mercury*, July 1925, p. 354.]

Love in America

LOVE is to the poet the one and only glamorous and important thing in the world. There are few poets in America—real poets of the emotion, I mean, not men who pass themselves off as poets by writing voluminous rhymed treatises on operatic characters, anti-slavery leaders and the Chicago stockyards—and as a consequence love has been so insufficiently and ineloquently interpreted to the American that he knows nothing more about it than a schoolboy or a vulgar alley-cat. American love is ridiculous, even in the high places. Consider the revelations in the instance of that book written by the Britton woman about Harding. It was, you will recall, argued against the publication of the book, first, that, even if wholly true, it was in deplorable taste; second, that a President of the United States, however indiscreet, should, in the higher interests of the State, be held sacrosanct in such cases; third, that—but I need not enumerate; the objections were sufficiently typical to be recognizable. What is more, they were also uniformly idiotic. The book in question was in no more deplorable taste than, say, Sainte-Beuve's *Mes Poisons*, yet there have been few protests against the latter. It was, further, no more justly to be condemned for casting reflections on a President of the United States—and a very inferior one, to boot—than would be the several recent lives of Washington, the greatest President the nation has had. Objection to the book on these grounds and on the others that they connote were essentially dubious, and plainly hollow. There was just one sound objection that might have been made against the book and that—brushing aside its spurious posture as a plea for more merciful laws in relation to illegitimacy—was that it offered itself as a great love story and contrived only to be a very cheap and very shoddy one. Harding may or may not have been an estimable man in other ways, but one thing is certain and that is that he was a dull and unimaginative lover. Nor, forgetting momentarily my rôle of gallant and remembering only my rôle as critic, does Miss Britton seem to have been any better. To offer to the public a book recounting the mewings, purrings and back-fence carnality of such a couple, and at a price for which the public might buy the *Divina Commedia, The Autobiography of Benvenuto Cellini* or even *The Life of Gaby Deslys,* is a leap far beyond the reasonable. Poor Harding! He deserved what he got. Yet he did nothing that George Washington didn't do, and neither of them did anything that Napoleon Bonaparte didn't do half a dozen times.

[From *Monks Are Monks,* 1929, pp. 150–2.]

ON SEX

The New View of Sex

THE DOCTRINE that there is a very considerable humor in sex, long upheld by the small minority of men and women who were able to think with their emotions, has spread so rapidly and so widely in the last decade that it is difficult to find more than one man or woman out of every dozen who doesn't currently believe in it. It used to be thought pretty generally that sex was a grim, serious and ominous business, to be entered into only by those duly joined in holy wedlock or by those lost souls already in thrall to the devil. Sex was synonymous with danger, tragedy, woe or, at its best, with legalized baby carriages. This view has gone out of style with such other delusions as French altruism, British honor and making of the world safe for democracy. I do not argue, plainly enough, that back in the cow pastures of the Republic the old view of sex does not still prevail, for it does; but wherever lights are brighter and there are paving stones and so much as a single street-car, wherever a band, however bad, plays on Saturday nights, there you will find a change in the old order. Sex, once wearing the tragic mask, wears now the mask of comedy. And whenever one laughs at a thing, one is no longer afraid of it. . . .

Many years ago, in my university days, I had a friend who played left end on the football team. It was my friend's technique—he was gifted with an irresistible talent for low comedy —to tell funny stories to the end playing opposite him on a rival eleven, weaken the latter with laughter, and thus easily dispose of him. Since sex has become the playing-ground of conversational humor, we may believe that the technique of my football friend is often adopted in other directions.

What has brought about this view of sex as a humorous business is problematical. It is possible that the altered view has come about in due course of time and nature, that all such things move in inscrutable cycles and that once again we are in the midst of a quasi-Restoration turn of the clock. However, I make a guess in another direction. After a long and uninterrupted period of serious regard of anything, the wind always changes and there is born a sudden and recalcitrant laughter. Human nature is such that it cannot stand monotony; it demands relief. And history shows us that as surely as a period of high gaiety is followed abruptly by one of desolation and as surely as a period of misery is followed by one of prosperity, so, too, does a psychically and philosophically glum period inevitably soon or late give way to one of psychic and philosophical revelry. Thus, it is probable that the humorous view of sex has come about as a direct result of the long serious view of sex, that human nature simply demanded a change. As it deposed czars and kings and set up Yiddish pants-cutters and Wop soap-box spielers in their places, so it deposed the tragedians and tragédiennes of sex and set up comedians and comédiennes.

But the change in the approach to the sex question has not, as might be inferred, been an arbitrary one. It is based upon a thoroughly clear and intelligent view of sex. Sex, in the great majority of instances, is a much more casual and unimportant thing than it is customarily admitted to be. An idiotic conspiracy has sought, with almost uniform success, to make the world accept it as something of paramount consequence in the life of man, the ground of his happiness or unhappiness, of his triumph or defeat, of his joy or his affliction. Yet the reflective man has long known that it is nothing of the kind, that it is, in fact, of considerably less importance in his general scheme of life than, say, his tobacco or his schnapps. Sex is purely and simply the diversion of man, a pastime for his leisure hours and, as such, on the same plane with his other pleasures. The civilized man knows little difference between his bottle of vintage champagne, his Corona Corona, his seat at the "Follies" and the gratification of his sex impulse. They all fall much under the same heading. He takes sex no whit more seriously than he takes, to put it superlatively, a symphony concert. He sees in it simply something always amusing and sometimes beautiful, and lets it go at that.

Well, the world itself grows more and more civilized as century chases century down the avenue of time and gradually it works itself up to the level of its more civilized inhabitants. And thus gradually the newer view of sex gains recruits. And what men believe, women in due time also believe. I do not say that such beliefs are commendable, for I am no judge, but merely an historian. I simply say that so long as men and women merely *felt* about sex, it was what it was yesterday. The moment they began instead to *think* about it, it dropped its mourning and wore vine leaves about its head—and painted its nose red.

In the course of man's contemplation of sex, one phenomenon has gradually impressed itself upon his consciousness above all others, and it is this one phenomenon that, more than anything else, has influenced him in his present attitude toward the subject. That sex is a relatively trivial and inconsequential event in life, that it is of infinitely less permanent significance in his scheme of things than his work in the world, however humble the nature of that work, or than his material welfare or his physical comfort or, as I have hinted, even certain other of his diversions, is clearly borne in upon him after a meditation of the history of sex life as it has directly concerned him.

One of the first things that strikes such a reflective man is the manner in which the brain cells themselves peculiarly operate to demote sex to a plane of unimportance. Such is the curious functioning of the male cerebral centres that the sex act, once it is so much as twenty-four hours past, quite passes from the memory or, at all events, from the direct consciousness. Although the fact, so far as I know, has never been articulated, it remains as an actuality that nothing is so quickly erased from masculine tablets of memory as the sex act accomplished. It is a mental idiosyncrasy, indeed, that the association of the act with a specific woman vanishes within an unbelievably short space of time, that so evanescent is the recollection that the woman actually seems a physical stranger to the man. What remains in the masculine mind is not the consciousness of the sex act, but only what may have proceeded from it, to wit, affection, companionship, friendship or spiritual, as opposed to physical, love. It is not an easy matter to set down delicately in type the almost incomprehensible degree to which this post-consciousness of sexual indulgence evaporates. Yet there is no man, if he will view himself honestly in the light of his experience, but will recall at once the peculiar sense of remoteness that has generally and quickly enveloped the woman with whom he has been on terms of physical intimacy. It would seem that nature, operating through the human mind, has contrived thus to make the world frequently a happier and more peaceful place than it otherwise might be. In man's defective memory lies woman's symbol of chastity.

If sex were the important event in a man's life that some hold it to be, his mind would surely be influenced by it quite differently than it is. A woman, instead of so quickly and unintelligibly taking on the aspect of a complete physical stranger to him, would remain fixed in his sex consciousness. Sex would surely retain a vividness after its performance that it actually does not retain. Yet, such is the baffling drollery of human nature that a man's wife ever seems to him a virgin.

[From the *American Mercury*, April 1926, pp. 492–4.]

Attitude toward Sex

IF I were asked to suggest in a single sentence the essential difference between the Latin and the Anglo-Saxon, I should perhaps put it this way: to the Latin, sex is an *hors d'œuvre;* to the Anglo-Saxon, it is a barbecue.

2

In the current oppressively ubiquitous cackling about sex, one finds the intelligentsia inclining more and more to the view that sex, far from being the sour-visaged tragedy that it is commonly supposed to be, is really of the essence of pure comedy. While this point of view is, of course, anything but new—having been the established philosophy of all bachelors and Turks over the age of sixteen since the beginning of the Eleventh

Century—it seems to me that, for all its major authenticity, it is not without its suspicion of a hole. Sex is a comedy, true enough; it borders, indeed, upon farce; but, like a comedy or a farce, it is played upon something approximating a theatre stage. The parties to the performance, the actors, are most often entirely serious about it, as are the actors of comedy and farce ever. The humor of sex is enjoyed not by the actors directly concerned in it, but by the onlookers, the audience. The bridegroom is not a comedian in his own eyes; he is a comedian in the eyes of his audience. The bride herself is wistful and a bit wet of eye; the wheezes are reserved for the mob around the punchbowl.

Paraphrasing Horace Walpole, sex is a tragedy to him who feels and a comedy to him who thinks. In the grip of sex, no man has ever thought. Sex, to the participant in its theoretical excitements, is thus ever purely emotional and hence removed, at least for the time being, from the domain of low comedy. It may be funny in retrospect, but so too in retrospect are three-fourths of the tragedies of the world.

3

Beware the sexlessness of those who talk most of sex!

4

In the midst of all the somewhat obstreperous discussion as to whether it is the man or the woman who is the aggressor in matters of sex, it seems to me to be the most reasonable assumption, based upon a studious and careful investigation of the statistics, that the thing is less a tug-of-war than a tandem. There is no victor; there is no vanquished. The keystone bears engraved upon it the motto, "*Ab hoc et ab hâc.*" As well speak of the aggressor in a piano duet.

5

I can never understand the critic who takes moral objection to sex treated humorously. It is comprehensible that a certain type of mind, so to speak, may find disrelish in certain serious treatments of sex, but my powers of understanding are insufficient to grope with the type of mind that can find offense in any intelligent laughter at sex. It is the outstanding mark of the Anglo-Saxon's philosophical provincialism that he places sex on the farcical index expurgatorius along with his God, his wife, and his pet dog.

[From *The Autobiography of an Attitude*, 1925, pp. 235–7.]

Marriage, Sex, and Divorce

In this age of gossip and scandal it has come to be an accepted fact that the breaking up of at least nine-tenths of marriages is due to *outside* fooling around by one or another of the parties to the marriage. For one such marriage that disintegrates for that reason, I hazard the guess that there are a dozen that go to pieces because of *indoor* difficulties on the part of the married couples themselves. What are these difficulties? They are the difficulties bred not of physical intimacy, as most persons argue, but, more importantly, of emotional intimacy. A wife may delight in the sex intimacy of her husband—and vice versa—for many years, but in the meantime she or he is hard put to it to live with his or her extra-boudoir emotions. A married couple that fights in bed is as rare as a married couple that does not fight at the dinner-table. Illusion, the *sine qua non* of a male and female relationship that endures, has nothing to do with sex. A man and woman are completely happy in sex only when they have sagaciously rid themselves of illusion, when they are as realistic, on the woman's side, as Margaret of Navarre and, on the man's, as Balzac. But sex, for all our modern novelists who write like castrated longshoremen, plays very little part in any lasting relationship—perhaps, if exact statistics were available, not more than two or three hours out of a week's one hundred and sixty-eight. That, incidentally, is why a young boy and girl, to whom sex is relatively new and novel, tire of each other so quickly after they have indulged themselves and seek illusion in the eyes and hearts of other girls and boys.

All these arguments about the failure of marriage do not convince me, though I surely believe that it is a failure. Take, for example, what they say about the modern apartment house.

The apartment house is frequently charged with breaking up the old spirit of home life in our larger cities and contributing toward marital *débâcle*. The idea strikes me as foolish. The notion, commonly promulgated, that a wife who orders dinner up from the restaurant, or gets it at the delicatessen around the corner, or is able quickly to prepare it with newfangled mechanical appliances is bound for some occult reason to be a less meritorious and gradually less contented and happy spouse than the one who stands half a day over a sweltering stove does not penetrate too smoothly into my logical centres. The wife who washes dishes may contribute to keeping her husband's and children's home intact—in fact, she generally does— but it is a home sordid, rebellious and miserable. The so-called old home life was often largely a sentimental legend, cherished by outsiders. Its disappearance has done more to argue for the success of marriage, relatively speaking, than anything else one can think of.

[From *Monks Are Monks*, 1929, pp. 156–7.]

From the Sublime to the Ugly

SEX is most thrilling and beautiful only when it is ugliest. I am not fashioning a cheap epigram, believe me, dear lady. As I said before, sex—in actual life—touches the heavens only when it simultaneously touches the gutter and the mud. Love and sex are two different things, as different as a violin and a bass-drum, though both may be in the same orchestra and play their share in the same melody. In the arts, it has taken sex in its ugliest phases to produce the most thrilling and beautiful master-pieces—like *Oedipus, Phedre, The Cenci* and *La Citta Morte* in drama, *Die Walküre* in opera, *Jupiter and Io* and *Leda* in painting. One of Shakespeare's most beautiful works deals with the passionate love of a black man for a white girl, and another with the incestuous concupiscence of a man for his brother's widow. Among the greatest novels, from Fielding and Gautier to Proust, you'll find sex at its foulest converted into artistic majesty.

[From *Monks Are Monks,* 1929, pp. 157–8.]

ON PARENTS AND CHILDREN

A PARTICULARLY bitter pill to children is their parents' insistent resolve that they should have musical training of one sort or another, whether they are able to distinguish between a piano and a go-cart or not, or whether they are in full possession of all ten digits or have had six of them shot off by the neighbor boy's grandfather's blunderbuss. I mention the piano specifically because, though there are many other instruments to choose from among them a number that might be more pragmatically profitable in after years, it is generally the art of the pianoforte with which parents confront and challenge their progeny, nine-tenths of whom are destined to end up as insurance salesmen, shyster lawyers, bus boys, or wives of men who venerate the phonograph.

It is the parental theory in the case of male offspring that an acquired ability to play even the simple scales, followed possibly by a one-finger mastery of "Coming Through the Rye," will inevitably contribute a touch of high refinement in later years and that, in the case of girls, it will enhance their sweet womanliness and desirability in the eyes of the male of the species. Let a cynical boy contravene his parents' fond belief by casually pointing out to them that, with the sole exception of Paderewski, the world's greatest pianists from de Pachmann to Moriz Rosenthal had not been inoculated by their art with a personal refinement any more voltaic than that enjoyed by the average stockbroker, or let a realistic little girl try to explain that it seems that the average female who pounds a piano drives her husband into the arms of the first woman he can find with a severe case of digital rheumatism—let a boy or girl attempt to do any such thing and it's bed without supper.

Though parents infrequently have in mind future pecuniary advantages to a child (and to themselves) in connection with this early musical instruction, it would often be wiser if they did. The more unselfish idea that the child will derive from his piano playing an inordinate personal and private pleasure in his maturer years is—in view of the fact that not one child out of a hundred ever continues an interest in subsequent years and in view of the second fact that the exceptional hundredth who does so usually attains to a virtuosity barely equal to that of the colored professor in a Jersey City bordello—hardly tenable. It is not tenable, that is, save the youngster when grown up retains an ear for music that is equally satisfied by such equivalent performances as are vouchsafed by jukeboxes, sound films, musical beer mugs and Sigmund Romberg.

It would, as noted, accordingly be much better if parents looked the situation unsentimentally and realistically in the face and surrendered their prejudice against other and theoretically more vulgar musical instruments that their offspring are generally attracted to and that presently make even a father and mother who can't differentiate between the tone of a piccolo and that of a harp gnash their aesthetic teeth and openly ventilate the fear that their offspring will grow up to be bums.

Let a child suggest that his predilection runs to the saxophone, the cornet or the drum, for example, and parents customarily comport themselves as if they had just received news that their own mothers and fathers, who used to beat the pants off them for devoting themselves musically to hair combs wrapped in toilet paper, had been killed in a bomb raid. While it is to be freely allowed that the sounds emanating from a saxophone, cornet and drum are, when those instruments are negotiated by the untutored and overly enterprising young, hardly conducive to the household peace and tranquillity, it is also to be meditated that they are scarcely more painful than the piano banging. But that is not the point, though truth argues it is a pretty good one. The point is that there is nothing particularly *infra dignitatem* in the instruments in question and that, all things considered, it is better, if a child has an unmistakable urge to do so, that he grow up to be a good saxophone or cornet player or drummer than a pianist so bad he will have beer bottles heaved at him.

There are, God wot, artistic professions and even light diversions somewhat superior to the saxophone, cornet and drum, but—the professions aside and the diversions considered—I, for one, am not altogether sure that playing a saxophone is any more derogative of self than dissipating time on cards, tooting a cornet any more ignominious (except maybe in the ears of the deafened and indignant residents in the block) than turning the radio dial to soap operas, male blues singers and the Indianapolis Symphony orchestra, or beating a drum any more demeaning than playing what is called "the game," which consists in figuring out the word a participant who grimly gets down on the floor and bends himself like a corkscrew is pantomimically trying to interpret.

2

It is always well to bear in mind what interests a child and what does not, and this brings us to the question of his general education. The indignation of parents when their offspring bring home from school low marks in certain studies and when the low marks continue is ill taken. Most often, if parents will take the trouble to study the low marks in relation to the higher ones, they will gradually gain the knowledge not that a child is necessarily backward or lazy in the particular studies but simply that he is not interested in them and is accordingly inattentive, and that no amount of forced study will, however high the grades he achieves, ever make him regard them as other than dismal chores.

Looking back on my own childhood, I recall that I thus always brought home such abysmal marks in arithmetic, for instance, that my father, getting to the bottom of the card, had to look on the other side to find them, and then couldn't believe his eyes. My explanations that arithmetic did not interest me failed to persuade him and I was forced to continue my study. But though I did continue—it was necessary in those days to offer mathematics later on for college entrance—and though at college itself it was demanded of me further to pursue the cursed subject, I was always more or less a bored dud at it, never profited by it either then or since, and still today cannot, for all my acclaimed and staggering talents in other directions, even multiply seven by nine without putting seven down nine times and adding up the sevens singly.

There is altogether too much parental shortsightedness and misapprehension in the matter of the education of their young. Teachers who, for example, cram the latter's little heads with innumerable historical dates, not one out of fifty of which they can remember a day afterward, should be taken right out into the yard and be drawn and quartered. They waste children's time and, worse, make the kids regard school as a doubly irksome institution. The average youngster, even when he reaches the age of fifteen, remembers hardly more than three or four dates out of all the wholesale dose that has been fruitlessly and, in all good truth, unnecessarily imposed upon him— 1492, 1775, 1861 and, possibly, 1898. And these, added to the obvious January 1, February 12, February 22, March 17, May 30, July 4, the last Thursday in November, and December 25 are to all intents and purposes sufficient. Not one child in thirty thousand ever finds it immediately or subsequently profitable to be in rapt possession of the exact knowledge that the British surrendered at Yorktown on October 19, 1781, or that it was on May 2, 1863, that Stonewall Jackson was mortally wounded during the battle of Chancellorsville. Such knowledge is commodious only to children doomed to grow up to be eighteen-dollar-a-week school-teachers and to the depressing species of youngsters who offensively disport themselves on radio quiz programs.

A child's teacher's horror of slang, duly echoed by its parents, is yet another problem imposed upon the helpless young. Let a teacher or parent say to a youngster, "Willie, now tell me the difference between a flower and a weed," and let Willie reply, "The flower has a sweet smell, but the weed has a lousy one"—and Willie's teacher or parent will not recover his composure for at least ten minutes. It is, of course, a bit early in his life for the youngster to inform the aggrieved ones that what was good enough for Shakespeare should be good enough for them, to say nothing of for himself. And it will be some time yet before he will be able to apprise them of the fact that a great deal of the slang which so seriously affronts them when he indulges in it has similarly the sanction of the literary elect. All of which is to be deplored, since the tendency to frown upon free expression and to starch the child into a lingual stuffed-shirt can do little but convert him into a lamentable rubber-stamp, eventually, if pursued and insisted upon, making him of a dull piece with his school-teacher and the family undertaker. Lousy is a good and valuable word. And so, for example, are such as noodle, pooped, stink, croak, pash, stewed, nose-paint, pizzle, shrimp, guts, bum, mum, piece of cheese, cold as hell, bellyful, whale, bung, fishified, punk, kicky-wicky, bull, piss, soused, all wet, crack, goose, tripe, dump, slop, blab, peach, goat, dame, and many another. They had, all of them, the full approval of the most illustrious man of letters who ever lived.

It is far better to have a possibly incipient George Ade or Ring Lardner around the house than a definitely incipient Clayton Hamilton or Mortimer Adler.

3

Nothing is more humorous to the average child than his parents' excessive caution in the preservation of his innocence from what are euphemistically called the facts of life. The processes of circumlocution, evasion and downright prevarication entered into by them entertain him enormously, although he finds it incumbent upon him, as in the case of Santa Claus, to relieve his acute embarrassment and to safeguard his interests and behind by pretending to a wholesome ignorance.

The stork and cabbage leaf period in a youngster's life ends very much sooner than fond parents are disposed to imagine, and it ends, peculiarly enough, earlier in girls' than in boys', as any boy in later years will affirm. The persistence of parents in believing the opposite is no tribute to their own powers of personal recollection. The child of nine or ten may not know the aforesaid facts in exact elaboration; there may be—and unquestionably are—various nuances and details to which he is not privy; but one thing he does know, and that is that the mythology imparted to him by his parents is a lot of nonsense. And it is consequently a rare child living within a mile of a hayloft or who has been willingly inveigled into the game called "playing house" who does not have difficulty suppressing a chuckle when his sire one day takes him solemnly aside and ambiguously enters into a discourse about the bees and the flowers.

4

One of the deepest concerns of parents is the safeguarding of their young from what they are pleased to regard, in their own terminology, as bad associates. These bad associates are usually indigenous to the same neighborhood and it is a notable paradox that one of the deepest concerns of *their* parents in turn is the safeguarding of *them* from association with the first mentioned little Machiavellis.

Just how parents, in their infinite wisdom, arrive at the low estimate of their children's favorite companions remains something of a rebus to the kids, since the latter are not long in appreciating that their suspected and condemned boon buddies are no worse in conduct, morals, tastes and dog-tail can-tying than they themselves are, but are, in point of fact, often a lot better.

Looking back on my own childhood, I remember three specific little boys whom my parents were especially solicitous in cautioning me against. One—and I mention real names—was a youngster hight Charles Buchanan Stuart, popularly known in our gang as Buck. This Buck was a powerfully built boy of some one hundred and fifty pounds whose strength was the marvel of the rest of us. His feats of physical prowess, such as singlehanded upsetting the phæton in the family stable, batting a baseball through the window of the clergyman's house in the next block, and wrassling the much bigger laundry delivery boy onto his backside, were our gaping awe and admiring envy. Yet it was Buck's parents' frequently expressed conviction that he was a delicate child and that his association with the rest of us, all but one of whom weighed under ninety and none of whom failed regularly to catch his death of cold merely from having stepped into a minor rain puddle, was something to be regarded as inimical to his health, social well-being, and high aesthetic interests. "You know, boys," I well recall his mother admonishing us, "Charlie isn't as strong as you are, and he can't do the things you do, so I must ask you either to stay away and let him rest or, if you are with him, to watch out for him carefully." Whereupon the shamefaced Charlie would shuffle into the house behind his protective mother and, the moment she turned her head, would sneak out the back door into the back yard and delicately entertain himself heaving large hunks of brick at the milk cans in the yard next door and, that done and the contents of the cans duly upset, busting open the stable door with his shoulder and sending the family surrey rolling hell-bent down the side drive.

The second stern warning was directed against a boy named Randall Crawford, known to the gang as Butch. The parental criticism of this Butch was, one gathered, that he was on the lewd side and given to pulling the girls' pigtails, rubbing noses with the more personable ones, and thus otherwise competing with the doom of Casanova and suchlike loafers. The truth about this Butch was, however, as we soon found out, that he was scared to death of girls and would run a block to avoid contact with one of them. The low opinion that my parents had of him was based solely upon my own ignoble explanation, when some little girl came in crying that I had mussed her up, that it was Butch who was the guilty party. As I delivered such explanations no less than three times a week and as the other boys indulged in similar shameless evasions to their parents, it was poor Butch who suffered the blame and gained the reputation of being an adolescent synthesis of Kyrle Bellew, Jim Fiske and Jack-the-Ripper.

The third boy association with whom alarmed my parents to the point of aghast horror was one Billy Morris. Billy, it appeared to be their self-persuasion, was what they designated a "sport." For some reason or other, logical antecedents unknown, they viewed him as one alone given to crap shooting for stakes, Sweet Caporal inhaling, sophisticated whistling at passing puellæ, and like attributes and divertissements of a practitioner of the gay life. It was true that Billy had a passion for craps, but it was no less true that he was a sucker at the game and that the rest of us sacrosanct angels regularly took him at it for what nickels and dimes he could dredge up. It was also true that he relished Sweet Caporals, if and when he was able to beg them from the rest of us. And it was again true that he would whistle loudly at the girls, yet such whistling was imposed upon him by the rest of us, none of whom could maneuver his lips beyond a feeble whew, and for his services always had to be recompensed with one of the nickels we had achieved from him via the dice.

5

A male parent's witticisms and jokes are yet another source of agony to his offspring. The average father usually has two or three pet facetiæ and it is a rare week that does not witness their reiteration at the expense of his poor wife and children. Since the latter are expected each time to laugh immoderately, lest the old man be offended and not come forth with the conventional weekly gratuities, the strain soon becomes trying, and it is not long before the mother and her chicks look upon the advent of dinner with its concomitant of paternal humor as akin to ordeal by fire.

My own dear father, otherwise a paragon of all the virtues— or maybe three or four—entertained a peculiar fondness for three especial whimsies and had at us with them on every possible occasion. We must have heard them no less than a thousand times, and each time it was incumbent upon my small brother and myself, and now and then even our mother, to pretend to laugh our heads off at his enormous comedic gifts. One overwhelming jocosity consisted in referring to a puddle as a poodle. The second, a general great favorite of that remote period, had to do with the necessity of rolling up one's trousers at the bottom as it was raining in London. The third was an allusion to the piano as the pioneer. It got to be so that one day when he came home with a new one that enjoyed some authentic novelty and merit we were so depressed from long contact with the established trio that we couldn't summon up the strength essential to its appreciation and so were the recipients of indignant spankings for our failure to show our father the proper veneration and respect.

6

Altogether too much washing is imposed upon the young, and nothing could be more ridiculous. The moment a parent detects the faintest smudge upon a child's face, it is demanded of the child that it submit to an immediate laundering, with not only the smudge as the ablutionary object but, gratuitously, the entire corpus. Parents seem to regard a child as being constantly half-way between a garbage can and a particularly trenchant sewer. Let a youngster come in from playing even a mild little game of hide-and-seek and the bathtub is instantly set to so furiously steaming a roar that the whole neighborhood blacks out under the impression that at least six hundred enemy airplanes are already overhead.

What appears to inflame the mysophobia of parents especially is the scrupulosity of that area of a child behind the ears. For some reason or other parents are firmly convinced that the aforesaid area accumulates dirt more quickly and in greater volume than any other, including even the fingernails and the inside of the nose, and accordingly and constantly assault it, to the humiliation of the child's higher sensibilities and personal pride, with such an outlay of soap and water as is more logically to be reasoned in the case of a Tuskegee gymnasium after a particularly ebullient possum hunt or a Russian ballet's première danseuse. What has inspired the common belief that the miniature expanse behind a youngster's ears is more magnetic to dirt than the area in front of his ears and so prehensile that, however regularly it be bathed, it is hard to distinguish it from a coal dump, scientists have never been able to deduce. Yet so determined are parents to improve and rectify the non-existent condition that it is an uncommon child who, upon arriving at the age of eleven, hasn't ears the back of which more or less resemble steaks Tartare.

Nothing would affront such parents more greatly than their child's suggestion that they are in all probability just as dirty as he is alleged to be and that it would hence be reciprocally suitable to wash themselves every hour. Nevertheless, these same parents who esteem their cleanliness as being not merely next door to godliness but right in godliness' front parlor often consider the technique of a single bath a day sufficient unto their celestial faith.

7

The heavily elaborate efforts of parents to conceal from their offspring the occasional coldness and even hostility that springs up between them seldom achieve their purpose. A child cannot be fooled in such matters, for the symptoms are unmistakable to him. He senses almost as soon as his mother that his father has been caught out with an inebrious old college chum or a high yaller girl and he can foretell with a surety the reception papa is going to get when he opens the front door. His mother's histrionic attempts to conceal her indignation in such subterfuges as informing him that her high-strung condition is due to a sudden severe headache or her fear that papa may have been run over by a street car while on the way home only make the child laugh sardonically, if a bit sympathetically and sadly, in his sleeve.

Even if the child be somewhat backward and not possessed of the sophistication so paradoxically peculiar to most of the young of the species, it is not very long before he appreciates that something is up. He detects something suspicious in the sudden and unusual solicitude of his parents for him, in their unwonted geniality toward him, and in the strange and even eerie combination of his father's grandiose bestowal upon him of an unexpected whole half-dollar and his mother's furtive tear. The moment a child observes that he is being treated to an overdose of love and affection by his parents, he knows that there is going to be an awful scene that night as soon as he is safely asleep and they have locked themselves in their room.

8

The childish prejudices and superstitions habitual with parents take some time for a youngster to digest and, when digested, arouse his profound scorn. Experience quickly teaches him that there is nothing in them and that his parents must be even greater idiots in believing in them than he hitherto generously had deemed them.

For example, the child sees his parents knock on wood to ward off ill luck. This goes on so often and so steadily that he sometimes doesn't know whether he is living in a house or in a xylophone. At the beginning naturally making some impression on him, despite his native skepticism, he subsequently tries it and ten minutes later falls off the front stoop, bruises both his knees, and suffers a black and blue behind. He thereupon promptly and disgustedly concludes that the next time his father after two glasses of wine modestly allows at the dinner table that he has always detected a slight resemblance between himself and Frederick the Great, or even Martin Van Buren, he will heave the pea soup at him. And that if his mother so much as beams an eighth of an inch beam of approval at the old man he will follow up the pea soup to his right with the Nymphenberg centre-piece.

The child, discovering the knockings on wood are recalcitrantly inefficacious in safeguarding him from ill fortune, next deigns to mimic his parents to the same end by crossing his fingers. After having crossed them so often that his little hand begins to take on the permanent aspect of a pretzel and finding that for all his digital Yoga he still somehow tears his pants on fence nails, loses his pennies down iron gratings, and is cruelly kept in after school merely for applying a match to the pigtails of the little girl sitting in front of him—after such pains, indignities and disappointments his combined faith in the occult and in the sapience of his parents is not worth a Canadian penny on the street-corner bourse.

To all such sundry superstitional didoes of his parents a kid gives early hospitable ear, and soon discovers his hospitality rewarded only with dolour and regret. He duly smears himself up with oil of pennyroyal until he looks like a baba au rhum in a French eighty-five cent table d'hôte restaurant, and smells even worse, and still the mosquitoes are not fooled for a moment that he isn't a particularly appetizing smörgåsbord. He obediently never goes out directly after having had a hot bath, always takes off his wet shoes when he comes back into the house after being in the rain, and acquiescently wears heavy woolen underwear in winter, yet he catches the same old colds at least six times a year. He breaks a mirror and finds that no especially horrible calamity befalls him; in fact, he seems to break mirrors all through the feared seven years of superstitional schedule and nothing catastrophic out of the ordinary happens. He tries time and again to get a cinder out of his eye by rolling it furiously in an outward direction and simultaneously and loudly blowing his nose—it never fails, according to his parents—but the cinder apparently is not privy to the technique. He abstains, per parental injunction, from touching hop-toads, yet the warts come just the same. He hears a dog whining in the middle of the night and confidently expects his rich Uncle Anatol to die within the fortnight and leave him, as he always promised, some money, yet not only Uncle Anatol but all his other well-heeled relatives disgustingly live on to a ripe old age.

Harking to his parents' admonitions, the offspring also abstains, at least at such moments as they are looking, from negotiating such putative bellyache inducers as doughnuts, pickles, green apples and drugstore cinnamon drops. His appetite for these delicacies is discouraged by his elders with horrendous accounts of the effect they will unequivocally have upon his insides, embellished with frightening pictures of the accompanying malaises and bubonic agonies. Nor are these the only dire warnings. Eating a handful of snow, it seems, will make the gourmet a victim of diphtheria. A mastication of cucumbers followed by a wolfing of ice cream of whatever flavor will result in cholera morbus, just as eating anything at all before going in swimming will nigh bring on the grim reaper. And more than one slice of watermelon, to the overwhelming consternation of the child's little colored friends, whose parents seem not to have been reading the right papers, is guaranteed to produce such an internal revolution as is not otherwise known to medical science, while the swallowing of so much as a single seed thereof will bring on appendicitis almost immediately.

Having duly and indefatigably experimented with the great dangers and having discovered that the only resultant pain in his tummy has come from the tightness of his belt induced by too wholesale a relish of them, the youngster is at a loss to comprehend his parents' alarms. How is it, he wonders, that they themselves pleasure themselves with exactly the same savouries, excepting only the handful of snow, and yet retain a perfect tranquillity of the middle regions? It is not long, therefore, before he makes up his mind that they are just as uninformed in this particular quarter as they are in most others, and thenceforth banquets himself, in entire physical peace, to his heart's and stomach's delight. If perchance one day he does get a bellyache, he appreciates it is not the forbidden delicatessen that are responsible but maybe the colored soda pop or lemonade that he has swilled simultaneously. So he simply leaves off the tipples.

The child engages such further superstitional tenets as the throwing of a pinch of spilled salt over the shoulder by way of making certain that the house is not going to fall down or some similar stroke of evil fortune not befall him. It doesn't work. The house may not fall down, true enough, but the salt does not seem to be otherwise any more brawny in talismanic powers than the knocking on wood or the crossing of fingers. And his parents' stout faith that, when he has nose-bleed, the gore may be instantly checked by dropping the key to the booze closet down his back makes him so wrath after their experiment with his nineteenth nose-bleed, after his back has suffered copious back-bleeds from the sharp key and after the nose-bleeds remain sublimely indifferent to his parents' therapeutical exercises, that he throws up his little hands, looks despairingly and cynically at his elders, and moans whatever is the ten-year-old equivalent of what the hell!

9

The small boy's rebellion against going to dancing school for fear that other boys will consider him a sissy deserves the sympathy from his parents that they customarily withhold from him. It isn't that the ability to dance will not come in handy for him in his later life. It will, for in few other ways will he be able to get a quicker inside track with the girls. It is rather that the other boys, most of whose girls he will steal when he grows a little older and cuts fancy with them on the hoofing floor, *will* look upon him as a sissy, which will sorely embarrass him in his present years and probably lead to fist fights with their usual concomitance of bloody nose (of the species allergic, even in the parents' pharmacopoeia, to booze closet keys), black eye, torn ear, busted shin, and maybe even profanity.

The wiles wherewith parents seek to cajole the mutinous youth into an acceptance of his terpsichorean fate seldom succeed in even halfway persuading him. A knowledge of the dance, they inform him, is a mark of the compleat gentleman.

But he doesn't, dammit, want to be a gentleman; he wants to be a regular guy like all the other boys he goes with. The dance will bequeath physical ease and grace to him. So, he snorts, will baseball, and it's a lot more fun. George Washington, the father of his country, was a good dancer. So what? Jack Dempsey isn't; Babe Ruth isn't; Joe Louis and Douglas MacArthur ain't. An ability to dance well is the open sesame to society. So Bill Robinson and Whitey's Lindy Hoppers are members of the smart set. Dancing is part of fine manners. Maybe his parents haven't heard they are dancing hot jazz primarily nowadays and not the minuet and quadrille. But nonetheless dancing is part of his education. So, the youngster is at pains convincingly not to retort, is the French taught him at school by a young graduate of the local girls' manual training school.

10

Then there is papa's pride and delight in his hypothetical physical strength and manly prowess. He does not always project the idea directly, but maneuvers it into his offspring's and his wife's consciousness with divers elaborate intimations and hintings. Sometimes, however, bored by his generous reticence, he demonstrates, to the politely concealed misgivings and internal humors of both members of his audience in concert. He is, it would seem, in his own estimation a cross between Sandow on the one hand and Jack Sharkey in his prime on the other, with overtones of the Cardiff giant, Geronimo and Bernarr Macfadden. The tall tale of his triumph in fisticuffs in 1915 when he was simultaneously set upon by two dozen Yale students in Mori's (if he is a Yale man, it was Harvard muckers) and how singlehanded he knocked the two dozen flat as pancakes and then threw them one by one through the plate glass window—his poor wife and poor heir are regaled with it every time the old boy has had a snifter too many. And so, too, with the equally tall tale of how he once with his left hand grabbed a three hundred and forty pound ruffian by the throat and held him helpless until a squad of police arrived and with their combined force managed to subdue him and put him under arrest, to say nothing of the other time he lifted an Adams

Express truck weighing not less than two tons with his shoulder and rescued from underneath it an injured dog.

In view of the fact that his contemporary proof of his Ajaxian muscular magnificence—on the occasions he challengingly sees fit to demonstrate it—consists for the most part in vainly trying to pull a tight cork out of a bottle of Scotch and spraining his thumb in the process or in landing on his posterior in an effort to pull open a stuck bureau drawer, the skepticism of his loved ones may be pardoned. Yet it is nevertheless an unprecedented wife and child who the very next evening haven't again to serve as audience to the tale of how the champ once achieved a gold medal for his all-around gymnasium virtuosity and how he at a slightly later period, though he wasn't feeling so well at the time, floored a six-foot bartender who had passed a disparaging remark on his protuberant middle.

11

Parents seem often to be openly distressed by their child's habit of scratching his head. Examining his scalp for possible unpleasantnesses and discovering nothing, they are at a loss to understand the habit. I have the honor to provide them with the explanation. The child scratches his head in constant meditation of their unbelievable imbecility.

[From *Beware of Parents: A Bachelor's Book for Children*, 1943, pp. 107–30.]

ON BACHELORS

ONE of the many things that amuse the bachelor is the prevalent and apparently irrevocable idea, entertained chiefly by very young girls and the older married folk, that he is always having a hell of a gay time. The circumstance that the idea in point is encouraged by the vainer idiots among bachelors themselves only adds to the diversion of the more realistic and self-analytical bachelor. As a member of the latter order in long and at least comparatively honorable standing, I take the liberty of dispelling several of the more popular misconceptions.

The first of these is that it must be wonderful not to be tied down to any one woman and with the field constantly to choose from. On the joys of connubial bliss I am, of course, unqualified to speak, but on the theoretically superior and overwhelming joy of being free to keep company with a plurality of women I should like to say a few words.

Out of every fifty women of all ages and conditions whom a bachelor meets, he is lucky if he can find one of sufficient charm, intelligence, and loveliness to interest him in the slightest. That is, for any length of time and presuming him to be moderately intelligent and of any experience and accuracy of taste. More bachelors spend evenings alone at home, or at their clubs, or having dinner with other lonely bachelors than the generality of legend-lovers imagines, and it isn't always because they wish to. It is because, against their will, they do it rather than sit around with nine-tenths of the women available to them and listen to the same routine feminine chatter on all the same routine subjects from sex, Dorothy Thompson, and the novels of D. H. Lawrence on the one hand to the ineffable delights of the conga and the deep problem dramas of Noel Coward on the other, not forgetting, of course, how come such a charming and interesting man as oneself (that is, if one has ordered ten dollars' worth of caviar and a bottle of vintage Bollinger and has brushed one's hair that day) has never married but how wonderful it must be anyway not to be tied down to any one woman.

A second misconception is the bachelor's enormous popularity with hostesses, it apparently being the theory that, simply because one happens to be a bachelor, hostesses constantly fall all over themselves in a mad scramble for one's company. That bachelors, by virtue of their estate, are relatively easy and available prey for hostesses seeking to fill out dinner tables, dance floors, and the attentions of the more silly, voluble, and neglected dowagers, is not to be denied. But that any hostess of experience doesn't in turn know from that experience that a bachelor is something of a problem and maybe even an instrument of disconcerting pain is to be doubted only by those whom the aforesaid hostess has never taken into her confidence.

The trouble with bachelors in this respect is threefold. In the first place, they usually seem to have mysterious engagements of one kind or another, not always entirely mythical, which remove them from the party at least an hour of two before the hostess has reckoned, thus leaving a number of extra women seated forlornly in corners with no one to talk to and with the hostess herself, to her distress, compelled to weary herself being solicitous about them. In the second place, the bachelor is more inclined to be quickly bored than the non-bachelor, and is hence a further concern to his hostess. The reasons for the bachelor's relative ennui are several. Whereas a married man finds diversion in mingling for a change with women other than his wife, the bachelor, to whom such mingling is a commonplace, finds neither novelty nor any particular excitement in it. Again, whereas a married man has from long training in the art made himself adaptable to formality and as a matter of fact secretly likes it, the bachelor finds it rather uncomfortable and tedious and prefers his own somewhat looser punctilio. And in the third and final place, the bachelor is above all an irritatingly selfish fish and demands twice as much attention from a hostess as a married man. He feels, doodle that he essentially is, that he is doing her a favor by the mere act of contributing his presence and he expects it to be appreciated. This is especially true if he falls into the social category of the "extra man," that is, the bachelor equivalent of military reinforcements, the fellow who is called upon at the last moment to fill in the dinner chair next to some particularly dull female (the aforesaid chair having been deserted, also at the last moment, by some more independent and assertive bachelor), to sit through a show he has already been summoned to sit through at least five times, or to attempt to loosen up some visiting duchess's joints sufficiently to persuade the onlookers that it is a rumba and not a minuet that is being danced.

A further popular misconception is that a bachelor is extremely fortunate in being able to go home late at night, lock himself in from outside bothers, be alone with himself, and meditate quietly to his heart's content. Anyone who believes that doesn't know the truth by half. The telephone companies' records will attest to the fact that most of the peremptory requests for changes of phone numbers come regularly from bachelors. The bachelor who, when he gets home at night, finds peace and quiet is largely a product of others' romantic imaginations. If he isn't awakened by telephone calls of all varieties, he is disturbed by all kinds of friends in the shape of visitors and droppers-in who somehow imagine that a bachelor is synonymous with a bartender, a guide to the night life of the city, a confidential directory of all the great stage beauties since Lily Langtry, a prestidigitator of sandwiches, and a sweet reprobate generally. The biggest laugh the poor bachelor can evoke on such occasions is to remark that he has to get up early the next morning and work.

The notion that a bachelor is especially blessed by Providence and is a combination William Wycherley, Casanova, and recherché maître d'hôtel, with slight overtones of Florenz Ziegfeld, Basil Zaharoff, and Moët and Chandon, is shared even by the world's law-makers, who every now and then seek to make him conscious of and pay for his theoretical great privilege. Taxes on bachelors are regularly proposed in the various nations; in Italy, in Germany, and in Greece today, indeed, a considerable fee is ordained; and in other countries the right to make him cough up handsomely is making big strides. But the last straw came recently in a press dispatch from Dover, Delaware, in this, our great republic. The dispatch was as follows: "The Legislature has received a proposal to tax bachelors for the support of a home for unwed expectant mothers. A bill introduced recently by Representative William R. Ringler would require all bachelors over thirty to pay fifty dollars a year."

There are, of course, it is to be admitted, certain compensations, hereinafter to be duly and gratefully noted, which the bachelor enjoys, but they are assuredly not the ones that the layman, in his ignorance, conjures up. The bachelor's admired freedom is often a yoke, for the freer a man is to himself the greater slave he often is to the whims of others. The bachelor as envied Lothario is frequently a migraine to the bachelor himself, for Lotharioism is simply monogamy's doldrums multiplied, and with thrice monogamy's duties, penalties, and wear and tear. And the bachelor's respected privacy, as observed, is frequently the privacy of a monkey in a zoo. The day when everyone begins properly laughing at bachelors instead of envying and admiring them will see a wholesale bachelor stampede to the altar, God forbid.

[From *The Bachelor Life*, 1941, pp. 1–9.]

ON COUNTRY LIFE

In New York

COMES summer and the influx of city folk into bucolic New York reaches its height. The lure of the good old country brings in residents of such municipalities as Pugh's Corners, Connecticut, Five Forks, New York, and the like by the bus- and train-load. For it is in Manhattan that they can find all those attributes and delights of real country life which are denied them in their pastoral retreats.

The first joy of the thitherward rustics in New York lies in the good, honest country food which is to be found in abundance. Unable to get fresh corn, peas, string beans and other such vegetables at home, and forced to use the canned variety because all the fresh stuff is bought up by the New York markets, they here can revel in them to their starved hearts' content. Fresh and juicy meats, which are a rarity down on the farm, are the natural order of the day, and so is all the fresh fruit that is shot out of the hinterlands on express trains the moment it is picked.

Worn out by lack of sleep because of the loud noises made by birds, frogs, and crickets, the country visitor to the city revels in the quiet and peace of hotel rooms, and soon discovers his health and mental well-being restored. For the first time in months, his slumbers are serene. He may sleep his fill, safe from dawn disturbances by crowing roosters and mooing cows, and safe as well from the early sunlight's intrusion through broken window shades and cracks in the wall.

The absence of mosquitoes is another source of comfort to him. If in his countryside he so much as sticks his head out of doors after dark, he will look like a violent case of measles, somewhat complicated with hives, the moment he draws it in again. But in the city no such agony awaits him. He may freely walk miles or sit outdoors for hours on end without a single bite. Nor is there the busy bee to buzz him and maybe painfully sting him into profuse profanity.

The rural scenery of the city is still another big drawing-card for the country boys and girls. Condemned for eleven months in the year to live in localities where most of the trees have been cut down to make room for farm land and where flowers are as rare as bathtubs, they find an especial thrill in the wooded parks and squares, in the real trees and blooms of Rockefeller Center, in the profusion of flowers in the windows and shops of the countless florists, and in the blooms and blossoms in innumerable window-boxes along the streets and on the terraces of an endless number of apartment houses and hotels. The waterfalls which they behold in various restaurants, and the running streams and brooks which they encounter in some of the Italian spaghetti eating places, similarly bring the feel of the real country to them, a feel which they seldom get where they come from.

The cool days and nights maneuvered through air-conditioners, refrigerating devices, etc., are yet still another rustic feature that only the city can vouchsafe them. In what passes for the actual country, there is no escape from the hot days and hotter nights. But in the city the fresh, cool country breezes are the yokel visitor's gift at a mere button's press. If he wanders in the open, the backwoodsman may additionally get all the real country breezes, hitherto denied him and which he longs for, by sitting in one or another of the many roof gardens, or standing on the balcony of one of the many skyscrapers, or simply getting into a speeding taxicab or climbing atop a bus.

One of the theoretical contentments of living in the country is the rocking chair. A farmhouse porch and its inevitable rocking chair have long been hymned in fiction as the ultimate in physical ease and peace. But anyone who can discover a rocking chair in the rural regions that isn't lopsided or busted is worthy to have his statue placed in the world's Hall of Fame alongside those of Amerigo Vespucci, Balboa, and Stanley. In the city, on the contrary, country folk may have thousands of rockers in perfect condition and may rock and lull themselves into an authentic and ecstatic bucolic complacency.

And do not overlook the good old bucolic smells! Deep in the sticks, the good old bucolic smells that you read about are as hard to find as a copy of today's newspaper. Aside from the time-honored manure, whose rich fragrance is an acknowledged pleasure, there isn't a genuine country odor within sniffing distance. The flowers, as I have pointed out, are negligible; the trees, where they exist, have been so doused with insecticides and whitewash that all their olfactory delights have vanished; the droughts banish the smell of fresh earth; and about the only real rustic smell left is that provided by the garbage cans in the backyards. In the city, however, you get the beautiful country smells by the wholesale. The potted palms in even the cheapest hotel corridors give out a fragrance of foliage that comes as a godsend to the visiting farmers. The flowers in the little side vases in automobiles and taxicabs regale their famished nostrils. The fountains in parks and restaurants and plazas splash their dews on the grass below and enchant their senses. The trees in the side streets and elsewhere, left largely to their own devices, retain a leafy freshness. And the fresh, moist smell of earth fills the circumambient atmosphere in countless little back gardens, in many well-tended districts like Gramercy, Mount Morris, Madison Square and other such small parks, in the hundreds of shops where seeds and bulbs are for sale, in the thousands of markets and grocery stores with their loads of vegetables only recently pulled out of the still-clinging but here carefully sprinkled soil, and in even the five-and-ten stores where soil demonstrations are conducted on behalf of ambitious city gardeners by lovely and provocative salesgirls.

That long-celebrated concomitant of country existence, the personal column in the hick newspaper, in which country folk could read of Mrs. Jones' purchase of a new washing machine and of Mrs. Terwilliger's anticipated baby, has gradually disappeared along with most of the other long-celebrated and hypothetically indigenous country institutions. It is now but a slim shadow of its former self. But in the city it has flowered into full bloom at the hands of the new order of columnists. In the city the yokels can now read that Mrs. Jones has not only bought the new washing machine but that she is washing in it the socks of Mr. Smith, about whom she is that way, and that Mrs. Terwilliger is not only anticipating the baby but that it will be born at exactly four and one-half minutes past 6 a.m. on February 15, that it will be a boy, that it will be named Maximilian, and that Mrs. Terwilliger will thereupon divorce her husband, who has been running around with Brenda Frazier's maid's stepbrother's boss's cousin's stenographer and will marry Mrs. Jones' husband when he in turn gets a divorce because of the noise made by the aforementioned new washing machine.

[From *The Bachelor Life,* 1941, pp. 231–9.]

In the Country

IT seems a whole lot of city folk have just recently heard of the old philosophy that every man, for his true and ultimate peace and contentment, should own and cultivate a bit of land. The resulting back-to-the-earth stampede has been something to behold. Even I, a notoriously urban fellow, felt the call not long ago. I bought me a minute slice of the Western Hemisphere in northern Connecticut, went out to look at it early one afternoon, sat down under a tree and got into the mood by reading Thoreau for ten minutes, and then—not more than twenty-two miles by motor—found an inn with a bar presided over by Jimmy Brennan, who had been at the Waldorf up to May 15, and with such mint juleps as would have made Grant happily surrender to General Lee before even Bull Run. Vastly exhilarated by the country air, I got back to town just in time to catch the opening of *Hold on to Your Hats,* a good show, and I haven't been back to look at my schnitzel of Good Earth since. As for Jimmy, he went back to the Waldorf two days later. It seemed he was delayed. Two of his old New York customers who had also gone back to the land for a few hours had bribed him to stay on the job and alleviate their urban nostalgia with his Kentucky masterpieces.

I suppose the country is great stuff for people who have been born in it and don't know the difference, but for anyone who can't tell a redwood tree from Hendrik Willem Van Loon I'm not so sure. Of course, it's nice to motor out and take a look at it once in a while, and it may not even be so bad to visit some of your rustically inclined friends now and then (for an extremely brief period), but as a steady dose I'll debate for the negative side free of charge. Nor do the innumerable recently published books arguing the opposite in the least persuade me. All except one of them that I have read in the last six months are by authors who believe they are big authorities on the subject because two of their tomato vines came out all right and because they've discovered no noisy bus-lines in their rural neighborhood. As for that, you can successfully raise all the tomato vines you have a mind to in any penthouse garden right here in Manhattan, and there are hundreds of streets where the noise of a bus never penetrates.

But, they say, the good old smell of the earth! Well, they can have the good old smell of the earth. Nine times out of ten it isn't the good old smell of the earth that they smell so much as the good old smell of wet chicken feathers, stagnant pools of water, outhouse perfumes, cooking odors from badly designed kitchens, and damp wall plaster.

Any realistic person who hasn't been influenced in his view of country life by New England naturalists who operated in the days before open plumbing knows that once you leave the city you leave behind you all the true peace and comforts of civilized man. As to the comforts there isn't, I take it, much doubt, except maybe on the part of such fish as prefer cornhusk mattresses to Ostermoors, love the exercise involved in trying to open wardrobe drawers that, once they get to the country, refuse to open unless you reward them with a strained back, a sprained wrist, and a bruised toe, and cherish walking half a block to a certain necessary retreat which at home is just a couple of feet removed from the cheval glass. And as for the peace there can be even less doubt, save perhaps in the case of those who think it is infinitely more peaceful to lie in bed at night and listen to the rain pour down romantically on a tin roof and then drip through the ceiling and weewee all over your sheets than to roll over quietly in town and sleep dry.

I will not be so banal as to mention bugs, bees, caterpillars, gnats, bats, wasps, spiders, mice, rats, water roaches, and ants. Even the most rabid endorsers of country life, I discover, have to admit that there are certain other slight inconveniences. For instance, the servant problem. It seems that a cook or a maid has never been brought up properly for country existence. She will behave all right for about a week or two, and then the trouble will begin. The trouble, it appears, is that if you are far enough away in the rural regions there is no place for her to go at nights where she can see Clark Gable. It is never long before the cook or maid just has to see Clark Gable or know the reason why. The whole difficulty, of course, will readily be solved as soon as Louis B. Mayer sees to it that a movie theatre is built just around the corner from every chicken farm, apple orchard, and tomato patch, but Louie has been awfully remiss up to now and so there is hell to pay.

Another inconvenience about idyllic country life, they reluctantly allow, is the electric lights. When you buy or rent the house and try out the lights, everything is ups-a-daisy. Turn on the switch and it all looks like Roxy's. But about two nights later, after your check has been cashed, turn it on again, sucker, and then hurry for the oil lamp and the candles. An electric light system in the country invariably declines to do any business for you after you get all your trunks unpacked and conclude that you are settled down. Sometimes it fools you by working a little longer than you hoped, but at the first faint sound of a thunderstorm—flooie! If you have ever tried to shave by candlelight, or read a novel by the light of an oil lamp, or tried to locate your pet poodle, out in the barnyard with a box of matches, and if you still feel that night in the country is superior to night in your town apartment, all I can say is that one of us is dotty.

But, persist the sentimentalists, the joy and pleasure in watching things grow! That is the favorite big card they play. Well, I've tried it, once. I once hung around patiently for three weeks watching a squash grow (of course, I motored into town every night and returned to the vigil the next afternoon), and in all that time it didn't do much but pop a scant eighth of an inch out of the ground. All I could see was something that began remotely to resemble a small greenish-white worm and that didn't look anything like a squash. I figured out that if the squash didn't grow more than an eighth of an inch every three weeks it would be June 19, 1954, until I saw the squash really develop—so, as I planned to begin writing another book in February, 1950, I decided to motor back to town—and not return the next afternoon for any more such joy and pleasure.

When I got to New York, I found I could buy a squash, already full grown and not necessitating any daily scrutiny, for fourteen cents.

[From *The Bachelor Life*, 1941, pp. 245–50.]

ON NEW YORK CITY

In a review of a recently published novel, I find the phrase, "the artificial window-box life of New York." It is a phrase that, in one form or another, one constantly encounters in the writings of men who live in the hinterland or of others who, imported to New York, long still in their hearts for the great open cow-pastures. What is in the phrase? So far as I can make out, after prolonged conferences with myself, absolutely nothing.

The notion that life in New York is in the aggregate any more artificial than life in a small town is the not uncharacteristic reasoning of such persons as have been born to believe that human nature is forthright and honest in a farmhouse but is quickly perverted if it takes a suite at the Ritz. That there is an artificial side to life in the metropolis, no one disputes. But this phase of life is confined very largely to more or less temporary visitors who are no more really New Yorkers than real New Yorkers are Parisians when they cut up in the Paris cafés and peepshows. The New Yorker, by and large, leads a life that is no more artificial, when you come to look at it closely, than the life led by the average country-town lout. What is more, even the good-time-Charlie New Yorker, the flashier type of New Yorker, isn't at bottom much different from his country-jake cousin. He dresses better and he spends more money (because he makes more), but in other ways Julius O'Grady and this lady's Colonel—jake and sophisticate— are birds of a feather. Both, to get to the main point at once, are ignoramuses. They have little education, little taste, little distinction—and not the slightest perception of refinement or beauty. Both are dolts. But their lives are cast upon much the same intrinsic plan, however varying the details. The rube lives in a frame house with the *châlet de nécessité* a block away; the New Yorker lives in an apartment with the *cabinet d'eaux* three feet from his bed. The New Yorker drinks genuine

Holloway gin; the rube, homemade applejack. The New Yorker dances jazz to Paul Whiteman's jazz band; the rube dances the polka and the Virginia reel to the grocery boy's fiddle. The New Yorker negotiates his rendezvous on the Albany night boats or in Atlantic City; the rube negotiates his in his phaeton or in a hayloft, and he negotiates them oftener, if the statistics do not deceive us, than the city man. The New Yorker, when he tires of his wife and can't stand her any longer, kicks her out and divorces her; the rube, when he tires of his and can't stand her any longer, goes on living with her and making the rest of his own and her life miserable.

And so it goes. If life in New York is artificial, life in Newtsville and Sauk Centre is equally so. If the New Yorker pivots his life on the making of money, what about the farmer? If the New Yorker, in the pursuit of money, cheats and swindles, what about the farmer? If the New Yorker does not go to church on Sunday, how much does the rube consider God on Monday, Tuesday, Wednesday, Thursday, Friday and Saturday? If the New York flapper bobs her hair, rolls her stockings, smokes cigarettes and is indiscreet, so to speak, in taxicabs, what about the country girl when the lights in the front parlor have been turned down and pa has swallowed his chewing tobacco and gone to bed? If the New Yorker sits up at night listening to a cabaret hussy sing "Who Makes the Dressmaker's Daughter When the Dressmaker's Making a Dress?", what about the rube's sitting up at night to listen to the same flapdoodle over the radio? If the New Yorker thinks artificially, the rube doesn't think at all. When I read references to the artificiality of life in New York, indeed, I am reminded of the French peasant who walked two hundred miles to see Paris, who arrived at six o'clock in the morning, who saw a policeman patroling his beat in the chilly dawn and who, shaking his head sadly, observed, "Yes, yes, they are true. Alas, they are true, these stories of the dissipations and artificial life of Paris! What will happen to our army if its generals stay up all night and raise hell like that one there and don't go home until this time in the morning?"

[From *The Autobiography of an Attitude*, 1925, pp. 119–22.]

ON POLITICS

WHEN I am charged with not taking a sufficiently serious interest in politics, in the doings of the crowd of low thieves and mountebanks down at Washington—a parcel of men almost wholly devoid of truth, decency and honor—it is precisely as if I were asked to take a serious interest in the doings of a union of piano-movers over in Long Island City. I decline to pollute my mind with such obscenities. Even the consideration of politics as a species of buffoonery does not hold any enchantment for me. I can see nothing enjoyable in riding on the steam cars for several days to look at a thousand dudelsocks who believe that the way to pick out the best man for President of the United States is to rip off their undershirts, tote around banners labeled "Oh You Kid!", sing "Ach, Du Lieber Augustin," squirt tobacco juice on the chairs, and periodically yell "Three cheers for Kansas!" Compared with such a spectacle, a Broadway leg-show is a masterpiece of diversion. I would rather look at a pretty leg once than at Frank Kellogg twice—any day. And I would rather listen to a sightly wench warbling "Kiss Me on the Ear, Gus, My Mouth Is Full of Gum" than to a suffragette chromo reciting the virtues of William G. McAdoo.

I am told that my complete disinterestedness in politics causes me to miss a lot. What do I miss? I miss a lot of block-heads in behalf of a candidate who is generally a lot more of a blockhead than they are. I miss reading a lot of tripe about a lot of fourth-rate micks busying themselves with the noble enterprise of getting a third-rate job for a second-rate mick. I miss seeing democracy behind the scenes in its dressing-room, clad only in its chemise. I have no taste for such vulgarity. I prefer a good dog fight, or a burlesque show. The spectacle of a United States senator in the lavatory at a national convention, pickled to the ears and making an indignant speech on the League of Nations to three patriotic American delegates named, respectively Winckheimer, Eiersalat and Schnitzblauser, or of a candidate for the Presidency, boiled to the eyebrows, trying to make an impression on the newspaper correspondents, grabbing the edge of a table to steady himself and, missing it, landing plumb on his *Sitzfleisch*—such spectacles are only a cheap imitation of Robie's Crackerjack Burlesquers. And I prefer to get such a show at first hand. Why travel for days at the cost of hundreds of dollars to see something that I can see done much better down in Fourteenth Street for seventy-five cents? The clowns of politics are no whit more real than the clowns of the stage: a senator, or even a President, and Herman Krausmeyer are brothers under their skin; both are equally mummers. The slapstick that lands to the rear of a politician, however eminent, and the one that lands to the rear of a stage pantaloon are, to me, one and the same, and the respective seats upon which the slapsticks land are no less one and the same. And when it is argued that politics provides the greater and lewder show because in the theatre one has to pretend that the slapstické is someone of dignity and consequence in order properly to appreciate the humors of his embarrassment consequent upon the receipt of the wallop, I argue in turn that one has to pretend exactly the same thing in the case of politics. Thus, if in the pursuit of ribald jocosity I have to imagine for the time being that some burlesque show ham is the Count de Roquefort, owner of the Deauville Casino, the lover of politics in turn has to imagine that some erstwhile shyster lawyer from Sandusky, Ohio, or Kraus Creek, Minnesota, is a purple toga'd Mark Antony with a liberal soupçon of Roman in him. The buffoons of politics, in good truth, are less real than the buffoons of the stage. Which, for example, is the more convincing: William H. Crane's United States senator or J. Thomas Heflin's? If the essence of humor lies in the sharp contrast between dignity and importance on the one hand and sudden disaster and ignominy on the other, one may inquire as to the dignity and importance of the politician. That dignity and importance exist simply in the mind of the spectator, through a voluntary remission of judgment, exactly as in the case of the stage actor. If, in order to pave the way for a good loud belly-laugh, I have to pretend to myself that Louis Mann, say, is a millionaire steel magnate, a lover of rare books and a powerful thinker, the devotee of politics has to pretend to himself that a United States ambassador to a great European capital is a sagacious statesman and diplomat, and not—as he more often actually is—merely an American who can wear a silk hat without looking like a French hack driver, who can stand on a polished hardwood floor without slipping, and who has learned how to say "This soup is delicious" in two foreign languages.

As it is pretty well agreed, even by the most enthusiastic followers of political phenomena, that about 95 per cent of politicians are idiots, I cannot quite grasp the pleasure that these followers derive from watching them swell up and explode. In Matteawan perhaps 95 per cent of the incarcerated idiots imagine themselves to be senators, ambassadors, governors and even Presidents. I might thus get the same degree of amusement contemplating these poor fellows as I can get contemplating those of their brothers who are still at large. The circumstance that a politician is gravely accepted by three of four hundred thousand dinkelspiels for the sage he pretends to be, and that he deceives himself in the same direction, surely does not make him any better material for a cultivated man's risibilities than a mere stage anticker. There were just as many dolts who believed that Richard Mansfield was a great intellectual and great art force as there were dolts who believed that Woodrow Wilson was a Gladstone and Bismarck. The mob may regard a Governor of Tennessee as a more important man than Cabell, or Borglum, or even Bach, but the same mob in turn regards Charlie Chaplin as a more important man than a Governor of Tennessee—and I am not certain that, here at least, the mob isn't partly right. Carrying out to its logical conclusion the contention that the humor of politics lies entirely in the accepted eminence of politicians and the consequent relatively more emphatic report that issues from the collision of their seats with the pavement, it might be said that Elihu Root, whom hundreds of thousands of Americans soberly consider a Socrates, is by that fact, and that fact solely, a droller pickle than Al Jolson, whom the same number of Americans frankly consider a clown. Therefore, in conclusion, I fear that it would be silly for me to waste years trying to acquire a talent for laughing at politicians. The thing would be just as insane as for Beethoven to have given up music and to have devoted ten or twenty years to learning how to paint on china.

[From *The Autobiography of an Attitude*, 1925, pp. 32–7.]

ON VACATIONS

Approaches the ghastly time when people who have been perfectly happy and comfortable all year feel it their duty to do something about a vacation, however much they may gag at the idea. There are, of course, it is regretfully to be admitted, folk who delight in vacations, but they are generally found to be the same who delight in putting tacks on chairs, tying cans to dogs' tails, sprinkling sugar on cantaloupe, and other such tortures and atrocities. The majority of normal and rational folk deep down in their hearts look upon vacations with the same disquiet and even disgust that they look upon any other gratuitous and wholly unnecessary interference with their average way of being.

Driven by fatuous tradition, I have now been taking vacations once a year for more than a quarter of a century, and I long for the day when I shall at length have achieved sufficient independence and common sense to give up the melancholy practice. Each year—come the approaching time—I duly like a robot pack a lot of bags and start off to some place to which I do not at all wish to go and where I damn well know I will not be in the least comfortable or amused simply because tradition says I must.

It all starts sometime in April. Dozens of friends and acquaintances, doubtless not knowing what else to say, begin it by asking where I am going for the summer. Not wishing to go anywhere for the summer, being wholly and beautifully content to remain just where I am, but also not knowing what else to say, I casually answer, at least in peace time, "Oh, I suppose Europe, as usual." I keep on casually answering, "Oh, I suppose Europe, as usual" for the next two months, and then—though, as I have said, I do not want to go to Europe or any place else as usual—off to Europe or some other place I find myself going, all because I do not wish to be thought a poseur or a liar. If only they'd stop asking me in April where I am going in June, my problem would be over. I could stay quietly, peacefully, and happily in New York and have the time of my life.

It isn't that I have grown tired of vacations since I have grown older. I have never liked them. As early as the age of ten (being an extraordinarily sagacious child), I failed to perceive the sense in running away from a place I liked, and where I was supremely contented and happy, to some other place where I knew I would be taking chances and where, four times out of five, I subsequently discovered my intuition was correct.

The theory behind the vacation idea is a fourfold one. First, it is so interesting, they say, to see new faces and meet new people. Well, I have seen thousands upon thousands of new faces in my long vacation experience, and I have met hundreds upon hundreds of new people, and you can have all but maybe six or seven of them for a nickel. Secondly, it is so good, they say, to have a change once a year. Why? If what you already have is sufficiently agreeable and pleasing, what value is there in getting away from it? Thirdly, they tell you, it is great to throw aside all your cares and just take things easily for a while. That is the sourest quarter of the whole theory. The more leisure you have, the more your cares will recur to you. In the thick of one's worries at home, one often paradoxically succeeds in putting them out of mind for a spell, but try to run away from them altogether, and they will follow you like bloodhounds. Fourthly and finally, it is all such fun, they assert, to kick over the traces and let go. Very well. It's fun for a few days—and then does it become a bore! You drink too much; you eat too much; you flirt, as the euphemism is, too much; you spend twice as much money as you should; you do everything, in short, that contributes to a magnificent case of physical, emotional, financial, and spiritual katzenjammer.

A drunk was standing at a bar. " 'Nother Martini!" he roared. Whereupon he downed it, cracked the stem off the glass, threw it aside and chewed the top of the glass to bits. " 'Nother Martini!" he yelled. Whereupon he downed it, cracked the stem off the glass, threw it aside, and again ate the top of the glass. A second drunk staggered up to him. "Say you!" he asked. "How

long you been doing that?" The other glowered at him. "All m'
life," he retorted. "And do yuh wanna make something of it?"
"Naw," said the other. "I just wannad t' tell you you're throwin'
away the best part!"

There's no accounting for tastes. Vacations and those stems
have a great deal in common.

However, I wish to qualify slightly the aspersion which I
have cast. There was one vacation I enjoyed immensely. I have
taken vacations all over the world, and none of them even
faintly approximated the satisfaction I derived from that one.
It happened just ten years ago. I booked passage to Europe on
one of the German ships then docked at and sailing from Hoboken at midnight. Several of my friends gave me a farewell
party that started at 3:15 p.m. sharp at "21" with double Old
Fashioneds, proceeded to the Oak Room at the Plaza at 6:04
and continued with triple Daiquiris, and wound up at the Colony and began at 8:19 with Moët and Chandon. Around ten
o'clock I sneaked out, got into an automobile, and headed for
my ship. Passing through Hoboken, the car halted briefly for
the traffic lights, and on the curb I saw standing what seemed
to me, in my exalted imaginative condition, to be the most
beautiful girl I had ever seen not only in Hoboken but in my
life. And, wonder of wonders, the most beautiful girl I had ever
seen not only in Hoboken but in my life smiled at me! or, anyway, in my exalted imaginative condition, I thought she did. I
descended from the car, bowed low, beseeched her gracious
indulgence, and introduced myself. Would she, I privileged
myself the unheard-of presumption and audacity to ask her,
consider joining me briefly for a glass of wine at Meyers' café?
She sweetly smiled her acceptance; I gave her my arm; I deposited her in the car; I commanded the chauffeur: "Meyers',
James!"

Arrived at Meyers' my fair companion and I quaffed a glass
seriatim to the various crowned heads of Europe, to the Presidents of the South American republics, to the Shah of Persia
and the Sultan of Turkey, to the President of the United States,
to the Vice-President of the United States, to the Speaker of
the House, and to Nicholas Murray Butler. Then we drank a
couple to ourselves and, arm in arm, went over to the dock.

There I kissed the most beautiful girl I had ever seen not only in Hoboken but in my life auf wiedersehen, mounted the gangplank, stood a moment at the rail of the ship to wave her a fond au revoir, and started for my stateroom. Someone grabbed me by the arm. "Where do you think you're going?" he wanted to know. "To Europe," I loftily replied. "Well, if you are," he answered, "you're on the wrong boat. There's the one going to Europe steaming down the harbor. This one got in from Europe just six hours ago!"

I rushed down the gangplank and kissed the most beautiful girl I had ever seen not only in Hoboken but in my life hello.

❃   ❃   ❃

It was a wonderful vacation.

[From *The Bachelor Life,* 1941, pp. 231–9.]

ON DOCTORS

As one who, man and boy, has liberally patronized the medical profession for more than forty years and paid its bills on the first of each month, swear-words notwithstanding, I have arrived, somewhat belatedly as must be apparent, at the conclusion that the good health of Frenchmen must be due to the notorious badness of French doctors and to the correlated fact that a Frenchman seldom calls one in to look after him. Like most human beings I have been assailed by the average repertoire of malaises; like most human beings I have on such occasions called up a medical gentleman for professional advice; and, like most human beings, I have nine times out of ten subsequently found that I might just as well have saved the money. There are, of course, occasions—the tenth time in ten—when a doctor is not only necessary but highly profitable. I am not so physiologically bumptious as to venture to deny that. But in the general run of things—at least so far as my own experience has gone—he may, I believe, very safely be left either at home or on the golf links. Let me, by way of illustration, display a few lantern slides of my personal adventures with the profession.

Since the age of fifteen, I have been a periodic sufferer from neuralgic pains in the left eyeball. Seeking relief, I have consulted, by actual count, seventy-one different doctors not only in America but in England, France, Austria, Germany and Italy and I have the honor to report that, for all their wisdom and bills, the damned pain is still there. This pain has been variously diagnosed—with appropriate treatment subsequently undergone—as resulting from acute astigmatism, an infection of the fifth facial nerve, sinus congestion, stiffness of the muscles at the back of the neck, lead poisoning, malnutrition, poor circulation, streptococcicosis, something wrong with the nasal passages, tonsils, teeth, eye-strain, acidity, tobacco, acute nervousness, a bone pressing against a nerve, a trigeminal tic, too much coffee, improper assimilation of certain foods, principally fish, not enough fresh air, climatic conditions, kidney trouble, the use of poisonous hair tonics, overwork, the use of alcohol, and sleeping on too high a pillow, together with any number of other causes, each separate cause being profoundly enunciated in turn by each of seventy medical gentlemen. There were some agreements, however—chiefly as to coffee, alcohol, tobacco and fish. Only one doctor, the seventy-first, a distinguished member of the staff of the Johns Hopkins Hospital, was frank enough to admit that he didn't know what caused the neuralgia, couldn't find out and wouldn't know anything to cure it if he did.

As I say, I went through thousands of dollars' worth of treatments for the alleged causes of my neuralgia and not a thing happened. I have always felt just as badly after it was all over as I did before the doctor began feeling my pulse, looking at my tongue, taking my temperature, and making an omniscient face. I have had my teeth X-rayed, my arm scratched in food tests, my blood examined, my eyes examined, my spine massaged, my nose operated upon, my sinuses punctured and everything else done to me as recommended, and by the dawn's early light the pain was still there. One eminent doctor insisted the neuralgia was due to lead paint on the wallpaper in the room in which I slept. I had the paper removed and the pain gradually got worse. Another, after six visits, stated that it was his conviction that my trouble was due to overwork, the aforesaid conviction failing entirely to convince me as, at the time, I happened to be in Austria where I had been resting and taking life easily for five months. Still another informed me that I had undoubtedly inherited the neuralgia from my father or mother, neither of whom had ever had any such neuralgia.

A man, feeling out of sorts, went to see a doctor. After the examination, the latter admonished him: "No more meat, lots of vegetables and three cigars a day; mind you, just *three* a day—no more!" Several days later the man returned, looking and feeling terribly. "What's the trouble?" asked the doctor. "I don't know," replied the customer. "But it must be those cigars. I never smoked one before." It's an old story, but it seems to fit my case.

Then there are colds. Like everybody else, when I don't know what else to do, I seem to go in for catching colds. I have had some beauties and they have been just as beautiful after doctors got through with them as they were before I was fool enough to telephone. If there ever was a doctor who could actually shut up a cold in less time than it takes a cold to shut itself up, I do not know his address—and I know a lot of doctors' addresses. Among the doctors' recommendations that I have followed and paid ten dollars apiece for have been everything from quinine to creosote, and from hot-drinks at bedtime and magnesium carbonate to belladonna and pyramidon, and I have continued to sneeze my head off and groan notwithstanding. I have listened to medical patter on the subject of my colds for years and I have obeyed instructions to the letter, but my colds haven't seemed to pay any attention to the imparted medical sagacity. My memory whimsically recalls the professional chatter: "Avoid draughts . . . keep the bowels open . . . keep the temperature in your room even, not too hot, not too cold . . . keep your window open at night but be careful to cover up well . . . don't go into crowded places . . . gargle bi-carbonate of soda every two hours . . . bundle up well if you go out . . . don't overexert yourself . . . a mild nasal spray would be a good thing . . . take this medicine every three hours . . . and you'll be all right again in a couple of days." In other words, so far as my colds have been concerned, sausage! I have been all right again in a week or nine days, maybe, when the cold has just naturally got tired of me and has gone somewhere else, but not a minute before.

The trouble with doctors, I find, is that they seldom admit that anything stumps them. When they don't know what is wrong with you or, knowing, of the way to cure it, do they confess as much? They do not. With the ten dollar fee in sight, they invariably proceed to mask a guessing contest as science. For several years I had neuritis in my right arm and sought counsel upon the subject from various big pill and pulse men. Not one hesitated a moment in his diagnosis of my trouble, although the diagnoses had all the variety of an old-time vaudeville bill. One said it was due to sleeping with my right arm under me. I have, since cradle days, slept on my left side. Another said it was due to high acidity, which subsequent tests showed I didn't have. A third, after three months of mystic hocus-pocus involving heat rays, electric pads and muscular massage, insisted that my neuritis was caused by a sesquipedalian and rather exotic term that he somehow didn't seem to feel the need of elucidating to me and for which he announced the only cure was more heat rays, electric pads and muscular massage which, during the previous three months, hadn't done a thing to my neuritis. When I mildly protested, he took off his glasses, eyed me majestically and observed that he could do nothing for me if I didn't whole-heartedly believe in his treatment.

I have a friend who has had hay-fever for thirty years. He has tried dozens of doctors for it and dozens of their cures and he is still watering at the nose and eyes and sneezing as handsomely as thirty years ago. I have another friend who used to get an ear-ache every Summer and who, after twelve years of vain trying to learn from doctors what the trouble was and dosing himself up with a hundred and one philtres, finally kicked the last doctor out and relieved himself of his pain by the simple expedient of thinking to put a small piece of ice close to his ear.

When a doctor is at a loss to figure out what is wrong with the average patient he will pretty generally be found falling back on the clichés, tobacco, liquor, coffee, too much red meat, or "When did you last have your teeth examined?" I myself have paid out a sum of money I hate to think of just to hear one or another item in this venerable catalogue of flim-flam. Like many another sucker it has also cost me good money to be made privy to the esoteric news that it is bad to get one's feet wet, that one ought to eat more fruit, that it is bad to keep one's rooms too hot and that steam heat robs the air of its moisture, that if one has a headache one shouldn't wear a tight hat, that it isn't good for one to go out immediately after a hot bath, that one shouldn't drink too much alcoholic liquor, that during an influenza epidemic one should be careful to keep the bowels in good condition, that deep breathing is to be recommended, that a little bi-carbonate of soda in half a glass of water is good for a stomach that doesn't feel just right, that water is the most healthful thing one can drink, that one's bedroom should be well aired, and that one thing is certain and that is that you've got to get enough sleep.

That medical progress has in a number of directions in the last quarter of a century been very considerable, I am surely not one to deny, but the progress doesn't strike me as having been fully shared by most family doctors. The majority of the latter that I have come into contact with—I wish to except one in whose bad graces I do not wish to find myself when I next call up about my lumbago—are still delivering themselves of all the stenciled nonsense that has been in operation since the days of our grandfathers. Medical science may have succeeded in mastering many hitherto major and occult problems, but the average ills of the average man still elude the ordinary practising medical gentry as they always have. The MM. Nicolle and Ricketts have done things about typhus fever, Finsen has done things about tuberculosis of the skin, the Dicks have done things about scarlet fever and other such highly talented investigators have also done splendidly in various fields, but old Dr. Jones, the family's friend, is still where he was years ago. True enough, he has added some fancy new words and phrases to his vocabulary, such as *vitamins, proteins, chemotherapy, pituitary gland, puerperal sepsis,* etc., but he still prescribes small doses of codein for a stubborn cough, quinine for a cold in the head or—if quinine causes ringing in your ears—perhaps something else with ammonium salicylate or camphor in it, hot-water applications or else an ice-bag for headache, an iron tonic and plenty of spinach for a run-down condition, some kind of rubbing oil for back pains, and the second-latest widely advertised gargle for sore-throat, the latest, he allows, "not having as yet been carefully investigated by him."

One of the favorite arguments of the average doctor is the tonsils. If you aren't sure, blame it on the tonsils: that seems to be the policy. I have had ten doctors strongly advise me to get rid of my tonsils and ten others urge me as strongly to do nothing of the kind, as they were atrophied anyway. An equal pet is blood-pressure. Nobody's blood-pressure ever seems to be just right: either it is too high or too low. If it is too high, it costs you ten dollars to be told to lay off liquor and if it is too low it costs you ten dollars to be told to lay off tobacco. The suggestion that you had better also lay off meat in the first instance and eat more meat in the second is sometimes thrown in gratis, although often it takes another ten-spot to buy the extra sliver of wisdom. Then there is exercise. Either you are overdoing it or you are not doing enough of it, depending upon how much news on the subject the doctor has succeeded in slyly coaxing out of you. "Exercise is a good thing in moderation, but it mustn't be overdone"—that also puts you back ten dollars. If you are in the habit of playing eighteen holes of golf, cut it down to nine; if nine, raise it to eighteen—no matter how you feel or where the seat of your trouble lies. Then—people don't drink enough water these days, it appears. It has cost me hundreds of dollars to learn this, although I have always drunk enough water daily to float a rowboat. "But," I have protested, "I already drink all the water I can hold!" Undismayed and unruffled has come the reply, "Well, drink more."

Some years ago I found myself suffering from a pain near the base of the spine. I sought out four doctors in pursuit of explanation and relief. One diagnosed my difficulty as bladder trouble and put me through an elaborate cure. I still had the pain. The second diagnosed the case as a nervous condition and prescribed treatments with some kind of new-fangled light. I still had the pain. The third, after much professorial monkey-business, decided that the trouble was with my vertebræ and put me in the hands of a chiropractor who manipulated my back two hundred and fifty dollars' worth. I still had the pain, only a little worse than it was before. The fourth had me come around to his office three times for examinations and then told me that the pain was doubtless due to an abscess under one of my back teeth. So I went to a dental surgeon, had thirty-five dollars' worth of X-rays taken, learned that my teeth were all right, and still had the pain. Achieving by this time a small measure of sense, I decided to take my pain to some place other than a doctor's office. An athletic trainer whom I knew in my college days happened to be in town and I called him up and asked him to come around to my house for a drink. Over the fourth cocktail I told him of my pain and asked him what he thought. "Give me a hard one!" he exclaimed. "This is too easy. Like a lot of you writing guys, you put a cushion under you on your desk chair when you're pushing a pen. Get rid of the cushion, sit on the hard chair and your pain'll vamoose." I got rid of the cushion and I have never had the pain since.

I subsequently asked my friend how he had known so immediately what caused my pain, and recounted to him the failure of the four professional medicoes to diagnose it. "In the early days of crew training," he said, "they used to have pads on the oarsmen's seats. The oarsmen often used to complain of pains like yours. So they investigated and found out that the pads were to blame. That's that."

I had an uncle, now dead, who for many years was bothered by a burning sensation on his tongue. It didn't amount to much, but it worried him and he patronized many doctors in this country and abroad in an effort to learn what caused it. The doctors diagnosed the trouble as this and that and prescribed various treatments which my late lamented relative took, each and all to no avail. One day, eight years after he began consulting doctors and taking their futile treatments, he happened to mention the burning sensation to an old German bartender in a well-known Philadelphia comfort parlor of the period. "Put half a teaspoonful of salt in a glass of warm water and wash your mouth out with it about six times a day and you'll be all right again in a few days." My uncle followed the bartender's instructions and the burning sensation on his tongue disappeared.

[From *The Intimate Notebooks of George Jean Nathan*, 1932, pp. 280–8.]

ON ALCOHOL

In the words of a friend of mine, I drink to make other people interesting.

2

Of the infinite and various philtres devised out of the imagination and ingenuity of the world for the decoration and enchantment of the inside of mortal man, the cocktail, it seems to me, is the most estimable. It has a humor that no other drink has, and it has, in addition, a charm—aye, and romance—that are considerably absent from vessels of other content. The very schedule of its drinking suggests its intrinsic grace. Unlike bibbables that are guzzled either during or after one's moments of pleasure and joy, the cocktail is ever drunk before: a promise and harbinger of happiness to come. It is the aristocrat of tipples. It does not associate with fish, like sherry, or with cow meat like claret, or with cheese, like Tokay. It is the drink of friends; one seldom, if ever, engages it with a stranger. It is a drink that is reserved for those we like and those who like us. There is no record of a quarrel or fight that has followed its absorption. Such things are reserved for whiskey and the lower elixirs. It has breeding. Unlike champagne, it cares whom it associates with. It is quiet, unostentatious; it avoids flashy places; it is the only drink in the world whose birth is accompanied by tinkling music. Champagne comes into our presence with a loud and vulgar report; whiskey with a common gurgle; the cocktail with a sweet and cool and silvery rattle, as of Eskimo babies at play. It is only when these other potions abandon their genealogical pretensions and engage in miscegenation that they share the cocktail's glory.

The cocktail, once averred George Ade, follows the American flag. That was twenty years ago. The flags of all nations today follow the cocktail. Its fame has spread over the globe, and justly. It has captured the English and the French, the Danes and the Italians. Five o'clock in Piccadilly brings its gin and vermouth and dash of bitters as five o'clock along the grand boulevards brings its iced brandy and gum syrup and dash of Byrrh. It is the gift of smiling America to lackadaisical Europe. It is the international alcoholic Esperanto.

What, strictly speaking, constitutes the charm of the cocktail? Above everything else, its brevity. It is swallowed at once and *in toto*. Here-it-is-there-it-was! The idiotic hocus-pocus of seidel bumping and of highball sipping is missing entirely. It has the swiftness of a foil's lunge, the directness and point of a witty retort. It is of the very essence of pleasure: it is beautiful and it doesn't last. It claims its all and gives its all in one lovely, fleeting moment. Consider, too, its manner of delivery. The cocktail glass—one should say glasses, so diversified are the kinds that the true connoisseur employs—is perhaps of all drinking vases the most caressing to the eye. Its very shape is appetizing, for in it are lacking the topheavy rotundity of the champagne glass, the stark cylindrical quality of the julep and rickey and highball jardinières and the effeminacy of the sherry and port glasses. The cocktail glass is in aspect for all the world like the opening measures of a Strauss waltz; it is of insinuation, rhythm and melodic promise all compact.

There are, as I have implied, sixty-three different varieties of cocktail glasses that the genuine cocktail professor uses as residences for his divers brews, of which latter, in turn, there are one hundred and eighty-four different and equally delicious species. Roughly speaking, there are therefore only three kinds of cocktails that may be served in a single kind of glass without grievously offending the cognoscenti. To serve a Florestan cocktail, for example, in a Peloponnesus cocktail's glass is, in the eye and palate of the cocktail Corinthian, akin to serving Pilsner in a punch glass. And to see in this discrimination only an affectation is to set one's self down at the outset as one who knows nothing at all about cocktail æsthetics. One would not think of serving champagne in a Burgundy glass or Burgundy in a champagne glass, though both are wine. Similarly, one should not think of serving Daiquiri cocktails in a Martini cocktail glass or Martini cocktails in a Daiquiri cocktail glass, though both are cocktails. It is the same, obviously, with the other cocktails; every third kind calls for its special container. I personally have collected cocktail glasses for the last twenty-five years, my collection at the present time numbering no less than three thousand and eighteen different sets. With these various glasses I have conducted experiments which prove beyond the peradventure of a doubt that the disesteem in which the cocktail is held in certain bourgeois quarters is due in no small degree to the manner of its serving. Indiscriminately to serve different kinds of cocktails in one kind of glass is to offend and disgust the drinker as certainly as if the various dinner-table wines were all to be served to him in one kind of glass. Thus, when you hear a person say that cocktails do not agree with him, it generally means that it is the glass the cocktails have been served in that does not agree with him. The noblest stomach would in time rebel against Rhine wine served in a beer mug or Chartreuse served in a sherry glass. A Bachelor of Cocktails himself similarly cannot long go Twelve Apostles cocktails in a Cleopatra's Ear cocktail glass. Both glasses may be exactly of a size—as, in truth, they are; it is not the size that matters. What matters is the thickness or thinness and the contour of the glass. Imagine drinking Würzburger out of a thin cutglass tumbler. Imagine drinking Charles Heidsieck 1914 out of a pewter mug. Imagine drinking a Montezuma cocktail out of a Tolstoi's Nipple cocktail glass! The thought staggers one.

The most charming hour of the day, I take it we all agree, is the twilight hour, and the twilight hour is the hour for that most charming of all toddies, the cocktail. What other beverage, indeed, conceivably fits the hour? The day is fading; the evening is dawning. Work is done, and relaxation looms ahead. The factory whistles are losing themselves in the strumming of guitars. A different mood is hovering over the earth, and about to alight. The cocktail baptizes the evening. And the evening slides down the runway, smoothly, gracefully, into the rippling sea of music and laughter and banter and heart's ease.

It is the soundest philosophy of alcoholic conduct to drink only with men who have been interesting and women who may be. The waster is not he who wastes his time drinking but he, rather, who wastes his drinking. We owe it to the cocktail to keep it safe from democracy. In short, from that atrocity of atrocities, the cocktail "party."

3

The emotional effects of alcoholic liquor upon the human nerve centres and psyche generally, it seems to me, misjudged and misstated. For example, it is maintained that the drinking of alcoholic beverages induces in the drinker a pervading spirit of democracy—that love of one's fellow man and a genial desire to embrace him with both arms and hail him as brother are the distinguishing phenomena of alcoholic indulgence. This is surely not the case. For one man upon whom alcohol exercises this effect, there are fifty in whom drinking inculcates not a democratic, but an aloof and aristocratic, mood. The general effect of alcohol, indeed, is to invest the indulger with a superior air, to make him feel stronger, wiser and more important than he felt before and than he actually is, to create in him a sense of vast *brio* and personal grandeur. This accounts for the frequency of arguments and fights on the part of the partaker. If he were made to feel democratic by alcohol, there would be no such arguments and fisticuffs. Made rather to feel the monarch of all he surveys, he resents the intrusions of lowlier and more sober men, and quickly shows that resentment. Geniality and democracy may lie at the bottom of the first, and sometimes the second, glass, but in the bottom of every glass beyond lies the mood aristocratic.

Another fallacy has to do with the effect of liquor upon women. It is maintained, particularly by fearful old maid schoolteachers in the corn, alfalfa and *New Republic* belts, that a partaking of schnapps weakens a woman's morals and places her in a condition where she is unable, mentally and physically, to resist the advances of the predatory male. If this be true, no predatory male has ever noticed it. Instead of weakening a woman's moral defenses, alcohol strengthens them. Alcohol lowers a man's morals and raises a woman's. It places her doubly on guard, intensifies her alertness, takes from the man and gives over to her the reins of leadership and superiority in the personal equation. Whenever you see a Lothario with a black eye, it is a pretty safe assumption that he has got it from some mildly stewed but decidedly wide-awake damsel.

4

Prohibition is legislative birth control applied to rabbits.

5

One encounters them in all corners of Europe, men forlorn of hope, the lines of sorrow upon their faces, the marks of grief and disappointment in their hearts. There is an ache, a longing, in them, and their voices are no longer gay. They are far from home, in happier lands that yet are alien and so are, to them, sad. One I found at Skindle's in Maidenhead, England, a fine fellow whose heart beat bitterly under his striped silk shirt. Another I encountered in a little inn in Vlissingen on the Holland coast, with tears in his fine Celtic blue eyes. Still another, erst a jolly soul, was grumbling in the Rue de Rivoli in Paris, and another still in a large café in Dresden. I found them, these melancholy and transplanted exiles, in Milan, in Buda-Pest, in Lucerne, in Brussels, in far-off Athens, working, but heavy-hearted and morose and wounded behind their forced smiles. They are the last remains of the great and noble White Company, soldiers and gentlemen all, the bartenders of the good old days in America.

[From *The Autobiography of an Attitude*, 1925, pp. 143–51.]

ON EXERCISE

MORE and more, it seems to me, the delusion that physical exercise is the valuable thing it is cracked up to be is dawning upon that portion of the public which is gifted with a share of common-sense. That exercise is valuable to a boy or girl in the younger years may or may not be argued with some conviction. But that it is good for anyone beyond those years is, if statistics and observation prove anything, another story. In my own wide range of acquaintance I have known only two men who have been devotees of the exercise theory who haven't shown the evil effects of it when they crossed the line of forty. There may be statistics in the medical and health books and other propaganda organs that demonstrate the benefits of exercise, but my own personal experience and my observation of other men—hundreds of them—convince me that there's a lot that's bogus in the figures. For example, out of fifty-six men I knew intimately in my college days, thirty-eight were athletes and the rest, eighteen, cared no more for exercise of any sort than a Zulu cares for French perfume. Of the thirty-eight, fourteen died from natural causes between the ages of twenty-five and forty-two. Of the remaining twenty-four, eight today are invalids, six have periodically suffered serious nervous breakdowns, and one is able to work not more than five hours a day because of a weakened heart. Of the eighteen who didn't believe and haven't since believed in exercise, two were killed in the war, two died from natural causes, and the rest are today as thoroughly healthy, active and alive as so many fighting cocks. Of these latter, I have at least the temporary honor to be one.

In my college days I was a bit of a backslider and actually did exercise a little—chiefly on a toboggan slide—but of exercise in the commonly accepted sense I knew little, and since that time my exercise has consisted chiefly in sedulously avoid-

ing all forms of exercise. I pose as no professor in the philosophy of exercises. I simply tell you my personal observations
and certain facts that have come to my attention. But it seems
to me that such observations and facts have quite as much
merit as the observations and records of those who choose to
pose as authorities. If I printed what I am saying, I'd expect
to receive letters from golf fiends, rubber-apparatus pullers,
men who touch the floor with the tips of their fingers fifty
times every morning and night, and other such self-doctorers
arguing that I was first cousin to the jackass for exposing such
a contention to the public gaze. But the facts as they have
presented themselves to me remain, and these facts cause me
to conclude that many of those who believe that exercise is
benefiting them are actually being benefited very little, and,
further, that they would in all probability be a whole lot better off if they hung their golf clubs over the mantelpiece as
mural decorations, converted their rubber-pullers into chewing gum and devoted the time they spend at present in touching the floor with their fingertips to reading *La Vie Parisienne*.
Such exercise as they currently indulge in may give them the
sense and feel of health, but I doubt that it gives them actual
health—at least, in the long run. When a man finishes eighteen
holes of golf, he may feel like a lion; but a man feels no less
like a lion, for that matter, when he has finished six cocktails.
Exercise imparts a superficial feeling of health, but keep it up
and in time it will give you biological delirium tremens.

While not in the inside confidence of the Deity, I seriously
doubt that God, when He put His children on earth, designed
the perpetuation of their health and well-being after the same
principle that He designed the perpetuation of the health and
well-being of chipmunks. There is an old phrase, "As healthy
as a barber." I have known many barbers in my life, but I
have yet to know one who ever played golf or tennis, was a
member of a baseball club, rode horseback, played polo,
basketball or any other kind of ball, ran cross-country, climbed
telegraph poles, or walked home from his work at nights.
There is probably no more sedentary occupation than that of
the tonsorial professor, and few occupations that are conducted where the air is so bad; yet the average barber, who,

even on his day off, takes no more exercise than is involved in riding on a Coney Island roller-coaster or in going to a movie show, is generally in an enviably fit physical condition.

Every man, of course, takes a certain amount of exercise unconsciously, and this, as I see it, is enough for him. Whether he believes in exercising or not, he still walks more or less, climbs stairs, lifts weights of one sort or another during his daily round, jumps on and off busses and street cars, pushes doors open and shut, waves his arm to friends across the street, and otherwise loosens up his muscles. The theory that this exercise is vastly more beneficial if he does it in a plus four suit, I can't grasp. But the majority of men think otherwise, which accounts for the prosperity of salesmen of oil stocks, divining rods, horoscopes, wall-papering lessons by mail, perpetual motion machines, genuine diamonds for $3.25, and other such sucker bait. The average man believes that exercise is valuable only if it is something that is described in one of Spalding's "Guides."

The time-honored saying that England's great battles have been won on the playing fields of Eton is a lot of hooey. England's great battles have been won out of the shops and factories of the cities, the same as the great battles of almost any other nation. For one English boy who could and can afford the athletics of Eton, there were and are a thousand who get no more exercise than an occasional holiday permits them to— and in these thousands lies England's military glory, as in other similar thousands lies the fighting glory of other nations. Athletics, to repeat, are for athletes. The great work of the world is not done by men with biceps as large as Smithfield hams or by proficient pole vaulters and water polo players, but by men who let their bodies quietly store up enough energy so that their minds may exercise themselves to their infinite content. Bismarck's chief exercise was eating. Anatole France said that his was sleeping. Van Cortlandt Park's tennis courts and golf links are full of curb brokers, shoe clerks, and automobile salesmen.

[From *Monks Are Monks*, 1929, pp. 177–82.]

ART AS A CORRUPTER OF MORALS

It has always been the mission of the theatre to reduce, insofar as it lay within its power, the manners and morals of the community. Obviously, I do not speak of the debased, uncivilized theatre, but of the theatre that is artistically on the highest and finest level. That for more than two thousand years men who have not gone to the trouble to understand the theatre have sponsored the opposite point of view and have seen in the playhouse a medium for the uplifting of the human psyche and table manners, indicates only that it has taken the twentieth of the centuries to arrive at astonishing discoveries in the world of high art other than the radio, colored moving pictures, and the Czech drama.

When I speak of the theatre as a corrupter of morals, it is of course as a synonym for drama. And when I speak of drama, I speak at the same time of most of the other arts, for the accomplishment, if perhaps not always the intention, of all art is the lowering of human virtue, in the commonly accepted sense of the word, and the conversion of men from metaphysical and emotional Methodism to metaphysical and emotional Paganism. To believe the contrary, to believe that great art is an inspirer of virtue, is to be so vealy as to believe that *Tristan* makes its auditor feel like St. Francis of Assissi, that Byron and Swinburne conjur up Sunday-school memories, that the Venus of Cnidus makes one think of entering a monastery, and that *Lysistrata* is the most eloquent argument for continence ever written. Only the fly-blown and ignorant, however, longer suffer any delusions about the purposes of art. Such fowl hit upon a few obvious kindergarten exceptions to the general and seek to build their case upon them. Unacquainted with nine-tenths of the world's best music, literature, painting, sculpture, poetry and drama, they imagine that all art has the same effect upon the human spirit as Chopin's E flat major nocturne or the slow movement of his B flat minor sonata—or Botticelli's "Madonna and Child" and *Romeo and Juliet*. Yet if art were what these fowl imagine, it would have died from the cosmos hundreds of years ago. It has been kept alive by man's unregenerate sinfulness alone. Its greatest patron saints, the men who with power and gold and favor have encouraged and assisted its craftsmen, have almost without exception been the more dissolute kings and emperors, lechers, millionaire crooks, fleshpot fanciers, and followers of Pan. And its greatest lovers and stoutest champions have ever been the men who most truly appreciated that behind its pretence of divine origin there curled a red and forked tail.

Art ennobles? Then tell me what, precisely, is the ennobling nature of—and how, precisely, one is made to feel *Corpsbruder* to the angels by—*Macbeth*, Rembrandt's portrait of his sister, *Madame Bovary* or Richard Strauss' *Salome*. The simple truth, of course, is that, aside from a purely critical gratification, *Macbeth* exalts the cultured and intelligent man just about as much as a modern Edinburgh bathtub, that the chief thought that enters his mind when he gazes upon the Rembrandt portrait is that it would be charming to give the old boy's sister a hug, and that Flaubert and Strauss induce in him much less an overwhelming desire to lead a better and nobler life than a worse and more lamentably agreeable one. Such a contention, plainly enough, will be set down as a mere showy bout with paradox, since it is ever the custom of otherwise estimable folk to laugh off as unsound paradox any perfectly sound but more or less novel argument whose surface has upon it regrettable, but unavoidable, ripples of smart-aleckry. Yet that the thesis is deeply imbedded in fact may readily be determined by examining the lives and history of professional dramatic critics, for example, since the first and greatest of the craft saw the light of day at Stagira. If dramatic art is capable of ennobling the spirit, it is reasonable to suppose that men most constantly in audience with it should be among the blessed of God and that the dramatic critic, accordingly, should soon or late find himself on a hyperphysical plane along with St. Peter, Emanuel Swedenborg and the Rev. Dr. S. Parkes Cadman. Yet it is well known that, with the exception of music critics, there has been and is no more spiritually disreputable body of men on earth than these very dramatic critics, beside whom an aisle full of Bobadils would be paragons of virtue. If the influence of classic art is so powerful in the direction of the uplift, why have not those who have come most directly under the spell shown some of the good effects? However, glance at the leading subjects of the influence and observe what happened to them! Scaliger, of the famous *Poetices Libri Septem,* was one of the foulest liars of his time (he lied about everything from his mythical noble patronage to his conquests among women), was charged with heresy, and found himself shunned by all the decent people of his day. Castelvetro, knowing that the authorities would get him for heresy, ran off like a frightened cur to Chiavenna and was later disgraced by excommunication. Sebillet, of the *Art Poetique,* was a scurvy political crook; Cervantes was a jailbird and in his later life was caught by the government in bizarre financial dealings and was kicked out of his job; Lope de Vega was banished from Spain for dirty libels, later raped the daughter of a Madrid government official and, entering a monastery in 1614, promptly brought obloquy upon the order by his various sexual peccadilloes; and Gabriel Tellez's chief amusement lay in the *Cigarreles de Toledo,* at some of which even Abe Lincoln would have blushed.

Coming to the Sir Philip Sidney of *A Defence of Poesie,* we find an unmitigated snob and one whose questionable adventures among the fair sex are well known. Ben Jonson was sent to jail on three different occasions and had the killing of a man to his credit. Scudéry was guilty of unremitting personal dishonesty; among other noble acts, he based his hostile attitude toward Corneille entirely upon personal reasons and went far beyond the truth in calling the latter a thief. Chapelain was so drunk that Richelieu had a hard time getting him to rewrite his report on *Le Cid* so that it made clear reading. Racine was lazy, lived on pensions and at one time in his life was actually little better than literary gigolo to Madame de Maintenon. Saint-Evremond had the manners of a cheap boor, lost an army commission because of the execrable taste of a joke he tried to play on his quondam friend Condé, and was later sent into exile. John Dryden was once taught a lesson in manners by being beaten up on the streets by the Ku Klux of his day; Milton treated his wife so badly that she left him a short time after their marriage, and he was subsequently clapped into the hoosegow as a public menace; Congreve, a gross fellow, was a victim of the gout from loose living and eventually went blind, according to report, from a lewd disease; and Farquhar got into a brawl with an actor and seriously wounded him, carried on loosely with Nance Oldfield, squandered his last shilling and died leaving his wife and two daughters to live on the charity of others.

Goldoni, to continue, was feared by the mothers of the Italian countryside to such a degree that, whenever news of his approach was had, they locked their daughters in the attic and kept them there until he had gone on his way. Samuel Johnson was twice lodged in the cooler as a dead beat, and Oliver Goldsmith ate with his knife and gambled incessantly. Lessing didn't pay the contributors to his review, *Litteraturbriefe,* and, during the writing of the criticisms which were subsequently to be known as the *Hamburgische Dramaturgie,* ran up such malt bills at the Hamburg *Bierstuben* that his credit was stopped on no less than four different occasions. Voltaire's record is familiar. He was thrice booted out of France, was lodged in the Bastille, wrote books that had to be suppressed by the authorities, violated confidences right and left, published private letters, was arrested in Frankfurt, and broke the laws of Geneva. Diderot once actually stole money from a priest, kept a woman who took all his funds and who almost broke up his married life, and found himself in jail at Vincennes in 1749. Beaumarchais was constantly involved in all sorts of law suits, in 1765 was almost killed by a husband upon whose wife he had clapped a wicked eye, was chased a mile by an indignant father whose daughter he had made certain overtures to, later was sent to the lock-up, lost his reputation completely after the famous Goezman trial, and then again found himself in a prison cell in 1795. Schiller was arrested for insult amounting to libel; Goethe carried on with the girls and lived with la Vulpius many years before leading her to the altar; Schlegel got into amorous difficulties and found himself in the divorce court; and Freytag was such a boozer that it took two men and a chambermaid to get him into bed at nights.

As for Victor Hugo, he was banished from France because of questionable political dealings, entered into double-dealing with both political parties upon his return after the upheaval of 1870, and was driven from the country again. Dumas *fils* was always in debt and led a dissolute life; Sarcey periodically grafted on the leading personages of the theatre of his time; Brunetière was an absinthe fiend; and Zola was twice sentenced to a year's imprisonment and the payment of a heavy fine. Coleridge took opium to forget the ugliness of the world and once went around getting money for subscriptions to a paper which failed and didn't pay it back. Hazlitt, after one round in the divorce courts, found that his second wife also couldn't stand him and his temper became so bad and his meanness so marked that he got into nasty quarrels with such of his best friends as Coleridge, Southey and Wordsworth. And, to come to a conclusion, Charles Lamb was actually driven crazy from application to the presumably exalting classics and, having got his sister Mary similarly to apply herself to them, also succeeded in driving the poor girl to a point of insanity where she lost all reason and killed her own mother. My own remaining infinitesimal share of manners and morals after something like twenty-five years spent under the influence of the art of drama keeps me from going into the question of the more modern critics, many of whom are still alive. I therefore simply wink meaningly, and bow myself politely out. As for music critics, I content myself with refering you to the police records.

If fine art has in it the power of spiritual exaltation, I should like to ask the greatest aesthetician living in the world today just what is the nature of the psychic uplift he gets from such things as Rembrandt's "Old Woman Cutting Her Fingernails," Boethus' sculptures of the boy choking a goose and a little girl playing with dice, Fielding's *Tom Jones* and Zola's *La Terre*, Brahms' variations on a theme by Haydn or Molière's *Le Bourgeois Gentilhomme*. The truth is that the inspirational value of art has become a proverb, a phrase for promiscuous mouthing, a something taken for granted, and has been brought to apply to all art when in reality it applies only to a negligible fraction of art, and that fraction not always of the highest level. It may be true that such eminently estimable, if become obvious, works as the *Ave Maria* instil in the heart of man a feeling that was not there before and that such others as the crucifix of Spirito, the "Coronation of the Virgin" and the Rheims Cathedral accomplish a like end, but for every *Ave Maria* one finds no difficulty in naming a half dozen equally eminently estimable compositions by the same Johannes that do nothing of the kind and that make one feel considerably less devout than thirsty. And if the crucifix of Michelangelo, or the painting of Raphael alluded to, or the ecclesiastical architecture of a forgotten genius of the Middle Ages induces in the spectator one kind of feeling, you may be sure that Michelangelo's great cartoon of the Battle of Cascina, or certain of Raphael's frescoes, or the secular architecture of a forgotten genius of an earlier age in the instance of the Porta Martis induces quite another and vastly more material kind.

It is, in short, not art in its fullest bloom that uplifts and ennobles mortal man, but only art of a relatively mediocre quality. *Oedipus Rex* by no stretch of honest imagination can conceivably have the slightest inspirational effect upon any even half-way intelligent emotionalism, yet *Old Heidelberg*, a comparatively tenth-rate piece of work, can. The so-called dramatic catharsis of *King Lear* isn't one-fifth so strong as that of even *Peter Pan*. "Das Wohltemperirte Klavier," from 1 to 48 inclusive, can't gild or stimulate the heart and fancy and make them better and braver than they were before, whereas "Der Alte Dessauer," "Madelon" or "Home Sweet Home" conceivably may. For what is the effect of truly great art? The effect of truly great art, I persuade myself to believe, is to induce in the beholder a sense of inferiority, a sense of the pettiness and futility of his own life, and, inducing these, to cause him to try to forget his triviality and despair in rash, imprudent and deplorable acts, manners and thoughts from which otherwise he would abstain. It stings him to the quick, challenges him, jeers at him. "Come on, worm!" it cries. "*Try* to look into Paradise!" The worm, humiliated but rambunctious, thereupon digs his toes into the ground, cocks back his head, strains the heavens with his eyes—and has his pocket picked.

[From *The House of Satan,* 1926, Chapter i.]

SELECTIONS FOR A GUITAR

Tempora Mutantur

THEY couldn't understand why he married her, but the ironic little gods who have such matters in hand knew it was because she had a little way of swallowing before speaking, because she had a little way, when she came to him and saw him standing there with arms open to clasp her tight and kiss her, of sweeping her hat off and sailing it across the room, because she had a way of twining her little finger in his.

They couldn't understand why he divorced her, but the ironic little gods who have such matters in hand knew it was because she had a little way of swallowing before speaking, because . . .

Sic Transit . . .

"EVERYONE likes me," said the man.

"That is Popularity," whispered the little star.

"Everyone likes me and envies me," said the man, a year later.

"That is Fame," whispered the little star.

"Everyone despises me," said the man, a year later still.

"That is Time," whispered the little star.

The Severer Sentence

HE had done a great wrong to a good woman, and the congress of the gods sat upon his punishment.

"Be it decreed by us," spoke the god at the far end of the table, "that he be compelled to walk, with the pace of a tortoise, through Hell."

"Be it decreed rather by us," spoke the god at the head of the table—and all the gods, hearing him, nodded grimly their approval—"that he be compelled to race, with the pace of a hare, through Paradise."

Rache

"I HATE my enemy with a hate as bitter as the hate he bears me, and I would do that to him that would for all time weaken both him and his power against me," muttered the man.

"That is easy," whispered Revenge in the man's ear. "Flatter him extravagantly for the qualities he knows he doesn't possess."

Temperament

THE RAGE of the artiste knew no bounds. That she should be thus annoyed just before her appearance in the great scene! She stamped about her dressing-room; she threw her arms heavenward; she brushed the vase of roses from her table; she slapped her maid for venturing at such a moment to speak to her; she sank exhausted into an armchair, a bottle of salts pressed to her nostril.

It was full fifteen minutes before she recovered.

Then she went out upon the stage and began her famous interpretation of the great scene in which she chloroforms the detective, breaks open the safe, shoots the policman who attempts to handcuff her, smashes the glass in the window with the piano stool and makes her getaway by sliding down the railing of the fire-escape.

Inspiration

A POET, searching for Inspiration, looked into the hearts of all the women he knew. But all the hearts of these were empty and he found it not. And then, presently, in the heart of one woman whom he had forgotten, at the edge of a deep forest, he found what he sought for. For the heart of this woman was full. And as he looked at this heart, it seemed to him strangely familiar, as if, long ago, he had seen it before. And as he looked, the truth dawned fair upon him. The heart was his own.

The Good Fairy

A FAIRY, in the form of a beautiful woman, came to a young man and whispered, "One wish will I grant you."

The young man gazed into the deep eyes of the beautiful woman and, with thoughts playing upon her rare loveliness, breathed, "I wish for perfect happiness for all time!"

And the fairy in the form of the beautiful woman granted him his wish.

She left him.

Reputation

THE famous comédienne, suffering a sudden cramp, made a face.

"How wonderfully she expresses the feeling of homesickness," observed the gentleman seated in E 10.

"How wonderfully she expresses the feeling of wanderlust," observed the gentleman seated in M 7.

The Judgment of Solomon

To his court spake Solomon: "I seek another woman for wife. But I have at length learned wisdom in these matters. So go you bring before me fifty or more you deem most suitable. And from these I shall select with deliberation and care and wisdom that one that will best be fitted for my throne-side and the bearing of children." And they went forth into the kingdom and brought before Solomon women who were strong and women who were wise and women who were gentle and women who were serious with the grave problems of life— the pick of the women of all the great kingdom who best were suited to the king. . . . Solomon, weighing studiously the merits of each and pondering the one whom he might most appropriately take unto him as best fitted for wife and mother, suddenly caught sight, on the far edge of the crowd, of a little flower girl with a cunning dimple in her ear. . . .

The Supernatural

"WHAT is my name?" asked August Kraut of the Ouija board, as his hands guided the apparatus hither and thither.

"August Kraut," responded the Ouija board.

Vade Mecum

AN infatuated young man sought counsel at the bazaar of an ancient and prayed the ancient tell him how he might learn of his fair lady's faults.

"Go forth among her women friends," spake the venerable one, "and praise her in their hearing."

Advice

"BEWARE," warned the Mind, solemnly.

The Heart, whistling a gay tune, cocked its hat upon one ear, gave a twist to its cravat, and kicked the old savant downstairs.

Veritas

THE KING was desirous of obtaining the most truthful man of his court for Lord of the domain's Exchequer. One by one the king had tested the aspirants and one by one had consigned each in his turn to the headsman; for they had all proved themselves liars. Three, and three only, remained.

Said the king to the first of these, "Have you ever in all your life written, or tried to write, a poem?"

"No, your majesty," replied the fellow.

Whereupon the king signaled promptly the headsman.

Said the king to the second of these, "Can you sit in a rocking-chair without rocking?"

"Yes, your majesty," replied the fellow.

Whereupon the king signaled promptly the headsman.

Said the king to the third of these, "Have you ever used a hair tonic of any kind?"

"No, your majesty, never!" replied the fellow.

Whereupon the king signaled promptly the headsman. And to this day the post of Lord of the Exchequer is vacant.

Fatalism

THE STOCKBROKER's wife, mother of six children and portly, was a fatalist. "Why worry?" she was wont to say. "When the time comes for me to die, it will come properly enough, and that's all there is to it."

That afternoon, she was run over by a brewery wagon while on her way to see a singing teacher about having her voice cultivated.

Technique

THE STAR actor, unable to restrain his mirth at the astounding satin décolleté worn by his leading woman in the scene where she, a street waif, pleads with him to give her a farthing that she and her widowed mother may not starve, turned his back to the audience. So uncontrollable were his chuckles that his shoulders heaved up and down, and his head shook, and his neck got red, and his eyes watered.

"A master of the acting technique," thought the audience. "How wonderfully he expresses the emotional outburst of grief!"

[From *A Book without a Title*, 1918, *passim*.]

SELECTIONS FROM
THE NEW AMERICAN CREDO

SOME years ago, in collaboration with Mencken, I undertook a modest contribution toward the understanding of the democratic penetralia mentis, incorporated into a slender volume entitled *The American Credo*. In it were listed 488 different articles in the philosophical faith of the American people, basic assumptions from which many of their higher rational processes took root. The foreword to the inventory presented the following injunction: "The superficial, no doubt, will mistake this little book for a somewhat laborious attempt at jocosity. Because, incidentally to its main purpose, it unveils occasional ideas of so inordinate an erroneousness that they verge upon the ludicrous, it will be set down as a piece of spoofing, and perhaps denounced as in bad taste. But all the while that main purpose will remain clear enough to the judicious. It is, in brief, the purpose of clarifying the current exchange of rhetorical gas-bombs upon the subject of American ideals and American character, so copious, so cocksure and withal so ill-informed and inconclusive, by putting into plain propositions some of the notions that lie at the heart of those ideals and enter into the very substance of that character. 'For as he thinketh in his heart,' said Solomon, 'so *is* he.' It is a saying, obviously, that one may easily fill with fantastic meanings, as the prevailing gabble of the mental healers, New Thoughters, efficiency engineers, professors of scientific salesmanship and other such mountebanks demonstrates, but nevertheless it is one grounded, at bottom, upon an indubitable fact. Deep down in every man there is a body of congenital attitudes, a corpus of ineradicable doctrines and ways of thinking, that determines his reactions to his ideational environment as surely as his physical activity is determined by the length of his *tibiae* and the capacity of his lungs. These primary attitudes, in fact, constitute the essential man. It is by recognition of them that one arrives at an accurate understanding of his place and function as a member of human society; it is by a shrewd reckoning and balancing of them, one against another, that one forecasts his probable behavior in the face of unaccustomed stimuli."

.   .   .   .

Pursuing this research into the beliefs that, in sum, constitute the doctrinal body of contemporary American philosophy, one continues to encounter convictions that will be put down by the unthinking as exaggerated and even ridiculous, and duly dismissed as such. That these convictions are, forsooth, actually what such persons will hold them to be is not to be gainsaid. But that, nevertheless, they represent the reaction of the American cerebrum to the phenomena of life is surely not to be denied by the observant student of the native scene. If the beliefs of the American people are grotesque, it is not for the statistician to criticize or protest; it is merely his business to set them down, that professors of the American mind may have at their elbows material for a more extensive, more profoundly analytical and more acutely penetrating interpretation of that mind, the most curious and remarkable, perhaps, ever heard of in Christendom.

Before engaging in the amplification of the catalogue, I take the liberty of quoting a few more words from the introduction to the original tome wherein the bare plotting of the field was undertaken:

"What the psychologist will find to admire in this work is not its learning and painstaking, its laborious erudition, but its compression. It establishes, we believe, a new and clearer method for a science long run to turgidity and flatulence. Perhaps it may even be said to set up an entirely new science, to wit, that of descriptive sociological science. We believe that this field will attract many men of inquiring mind hereafter and yield a valuable crop of important facts. The experimental method, intrinsically so sound and useful, has been much abused by orthodox psychologists; it inevitably leads them into a trackless maze of meaningless tables and diagrams; they keep their eyes so resolutely upon the intellectual processes that they pay no heed to the primary intellectual materials. Nevertheless, it must be obvious that the conclusions that a man comes to, the emotions that he harbors and the crazes that sway him, are of much less significance than the fundamental assumptions upon which they are all based."

Credos

THAT tight corsets used to be the cause of many female ailments and that since women abandoned the wearing of them their general well-being has increased 100 per cent.

That a great many fires are caused annually by mice playing with matches.

That all the difficult feats ascribed to movie stars in the films are really done by doubles.

That the Irish are enormous consumers of whiskey, and that the average Irishman can singlehanded drink five Frenchmen, seven Englishmen and ten Jews under the table and then polish off the evening with another quart.

That too many soft foods are ruining the teeth of the race.

That when a society woman has a baby she is a complete wreck for months afterward, but that a washerwoman can have one at eleven o'clock in the morning and with perfect comfort go to a movie the same afternoon.

That General Robert E. Lee was exceptionally meticulous in the matter of dress and never went into battle without putting a clean collar on.

That every man should, if possible, read a little law, as it will safeguard him against swindlers.

That mathematics, while of no great practical value, are excellent discipline for the mind and will make one a deeper thinker.

That if you hurt your finger and promptly hold it under the hot water faucet, the pain will immediately vanish.

That a child who is brought up in filth is always more robust and lives to a greater age than one who is hygienically cared for.

That there are hundreds of letters in the Dead Letter Office whose failure to arrive at their intended destinations was instrumental in separating as many lovers.

That a man's stability in the community and reliability in business may be measured by the number of children he has.

That a doctor knows so much about women that he can no longer fall in love with one of them.

That when a comedian, just before the rise of the curtain, is handed a telegram announcing the death of his mother or. only child, he goes on the stage and gives a more comic performance than ever.

That the old ladies on summer hotel verandas devote themselves entirely to the discussion of scandals.

That all one has to do to gather a large crowd in New York is to stand on the curb a few moments and gaze intently at the sky.

That if a man takes a cold bath regularly every morning of his life he will never be ill.

That every circus clown's heart is breaking for one reason or other.

That when cousins marry, their children are born blind, deformed, or imbecile.

That the accumulation of great wealth always brings with it great unhappiness.

That a cat falling from the twentieth story of the Singer Building will land upon the pavement below on its feet, uninjured and as frisky as ever.

That a very small proportion of beggars posing as blind are actually blind.

That women with red hair or wide nostrils are possessed of especially passionate natures.

That when one twin dies, the other twin becomes exceedingly melancholy and soon also dies.

That French women use great quantities of perfume in lieu of taking a bath.

That whiskey is good for snake-bite.

That swearing is forbidden by the Bible.

That German peasants are possessed of a profound knowledge of music.

That a man married to a woman larger than himself is always henpecked.

That a Sunday school superintendent is always carrying on an intrigue with one of the girls in the choir.

That a policeman can eat *gratis* as much fruit and as many peanuts off the street-corner stands as he wants.

That onion breath may be promptly removed by eating a little parsley.

That whenever a woman receives a gift, she immediately goes downtown and prices it.

That if one drops a crust of bread into one's glass of champagne, one can drink indefinitely without getting drunk.

That if a dog is fond of a man it is an infallible sign that the man is a good sort, and one to be trusted.

That a nurse, however ugly, always looks beautiful to the sick man.

That the average New Yorker, under his sophisticated and sinful exterior, is really an innocent, sentimental sucker.

That the more modest a young girl is, the more innocent she is.

That what a woman admires above everything else in a man is an upright character.

That the wife of a rich man always wistfully looks back into the past and wishes she had married a poor man.

That all criminals get caught sooner or later.

That crossword puzzles measurably increase one's store of knowledge, in addition to improving the mental faculties.

That the mistresses of monarchs in the old days always dictated the policies of the country.

That children were much better behaved twenty years ago than they are today.

That each year a man volunteers to take his children to the circus merely as a subterfuge to go himself.

That one feels very humble and insignificant when looking at the Grand Canyon.

That the chicken salad served in restaurants is always made of veal.

That all country girls have clear, fresh, rosy complexions.

That chorus girls spend the time during the entr'-actes sitting around naked in their dressing-rooms telling naughty stories.

That many soldiers' lives have been saved in battle by bullets lodging in Bibles which they have carried in their breast pockets.

That Jules Verne anticipated all the great modern inventions.

That a man of fifty-five is always more experienced than a man of thirty-five.

That all French women are very passionate, and will sacrifice everything to love.

That the late Elbert Hubbard's "Message to Garcia" was read by all the monarchs of Europe, and that it made a very deep impression upon them.

That a pretty stenographer is never as competent as a homely one.

That newspaper reporters hear, every day, a great many thumping scandals that they fail to print, and that they refrain through considerations of honor.

That, in a family crisis, the son always sticks to the mother and the daughter to the father.

That a girl who has made one misstep is sure to make another.

That a woman who has led a loose life is so grateful for the respect shown her by the man who asks her to marry him that she makes the best kind of wife.

That fish is a brain food.

That street-corner beggars have a great deal of money hidden away at home under the kitchen floor.

That all girls educated in convents turn out in later life to be hell-raisers.

That all celebrated professional humorists are in private life heavy and witless fellows.

That whenever a will case gets into the courts, the lawyers gobble all the money, and the heirs come out penniless.

That every female moving-picture star carries on an intrigue with her leading man, and will marry him as soon as he can get rid of his poor first wife, who took in washing in order to pay for his education in the art of acting.

That oysters are a great aphrodisiac.

That appendicitis is the result of swallowing grape seeds.

That the average French housewife can make such a soup out of the contents of a garbage-can that the eater will think he is at the Ritz.

That in New York one never knows one's nextdoor neighbor.

That if a boy is given all he wants to drink at home he will not drink when he is away from home.

That thin wrists and slender ankles are unmistakable signs of aristocratic breeding.

That all the young men from the Argentine have sleek black hair, are excellent tango dancers and earn a living as gigolos.

That consumptives are always perfectly confident that they will recover, and are extremely happy and cheerful up to the moment they die.

That a bachelor never has any one to sew the buttons on his clothes.

That an Italian street laborer can do a hard day's work on one large plate of spaghetti.

That old baseball players always take to booze, and so end their days either as panhandlers, as nightwatchmen or as janitors of Odd Fellows' halls.

That all Catholic priests are very hearty eaters, and have good wine cellars.

That politics in America would be improved by turning all the public offices over to businessmen.

That the chief duty of a fireman, when not engaged in answering alarms, is to sit next to a warm fire in the hose-house and play checkers.

That only about one out of every hundred American citizens has any idea of the real issues of the campaign when he votes on election day.

That one can infallibly tell a cigar is a good one if the ashes remain on the end and don't fall off.

That millionaires who collect rare first editions never know anything about literature, merely buy them to embellish their libraries, and actually read nothing but *The Saturday Evening Post* and the *Detective Story Magazine*.

That an elephant in a circus never forgets a person who gives him a chew of tobacco or a rotten peanut, but will single him out from a crowd years afterward and bash in his head with one colossal blow.

That all actors sleep till noon, and spend the afternoon calling on women.

That one can never understand the names of stations or streets when they are called out by railroad or street-car conductors.

That if a woman gives a man a letter to mail, it will remain in his pocket for a week.

That being in love with a beautiful woman is a great inspiration to an artist.

That if a sailor dies on board a ship, a shark becomes promptly cognizant of the fact and proceeds to follow the ship all the way across the ocean.

That a sharp man may for ten cents often pick up in a second-hand bookstore a book that is worth a hundred dollars.

That when a man brings home flowers or a box of candy to his wife he has been guilty of something naughty.

That a widow is invariably expert in the arts of amour.

That home cooking is far more appetizing than that in the best restaurant.

That neither of the parties to a stage kiss derives any enjoyment from it.

That no one ever gets a full night's sleep in a sleeping-car.

That opportunity comes at least once to every man.

That all artists are impractical.

That people who live in New York never have a moment to themselves.

That a bachelor is a very untidy fellow, and that the floors of his living quarters are always a mess of soiled linen and cigarette butts.

That it is impossible to raise children properly in a large city.

That if you cut a worm into three or four pieces, each piece will presently sprout a new head and there will be three or four worms where before there was only one.

That seagulls fly around and around, never alighting until they drop dead from exhaustion.

That women who are able to afford servants wear kimonos during the greater part of the day and read the best sellers.

That the woman writer in an evening newspaper who gives advice to the lovelorn is invariably a man with a flowing beard.

That if a demi-rep really falls in love with a man she is always faithful to him to the bitter end.

That all policemen have unduly large feet.

That old ladies enjoy attending a funeral and that they always obtain front-row seats.

That people of Oriental blood always have very wily natures and that they glide about without making a sound.

That middle-aged widows are very fond of college boys.

That when people who are unaccustomed to money inherit a fortune their existence is likely to become very miserable.

That cows have very sad eyes.

That when a hard-boiled guy gets married he usually becomes so respectable that it hurts.

That Darwin said the human race was descended from monkeys.

That all star intercollegiate sprinters die of enlargement of the heart.

That professors are absent-minded, that they often come to their classes minus collar or tie, and that they sometimes walk into other people's homes by mistake while engrossed in deep thought.

That Edgar Allan Poe wrote all his stuff while sobering up after sprees, and that he was always drunk except when he took morphine.

That when women are together they tell stories just as smutty as the ones men tell.

That a girl who marries a man to reform him never succeeds.

That American men have more respect for women than the men of any other country.

That women who loll about the beaches in stunning bathing costumes never go near the water.

That a man who is sitting in front of one will turn around if one concentrates one's attention on the back of his head.

That baggage-men always take great delight in smashing trunks.

That people who sit in the gallery at a play are more discriminating than those in the orchestra.

That French actresses never hesitate to appear on the stage perfectly nude.

That many women who live in fashionable apartment houses have liaisons with the elevator boys.

That boys born in the neighborhood of a gas-house always grow up to be very tough mugs.

That summer romances are forgotten with the first frost.

That a married man never enjoys kissing his wife.

That when a girl who has been raised in poor circumstances marries, she demands a lot of expensive jewelry, four automobiles, three country houses, and a large staff of servants; but that when a girl who is accustomed to every luxury marries, she is perfectly willing to sew, cook, wash, take care of the baby, and darn her husband's socks.

That a criminal always returns to the scene of his crime, and usually in the dead of night.

That you can judge a man by what newspaper he reads.

That a few minutes before an atheist dies he usually changes his mind and becomes deeply religious, and that if he fails to do so he dies in great agony.

That people in the theatrical profession never take marriage seriously.

That eggs contribute to the vitality of great lovers.

That water drunk from the washstand faucet is not as pure as water drunk from the kitchen faucet.

That the life of a young man who marries an old woman for her money is always a very miserable and unhappy one.

That if all the money in the world were to be divided, within a year the same men would have it again.

That the Pennsylvania Dutch are all very rich, but that they never take a bath.

That persons with exceedingly high foreheads are always possessed of remarkable intelligence.

That it is almost impossible to find a person living in New York who was born there.

That when a bride and groom arrive at an hotel resort they never are able to disguise the fact that they have just been married.

That there is no future for a man who works in a bank.

That people who offer one a firm handclasp are very upright and honest.

That a beautiful woman never has any brains.

That if one were to read the dictionary ten minutes each day one would become very learned.

That a man who falls in love with a married woman is rotten to the core and is capable of any crime from murder to petty larceny.

That a great many society women use very profane language.

That a person who has little to say is very wise and a profound thinker.

That at a wedding nobody ever pays any attention to the bridegroom.

That no he-man ever uses talcum powder.

That a bride always looks very pretty.

That people who go to church a great deal are either fanatics or hypocrites.

That a young man must engage in a certain amount of deviltry before he settles down.

That it is easier to teach a mongrel dog tricks than a thoroughbred.

That a railroad conductor's watch is never one second out of the way.

That Benjamin Franklin discovered electricity.

That on his deathbed Robert G. Ingersoll repented and accepted Christ.

That everybody who signed the Declaration of Independence was a great man.

That hasty marriages are bound to end disastrously.

That it makes no difference when one drops tobacco ashes on the carpet, because the ashes help to preserve it.

That when one of the houris in a Turkish seraglio misbehaves, she is immediately sewn up in a sack and dropped through a trap-door into a subterranean river.

That nowhere is such hospitality found as south of the Mason and Dixon line.

That when people read a patent medicine pamphlet they immediately become convinced that they are suffering from all the ailments described therein.

That only a millionaire can afford to play polo.

That popular song writers always steal their melodies from well-known operas.

That men go in for college teaching because they couldn't get into anything else.

That de Maupassant wrote only smutty stories.

That the Empress Catherine of Russia fornicated continuously, and that every morning she would cause her regiment to line up outside the palace that she might survey the men and pick out the likeliest candidate for the night's pleasure.

That you can tell whether beer is good by the amount of foam at the top of the glass.

That nowhere in the world can one hear waltzes played as well as in Vienna.

That three-quarters of the men living in Wales are coal-miners.

That all the witty things about women have already been said by Frenchmen.

That many love affairs have been engendered by a mutual admiration for Robert Browning's poetry.

That Thomas A. Edison invented moving pictures.

That a pig eats all day long and never pauses so much as a moment for a breathing spell.

That a baby that laughs all the time will have a sunny disposition when it grows up.

That Irish descent insures the inheritance of a rich sense of humor and bright conversational gifts.

That it is very much easier to write a good play than a good novel.

That no one can sleep well when lying for the first time in a strange bed.

That John Paul Jones was an American.

That all auctions are fakes, and that the auctioneer always has a confederate in the audience to bid up prices.

That Buffalo Bill was an unerring marksman and a dead shot.

That nowhere in America can you get such mince pies as they make in New England.

That a doctor is not happy with a simple case, but is interested only when confronted by one of great complexity.

That boys at a western university are in the aggregate healthier than those at an eastern.

That if a bull spots a man with a red necktie on, it will go after him post haste, whereas a man with a blue or green one on will leave the bull cold.

That if you drink three glasses of water every day you will never have rheumatism or get kidney trouble.

[From *The New American Credo,* 1927.]

ESSAYS IN AUTOBIOGRAPHY

Souvenirs of Mencken, et al.

PAUL ARMSTRONG called Mencken and me on the telephone early one Sunday morning in a state of great excitement. "I have found something wonderful in the way of writing," he shouted over the phone, "and you two ought to hear of it!" We inquired sleepily what it was, but he wouldn't tell us, preferring, he insisted, to apprise us of his great discovery in person. Well, we said, we would be in our editorial offices around two o'clock (we often worked on Sundays) and to come around then. At two sharp, the door burst open and Armstrong rushed in. "Here," he yelled, "is the goddamnedest most beautiful stuff I've ever read! I got hold of it only yesterday and I tell you it's remarkable. You've got to read it right away and see for yourselves!"

Whereupon he thrust at us the Bible.

✿   ✿   ✿

Hugo Schemke is his name. He has been a table waiter at Lüchow's celebrated spa in East Fourteenth Street, New York, since the place opened in 1880 and during that time has been the favorite servitor of the elect in arts and letters who have waded in its foods and bathed in its exhilarating waters. One of his most devoted sitters was James Gibbons Huneker, that critic *par excellence*. It was Huneker who first introduced Mencken and myself in our younger days to Hugo, and it has been Hugo since Jim's passing who has regaled us with biographical data about him. Hugo admired the gay old boy as much as we did, and what fascinated, even awed, him was Jim's successful way with the ladies.

"Do you know," Hugo once leaned over the *bratwurst mit*

sardellen klops confidingly to whisper to us, "that some of those famous Metropolitan Opera House singers were so awful jealous of him they would come down and press their grease-painted noses so hard against the windows to spy what other singer he was maybe lunching with that Otto, the window-washer, had to scrub off the panes with sandpaper?"

❈   ❈   ❈

Of the literati with bibbing talents, Frank Harris was not the least. One of his favorite tipples, peculiarly enough, was the Orange Blossom cocktail, a concoction of gin and orange juice more suited to the feminine palate than to a toughly experienced one like his. When we used to convene with him of late afternoons at the old Holland House bar, he took pleasure in downing at least a dozen or more of the things at a single sitting and the only reaction noticeable in him was an increased flow of conversation, at which he was a master.

Few men I have met in my lifetime were as fascinating as he when his tongue started wagging. "Wilde's wit," he would observe, "was the wit of calculation and excellent acting. He could manage an impromptu air though one well appreciated that not only had he carefully prepared his rejoinders beforehand but had rehearsed their timing and delivery." Or, "Shaw's skill lies in persuading one with his personality before trying to persuade one with his words." Or again, "I am, really, a great writer; my only difficulty is in finding great readers."

These are merely some random samples that stick in my memory. Harris' conversations were cataracts that splashed one in all directions. It was nigh impossible to put in a word edgewise, for two good reasons. In the first place, he would talk so rapidly and steadily that, had one wished to put it in, one would first have had to hit him over the head with some blunt instrument. And in the second place, he was altogether too interesting for anyone to wish to interrupt him.

❈   ❈   ❈

Jack Barrymore, or John as he more dignifiedly called himself when he abandoned musical comedy for the drama, took an instant dislike to me when I met him for the first time at a small supper party given for Mencken and myself some thirty years ago by Zoë Akins, an old friend of ours, in her atelier on lower Fifth Avenue. He said nothing, but contented himself with fixing his bulging left eye on me and looking at me with an expression which was a mixture of that of a philatelist studying a counterfeit Peruvian stamp through a microscope and that of a small boy unbelievably beholding his first giraffe. Why he disrelished me, I had no idea, other than the distaste of the Barrymore family since the days of Papa Maurice for dramatic critics *in toto*. Maurice, incidentally, will be remembered for his remark to one of the species whom he encountered in the men's room of the old Hoffman House in the process of straining himself desperately to negotiate a normally simple act of nature. "Ah," drawled Maurice, "the strictures of the press!"

I didn't again encounter Jack, or John as he then was, until twenty years later, when I had a supper engagement at the Monte Carlo and was waiting for the appearance of my fair guest. Barrymore, as drunk as a lord, staggered through the door and spotted me, "George," he mumbled, wrapping an arm affectionately around my neck, "you're just the one I've been wanting to run into!" Whereupon he proposed that, while we were both waiting for our engagement to show up, I buy him a drink, and shakily deposited both his person and mine at one of the bar tables. "Yes, Georgie," he belched, "you're the one I've wanted to see, 'cause I got something to tell you." And then, propping himself against the table as best he could and steadying himself against one of the noblest jags of modern times, he outlined to me, between hiccups, his new conception of the rôle of Macbeth, and a brilliantly intelligent one it was.

* * *

W. C. Fields was another clown whom we both venerated to the extent of one day inviting him to join us in a five o'clock drink. "It will be an amusing session," Mencken forecast. "He surely is a funny fellow and we will get some elegant laughs." Fields duly appeared at the appointed moment. In his pockets were all of Ibsen's published plays. And during the entire two hours we sat together he held forth very solemnly on the dramatist who, it seemed, was his particular enthusiasm.

* * *

Lord Dunsany had been a valued contributor to *The Smart Set* and, when he came to this country on his maiden visit, Mencken and I started out to entertain him a bit. At our first personal meeting with him, we asked him at luncheon what he would like to start off with. "I have heard much about your American oysters and would relish trying them," he replied. The waiter brought him the customary half-dozen. "Oh, no, I should like to begin with two dozen," he corrected the waiter. When the two dozen were served, Dunsany waved aside the proferred salt shaker, demanded the sugar bowl, doused the bivalves with its entire contents, and one by one gobbled them. A broad smile enveloped his features. "Excellent!" he proclaimed. "But I would not be so sure of them without the sugar."

* * *

When he was preparing for production the revue, *The Seven Lively Arts,* Billy Rose got into touch with me about one of the sketches, the work of Moss Hart, which dealt with me in what he thought was a Torquemada manner, detailed it to me, and allowed in a friendly and gracious spirit that, if I wished, he would see to it that it was toned down. I told him that the sketch seemed to me, on the contrary, to be much too mild and offered him several suggestions as to how to make it much tougher. For some reason, he didn't accept them and the sketch was unfortunately played as Hart had written it, to the disappointment of many in the audience, who appeared to agree with me that it was altogether too gentle.

* * *

Cedric Hardwicke, himself an actor and a good one, is one of the best critics of acting I have encountered. Speaking of the difficulty of a mature actress' playing a young girl rôle, he explains, "And small wonder. A mature actress who plays such a rôle must first strip herself completely of everything she has built herself up to be and must start anew. The struggle

is one between herself as she is and technical skill that camou-
flages it. Most adult actresses who try to play young girl rôles
fail to be convincing because they are concerned with the
looks and voice of the rôle alone and not with the all-important
essential spirit."

✿   ✿   ✿

The self-confidence of amateurs is the envy of professionals.

✿   ✿   ✿

On my visit to Hollywood, mentioned in an earlier installment
of these memoirs, I was introduced to the movie director,
David Butler, a genial soul who seemed to be more than normally pleased to meet me. Noticing my amazement, he explained his interest. "You are," he said, "the only critic in
the last half-century who has ever mentioned my mother's
name." Observing my continued puzzlement, he went on to
say that his mother was one of the few women on the American stage who had ever played Hamlet.

[From the *American Mercury*, December 1950, pp. 739–43.]

Stray Notes

ONE of the most vituperative letters that has ever come my
way was from my former old and good friend, St. John Ervine.
In reviewing his play, *Boyd's Shop*, his most inferior and luck-
less dramatic effort, I allowed—generously, I thought—that it
had probably been a left-handed effort and with the box-office
perhaps in his usually independent mind. Evidently, if puz-
zlingly, convinced that the play was everything it plainly was
not, he took such offense at what I meant to be a charitable
view of it that in all these long, intervening years he has never
again spoken to me.

✿   ✿   ✿

Eugene O'Neill, attempting to cast his play, *A Moon for the
Misbegotten,* found himself stumped in the instance of its heroine: an inexperienced girl of the soil in her twenties, tall and

of powerful physique, but withal of an inner gentleness and maternal warmth. He asked me if I knew of any young actress who could possibly play the rôle and I mentioned one, an unknown, whom I had seen in a summer stock performance of, oddly enough, *Little Women*. He tried her out in the difficult part but found that she lacked the acting experience for it, as he had also found in the cases of several other girls who had been recommended by others. "What I'll evidently have to do if the play is produced in the future," he concluded, "is to abandon the hope of discovering a young girl for the rôle and cast it with a mature actress of, say, forty or more and have her play it down in the age scale. The rôle of a young girl who is supposed to be lacking in worldly experience takes a woman of considerable worldly experience to make the lack seem convincing." But the search for even such an actress was fruitless, and the play remains still in abeyance.

✻　✻　✻

Some years ago I was fetched by the idea of dramatizing in Shakespeare's own terms the story of Romeo and Juliet had they lived. To this end I employed and orchestrated the early portions of *Romeo and Juliet*, the middle portion of *Othello*, and the last portion of *The Taming of the Shrew*, and cast the result naturally into three acts.

Each and every word and line was Shakespeare's; I added not a syllable of my own. The play was published under the title, *The Avon Flows*, and was duly reviewed in the public prints by the late Charles Hanson Towne. "Though I have known him for many years," Towne wrote, "I never suspected and was overwhelmed to find that Nathan is the possessor of rich poetic gifts; many of his passages would do credit to the Bard himself." There were some other passages of Shakespeare, however, that Towne lamented as being unworthy of me and my remarkable talent.

✻　✻　✻

In my early days as a writer, I was at one time bothered by the circumstance that my work was being published in an inferior magazine of relatively small circulation. "Don't fret,"

Finley Peter Dunne counselled me. "If your stuff is any good, the right people are sure to see it." It was one of the two best pieces of advice I have ever received. What the other was, I don't remember.

* * *

I once wrote a lengthy review of one of Augustus Thomas' philosophical dramas in which I demonstrated through direct quotation of the plot and dialogue that it would make much more sense and be a more intelligent play if it were played backwards. Thomas never forgave me.

* * *

George C. Tyler, the well-known producer of another day, once got in touch with me on my return from an annual trip to Europe and asked me if I had seen any play that had made a considerable impression on me, since he was at a loss for a good script and was eager to get busy at once with a new production. I heartily commended to him George Birmingham's satirical comedy, *General John Regan,* which I had seen in London and which had had me laughing for fully two hours. He got hold of the play, liked it as much as I did, and lost no time in putting it on in New York. Most of the newspaper reviews were poor and the play lost money. Some years later, he again sought me out for a suggestion, since again he could not find anything that tickled his fancy. "Then why not put on *General John Regan* again?" I asked him. Admiring the play as he did, he replied, "An excellent idea. I'll do it!" He promptly went about preparing a second production and presently opened it on the road. Again the reviews were unfavorable and the play failed and lost even more money. "Well, anyway," he said to me, "*we* like it." There was a period later in his life, indeed, when only lack of funds prevented him from producing the play for a third time.

* * *

The French have never been particularly noted for their indifference to American dollars and have always exercised themselves craftily to please the tourist into parting with them.

In the attempt to demonstrate their warm friendship for him, they resort to many ingratiating devices. The most peculiar of these came to my notice one night many years ago when I attended a revue in one of the Left Bank music halls. The finale brought on the customary quota of nude women who, after parading down to the footlights, turned around and affectionately disclosed the American flag surmounted by a likeness of President Calvin Coolidge painted on their behinds.

❀   ❀   ❀

Quite a few of my friends among the novelists at one time or another in their lives have essayed the dramatic form and have asked me to read and criticize their efforts. I may say proudly that, though I agreed to oblige them, not one has paid the slightest attention to any suggestions I may have imparted and all save one did not volunteer any thanks for my trouble. The one exception was F. Scott Fitzgerald, who had written his sole attempt at drama, *The Vegetable,* and who, as a token of his gratitude for my reading the script, presented me with the gift of a linen handkerchief, neatly lodged in tissue paper. When finally I got around to wearing it in an outer coat pocket, I noticed that several people were eyeing it with a puzzled expression. I discovered that it was one of Fitzgerald's initialed, used own which, though unwashed, had been scrupulously pressed into the semblance of a new one.

Looking over and discussing with Sinclair Lewis an act of a play he was in the process of writing, I intimated that it was much too talky and that a deal of the dialogue might be profitably eliminated in favor of more suggestive stage business and action. One whole long love passage, I pointed out, could well be reduced to a single look that the heroine would bestow on the hero. He put me in my place with the tart remark, "No dice! I like to hear people talk a lot."

❀   ❀   ❀

I met Eugene Brieux just once. Though he was then riding high as a playwright and had received Shaw's accolade, he was living in cramped quarters over a butcher's shop in a shabby section of Paris. I went to see him to discuss several short play scripts for the magazine I was then associated with editorially. During the whole two hours I visited with him, he never ceased talking for so much as one minute about a single subject: money.

*　　*　　*

When I returned from a five days' visit in Hollywood and recorded my opinions on the place, I was taken to task by some of its inmates for venturing the views after so brief a stay. "No one," they protested, "can possibly judge Hollywood in so short a time." While I was too considerate to offer the reply that anyone with any experience in observation should be able to appraise Hollywood in even less time than he would require to appraise a conflagration, flood, or any other such calamity, I speculated openly on just what it was that afflicted the denizens of the area. Hollywood itself, I found, was essentially a string of sideshows, some of them amusing, without, however, anything resembling an authentic circus, save only the sawdust and the smell. And its inmates, I determined, were for the most part men and women who, in their belief that they were God-given geniuses, seemed to be suffering nevertheless and paradoxically from a perverted atheism. They were, it seemed to me, arrogantly hiding behind their self-doubts. Their goals, once achieved, were privately seen by them to be nothing, wrapped in tinsel which lost its sheen in short order. They had money, but it was as counterfeit to them compared to money honorably earned in pursuit of any real art. They were, all of them except the youngest and more foolish, homesick for a home they knew they did not have.

*　　*　　*

Little is more offensive to a practicing critic than the feigned goodwill of persons whose work he has expressed contempt for. I have in my lifetime experienced several such hypocrites and on each occasion when they have offered me their pseudo-generous geniality they have made me sick at the stomach, though an equally hypocritical gentlemanliness has kept me from showing it in their presence.

*　　*　　*

I have seldom written a line I did not believe and, on the exceptional occasions when I have not believed one, I have found that I believed it after I had written it.

*   *   *

The biggest theatrical swindle I have encountered in my more than forty years of professional theatregoing was something named *The London Follies*, produced in Weber's Theatre in New York in the early years of the present century. The advance advertising heralded it as "England's wittiest revue with the original London cast"; the prices for opening night seats were raised for the event; and a representative and eager audience was on hand when the curtain went up only to reveal a bare stage with a secondhand piano on it around which stood eight seedy looking males and females (the entire company) who for the next hour alternately sang stale songs off key and cracked jokes of an even more ancient vintage. The disgusted audience began to file out of the theatre after the first half hour and not more than twenty people were in the house when the second half of the thing got under way. The atrocity closed down instanter.

*   *   *

As a young man, I wondered why the celebrated English critic, Arthur Bingham Walkley, whom I greatly respected and admired, seemed to like me, or at least was most hospitable to me while I was in England. Vain as I was, I concluded that it must be because of my critical writings which perhaps had made an impression on him. Unable longer to suppress my curiosity, I one day, while lunching with him in his pleasant cottage at Brightlingsea, edged cautiously toward a solution. "You are the only American," he explained to my crestfallen self, "I have met in some time whose voice hasn't been such as to knock most of the dishes off the table."

[From the *American Mercury*, November 1950, pp. 546–51.]

ON MONTHLY MAGAZINES

A MONTHLY magazine has been defined as something halfway
between a newspaper and a book. The only kind of such magazine that interests me editorially, however, is one which tends
to be nine-tenths book to but one-tenth newspaper. The daily
journalistic point of view which afflicts even some of the better monthly periodicals has been responsible for lowering their
one-time position in the cultural world. That position now is
getting closer and closer to zero. The curse of timeliness has
laid its heavy hand on magazine editing, with the result that
a magazine which in an earlier era could be read with satisfaction some months after its publication date presently becomes flat and stale a few days after it appears, and frequently
because of the printing lag even before it reaches the stands.

This is no argument in favor of arty magazines, which are
even worse than those edited by amateurs of politics, dolts
who are flattered at being invited to tea at the White House,
suburban cosmopolites, sponsors of sewer-digests with ambitions to literary genius, and other such recherché intellects.
Nor is it an argument for any ivory tower attitude. It is simply
a single editor's belief that a magazine worth its salt should
forego the common editorial preoccupation with journalistic
immediacy and devote itself instead to those materials of art
and life that are not necessarily bound strictly by the clock
and that deepen, whether seriously or lightly, a reader's understanding of his surroundings, of himself, and of his fellows.

To view the world of life and art with intelligence and
humor, to avoid indignation and platitude, and to keep upper-
most in mind good writing—that, as I see it, should be an
editor's credo. No pomposity, no itch for cure-alls, no cheap
sensationalism, no posturing in the interests of self-glorifica-
tion. Entertainment yes, and by all means, but entertainment
founded on the nimbleness of sharp brains, on original

thought, and on that wit which is distilled from experience and knowledge. A magazine has to make money to survive? Surely. But such a magazine, as has been proved, can and does make money. Not, of course, the fantastic amount made by some of the popular trash buckets, yet enough to suffice its and its editor's and publisher's appetites.

[Mr. Nathan wrote this specially for the present volume.]

RANDOM CONCLUSIONS

America

WHAT America needs are fewer rostrums and more picnic grounds. A nation that eats its sandwiches sitting on the grass is pretty generally a peaceful and contented one.

[From *Monks Are Monks,* 1929, pp. 253–4.]

Birth and Death

THE CEREMONIES presently attending birth and death strike me as being confused one with the other and, being thus confused and hence illogical, at odds with sound Christian doctrine. The birth of a human being, under the current ethical dispensation, is accompanied by a species of behavioristic jazz and the death of a human being by a behavioristic dirge. When a child is born the father celebrates the event by turning on Ben Bernie on the phonograph, dancing the hornpipe, and getting himself expansively stewed. When it dies, whether in infancy or in maturity, the father puts on crêpe, throws the whiskey bottle into the ash-can and delivers himself of mournful knells and hymns. Among all Christian people, only the Irish, knowing the Scriptures better, exercise a true discrimination in such junctures. When an Irish baby is born into this vale of tears, the ceremony is appropriate to the occasion. The father is sad; he drowns his unhappiness in drink; he fights with the neighbors. But when an Irishman dies and goes, as per Holy Writ, to bliss eternal, his relatives, mindful of Holy Writ, celebrate the enviable excursion of their loved one by holding a wake at which everyone for miles around has one hell of a good time. This, I have the honor to argue, is as things should be! To be gay in the presence of birth and sad in the presence of death is to be an infidel, a denier of the Bible's threats and promises, an ignoble disbeliever. The true Christian, mindful that birth is but for the moment and of pain and travail in its brief day on earth compact, should greet it befittingly with melancholy, and death, the beginning of close communion with God and everlasting peace, with appropriate high spirits. Let the band play the Funeral March when the doctor joyfully announces, "It's a boy," and "The Varsity Drag" or "Shaking the Blues Away" when, some years later, he lugubriously says, "It was gallstones."

[From *Monks Are Monks,* pp. 104–5.]

The Eye

PURSUING my series of suggestions to the Creator by way of aiding Him to make a more satisfactory job of things, I take the liberty of bringing to His attention the matter of the human eye. In the initial fabrication of this organ, it seems to me that he overlooked an important point and in the overlooking, contributed further to the unhappiness of His creatures. It is the current misfortune of mortals that their eyes remain relatively young while their bodies grow old. That is, in a psychological, not a biological, sense. The eye of a man of fifty remains youthful in its appraisal of feminine charms, plays the constant Iago to his corporeal self, and so tortures him. The eye of a woman of forty remains similarly girlish in its view of the boys, plays in turn constantly the derisory critic to her own waning charms, and so tortures *her.* Something should be done about it to bring peace and contentment to the hapless children of earth. I shall exert my influence with a negligent Almighty the day I arrive in Heaven.

[From *Monks Are Monks,* 1929, pp. 79–80.]

Humor

THE TRUTH in an intoxicated condition.

[From *The Theatre, the Drama, the Girls,* 1921, p. 132.]

Music in America

JUST as the American knows nothing of love, so does he know nothing of music—of the heart and soul of music, that is. The European regards music as a pleasure, as a joy; the American looks upon it as a course in education. Go to a symphony concert in Europe and you'll see the house listening; go to one here and you'll see half the house making notes and the other half waiting to explain something or other in the composition to its companion in the next seat. The American, as Stokowski said, always wants to know what music is about, as if it were something by Einstein; he wants to understand it, as the phrase goes. He doesn't appreciate that music is simply to be felt and loved. The one way to get Americans gradually and in time to accept music for just what it is is to abolish all the nosey music critics. There are only two music critics in all of Europe, from the Channel to the Mediterranean, who try to explain music and no one wisely reads them, that is, no one but book publishers, writers of novels who wish to cabbage esoteric allusions from them by way of posturing an intimate knowledge of music, and some old fogies of both sexes who have got beyond getting any emotional reaction out of music and, like men who have fought in the long ago in brilliant and adventurous battles, now nurse their rheumatism and speculate as to what the war was about. In England, there is a music critic and a good one, Ernest Newman. He is very widely read there. That is doubtless why Englishmen love music so little.

[From *Monks Are Monks*, 1929, pp. 162–3.]

Statues

SERIOUSNESS is so often false and absurd. Take the matter of statues, for examples. The trouble with the omnipresent statues to the great is that they invariably present their subjects in an arbitrarily serious and heavily solemn mood. One is thus as much like another as two peas. Surely there is room for a statue or two that will reveal its subject in a different humor. Let us have a Lincoln who looks less like a professional undertaker and more like the eye-twinkling Lincoln that he occasionally was. Let us have the Napoleon of balmy Malmaison evenings instead of the inevitable Napoleon of chill Elba. Why not the Wagner of the farcical "Der Berggeist" instead of the stereotyped Wagner of "An Weber's Grabe"? Let us have at least one George Washington winking at an imaginary pretty girl, at least one General Grant slightly inebriated, at least one Grover Cleveland with a fishing pole. If biography is becoming increasingly forthright and honest, why shouldn't sculpture to a degree follow suit? Let us have more authentically human statues and not this endless succession of frost-bitten marbles and bronzes.

[From *Monks Are Monks*, 1929, pp. 164–5.]

Capital Punishment

THE ARGUMENT most often advanced for the abolition of capital punishment is that it has not successfully deterred and doesn't deter persons from committing murder. One might with equal logic therefore argue for the abolition of all forms of punishment in that none so far devised has succeeded in deterring persons from committing theft, perjury, arson, assault, bigamy, hold-ups, rape, or anything else.

[From *Monks Are Monks*, 1929, pp. 119–20.]

The Manners of Our Presidents

JOHN ADAMS, disgruntled over his failure to be reëlected, refused to attend the inauguration of his successor and further flung an insult at the latter by noisily leaving the scene of the inauguration a few hours before the ceremony. Andrew Johnson, similarly bitter over his failure to be renominated, snubbed his successor by publicly declining to ride with him to his inaugural celebration. James Madison, miffed by his charming wife's admirers, periodically took to making *sotto voce* cracks about them behind their backs in his drawing-room and would on occasion get so sore over an unduly prolonged hand-kiss that he would bustle querulously out of the room. James Monroe used toothpicks in the presence of his guests, and Andrew Jackson relished smelly cheeses so greatly —he served them regularly at his White House dinners—that the ladies sitting near him at table had to use extra-large fans. John Quincy Adams perspired copiously and, after wiping the beads from his face, would dangle his wet handkerchief to and fro, spreading moisture over everybody about him. Martin Van Buren invariably drank coffee out of the saucer and was restrained from doing so when important visitors were enjoying his hospitality only by the preliminary entreaties of his son's wife, who was mistress of the White House during most of his term. William Henry Harrison, who died of pneumonia, was subject to heavy colds and was a prodigious and fortissimo noseblower. John Tyler was a victim of liver trouble and had a habit of discussing his more intimate symptoms with the ladies. James K. Polk, in turn, suffered from a certain complaint peculiar to most babies, which led him, unfortunately, into predicaments embarrassing to his White House guests. It was to this fact that observers of the period attributed his considerate wife's abolition of dancing at White House receptions.

Zachary Taylor was a victim of chronic indigestion, from which he eventually died, and was a Gargantuan belcher. Millard Fillmore, his successor to the throne, would frequently doze off and snore gently in the presence of his guests and had to be covertly poked in the ribs by his daughter, Mary Abigail, who acted as mistress of the White House. Franklin Pierce, a veritable movie actor in looks and carriage, had a habit of scratching his head in a peculiar manner. Like Taylor, he also suffered from indigestion and middle trouble, which led him to indulge in periodic loud throat splutters. James Buchanan, during whose reign the Prince of Wales, later Edward VII, was a White House guest, greatly embarrassed his royal visitor by inadvertently making a *mot* on avoirdupois, and Abraham Lincoln, God rest his noble soul, on several occasions appeared in public, to the dismay of the general, with his pantaloons unbuttoned. Andrew Johnson, already alluded to, who as youngster had worked as a journeyman tailor, was wont to comment on the cut and fit of his guests' clothes, much after the manner of present-day movie ex-cloak and suit magnificoes. Grant, like the good Methodist he was, used often to hit the bottle in private and to show up nicely enameled. A smoker of strong cigars, he liked to blow rings at persons with whom he was talking and almost suffocated them with his Pittsburghian exhalations. Rutherford B. Hayes, also a Methodist and married to a Methodist wife, refused to serve wine to his White House guests and on one occasion permitted his wife peremptorily so to inform the French ambassador when the latter, doubtless aching for a drink, politely and silently indicated his discomfort.

Garfield carried an ivory ear-pick and his successor, Chester A. Arthur, had a habit of clearing his throat like an auctioneer. Grover Cleveland, peace be to his august ashes, for all his heft liked to cock his feet up on the table, and Benjamin Harrison, according to persons who had watched him in action, never learned that one used the soup spoon in a thitherward rather than an approaching direction. McKinley, though a Methodist, was a gentlemanly host and allowed his White House guests the appropriate tipples but could never rid himself of the habit of eyeing them with critical disapproval when they reached the third glass. Roosevelt had no tact in mixing his guests and would thus often bring great embarrassment to his dinner table. In addition, he was given to an abrupt turning of his back upon anyone who momentarily displeased him and to a periodic curtness of speech toward his helpless inferiors. Taft, whose estimable sister-in-law acted as mistress of the White House during his wife's illness and who inaugurated the custom of five o'clock teas in the executive mansion, always was ill at ease with a tea cup and had a terrible time keeping the contents from spilling onto his lap, and the eminent Woodrow was given to taking off his glasses while chatting with a lady and, during her share of the colloquy, distractingly polishing them with his handkerchief. Harding, a snappy dresser, was extremely self-conscious of his clothes and, try as he would, could never hide the fact. Nor could he take his eyes off the clothes of men conversing with him, as if silently appraising their relative inferiority to his own.

The Hon. Calvin Coolidge not long ago received into the house of the First Lady in the Land the quondam Mrs. Charlie Chaplin.

[From the *American Mercury*, July 1928, pp. 370–1.]

Vice-President

IT is a long-held facetious notion that the Vice-President of the United States takes his place as an obscurity with the husband of an actress or with an artist in the American Institute of Arts and Letters. Among the Vice-Presidents since the establishment of the nation we find John Adams, Thomas Jefferson, Martin Van Buren, John Tyler, Millard Fillmore, Andrew Johnson, Chester A. Arthur, Theodore Roosevelt and Calvin Coolidge—all subsequently occupants of the Dais. Aaron Burr, General George Clinton, Elbridge Gerry, John C. Calhoun, John C. Breckinridge, James S. Sherman and Charles G. Dawes were others—none of them certainly suppressed violets. Daniel D. Tompkins, who served two terms and had been Governor of the State of New York for ten years, created a stir after his election by his vigorous fight for the abolition of slavery in New York. Senator Richard M. Johnson, true enough, didn't amount to much, nor did Senator William Rufus King, who had been minister to France. But George M. Dallas was a figure in international diplomacy—he subsequently became the representative of the United States at the Court of St. James, and Hannibal Hamlin, quondam Governor of Maine and a conspicuous Senator, loomed large in Congress, in State politics and subsequently in the diplomatic service. Schuyler Colfax, speaker of the House of Representatives from 1863 to 1869, when he was elected to the Vice-Presidency, at least was much heard of toward the conclusion of his term of office in connection with the Crédit Mobilier scandal. Henry Wilson was one of the organizers of the Republican party, was long a stormy petrel in politics as a leader of the Free Soil party, and came into fame as the author of the three-volume work, *History of the Rise and Fall of the Slave Power in America,* to say nothing of such treatises as

History of the Anti-Slavery Measures of the Thirty-seventh and Thirty-eighth Congresses and *History of the Reconstruction Measures of the Thirty-ninth and Fortieth Congresses.* Such men as William Almon Wheeler, Thomas A. Hendricks and Garrett A. Hobart cut little ice, but Levi P. Morton made himself heard and felt in financial matters and Thomas R. Marshall at least kept himself in the public eye by a prolific discharge of very snappy nifties. If the Vice-Presidency has had its obscure Adlai E. Stevensons and Charles W. Fairbankses, let us not overlook the fact that the Presidency has had its relatively no less obscure Polks and Pierces.

[From *Monks Are Monks,* 1929, pp. 293–5.]

Youth

"Beautiful is youth, it never comes again," goes the German saying. I beg leave to amend it by inserting "because" just after the comma. Youth is a nuisance. Only very old men become ga-ga lament that it is no longer theirs.

[From *Monks Are Monks,* 1929, p. 120.]

The Nonsense Fund

Every man over the age of forty should put aside a certain amount of money each year for use as a nonsense fund. It is a rare man, and a liar, who will not confess to the possession of certain occasional idiotic sprees of fancy which he is unable to gratify. The regular and constant suppression of such wish-jags makes in time for a measure of unhappiness, an unhappiness which, though fundamentally trivial, colors the man's days and life and philosophy. The wish-jags of every man need release, and this release they may find only through such a fund as I have indicated. The amount set aside for these annual sailor's debauches of the wish-complex need not be large in the instance of the majority of men, for the majority of men's absurd wishes are in the main of a not very considerable bulk. They take some such form as a five-dollar necktie or a dollar-and-a-quarter cigar or a bottle of Charente brandy. But, though they are not great, a man's failure to realize them gets to him, as the phrase has it, and contrives to lodge a fly in the ointment of his mood. The man knows that he can afford to buy the things, but that is not the point. He does not buy them, or anything else of the kind upon which his foolish fancy has alighted, for the simple reason that they seem a bit too extravagant and unnecessary. A nonsense fund would take care of such things and make the average fellow happy. It would be a fund for him to squander with a grandiose nonchalance; it would not figure in his strict finances; it would be viewed by him in the light of found money or money won on a bet or inherited from a forgotten uncle. With it he might buy that case of Clicquot Ponsardin 1911, or that green vest, or that gilt piano upon which he has long rested a longing and frustrated eye.

[From *The Autobiography of an Attitude*, 1925, pp. 48–9.]

Personal Attitude

Outline of the History of a Man's philosophical Knowledge from Early Youth to Old Age.—
1. I am wrong.   2. I am right.   3. I am wrong.

[From *The Autobiography of an Attitude*, 1925, p. 3.]

Gyneolatry

LIFE is full of surprises. But not to a women over twenty-five or a man over thirty.

[From *The Autobiography of an Attitude*, 1925, p. 70.]

Fairy Tales and America

No country can call itself entirely its own whose children must look to other and strange lands for their fairy tales and fables. We have yet to have our Lewis Carroll, like England, our Grimms, like Germany, our La Fontaine, like France, or our Hans Christian Andersen, like even Denmark.

[From *Monks Are Monks,* 1929, p. 254.]

Beauty

BEAUTY makes idiots sad as it makes wise men happy.

[From the *American Mercury,* September 1929, p. 119.]

Sentimentality in America

THE AMERICAN sentimentalizes everything but what is genuinely and honestly worthy of sentiment. He is like a valentine being constantly delivered on Labor Day. He cries tenderly over any sloppy poem about a dog and then passes laws muzzling every dog in sight. He weeps when the radio exudes a mammy song and then calls his old colored scrub-woman a dirty nigger and bawls the hell out of her. He gets drunk and tells everybody around him what a great little woman his wife is and how much he loves her and then goes home and flops into his twin bed.

[From *Monks Are Monks,* 1929, p. 279.]

Love on the Continent

THE VIENNESE writes of love at 5 p.m.; the Frenchmen of love at 1 a.m.

[From the *American Mercury,* September 1929, p. 121.]

Cynicism

THE CYNICISM that is born of defeat is pitiable and worthless. It is only the cynicism that is born of success that is penetrating and valid.

[From *Monks Are Monks,* 1929, p. 56.]

Creative Writing

OF all the definitions mouthed by a certain branch of the critical fraternity, that which has to do with creation in literary fields is the most completely bogus. It is the persistent theory of the branch in point that the phrase *creative writing* must be reserved for novelists, poets and writers of a kind, however bad, and that it cannot truthfully be visited upon any others, however good. Criticism, according to the definition, does not come under the heading of creation and, as a consequence, such things as Dryden's *Essay on Dramatic Poesy* are not creative writing whereas such things as Zane Grey's novels presumably are. Nor does journalism in any form meet with the favor of the definition, with the result that the late Richard Harding Davis' description of the entrance of the German troops into Belgium is consigned to limbo, whereas the same writer's worst short fiction gains the good graces of the definition. The whole business, like so much of critical theory, is the purest nonsense. Frank Harris' journalism has often been creative writing of a high order. So has Shaw's and Wells'. What, too, of Addison's, Steele's, Swift's and Lamb's? And as for critical creative writing, what of Philip Sidney's, Corneille's, Samuel Johnson's, Lessing's, Voltaire's, Schiller's and Zola's?

[From *Testament of a Critic*, 1931, pp. 19–20.]

Advice to God

I OFFER this suggestion to God when He sets about creating a new world. Let him make all men rich in the Springtime and poor in Winter. Thus may men be happy when they yearn most for happiness and be driven to hard, productive work and to the serious business of life in the naturally sad and bleak period of the year.

[From *Monks Are Monks*, 1929, p. 80.]

Truth-Telling

ANY vainglorious assumption of immoderate truth-telling is highly offensive to me; I never for a moment desire to posture as a critic who believes there is any special virtue in unduly forthright talk, for the man who cherishes that belief is found pretty generally to be a nincompoop who imagines himself a hero on the strength of his bad manners. The truth is a graceful and lovely thing; it may no more be shouted without debauching it than a song by Wolf may be played by a jazz band. The truth should ooze out as softly as Spring from the snow. Yelling it is, in a sense, a form of mendacity.

[From *Testament of a Critic*, 1931, pp. 55–6.]

The Blasé Critic

To dismiss a critic as blasé is to be at one with the donkey. The best critics have been and are blasé men. The very circumstance of being blasé implies experience and experience, in turn, implies patience only with what is worthy and complete impatience and contempt for what is not. The blasé critic is one whose emotional equipment has been so toughened by concussion with tin-pan art that, unlike that of the still enthusiastic idiot, it responds alone to the finest form of stimulant. No critic in his first days is blasé. He is tickled by almost everything, and indiscriminately. No critic in his first days is worth a hoot. It is the critic who has a hard time keeping awake at the Metropolitan, at the theatre or in an art gallery that is the critic whose opinions are worth reading.

[From *Monks Are Monks*, 1929, p. 9.]

Dirt

THERE is no such thing as a dirty theme. There are only dirty writers.

[From *Testament of a Critic*, 1931, p. 179.]

Beauty and the American

THE AMERICAN is never satisfied with what beauty may be immediately before his eyes. 'When he goes to the Grand Canyon, for example, he takes field-glasses with him.

[From *Monks Are Monks*, 1929, p. 254.]

Art

ART states what we know in terms of what we hope.

To be convincing, emotion may go so far and no farther. Emotion become never so slightly too intense skirts perilously the abyss of travesty. It is thus that the writing of tragedy calls for a more highly developed genius than any other form of literary or dramatic composition.

To speak of morals in art is to speak of legislature in sex. Art is the sex of the imagination.

[From the *American Mercury*, July 1926, p. 374.]

Profundity

ALL that is necessary to raise imbecility into what the mob regards as profundity is to lift it off the floor and put it on a platform.

[From the *American Mercury*, September 1929, p. 119.]

Gayety in America

THE AMERICAN's idea of gayety is synonymous with noise. His designations of it in the vernacular, such as *whoopee* and *hoopla*, are thus relevantly derived from the shouts of cowboys and circus acrobats. He cannot conceive of gayety in a quiet sense. In this he differs radically from the European. To him, the absence of a racket that accompanies an Englishman's, a Frenchman's, an Austrian's or a German's fun is incomprehensible.

[From *Monks Are Monks*, 1929, p. 257.]

Sherlock Holmes

A RE-READING today of Conan Doyle's celebrated Sherlock Holmes series brings one to a puzzled pondering of the enormous success that the stories enjoyed in their time. Read again after many years they not only seem very bald and crude in a literary direction, but for the most part ingenuous in their plot scheme. Holmes himself, though grantedly the most popular and most widely known character in modern fiction, is seen to be a character less of Doyle's creation than of Doyle's readers. Holmes, so far as Doyle's character analysis goes, is the merest shadow. His double-peaked cap and pipe apparently mark the limits of the author's power of character delineation. His speech is without definite mark or illuminating idiosyncrasy; his musings are associated solely with the hide-and-seek plots in which he is made to figure and disclose next to nothing of the man himself; his actions are the arbitrary actions of tin-pot melodrama. And so far as his outward aspect goes, it is suggested to the reader not by Doyle but by the illustrator, Steele, who drew the pictures for the stories. It is, in point of fact, Steele's Holmes rather than Doyle's that people visualize when they think of the detective.

The only explanation that one can advance for the great success of the Holmes stories lies not in their writing, which is bad, nor in their character dilineation, which is worse, but in their plot appeal. For all the insistence of professorial literary criticism that it is character rather than plot that makes for longevity in the field of fiction, we have here still another example in contradiction. Action that makes character, however indeterminate the character may be, has a greater and wider popular appeal than the finer literature in which character determines action. Robinson Crusoe, Uncle Tom, Little Red Riding Hood and dozens of other such plot-born characters continue, like Sherlock Holmes, to enrapture and engross the public where characters who are parents of their plots do so in minor degree. Holmes was and is a world success not because of himself but simply because he happened to be present when a shudderful hound howled on the dark moor, when a poisonous and terrifying snake crawled down a bell-cord, and when a deadly Hindu dart was projected from a blow-pipe.

[From the *American Mercury*, January, 1930, p. 114.]

In Memoriam

THE PINEAPPLE Daquiri cocktails at the Telegrafo in Havana . . . the musty ale at the little bar around the corner from the Alhambra in London . . . the Chateau Haut Brion '09 in the dinky inn near the waterfront at Marseilles . . . the dark beer in the Mathäserbräu in Munich . . . the vodka with a dash of peppermint in the café near the jail in Moscow . . . the Johannisberger Dorf '11 in the Café Bauer in Berlin . . . the chilled maraschino and brandy at the Cafe de l'Europe in Vienna . . . the Tokay up the alley near the railroad station in Budapest . . . the Bual Madeira in the roadhouse a mile and a half out of Barcelona . . . the brandy with grated cocoanut on the ships plying between Bahia and Buenos Aires . . . the Glenlivet Extra Special '88 in the bar to the left of St. Mary's Cathedral in Edinburgh . . . the pale pink chianti in the café around the corner from Dante's monument in Florence . . . the crême de rose at Shepheard's in Cairo . . . the Tangerine cocktails at the old Holland House in New York . . .

[From *The World in Falseface*, 1923, pp. 325–6.]

Olfactory Note

THAT most of the large cities of the world have not only a distinctive look, distinctive manner and distinctive tone but, more important, a very distinctive smell, may have impressed itself upon others before this; if so, I haven't encountered the reflections in type and hence address myself to the subject. In the instance of many such cities it has always seemed to me that, after some experience of them, it would be very easy to distinguish one from another blindfolded and by the exercise of the nose alone. Thus, landing by parachute in Paris on a dark night, it wouldn't be the scent of horsechestnuts, as is fictitiously believed, that would quickly identify the locality, but the asphalt odor that is peculiar to Paris and the exact like of which isn't to be sniffed in any other city I know of. Thus, too, London would be readily identifiable by virtue of a smell resembling oilcloth or linoleum drying in the sun; New York by a fragrance vaguely suggestive of dry rubber shoes; Vienna by an empyreuma remindful of a dusty straw basket; Berlin by the odor of wet talcum powder; and Philadelphia by the aroma of dry-lime. Constantinople smells like mouldy maple caramels; Havana, appropriately enough, like burning brown-paper cigarettes; San Francisco like damp pulp paper; and Chicago like rusty iron. Each large city assails the nostrils in a different manner. Of all those I am acquainted with, only two in this regard in the least resemble each other: Paris and Philadelphia.

[From the *American Mercury,* January 1930, pp. 114–15.]

America and the Artist

THE LAMENTATION, so often ventilated by incompetent and disgruntled craftsmen, that the United States treats its artists badly—if, indeed, it even so much as gives them a passing thought—is hardly borne out by the noticeable affluence of most of them, by the exaggerated amount of attention they get from the public press and by the abundance of invitations they receive to lend their not always too *soigné* presences to dinners, banquets, ladies' club teas, movie openings, lecture platforms, blindfold tests of cigarettes, dedicatory celebrations and booze parties on the ocean liners. I have grave doubts that in any other country in the world is a meritorious artist so rewarded and petted as he is in this one. And I entertain even graver doubts that he wouldn't be a blamed sight better off if well-intentioned idiots would let him alone, allow him to keep his mind solely on his work, and so permit him to function in peace and quiet to his greater glory. The United States not only does not disdain its artists; it goes to the extreme of coddling them so greatly, both in the way of personal attention and financial reward, that it often damn nigh ruins them.

The trouble with the lamenters, even those few who have a share of sense, is that they allege against the country as a whole an inattention and lack of sympathy that one actually finds mainly in a single quarter, and that quarter a high one. The American artist's chief neglect is not at the hands of what may be called the average American, but at the hands of Americans of wealth, Americans conspicuous in public affairs, Americans of position in what is dubbed society and Americans who might be presumed, however erroneously, to have some breeding, discrimination and taste. It is this class, which in another nation often offers a warming hospitality and cordiality to the artist, that here is hostile and apathetic to him or, if not precisely hostile and apathetic, that regards him with a sniffish casualness and unconcern. With the single exception of the later Henry H. Rogers, I can think of no rich American who has ever intelligently befriended a worthy American artist. The Maecenases of the present day decline to endorse artists like O'Neill and prefer to visit their patronage instead upon cabaret jazz bands and leg shows.

The American artist must look for his reward from the masses of the people, not from those who might ordinarily be expected, by the standards of other countries, to take a perhaps greater and more friendly interest in him. This reward the American in the mass accords him. But this reward is almost invariably withheld from him by the American of relative eminence. The Presidents of the United States, for example, for the last twenty years, with one exception, have proudly announced themselves to be devourers of cheap detective stories. The exception, Roosevelt, caused a national consternation by announcing that he had once read a novel by Owen Johnson and had liked it.

[From the *American Mercury*, September 1929, p. 116.]

There Lies Glamour; There Lay Romance

THE MALECON at two o'clock of a late Spring morning, with its tiara of amber lights, the harbor of Havana playing its soft lullaby against the sea-wall, and Morro Castle blinking like a

patient owl across the waters . . . the garden of the Hotel de
France et l'Angleterre at Fontainebleau in the twilight, with
the cannon of the French artillery in late summer manoeuvres
echoing dully in the outlying forests . . . Hampton Court on
a lazy afternoon in the late autumn of the year, deserted, still,
with the leaves falling across the withered flower-beds and, up
from the Thames, the sound of a lonely paddle . . . mid-
winter dawn in the Siegesalle of Berlin . . . the steps of the
Tcheragan Serai in Constantinople on a moonlit night trembling in the mirror of the Bosporus . . . the palm-bordered road
out of Hamilton, Bermuda, on a rainy day in May, with the
smell of the sea dripping from the great leaves . . . the hurri-
cane deck of a ship gliding noiselessly through the blue, star-
shot cyclorama of a Caribbean night, with the intermittent
click of poker chips from the smoking-room and the orchestra
below playing the waltz song from *Sari* . . . the Kärntner-
Ring in Vienna just after eleven of a November evening, with
its elaborately costumed police, and the hackmen bawling for
fares, and the young girls selling Kaiserblumen, and the
crowds in dominoes of a dozen colors on their way to the
Flower Ball, and cavalrymen kissing their sweethearts in
the middle of the street . . . the path of pines that winds up
the hill on the far side of Lake Mohegan, its carpet of moss
still damp from the retreat of April, an hour from Times
Square. . . .

[From *The World in Falseface*, 1923, pp. 296–7.]

Pilgrim Fathers

AMONG the Pilgrim Fathers who came over on the *Mayflower*
to settle America there was not a single artist, or the son of
an artist, or the grandson of an artist, or the great-grandson of
an artist.

[From *The World in Falseface*, 1923, p. 8.]

Life

LIFE is a conflict of principles. Drama, of emotions.

[From *The World in Falseface*, 1923, p. 9.]

Insanity

STRINDBERG, the cynic, they sneer, was insane. Well, so was Schumann, the sentimentalist.

[From *The World in Falseface*, 1923, p. 10.]

Great Art

GREAT art has outlived a score of gods. It is the only permanent and immortal religion.

[From *The World in Falseface*, 1923, p. 7.]

Criticism and Value

CRITICISM is the art of appraising others at one's own value.

[From *The World in Falseface*, 1923, p. 3.]

Clear Writing

ONE of the fallacies that hovers over the literary art is that the writer who thinks clearly will pretty generally write clearly, whereas the one whose thought is muddled will write in a muddled manner. Conan Doyle, when he enters the field of spooks and metaphysics, shows a mind as muddled as a tureen of potage Mongol, yet he writes simply, clearly and, so far as mere writing goes, effectively. The same is true of G. K. Chesterton when he goes in for religion, as it is true of Benedetto Croce when he tackles the higher metaphysics of criticism. On the other hand, a measure of the writing of the world's first and clearest philosophical thinkers is, from the viewpoint of mere writing as writing, ambiguous, defective, involved and clumsy. For one Nietzsche or Huxley who has written as clearly as he thought, you will find sufficient instances of clear thought transcribed groggily to paper—by way of example, some portions of Spinoza's *Ethics* and many more in the works of Kant.

The fallacy of the short sentence as a symbol of clear and direct thought is equally persistent. The clearest and most important philosophical thought that has been contributed to man has often been expressed in sentences so long that it is difficult to remember the beginning of them by the time one has plowed one's way past the middle. The most planless and idiotic thought of the most idiotic writers has been visited upon us in the crisp, short and speciously effective sentences of political diatribes, newspaper editorials and dime novels.

[From the *American Mercury*, June 1929, p. 244.]

Vulgarity in Literature

THE WORD vulgar, appearing promiscuously in American criticism, is the emptiest word in the critical vocabulary. Indiscriminately and with a supercilious snoot visited upon the writings of some of our best artists, its users betray simply their own shanty fastidiousness, to say nothing of their ignorance of the platitudinous fact that some of the grantedly greatest art that the world has known has been as vulgar as pigs' feet. What, may one ask, would these critics say today of an artist whose characters expectorated all over the place, talked of whores and intimate biological functions and discoursed on human sex indulgence in terms of animals; who treated of incest, named certain of his women characters after the social diseases and their consequences and descended to the lowest form of gutter speech; whose characters were Christened after the more esoteric portions of the human anatomy and after the act of copulation, drank themselves into a state of stomach sickness, indulged in a prodigious belching, never failed to speak of disgusting odors, and swore like bohunks? That is, conceiving a second coming, of an artist like Shakespeare?

[From the *American Mercury*, July 1928, p. 372.]

Woman's Charm

A WOMAN is charming in the degree that her body outdoes her mind in the matter of unsophistication.

[From *The World in Falseface*, 1923, p. 244.]

Man's Emotional Age

A MAN may, or may not, be as old as he feels, but a far more accurate thermometer of his emotional age or youth is to be had in the women he looks at. The man whose eyes are for women whom youth has deserted confesses automatically to emotional age. He is afraid of the intolerant and derisive challenge of youth; he seeks lack of conflict, coincidence in despair, faded concord—all the things that the reserve and cowardice of emotional age hold out to him as agreeable. The man whose eyes are for youth in women is still eager for the fray. He may be a consummate idiot, but he is still emotionally young, and young in the spirit of romance and adventure.

[From *The World in Falseface*, 1923, pp. 245–6.]

Love that Laughs

THE ENDURING love is the love that laughs. The man and woman who can laugh at their love, who can kiss with smiles and embrace with chuckles, will outlast in mutual affection all the throat-lumpy, cow-eyed couples of their acquaintance. Nothing dies so quickly in the heart of the woman as the love that has been orchestrated by the man upon the strings of the tear ducts. Nothing lives on so fresh and ever green as the love with a funny-bone.

[From *The World in Falseface*, 1923, p. 246.]

Woman's Laugh

THE FIRST thing about a woman that ages is her laugh. The laughter of twenty-three is never the laughter of nineteen. The laughter of thirty, for all the cosmetics in the world, is a laughter with lines and crow's feet. A woman may deftly deceive the approaching years: she may retain the face and figure of the youthful twenties: but her laugh will inevitably betray her. For the music of the laugh of the 'teens is the first thing in a woman that dies.

[From *The World in Falseface*, 1923, p. 250.]

The Neck

No woman is more beautiful than her neck.

[From *The World in Falseface*, 1923, p. 258.]

Justice

GOD is just. He has reserved most of the prettiest legs for homely women.

[From *The World in Falseface*, 1923, p. 273.]

God

LET the moralists, when they revile the sex dramatists, not overlook the boldest, the most conspicuous, the most indefatigable, and the most dangerous of them all. I allude, obviously, to God.

[From *The World in Falseface*, 1923, p. 43.]

Indignation

INDIGNATION is the seducer of thought. No man can think clearly when his fists are clenched.

[From *The World in Falseface*, 1923, p. 21.]

THE DRAMA AND THE THEATRE

Aesthetic Jurisprudence

ART is a reaching out into the ugliness of the world for vagrant beauty and the imprisoning of it in a tangible dream. Criticism is the dream book. All art is a kind of subconscious madness expressed in terms of sanity; criticism is essential to the interpretation of its mysteries, for about everything truly beautiful there is ever something mysterious and disconcerting. Beauty is not always immediately recognizable as beauty; what often passes for beauty is mere infatuation; living beauty is like a love that has outlasted the middle-years of life, and has met triumphantly the test of time, and faith, and cynic meditation. For beauty is a sleepwalker in the endless corridors of the wakeful world, uncertain, groping, and not a little strange. And criticism is its tender guide.

Art is a partnership between the artist and the artist-critic. The former creates; the latter re-creates. Without criticism, art would of course still be art, and so with its windows walled in and with its lights extinguished would the Louvre still be the Louvre. Criticism is the windows and chandeliers of art: it illuminates the enveloping darkness in which art might otherwise rest only vaguely discernible, and perhaps altogether unseen.

Criticism, at its best, is a great, tall candle on the altar of art; at its worst, which is to say in its general run, a campaign torch flaring red in behalf of æsthetic wardheelers. This campaign torch motif in criticism, with its drunken enthusiasm and raucous hollering born of ignorance, together with what may be called the Prince Albert motif, with its sober, statue-like reserve born of ignorance that, being well-mannered, is not so bumptious as the other, has contributed largely to the common estimate of criticism as a profession but slightly more exalted than Second Avenue auctioneering if somewhat less than Fifth. Yet criticism is itself an art. It might, indeed, be well defined as an art within an art, since every work of art is the result of a struggle between the heart that is the artist himself and his mind that is the critic. Once his work is done, the artist's mind, tired from the bitterness of the struggle, takes the form of a second artist, puts on this second artist's strange hat, coat and checkered trousers, and goes forth with refreshed vigor to gossip abroad how much of the first artist's work was the result of its original splendid vitality and how much the result of its gradually diminished vitality and sad weariness. The wrangling that occurs at times between art and criticism is, at bottom, merely a fraternal discord, one in which Cain and Abel belabor each other with stuffed clubs. Criticism is often most sympathetic when it is apparently most cruel: the propounder of the sternest, hardest philosophy that the civilized world has known never failed sentimentally to kiss and embrace his sister, Therese Elisabeth Alexandra Nietzsche, every night at bedtime. "It is not possible," Cabell has written, "to draw inspiration from a woman's beauty unless you comprehend how easy it would be to murder her." And—"Only those who have firmness may be really tender-hearted," said Rochefoucauld. One may sometimes even throw mud to tonic purpose. Consider Karlsbad.

Art is the haven wherein the disillusioned may find illusion. Truth is no part of art. Nor is the mission of art simple beauty, as the textbooks tell us. The mission of art is the magnification of simple beauty to proportions so heroic as to be almost overpowering. Art is a gross exaggeration of natural beauty: there was never a woman so beautiful as the Venus di Milo, or a man so beautiful as the Apollo Belvedere of the Vatican, or a sky so beautiful as Monet's, or human speech so beautiful as Shakespeare's, or the song of a nightingale so beautiful as Ludwig van Beethoven's. But as art is a process of magnification, so criticism is a process of reduction. Its purpose is the reducing of the magnifications of art to the basic classic and æsthetic principles, and the subsequent announcement thereof in terms proportioned to the artist's interplay of fundamental skill and overtopping imagination.

The most general fault of criticism lies in a confusion of its own internal processes with those of art: it is in the habit of regarding the business of art as a reduction of life to its essence of beauty, and the business of criticism as an expansion of that essence to its fullest flow. The opposite is more reasonable. Art is a beautiful, swollen lie; criticism, a cold compress. The concern of art is with beauty; the concern of criticism is with truth. And truth and beauty, despite the Sunday school, are often strangers. This confusion of the business of art and that of criticism has given birth to the so-called "contagious," or inspirational, criticism, than which nothing is more mongrel and absurd. Criticism is designed to state facts—charmingly, gracefully, if possible—but still facts. It is not designed to exhort, enlist, convert. This is the business not of the critic, but of those readers of the critic whom the facts succeed in convincing and galvanizing. Contagious criticism is merely a vainglorious critic's essay at popularity: facts heated up to a degree where they melt into caressing nothingness.

But if this "criticism with a glow" is not to be given countenance, even less is to be suffered the criticism that, in its effort at a fastidious and elegant reserve, leans so far backward that it freezes its ears. This species of criticism fails not only to enkindle the reader, but fails also—and this is more important—to enkindle the critic himself. The ideal critic is perhaps much like a Thermos bottle: full of warmth, he suggests the presence of the heat within him without radiating it. This inner warmth is essential to a critic. But this inner warmth, where it exists, is automatically chilled and banished from a critic by a protracted indulgence in excessive critical reserve. Just as the professional frown assumed by a much-photographed public magnifico often becomes stubbornly fixed upon his hitherto gentle brow, so does the prolonged spurious constraint of a critic in due time psychologically hoist him on his own petard. A writer's work does not grow more and more like him; a writer grows more and more like his work. The best writing that a man produces is always just a little superior to himself. There never was a literary artist who did not appreciate the difficulty of keeping up to the pace of his writings. A writer is dominated by the standard of his own writings;

he is a slave *in transitu,* lashed, tormented, and miserable. The weak and inferior literary artist, such a critic as the one alluded to, soon becomes the helpless victim of his own writings: like a vampire of his own creation they turn upon him and suck from him the warm blood that was erstwhile his. A pose in time becomes natural: a man with a good left eye cannot affect a monocle for years without eventually coming to need it. A critic cannot write ice without becoming in time himself at least partly frosted.

Paraphrasing Pascal, to little minds all things are great. Great art is in constant conflict with the awe of little minds. Art is something like a wonderful trapeze performer swinging high above the heads of the bewildered multitude and nervous lest it be made to lose its balance and to slip by the periodic sudden loud marvelings of the folks below. The little mind and its little criticism are the flattering foes of sound art. Such art demands for its training and triumph the countless preliminary body blows of muscular criticism guided by a muscular mind. Art and the artist cannot be developed by mere back-slapping. If art, according to Beulé, is the intervention of the human mind in the elements furnished by experience, criticism is the intervention of the human mind in the elements furnished by æsthetic passion. Art and the artist are ever youthful lovers; criticism is their chaperon.

II

I do not believe finally in this or that "theory" of criticism. There are as many sound and apt species of criticism as there are works to be criticized. To say that art must be criticized only after this formula or after that, is to say that art must be contrived only out of this formula or out of that. As every work of art is an entity, a thing in itself, so is every piece of criticism an entity, a thing in itself. That *Thus Spake Zarathustra* must inevitably be criticized by the canons of the identical "theory" with which one criticizes *Tristan and Isolde* is surely difficult of reasoning.

To the Goethe-Carlyle doctrine that the critic's duty lies alone in discerning the artist's aim, his point of view and, finally, his execution of the task before him, it is easy enough to subscribe, but certainly this is not a "theory" of criticism so much as it is a foundation for a theory. To advance it as a theory, full-grown, full-fledged and flapping, as it has been advanced by the Italian Croce and his admirers, is to publish the preface to a book without the book itself. Accepted as a theory complete in itself, it fails by virtue of its several un-developed intrinsic problems, chief among which is its neglect to consider the undeniable fact that, though each work of art is indubitably an entity and so to be considered, there is yet in creative art what may be termed an æsthetic genealogy that bears heavily upon comprehensive criticism and that renders the artist's aim, his point of view and his execution of the task before him susceptible to a criticism predicated in a measure upon the work of the sound artist who has just pre-ceded him.

The Goethe-Carlyle hypothesis is a little too liberal. It calls for qualifications. It gives the artist too much ground, and the critic too little. To discern the artist's aim, to discern the art-ist's point of view, are phrases that require an amount of plumbing, and not a few footnotes. It is entirely possible, for example, that the immediate point of view of an artist be faulty, yet the execution of his immediate task exceedingly fine. If carefully planned triumph in art is an entity, so also may be undesigned triumph. I do not say that any such latter phenomenon is usual, but it is conceivable, and hence may be employed as a test of the critical hypothesis in point. Un-schooled, without aim or point of view in the sense of this hypothesis, Schumann's compositions at the age of eleven for chorus and orchestra offer the quasi-theory some resistance. The question of the comparative merit of these compositions and the artist's subsequent work may not strictly be brought into the argument, since the point at issue is merely a theory and since theory is properly to be tested by theory.

Intent and achievement are not necessarily twins. I have always perversely thought it likely that there is often a greater degree of accident in fine art than one is permitted to believe. The aim and point of view of a bad artist are often admirable; the execution of a fine artist may sometimes be founded upon a point of view that is, from an apparently sound critical estimate, at striking odds with it. One of the finest performances in all modern dramatic writing, upon its critical reception as such, came as a great surprise to the writer who almost unwittingly had achieved it. Art is often unconscious of itself. Shakespeare, writing popular plays to order, wrote the greatest plays that dramatic art has known. Mark Twain, in a disgusted moment, threw off a practical joke, and it turned out to be literature.

A strict adherence to the principles enunciated in the Goethe-Carlyle theory would result in a confinement of art for all the theory's bold aim in exactly the opposite direction. For all the critic may accurately say, the aim and point of view of, say, Richard Strauss in *Don Quixote* and *A Hero's Life,* may be imperfect, yet the one critical fact persists that the executions are remarkably fine. All things considered, it were perhaps better that the critical theory under discussion, if it be accepted at all, be turned end foremost: that the artist's execution of the task before him be considered either apart from his aim and point of view, or that it be considered first, and then—with not too much insistence upon them—his point of view and his aim. This would seem to be a more logical æsthetic and critical order. Tolstoi, with a sound, intelligent and technically perfect aim and point of view, composed secondrate drama. So, too, Maeterlinck. Synge, by his own admissions adjudged critically and dramatically guilty on both counts, composed one of the truly firstrate dramas of the Anglo-Saxon stage.

In its very effort to avoid pigeonholing, the Goethe-Carlyle theory pigeonholes itself. In its commendable essay at catholicity, it is like a garter so elastic that it fails to hold itself up. That there may not be contradictions in the contentions here set forth, I am not sure. But I advance no fixed, definite theory of my own; I advance merely contradictions of certain of the phases of the theories held by others, and contradictions are ever in the habit of begetting contradictions. Yet such contradictions are in themselves apposite and soundly critical, since any theory susceptible of contradictions must itself be contradictory and insecure. If I suggest any theory on my part it is a variable one: a theory that, in this instance, is one thing and in that, another. Criticism, as I see it—and I share the common opinion—is simply a sensitive, experienced and thoroughbred artist's effort to interpret, in terms of æsthetic doctrine and his own peculiar soul, the work of another artist reciprocally to that artist and thus, as with a reflecting mirror, to his public. But to state merely what criticism is, is not to state the doctrine of its application. And herein, as I see it, is where the theorists fail to cover full ground. The anatomy of criticism is composed not of one theory, but of a theory—more or less generally agreed upon—upon which are reared in turn other theories that are not so generally agreed upon. The Goethe-Carlyle theory is thus like a three-story building on which the constructor has left off work after finishing only the first story. What certain aspects of these other stories may be like, I have already tried to suggest.

I have said that, if I have any theory of my own, it is a theory susceptible in practice of numerous surface changes. These surface changes often disturb in a measure this or that phase of what lies at the bottom. Thus, speaking as a critic of the theatre, I find it impossible to reconcile myself to criticizing acting and drama from the vantage point of the same theory, say, for example, the Goethe-Carlyle theory. This theory fits criticism of drama much better than it fits criticism of acting, just as it fits criticism of painting and sculpture much more snugly than criticism of music. The means whereby the emotions are directly affected, and soundly affected, may at times be critically meretricious, yet the accomplishment itself may be, paradoxically, artistic. Perhaps the finest acting performance of our generation is Bernhardt's Camille: its final effect is tremendous: yet the means whereby it is contrived are obviously inartistic. Again, *King Lear,* searched into with critical chill, is artistically a poor instance of playmaking, yet its effect is precisely the effect striven for. Surely, in cases like these, criticism founded strictly upon an inflexible theory is futile criticism, and not only futile but eminently unfair.

Here, of course, I exhibit still more contradictions, but through contradictions we may conceivably gain more secure ground. When his book is once opened, the author's mouth is shut. (Wilde, I believe, said that; and though for some peculiar reason it is today regarded as suicidal to quote the often profound Wilde in any serious argument, I risk the danger.) But when a dramatist's play or a composer's symphony is opened, the author has only begun to open his mouth. What results, an emotional art within an intellectual art, calls for a critical theory within a critical theory. To this composite end, I offer a suggestion: blend with the Goethe-Carlyle theory that of the aforementioned Wilde, to wit, that beauty is uncriticizable, since it has as many meanings as a man has moods, since it is the symbol of symbols, and since it reveals everything because it expresses nothing. The trouble with criticism—again to pose a contradiction—is that, in certain instances, it is often too cerebral. Feeling a great thrill of beauty, it turns to its somewhat puzzled mind and is apprised that the thrill which it has unquestionably enjoyed from the work of art might conceivably be of pathological origin, a fremitus or vibration felt upon percussion of a hydatoid tumor.

The Goethe-Carlyle theory, properly rigid and unyielding so far as emotional groundlings are concerned, may, I believe, at times safely be chucked under the chin and offered a communication of gipsy ardor by the critic whose emotions are the residuum of trial, test, and experience.

III

Coquelin put it that the footlights exaggerate everything: they modify the laws of space and of time; they put miles in a few square feet; they make minutes appear to be hours. Of this exaggeration, dramatic criticism—which is the branch of criticism of which I treat in particular—has caught something. Of all the branches of criticism it is intrinsically the least sober and the least accurately balanced. It always reminds me somehow of the lash in the hands of Œacus, in *The Frogs*, falling upon Bacchus and Xanthus to discover which of the two is the divine, the latter meantime endeavoring to conceal the pain that would betray their mortality by various transparent dodges. Drama is a two-souled art: half divine, half clownish. Shakespeare is the greatest dramatist who ever lived because he alone, of all dramatists, most accurately sensed the mongrel nature of his art. Criticism of drama, it follows, is similarly a two-souled art: half sober, half mad. Drama is a deliberate intoxicant; dramatic criticism, aromatic spirits of ammonia; the re-action is never perfect; there is always a trace of tipsiness left. Even the best dramatic criticism is always just a little dramatic. It indulges, a trifle, in acting. It can never be as impersonal, however much certain of its practitioners may try, as criticism of painting or of sculpture or of literature. This is why the best criticism of the theatre must inevitably be personal criticism. The theatre itself is distinctly personal; its address is directly personal. It holds the mirror not up to nature, but to the spectator's individual idea of nature. If it doesn't, it fails. The spectator, if he is a critic, merely holds up his own mirror to the drama's mirror: a reflection of the first reflection is the result. Dramatic criticism is this second reflection. And so the best dramatic criticism has about it a flavor of the unconscious, grotesque and unpremeditated. "When Lewes was at his business," Shaw has said, "he seldom remembered that he was a gentleman or a scholar." (Shaw was speaking of Lewes' free use of vulgarity and impudence whenever they happened to be the proper tools for his job.) "In this he showed himself a true craftsman, intent on making the measurements and analyses of his criticism as accurate, and their expression as clear and vivid, as possible, instead of allowing himself to be distracted by the vanity of playing the elegant man of letters, or writing with perfect good taste, or hinting in every line that he was above his work. In exacting all this from himself, and taking his revenge by expressing his most labored conclusions with a levity that gave them the air of being the unpremeditated whimsicalities of a man who had perversely taken to writing about the theatre for the sake of the jest latent in his own outrageous unfitness for it, Lewes rolled his stone up the hill quite in the modern manner of Mr. Walkley, dissembling its huge weight and apparently kicking it at random hither and thither in pure wantonness."

Mr. Spingarn, in his exceptionally interesting, if somewhat overly indignant, treatise on "Creative Criticism," provides, it seems to me, a particularly clear illustration of the manner in which the proponents of the more modern theories of criticism imprison themselves in the extravagance of their freedom. While liberating art from all the old rules of criticism, they simultaneously confine criticism with the new rules—or ghosts of rules—wherewith they free art. If each work of art is a unit, a thing in itself, as is commonly agreed, why should not each work of criticism be similarly a unit, a thing in itself? If art is, in each and every case, a matter of individual expression, why should not criticism, in each and every such case, be similarly and relevantly a matter of individual expression? In freeing art of definitions, has not criticism been too severely defined? I believe that it has been. I believe that there may be as many kinds of criticism as there are kinds of art. I believe that there may be sound analytical, sound emotional, sound cerebral, sound impressionistic, sound destructive, sound constructive, and other sound species of criticism. If art knows no rules, criticism knows no rules—or, at least, none save those that are obvious. If Brahms' scherzo in E flat minor, *op.* 4, is an entity, a work in and of itself, why shouldn't Huneker's criticism of it be regarded as an entity, a work in and of itself? If there is in Huneker's work inspiration from without, so, too, is there in Brahms': if Brahms may be held a unit in this particular instance with no consideration of Chopin, why may not Huneker with no consideration of Brahms?

If this is pushing things pretty far, it is the Spingarns who have made the pushing necessary. "Taste," says Mr. Spingarn, "must reproduce the work of art within itself in order to understand and judge it; and at that moment æsthetic judgment becomes nothing more or less than creative art itself." This rings true. But granting the perfection of the taste, why define and limit the critical creative art thus born of reproduction? No sooner has a law been enunciated, writes Mr. Spingarn, than it has been broken by an artist impatient or ignorant of its restraints, and the critics have been obliged to explain away these violations of their laws or gradually to change the laws themselves. If art, he continues, is organic expression, and every work of art is to be interrogated with the question, "What has it expressed, and how completely?", there is no place for the question whether it has conformed

to some convenient classification of critics or to some law derived from this classification. Once again, truly put. But so,
too, no sooner have laws been enunciated than they have been
broken by critics impatient or ignorant of their restraints, and
the critics of critics have been obliged to explain away these
violations of the laws, or gradually to change the laws themselves. And so, too, have these works of criticism provided no
place for the question whether they have conformed to some
convenient classification of the critics of criticism or to some
law derived from this classification.

"Criticism," said Carlyle, his theories apart, "stands like an
interpreter between the inspired and the uninspired, between
the prophet and those who hear the melody of his words, and
catch some glimpse of their material meaning, but understand
not their deeper import." This is the best definition that I
know of. It defines without defining; it gives into the keeping
of the interpreter the hundred languages of art and merely
urges him, with whatever means may best and properly suit
his ends, to translate them clearly to those that do not understand; it sets him free from the very shackles which Carlyle
himself, removing from art, wound in turn about him.

[From *The Critic and the Drama*, 1922, Chapter i.]

The Drama as an Art

IF the best of criticism, in the familiar description of Anatole
France, lies in the adventure of a soul among masterpieces,
the best of drama may perhaps be described as the adventure
of a masterpiece among souls. Drama is fine or impoverished
in the degree that it evokes from such souls a fitting and noble
reaction.

Drama is, in essence, a democratic art in constant brave
conflict with aristocracy of intelligence, soul, and emotion.
When drama triumphs, a masterpiece like *Hamlet* comes to
life. When the conflict ends in a draw, a drama halfway between greatness and littleness is the result—a drama, say, like
El Gran Galeoto. When the struggle ends in defeat, the result is a *Way Down East* or a *Lightnin'*. This, obviously, is

not to say that great drama may not be popular drama, nor popular drama great drama, for I speak of drama here not as this play or that, but as a specific art. And it is as a specific art that it finds its test and trial, not in its own intrinsically democratic soul, but in the extrinsic aristocratic soul that is taste, and connoisseurship, and final judgment. Drama that has come to be at once great and popular has ever first been given the imprimatur, not of democratic souls, but of aristocratic. Shakespeare and Molière triumphed over aristocracy of intelligence, soul and emotion before that triumph was presently carried on into the domain of inferior intelligence, soul and emotion. In our own day, the drama of Hauptmann, Shaw and the American O'Neill has come into its popular own only after it first achieved the imprimatur of what we may term the unpopular, or undemocratic, theatre. Aristocracy cleared the democratic path for Ibsen, as it cleared it, in so far as possible, for Rostand and Hugo von Hofmannsthal.

Great drama is the rainbow born when the sun of reflection and understanding smiles anew upon an intelligence and emotion which that drama has respectively shot with gleams of brilliant lightning and drenched with the rain of brilliant tears. Great drama, like great men and great women, is always just a little sad. Only idiots may be completely happy. Reflection, sympathy, wisdom, gallant gentleness, experience—the chords upon which great drama is played—these are wistful chords. The commonplace urge that drama, to be truly great, must uplift is, in the sense that the word uplift is used, childish. The mission of great drama is not to make numskulls glad that they are alive, but to make them speculate why they are permitted to be alive at all. And since this is the mission of great drama—if its mission may, indeed, be reduced to any phrase—it combines within itself, together with this mystical and awestruck appeal to the proletariat, a direct and agreeable appeal to such persons as are, by reason of their metaphysical perception and emotional culture, superior to and contemptuous of proletariat. Fine drama, in truth, is usually just a trifle snobbish. It has no traffic with such souls as are readily made to feel "uplifted" by spurious philosophical nostrums and emotional sugar pills. Its business is with what the match-

less Dryden hailed "souls of the highest rank and truest understanding": souls who find a greater uplift in the noble de-
pressions of Brahms' first trio, Bartolommeo's Madonna della
Misericordia, and Joseph Conrad's "Youth" than in the easy
buoyancies of John Philip Sousa, Howard Chandler Christy
and Rupert Hughes. The aim of great drama is not to make
men happy with themselves as they are, but with themselves
as they might, yet alas cannot, be. As Gautier has it, "The
aim of art is not exact reproduction of nature, but creation,
by means of forms and colors, of a microcosm wherein may be
produced dreams, sensations, and ideas inspired by the aspect
of the world." If drama is irrevocably a democratic art and
uplift of the great masses of men its noblest end, Mrs. Porter's
Pollyanna must endure as a work of dramatic art a thousand
times finer than Corneille's *Polyeucte*.

Drama has been strictly defined by the ritualists in a dozen
different ways. "Drama," says one, "must be based on character, and the action proceed from character." "Drama," stipu-
lates another, "is not an imitation of men, but of an action
and of life: character is subsidiary to action." "Drama," pro-
mulgates still another, "is the struggle of a will against obsta-
cles." And so on, so on. Rules, rules and more rules. Pigeonholes upon pigeonholes. Good drama is anything that interests
an intelligently emotional group of persons assembled together in an illuminated hall. Molière, wise among dramatists,
said as much, though in somewhat more, and doubtless too,
sweeping words. Throughout the ages of drama there will be
always Romanticists of one sort or another, brave and splendid
spirits, who will have to free themselves from the definitions
and limitations imposed upon them by the neo-Bossus and
Boileaus, and the small portion Voltaires, La Harpes and Mar-
montels. Drama is struggle, a conflict of wills? Then what of
Ghosts? Drama is action? Then what of *Nachtasyl*? Drama
is character? Then what of *The Dream Play*? "A 'character'
upon the stage," wrote the author of the last named, "has become a creature readymade—a mere mechanism that drives
the man—I do not believe in these theatrical 'characters.'"

Of all the higher arts, drama is organically perhaps the
simplest. Its anatomy is composed of all the other arts, high

and low, stripped to their elementals. It is a synthesis of those portions of these other arts that, being elemental, are most easily assimilable on the part of the multitude. It is a snatch of music, a bit of painting, a moment of dancing, a slice of sculpture, draped upon the skeleton of literature. At its highest, it ranks with literature, but never above it. One small notch below, it ranks only with itself, in its own isolated and generically peculiar field. Drama, indeed, is dancing literature: a hybrid art. It is often purple and splendid; it is often profoundly beautiful and profoundly moving. Yet, with a direct appeal to the emotions as its first and encompassing aim, it has never, even at its finest, been able to exercise the measure of direct emotional appeal that is exercised, say, by Chopin's C sharp minor Nocturne, op. 27, No. 1, or by the soft romance of the canvases of Palma Vecchio, or by Rodin's superb "Eternal Spring," or by Zola's *La Terre*. It may, at its finest as at its worst, of course subjugate and triumph over inexperienced emotionalism, but the greatest drama of Shakespeare himself has never, in the truthful confession of cultivated emotionalism, influenced that emotionalism as has the greatest literature, or the greatest music, or the greatest painting or sculpture. The splendid music of *Romeo* or *Hamlet* is not so eloquent and moving as that of *Tristan* or *Lohengrin;* no situation in the whole of Hauptmann can strike in the heart so thrilling and profound a chord of pity as a single line in Allegri's obvious "Miserere." The greatest note of comedy in drama falls short of the note of comedy in the "Coffee-Cantata" of Bach; the greatest note of ironic remorse falls short of that in the scherzo in B minor of Chopin; the greatest intellectual note falls short of that in the first and last movements of the C minor symphony of Brahms. What play of Sudermann's has the direct appeal of "The Indian Lily"? What play made out of Hardy's *Tess,* however adroitly contrived, retains the powerful appeal of the original piece of literature? To descend, what obvious thrill melodrama, designed frankly for dollars, has—with all its painstaking and deliberate intent— yet succeeded in provoking half the thrill and shock of the obvious second chapter of Andreas Latzko's equally obvious *Men in War?*

Art is an evocation of beautiful emotions; art is art in the degree that it succeeds in the evocation: drama succeeds in an inferior degree. Whatever emotion drama may succeed brilliantly in evoking, another art succeeds in evoking more brilliantly.

II

Although, of course, one speaks of drama here primarily in the sense of acted drama, it is perhaps not necessary so strictly to confine one's self. For when the critic confines himself in his discussion of drama to the acted drama, he regularly brings upon himself from other critics—chiefly bookish fellows whose theatrical knowledge is meagre—the very largely unwarranted embarrassment of arguments anent "crowd psychology" and the like which, while they have little or nothing to do with the case, none the less make a certain deep impression upon his readers. (Readers of criticism become automatically critics; with his first sentence, the critic challenges his critic-reader's sense of argument.) This constantly advanced contention of "crowd psychology," of which drama is supposed to be at once master and slave, has small place in a consideration of drama, from whatever sound point of view one elects to consider the latter. If "crowd psychology" operates in the case of theatre drama, it operates also in the case of concert-hall music. Yet no one so far as I know seriously maintains that, in a criticism of music, this "crowd psychology" has any place.

I have once before pointed out that, even accepting the theory of crowd psychology and its direct and indirect implications so far as drama is concerned, it is as nonsensical to assume that one thousand persons assembled together before a drama in a theatre are, by reason of their constituting a crowd, any more likely to be moved automatically than the same crowd of one thousand persons assembled together before a painting in an art gallery. Furthermore, the theory that collective intelligence and emotionalism are a more facile and ingenuous intelligence and emotionalism, while it may hold full water in the psychological laboratory, holds little in actual external demonstration, particularly in any consideration of a crowd before one of the arts. While it may be true that the Le Bon and

Tarde theory applies aptly to the collective psychology of a crowd at a prizefight or a bullfight or a circus, one may be permitted severe doubts that it holds equally true of a crowd in a theatre or in an art gallery or in a concert hall. The tendency of such a latter group is not æsthetically downward, but upward. And not only æsthetically, but intellectually and emotionally. (I speak, of course, and with proper relevance, of a crowd assembled to hear good drama or good music, or to see good painting. The customary obscuring tactic of critics in this situation is to argue out the principles of intelligent reaction to good drama in terms of yokel reaction to bad drama. Analysis of the principles of sound theatre drama and the reaction of a group of eight hundred citizens of Marion, Ohio, to "The Two Orphans" somehow do not seem to me to be especially apposite.) The fine drama or the fine piece of music does not make its auditor part of a crowd; it removes him, and everyone else in the crowd, from the crowd, and makes him an individual. The crowd ceases to exist as a crowd; it becomes a crowd of units, of separate individuals. The dramas of Mr. Owen Davis make crowds; the dramas of Shakespeare make individuals.

The argument to the contrary always somewhat grotesquely assumes that the crowd assembled at a fine play, and promptly susceptible to group psychology, is a new crowd, one that has never attended a fine play before. Such an assumption falls to pieces in two ways. First, it is beyond reason to believe that it is true in more than one instance out of a hundred; and, secondly, it would not be true even if it were true. For, granting that a crowd of one thousand persons were seeing great drama for the first time in their lives, what reason is there for believing that the majority of persons in the crowd who had never seen great drama and didn't know exactly what to make of it would be swayed and influenced by the minority who had never seen great drama but did know what to make of it? If this were true, no great drama could ever possibly fail in the commercial theatre. Or, to test the hypothesis further, take it the other way round. What reason is there for believing that the majority in this crowd would be moved the one way or the other, either by a minority that did understand the play, or did not understand it? Or take it in another way still. What reason is there for believing that the minority in this crowd who did know what the drama was about would be persuaded emotionally by the majority who did not know what the drama was about?

Theories and again theories. But the facts fail to support them. Take the lowest type of crowd imaginable, one in which there is not one cultured man in a thousand—the crowd, say, at a professional American baseball game—and pack it into an American equivalent of Reinhardt's Grosses Schauspielhaus. The play, let us say, is *Œdipus Rex*. At the ball game, let us say, the crowd psychology of Le Bon operated to the full. But what now? Would the crowd, in the theatre and before a great drama, be the same crowd? Would not its group psychology promptly and violently suffer a sudden change? Whether out of curiosity, disgust, admiration, social shame or what not, would it not rapidly segregate itself, spiritually or physically, into various groups? What is the Le Bon theatrical view of the crowd psychology that somehow did not come off during the initial engagement of Barrie's *Peter Pan* in Washington, D.C.? Or of the crowd psychology that worked the other way round when Ibsen was first played in London? Or of the crowd psychology that, operating regularly, if artificially, at the New York premières, most often fails, for all its high enthusiasm, to move either the minority or the majority in its composition?

The question of sound drama and the pack psychology of a congress of groundlings is a fatuous one: it gets nowhere. Sound drama and sound audiences are alone to be considered at one and the same time. And, as I have noted, the tendency of willing, or even semi-willing, auditors and spectators is in an upward direction, not a downward. No intelligent spectator at a performance of *Ben Hur* has ever been made to feel like throwing his hat into the air and cheering by the similar actions of the mob spectators to the left and right of him. No ignoble auditor of *The Laughter of the Gods* but has been made to feel, in some part, the contagion of cultivated appreciation to *his* left and right. "I forget," wrote Sarcey, in a consideration of the subject, "what tyrant it was of ancient Greece to whom massacres were everyday affairs, but who wept copiously over the misfortunes of a heroine in a tragedy. He was the audience; and for the one evening clothed himself in the sentiments of the public." A typical example of sophisticated reasoning. How does Sarcey know that it was not the rest of the audience—the crowd—that was influenced by this repentant and copiously lachrymose individual rather than that it was this individual who was moved by the crowd?

If fallacies perchance insinuate themselves into these opposing contentions, it is a case of fallacy versus fallacy: my intent is not so much to prove anything as to indicate the presence of holes in the proofs of the other side. These holes seem to me to be numerous, and of considerable circumference. A description of two of them may suffice to suggest the rest. Take, as the first of these, the familiar Castelvetro doctrine that, since a theatrical audience is not a select congress but a motley crowd, the dramatist, ever conscious of the group psychology, must inevitably avoid all themes and ideas unintelligible to such a gathering. It may be true that a theatrical audience is not a select congress, but why confine the argument to theatrical audiences and seek thus to prove something of drama that may be proved as well—if one is given to such idiosyncrasies—of music? What, as I have said before, of opera and concert-hall audiences? Consider the average audience at Covent Garden, the Metropolitan, Carnegie Hall. Is it in any way culturally superior to the average audience at the St. James Theatre, or the Théâtre de l'Œuvre, or the Plymouth—or even the Neighbourhood Playhouse down in Grand Street? What of the audiences who attended the original performances of Beethoven's "Leonore" ("Fidelio"), Berlioz's "Benvenuto Cellini," the original performances of Wagner in France and the performances of his "Der Fliegende Holländer" in Germany, the operas of Händel in England in the years 1733–37, the work of Rossini in Italy, the concerts of Chopin during his tour of England and Scotland? . . . Again, as to the imperative necessity of the dramatist's avoidance of all themes and ideas unintelligible to a mob audience, what of the success among such very audiences—to name but a few more recent profitably produced and locally recognizable examples—of Shaw's *Getting Married,* Augustus Thomas' *The Witching Hour,* Ibsen's *The Wild Duck,* Dunsany's *The Laughter of the Gods,* Barrie's *Mary Rose,* Strindberg's *The Father,* Synge's *Playboy?* . . . Surely it will be quickly allowed that however obvious the themes and ideas of these plays may be to the few, they are hardly within the ready intelligence of what the theorists picture as the imaginary mob theatre audience. Fine drama is independent of all such theories: the dramatist who subscribes to them should not figure in any treatise upon drama as an art.

A second illustration: the equivocation to the effect that drama, being a democratic art, may not properly be evaluated in terms of more limited, and aristocratic, taste. It seems to me an idiotic assumption that drama is a more democratic art than music. All great art is democratic in intention, if not in reward. Michelangelo, Shakespeare, Wagner and Zola are democratic artists, and their art democratic art. It is criticism of Michelangelo, Shakespeare, Wagner and Zola that is aristocratic. Criticism, not art, generally wears the ermine and the purple. To appraise a democratic art in terms of democracy is to attempt to effect a chemical reaction in nitrogen with nitrogen. If drama is, critically, a democratic art since it is meant not to be read by the few but to be played before the many, music must be critically no less a democratic art. Yet the theorists conveniently overlook this embarrassment. Nevertheless, if Shakespeare's dramas were designed for the heterogeneous ear, so, too, were the songs of Schumann. No great artist has ever in his heart deliberately fashioned his work for a remote and forgotten cellar, dark and stairless. He fashions it, for all his doubts, in the hope of hospitable eyes and ears, and in the hope of a sun to shine upon it. It is as ridiculous to argue that because Shakespeare's is a democratic art it must be criticized in terms of democratic reaction to it as it would be to argue that because the United States is a democracy the most acute and comprehensive criticism of that democracy must lie in a native democrat's reaction to it. "To say that the theatre is for the people," says Gordon Craig, "is necessary. But to forget to add that part and parcel of the people is the aristocracy, whether of birth or feeling, is an omission. A man of the eighteenth century, dressed in silks, in a fashionable loggia in the theatre at Versailles, looking as if he did no work (as Voltaire in his youth may have looked), presents, in essence, exactly the same picture as Walt Whitman in his rough gray suit lounging in the Bowery, also looking as if he did no work. . . . One the aristocrat, one the democrat: the two are identical."

III

"Convictions," said Nietzsche, "are prisons." Critical "theories," with negligible exception, seek to denude the arts of their splendid, gypsy gauds and to force them instead to don so many duplicated black-and-white striped uniforms. Of all the arts, drama has suffered most in this regard. Its critics, from the time of Aristotle, have bound and fettered it, and have then urged it impassionedly to soar. Yet, despite its shackles, it has triumphed, and each triumph has been a derision of one of its famous and distinguished critics. It triumphed, through Shakespear, over Aristotle; it triumphed, through Molière, over Castelvetro; it triumphed, through Lemercier, over Diderot; it triumphed, through Lessing, over Voltaire; it triumphed, through Ibsen, over Flaubert; it has triumphed, through Hauptmann, over Sarcey and, through Schnitzler and Bernard Shaw, over Mr. Archer. The truth perhaps is that drama is an art as flexible as the imaginations of its audiences. It is no more to be bound by rules and theories than such imaginations are to be bound by rules and theories. Who so allwise that he may say by what rules or set of rules living imaginations and imaginations yet unborn are to be fanned into theatrical flame? "Imagination," Samuel Johnson's words apply to auditor as to artist, "a licentious and vagrant faculty, unsusceptible of limitations and impatient of restraint, has always endeavored to baffle the logician, to perplex the confines of distinction, and burst the inclosures of regularity." And further, "There is therefore scarcely any species of writing of which we can tell what is its essence, and what are its constituents; every new genius produces some innovation which, when invented and approved, subverts the rules which the practice of foregoing authors had established."

Does the play interest, and whom? This seems to me to be the only doctrine of dramatic criticism that is capable of supporting itself soundly. First, does the play interest? In other words, how far has the dramatist succeeded in expressing himself, and the materials before him, intelligently, eloquently, symmetrically, beautifully? So much for the criticism of the dramatists as an artist. In the second place, whom does the play interest? Does it interest inferior persons, or does it interest cultivated and artistically sensitive persons? So much for the criticism of the artist as a dramatist.

The major difficulty with critics of the drama has always been that, having once positively enunciated their critical credoes, they have been constrained to devote their entire subsequent enterprise and ingenuity to defending the fallacies therein. Since a considerable number of these critics have been, and are, extraordinarily shrewd and ingenious men, these defences of error have often been contrived with such persuasive dexterity and reasonableness that they have endured beyond the sounder doctrines of less deft critics, doctrines which, being sound, have suffered the rebuffs that gaunt, grim logic, ever unprepossessing and unhypnotic, suffers always. "I hope that I am right; if I am not right, I am still right," said Brunetière. "Mr. William Archer is not only, like myself, a consistent one. I am sure he takes care that his practice agrees with his opinions—even when they are wrong." Dramatic criticism is an attempt to formulate rules of conduct for the lovable, wayward, charming, wilful vagabond that is the drama. For the drama is an art with a feather in its cap and an ironic smile upon its lips, sauntering impudently over forbidden lawns and through closed lanes into the hearts of those of us children of the world who have never grown up. Beside literature, it is the Mother Goose of the arts; a gorgeous and empurpled Mother Goose for the fireside of impressible and romantic youth that, looking upward, leans ever hushed and expectant at the knee of life. It is a fairy tale told realistically, a true story told as romance. It is the lullaby of disillusion, the chimes without the cathedral, the fears and hopes and dreams and passions of those who cannot fully fear and hope and dream and flame themselves.

"The drama must have reality," so Mr. P. P. Howe in his engaging volume of "Dramatic Portraits," "but the first essential to our understanding of an art is that we should not believe it to be actual life. The spectator who shouts his warning and advice to the heroine when the villain is approaching is, in the theatre, the only true believer in the hand of God; and he is liable to find it in a drama lower than the best." The art of the drama is one which imposes upon drama the obligation of depicting at once the inner processes of life realistically and the external aspects of life delusively. Properly and sympathetically to appreciate drama, one must look upon it synchronously with two different eyes: the one arguing against the other as to the truth of what it sees, and triumphing over this doubtful other with the full force of its sophistry. Again inevitably to quote Coleridge, " Stage presentations are to produce a sort of temporary half-faith, which the spectator encourages in himself and supports by a voluntary contribution on his own part, because he knows that it is at all times in his power to see the thing as it really is. Thus the true stage illusion as to a forest scene consists, not in the mind's judging it to be a forest, but in its remission of the judgment that it is not a forest." This obviously applies to drama as well as to dramatic investiture. One never for a moment believes absolutely that Mr. John Barrymore is Richard III, so that one may receive the ocular, aural and mental sensations for which one has paid three and one-half dollars. Nor does one for a moment believe that Mr. Walter Hampden, whom that very evening one has seen dividing a brobdingnagian dish of goulash with Mr. Oliver Herford in the Players' Club and discussing the prospects of the White Sox, is actually speaking extemporaneously the rare verbal embroideries of Shakespeare; or that Miss Ethel Barrymore who is billed in front of Browne's Shop House to take a star part in the Actors' Equity Association's benefit, is really the queen of a distant kingdom.

The dramatist, in the theatre, is not a worker in actualities, but in the essence of actualities that filters through the self-deception of his spectators. There is no such thing as realism in the theatre: there is only mimicry of realism. There is no such thing as romance in the theatre: there is only mimicry of romance. There is no such thing as an automatic dramatic susceptibility in a theatre audience: there is only a volitional dramatic susceptibility. Thus, it is absurd to speak of the drama holding the mirror up to nature; all that the drama can do is to hold nature up to its own peculiar mirror which, like that in a pleasure park, amusingly fattens up nature, or shrinks it, yet does not at any time render it unrecognizable. One does not go to the theatre to see life and nature; one goes to see the particular way in which life and nature happen to look to a cultivated, imaginative and entertaining man who happens, in turn, to be a playwright. Drama is the surprising pulling of a perfectly obvious rabbit out of a perfectly obvious, everyday silk hat. The spectator has seen thousands of rabbits and thousands of silk hats, but he has never seen a silk hat that had a rabbit concealed in it, and he is curious about it.

But if drama is essentially mimetic, so also—as Professor Gilbert Murray implies—is criticism essentially mimetic in that it is representative of the work criticized. It is conceivable that one may criticize Mr. Ziegfeld's "Follies" in terms of the "Philoctetes" of Theodectes—I myself have been guilty of even more exceptional feats; it is not only conceivable, but of common occurrence, for certain of our academic American critics to criticize the plays of Mr. Shaw in terms of Scribe and Sardou, and with a perfectly straight face; but criticism in general is a chameleon that takes on something of the color of the pattern upon which it imposes itself. There is drama in Horace's *Epistola and Pisones,* a criticism of drama. There is the spirit of comedy in Hazlitt's essay *On the Comic Writers of the Last Century.* Dryden's *Essay on Dramatic Poesy* is poetry. There is something of the music of Chopin in Huneker's critical essays on Chopin, and some of Mary Garden's spectacular histrionism in his essay on her acting. Walkley, criticizing *L'Enfant Prodigue,* uses the pen of Pierrot. Criticism, more than drama with her mirror toward nature, holds the mirror up to the nature of the work it criticizes. Its end is the revivification of the passion of art which has been spent in its behalf, but under the terms laid down by Plato. Its aim is to reconstruct a great work of art on a diminutive scale, that eyes which are not capable of gazing on high may have it within the reach of their vision. Its aim is to play again all the full richness of the artist's emotional organ tones, in so far as is possible, on the old cerebral xylophone that is criticism's deficient instrument. In the accomplishment of these aims, it is bound by no laws that art is not bound by. There is but one rule: there are no rules. Art laughs at locksmiths.

It has been a favorite diversion of critics since Aristotle's day to argue that drama is drama, whether one reads it from a printed page or sees it enacted in a theatre. Great drama, they announce, is great drama whether it ever be acted or not; "it speaks with the same voice in solitude as in crowds"; and "all the more then"—again I quote Mr. Spingarn—"will the drama itself 'even apart from representation and actors,' as old as Aristotle puts it, speak with its highest power to the imagination fitted to understand and receive it." Upon this point of view much of the academic criticism of drama has been based. But may we not well reply that, for all the fact that Shakespeare would still be the greatest dramatist who ever lived had he never been played in the theatre, so, too, would Bach still be the greatest composer who ever lived had his compositions never been played at all? If drama is not meant for actors, may we not also argue that music is not meant for instruments? Are not such expedients less sound criticism than clever evasion of sound criticism: a frolicsome and agreeable straddling of the æsthetic seesaw? There is the printed drama—criticize it. There is the same drama acted—criticize it. Why quibble? Sometimes, as in the case of *Gioconda* and Duse, they are one. Well and good. Sometimes, as in the case of *Chantecler* and Maude Adams, they are not one. Well and good. But where, in either case, the confusion that the critics lay such stress upon? These critics deal not with theories, but with mere words. They take two dozen empty words and adroitly seek therewith to fashion a fecund theory. The result is—words. "Words which," said Ruskin, "if they are not watched, will do deadly work sometimes. There are masked words droning and skulking about us just now . . . (there never were so many, owing to the teaching of catechisms and phrases at school instead of human meanings) . . . there never were creatures of prey so mischievous, never diplomatists so cunning, never poisoners so deadly, as these masked words: they are the unjust stewards of men's ideas. . . ."

As they are of men's lack of ideas.

[From *The Critic and the Drama*, 1922, Chapter ii.]

Literature and Drama

THE CONTEMPT exhibited by literary men for drama on the ground that drama, because of the intrinsic nature of the theatre, cannot be literature is analogous to a contempt that architects might affect for music on the ground that it cannot be made out of bricks. Aside from the painfully obvious fact that great drama actually is literature, and great literature, the literary gentlemen conveniently overlook the second and even more painfully obvious fact that the circumstance that drama may not necessarily be literature is no more valid criticism of it as art than the circumstance that literature need not necessarily be dramatic is valid criticism against literature as art.

Of all artists, literary men are the most self-sufficient, snobbish and, generally, the least catholic and critically sagacious. Whimsical fellows, they look scornfully upon a dramatist who must perforce resort to such ignoble and inartistic devices as the condensing of a character's lifetime into an arbitrary two hours while they themselves enjoy all of two hundred pages, which take two hours to read, for the same purpose. They laugh at the arbitrary demands of the stage in the matter of curtain falls, while they agreeably forget the arbitrary demands of the novel in the matter of chapters of similar necessary furloughs for the reading eye. They speak from a superior vantage point of bad actors, and overlook bad typesetters, bad proofreaders, bad binders. They think of theatre audiences, and double up as with a colic; but they do not recall that nine out of every ten persons who read their own work are similar bounders and pickleheads.

This attitude toward the drama on the part of literary men may easily be explained. It derives from their own inability to write drama when they try their hands at it and a subsequent attempt to apologize to themselves for that failure with the reassuring remonstrance that drama must be a very low art form, else they would be able to master it. It seems to be the literary craftsman's idea that drama is child's play, something to be taken up, largely as a joke, when his own more serious and important and difficult work is done. He does not realize that the two arts are as far apart as sculpture and painting. Thus, an

Arnold Bennett observes loftily that any proficient *littérateur* can write a good play with one of his hands tied behind his back and his eyes blindfolded—and turns out such stuff as *Polite Farces, Cupid and Common Sense, What the Public Wants, The Honeymoon, Mr. Prohack, Sacred and Profane Love,* and *Milestones.* The best that Frank Harris can manage is a *Mr. and Mrs. Daventry,* which is to his literary canon what *Papa Loves Mama* is to *Andromache.* Huneker, a champion of literature at the expense of the poor drama, tried to write a play called *Chopin* with sad results, and Sinclair Lewis is the author of *Hobohemia* and another opus, *City Hall,* that shall be enveloped in a polite silence. Dreiser would doubtless be loath to have anyone speak of his *Hand of the Potter* in the same breath with *Sister Carrie, Jennie Gerhardt* and other of his novels; and H. G. Wells is responsible in part for *The Wonderful Visit.* George Moore, a great scoffer at drama and one who has looked on it as being of a piece with making mudpies, when he condescendingly tried his skill at it succeeded in producing only a *Coming of Gabrielle* and a *Strike at Arlingford.* Heinrich Mann's literary talent gives birth to a *Die Grosse Liebe*; and Gustav Frennsen's to a *Sönke Erichsen.* What Knut Hamsun's plays are like, I don't know; I haven't read them; but I heard that they are very bad. Henry James' attempt to make a play out of his novel *Daisy Miller* is still a dolorous memory, as is his *Guy Domville,* and Joseph Conrad's *One Day More* is, considering Conrad, pathetic. David Graham Phillips, after much sincere trying, could manage only *The Worth of a Woman*; and Hergesheimer, after two separate attempts, appears to have given up. The short comedies and farces of William Dean Howells are of puny dramatic merit; Bret Harte's *Two Men of Sandy Bar* is drivel; and Robert Louis Stevenson's and W. E. Henley's attempts, *Deacon Brodie* and *Admiral Guinea,* are equally drivel. No need to multiply the list; dozens upon dozens of additional instances will readily occur to you, both of yesterday and today. The legitimate exceptions are few. Galsworthy, for example, is by his own confession a dramatist first and a novelist second: the dramatic form is closest to his heart. So with Maugham, though his plays are far beneath the quality of his novels. Thomas Hardy tried to make a dramatization of his *Tess of the D'Urbervilles* and failed to make one that was anywhere nearly so good as the antecedent one made by a more experienced theatrician.

The difference between a novel and a drama is the difference between music read and music played. The novelist peoples the imagination with ghosts; the dramatist peoples the eye and ear with living, moving forms and voices. This difference the literary man turned playwright seldom perceives, and as a result the drama that he fashions often too greatly neglects the eye and ear in favor of an overtaxed (and undersupplied) theatrical imagination. I speak here, of course, of the literary man who approaches the dramatic form seriously and not merely as a means to hornswoggle the box-office out of a bit of change. In the average play of the literary man, one can, in one's mind's eye, see the book leaves turning with the movements of the stage characters. One feels that the characters are reading their lines rather than speaking them. The dramatic personages move less in terms of sentences than in terms of paragraphs. They are less types than typography. A shoemaker should stick to his last. The composer of *Parsifal* is ill at ease in *Religion und Kunst*; the painter of the *Cenacolo* is lost when he woos the art of the composer; the author of *Romeo and Juliet* sloshes around uncomfortably in Ben Jonson's sock and buskin; the confector of the *Essays of Elia* only brings down a deserved booing upon himself when he confects a *Mr. H.*

Of the several recent instances of the condescension of literary men toward the drama that have come to my notice, none is more illuminating than that of the gifted Mr. Aldous Huxley. Mr. Huxley makes known his airy disdain in an essay called "Why I Do Not Go to the Theatre." The title, considering the ancient point of view which the essay sets forth, would be vastly more pat had the author omitted its first word. For the theatre which Mr. Huxley so contumeliously discourses upon obviously belongs to the early eighties.

Let us glance briefly at a few of our friend's antiquated opinions. First, that "the popular conventions are accepted in the theatre at their face value without any attempt being made to discover the psychological realities which lie behind them." Brushing aside as being too apparent contradictions of Mr.

Huxley's horsehair-sofa viewpoint the plays of such present-day dramatists as Shaw, O'Casey, Toller, O'Neill, Pirandello and a score of others, let us sample the hollowness of his contention by descending to even the Broadway commercial drama of a recent year. I list herewith a number of plays that, during that season along in the New York theatre, turned the popular conventions inside out and at least tried to make the very attempt which Huxley denies is ever made: *The Home Towners, Sour Grapes, Sandalwood, The Captive, The Good Fellow, God Loves Us, Gentle Grafters, This Was a Man, The Constant Wife, The Silver Cord, Lady Alone, Inheritors, Mariners, Spread Eagle* and *The Second Man*. During the same period, there were produced on Broadway such equally controverting examples of modern drama as the *Naked* and *Right You Are* of Pirandello, etc.

"There are only two kinds of love on the stage—the pure and the impure," continues Huxley in defence of his non-theatre-going attitude. "No hint is ever dropped that in reality sacred and profane love are inextricably mixed together; it is never so much as whispered that there may be a great many varieties of both kinds." Need I bring to our friend's notice a hundred and one modern plays that must make his statement ring loudly with foolishness, such, for example, as Porto-Riche's *L'Amoureuse,* certain of Arnold Bennett's later comedies, d'Annunzio's *La Città Morta,* Capus' *L'Oiseau Blessé* and *Les Passagères,* Strindberg's *The Dance of Death* and O'Neill's *Welded,* Sudermann's *Das Blumenboot,* Schnitzler's *Zwischenspiel* and *Der Ruf des Lebens,* and Lenormand's *Simoon?* "On the stage," concludes Huxley, "love is, moreover, always a function of the loved object, dependent exclusively on the blonde curls and the virtue of the heroine, the black shingle and the alluring impurity of the villainess. No allowance is ever made for the lover's state of mind and body. If there is one thing (on the other hand) that the novelist's exploration of reality has made abundantly clear, it is that love is, to a great extent, the product of the lover's imagination and desire and that it has comparatively little to do with the qualities of the beloved." It appears that Mr. Huxley is completely unaware of a multitude of plays like Schnitzler's *Countess Mitzi,* Sudermann's *The Three Heron*

Feathers, Barker's *The Madras House,* Strindberg's *To Damascus,* and the various Guitry and Dieudonné comedies, to mention but a few that come readily to mind.

[From *Art of the Night,* 1928, pp. 140–8.]

Intelligence and the Drama

ALTHOUGH we live in the enlightened years of the Twentieth Century, the talk of intelligence in the theatre continues. We hear still of "intelligent drama" on the one hand and plays that "insult the intelligence" on the other. The whole canon of dramatic criticism in the last thirty years, indeed, appears to rest snootily on the premise that the virtue of drama is predicated on this intelligence, and that, save drama possess it, and, possessing it, gratify intelligence in turn, the aforesaid drama may be dismissed from serious consideration without further ado.

Just how this notion of the consanguinity of intelligence and drama first got bruited about, one has trouble in ascertaining, for if intelligence were the chief desideratum in drama and if all the plays written in the world today were chock full of it from beginning to end, there wouldn't be a single theatre between here and the island of Amorgopula that could pay its rent next Saturday night. But, of course, everyone except most dramatic critics knows perfectly well that the last thing necessary and valuable to drama is intelligence, and so the theatre prospers today as it has never before. Intelligence is no more relevantly a part of drama than it is of music, painting, sculpture, hooch dancing, six-day bicycle racing or any other art or diversion; it is a tremendous handicap rather than a magnificent asset. The drama is not the place for intelligence but only for a deft and superficially deceptive counterfeit of intelligence. To speak disparagingly, therefore, of drama that insults the intelligence is to speak disparagingly of graphic art that insults the intelligence and to complain of, say, Veronese's *St. Anthony Preaching to the Fishes* that it is of absolutely no worth because any man who thought he could accomplish anything by addressing lake trout on the subject of Holy Writ was a damned fool.

All fine art, in fact, not only insults the intelligence; it deliberately spits in the eye of intelligence. The ennobling tragedies of Shakespeare ask us to believe in ghosts and witches; and the great drama of Ibsen asks us to believe that the world is savagely cruel to a woman who has violated the Seventh Commandment, that dishonesty must inevitably turn upon its practitioner and smite him with a blow from which he cannot recover, that a syphilitic is doomed to end his days as a lunatic, and that, symbolism or no symbolism, when amorous old gentlemen afflicted with vertigo fall off the tops of towers, the young folk standing down below hear a harp recital going on in the air. Mozart, in *Don Giovanni,* asks us to believe that a woman who could express herself in the harmonic beauty of a "Non ti fider, O misera" might be thought insane; and Wagner asks us to believe, in *Lohengrin,* that a *swan* can pull a boat, in *Tannhäuser,* that if a man speaks of physical love in high terms all the women will promptly leave the room, and, in *Siegfried,* that a sword can split an anvil in two and that birds can speak excellent German. Bellini, in the *Madonna, Child and Six Saints,* asks us to believe that an angel views the spectacle of a naked man with a puritanical Methodist concern; Raphael, in the *Victory of Leo IV at Ostia,* asks us to believe that soldiers are constantly mindful of the picturesqueness of their poses in the heat of battle; and Tintoretto asks us, in *Adam and Eve,* to believe that Adam looked like Bernarr Macfadden. To speak of intelligent art, which is to say, to demand that overpowering beauty be coincidently rational, is to speak of an intelligent Grand Canyon or an intelligent Granada or Lombard Plain, and to demand that moonlight and the summer stars satisfy the philosophical doctrines of Spinoza, William Lloyd Garrison and Herbert Croly.

In drama, a forthright metaphysic spells certain disaster. Nothing is so corruptive of drama as hard logic. What the drama calls for is not mental intelligence, but only emotional intelligence. No matter how poorly the characters of drama reason, the demands of drama are fully satisfied so long as their emotions are, or at least seem to be, reasonable. A great dramatic character may have the mind of an alley-cat or a congressman, but so long as his emotions are rational and logical, so long as he feels convincingly, so long as he doesn't become angry when someone hands him an excellent cigar or doesn't fall in love with a woman who is too fat, he may continue to be a great dramatic character. Macbeth is a simpleton, but his emotions are those of a great man, hence he is a great dramatic character. And it is the same with most of the other great characters of drama. It is almost impossible to imagine a fine play built around, say, Kant or Hegel as a philosopher. The theatre has no call for such heroes. Its heroes must think with their hearts and feel with their minds. (Bahr's *The Master*, on a not important dramatic level, may in this regard nevertheless be offered as supplementary reading.) To build a play around Kant or Hegel and hope to keep even the most intelligent theatrical audience in the world in its seats after nine o'clock, one would inevitably have to make up either Immanuel or Georg Wilhelm to look like John Drew, have him crawl under Fifi's bed when her husband unexpectedly came back from Detroit, and introduce a scene in the second act in which he eluded the Scotland Yard detectives by hiding in the cuckoo clock.

Fine drama, as a matter of fact, generally insults the intelligence, as the phrase goes, vastly more than gimcrack drama. *Hamlet* frequently impresses the logical mind as mere gorgeously beautiful drivel, where some such twentieth-rate piece of work as *They Knew What They Wanted* satisfied the rational sense more or less completely. Great art is as irrational as great music. It is mad with its own loveliness. Aeschylus and Richard Strauss are beer-brothers under their skins: the *Eumenides* is as drunk with the dazzling beauty of æsthetic scapulimancy on the one hand as *Also Sprach Zarathustra* is on the other. If you are looking for sense, go to the plays of Channing Pollock and the songs of Irving Berlin.

And so we come to Shaw's dramatic gigolo, Eugène Brieux. Brieux's chief fault as a dramatist is his intelligence, or, more accurately, his dervish-like belief that what he knows constitutes intelligence and his passion for inculcating it in his plays. Take the average Brieux play, cut out the names of its leading characters, run the text together, borrow an ice-water pitcher, and you have a first-class lyceum bureau lecture for use at the Town Hall. The flame of intelligent nonsense is never—or, at

least, very seldom—present in his work, as it is present in the
work of such greatly more intelligent men as, for instance, his
god-father, Shaw. He seizes upon an available theme for a good
play and then proceeds painstakingly to think it right out of
the theatre. Where a competent and persuasive dramatist
would take the same theme and carefully drain from it every
vestige of dialectic wind and every trace of polemic dulness,
Brieux goes carefully about the business of draining from it
every vestige of vagrant beauty and every trace of human
charm and boils it down to its elemental and vastly depressing
syllogistic bones. He seems to be of the theory that drama is designed to prove something to the human head, unaware completely that the highest aim of drama is rather to prove something only to the human heart. He burns with the fervor of a
shyster lawyer; like a movie comedian he is not content to be
what he is—in his case, a writer of plays—but must needs also
be regarded by the world beyond the theatre as a thinker. It
is thus that he goes about composing his plays with his eye
ever set upon convincing by stark logic, whereas the eye of the
real dramatist is ever set upon convincing by beautifully embellished equivocation. For in the theatre we believe not so
much what may be true as what may be merely plausible. The
logic of heredity, let us say, as we get it in some such drama as
Brieux's *The Escape* is never one-tenth so effective in the theatre as the romantic sophistry of heredity as we get it in a
Rostand's *L'Aiglon*.

There is no man so stupid, in point of fact, as the intelligent
dramatist who carries his intelligence full-fledged over into his
plays. His intelligence is of very great service to him before he
proceeds to the actual writing of his plays, since it tells him
what he should not write and since it further safeguards him
from writing the kind of plays that men less intelligent than
himself write; but when he sets himself to the actual business
of writing, he must leave his intelligence off stage and permit
it simply to criticize confidentially from time to time the
charming holiday from sound intelligence that is giving a show
out on the stage. To the Polichinelle secret, Brieux is seldom
privy, and as a result his plays generally disclose themselves to
be masses of platitudes, since by the time almost any philo-

sophic idea finds its way into the theatre it is, by the intrinsic nature of the theatre, already a great-grandfather. Brieux, however, constantly bemuses himself with the theory that because he has thought of something for the first time, it is therefore of a revolutionary newness and must so impress others; and his plays, as a consequence, generally take on the aspect of so many rush telegrams, delivered by a breathless messenger-boy, which contain information that the recipient has read in day before yesterday's newspaper, and not been the least interested in. Once in his life, Brieux forgot himself and wrote an excellent comedy, *Les Hannetons*. Once again, he partly forgot himself and came near writing a very good play, *Les Trois Filles de M. Dupont*. But for most of the rest of his life he has been writing such things as *La Robe Rouge*, *La Femme Seule* and *L'Avocat* which turn their stages into lecture platforms, Hyde Park soap-boxes and street-corner cart-tails, and their auditors into somnambulists groping their way to the exits.

The last named play has been shown in America recently by Mr. Belasco under the title of *Accused*. In a brochure published in commemoration of the great event, Mr. Belasco delivers himself of the following illuminating syllogism: "France, always conservative in her recognition of talent until talent is proved beyond question, has awarded M. Eugène Brieux two of the world's *supreme* honors—the decoration of the Legion of Honor [1] and admittance to the ranks of the Forty Immortals of the Académie Française . . . so it is no exaggeration to describe M. Brieux as the foremost contemporary author of his country, *if not of the world*." To which a dozen French, German and English dramatists—to limit Mr. Belasco's contemporary authors to the drama alone—must kneel, cross themselves, and join Toto, the Hippodrome clown, in saying Amen.

[From the *American Mercury*, December 1925, pp. 500–2.]

[1] Also awarded to Otto Kahn, Gertrude Atherton and James K. Hackett.

The Four Horsemen

FOUR HORSEMEN of the contemporary American drama are, Timeliness, Journalism, Cynicism, and Laughs. The mounts are critics, and the quartet is in large part responsible for much of the desolation in which that drama is finding itself.

Consider the marauders in order. The first, Timeliness, places a premium on the immediate chronological interest of a play's theme. A touching example of the degree to which the attitude goes was to be had in the New York Critics' Circle's award for last year's best play to the negligible *All My Sons*. The citation's most significant line read, "Because of the frank and uncompromising presentation of a *timely* and important theme." O'Neill's infinitely more important and superior *The Iceman Cometh* was dismissed by the awarders because, apparently, timeliness is considered a greater dramatic asset than timelessness. The O'Neill play deals with the spiritual needs of mankind unending; the Miller play with the corrupt wartime sale of some defective airplane parts and the consequent killing of a number of army fliers. It was therefore esteemed to be the finer specimen of dramatic art. If it was not esteemed principally on that score, we must believe that the awarding critics consider the novice Miller more expert in dramaturgy than the O'Neill who, by the same critics' paradoxical consent, is the foremost dramatist of the American theatre; that, for all its freely admitted faults, *The Iceman Cometh* is not more expert in character drawing than a play whose chief figure owns a factory that "looks like General Motors" yet who dresses, looks, acts and talks like a foreman's helper and who lives in a cheap little frame house with no servant to help his ailing wife run it; and that, because the O'Neill play consumes four hours and is not as compact as the two and one-half hour Miller play, the Miller play presumably for that reason is *ipso facto* more admirable in artistic economy than even the uncut four-hour *Hamlet*.

The veneration of timeliness is also clearly to be perceived in the case of other recent plays and has been instrumental, at its most preposterous, in according high critical favor to such a paltry example of dramatic writing as *State of the Union*, which carries timeliness to the extreme of altering nightly its references to the newspaper political headlines. A glance at last season's exhibits offers additional evidence of the tendency. Though *On Whitman Avenue* produced some critical qualms in other directions, the timeliness of its theme—injustice to the Negro—met with almost unanimous critical endorsement. In the same way, the opportuneness of the various themes of *A Flag Is Born, Temper the Wind, The Big Two, The Whole World Over* and other such poor plays was greeted with warm commendation, even if the plays themselves were here and there greeted with less. The same held true of experimental misfires like *The Wanhope Building, The Great Campaign, O'Daniel,* et al. And Sartre's *The Flies* got such notices partly because of its philosophical identification with the moment as had not been read locally since *Watch on the Rhine* similarly inflamed the critical enthusiasm some half dozen years ago. In the present season, plays like *Skipper Next to God* and *The Respectful Prostitute* continued to emphasize the general propensity.

All this, of course, is a consequence of the Second Horseman's journalistic attitude toward the drama. With minor exception, the drama most often depends for its life and livelihood not upon critics who view it as an art but upon newspaper reviewers most of whom regard it—perhaps properly and correctly in the nature of their jobs—through what they imagine are the eyes of the majority of their readers. It is these readers whose tastes, they please themselves to believe, are primarily for passing entertainment or, at the highest, "serious" drama with something of a "message." The message, they further allow themselves to think, is best and most acceptable when it has to do with something in the immediate minds of their readers and which has been lodged there by the news of the day.

There have been and there are still the exceptional daily reviewers who seek to operate on more independent and loftier principles. But they are not the popular ones and their opinions are accepted mainly by the minority of their readers who are biased in favor of drama of some repute, and even they at times cannot resist entirely the pull of what they are shrewd enough to realize is reader appeal. Compromise is accordingly not always beyond them. The more popular reviewers, on the other hand, are those who bear steadily in mind that the great majority of their readers have no use for the finer drama, that they cannot be persuaded to attend it even if the reviewers endorse it, that it is therefore the wiser course to accept the standards of the majority, and that in doubtful cases it is best to side with that majority's prejudices, real or imaginary. What all this naturally leads to is the reviewers' either quick or gradual surrender to the popular view of drama, again whether real or imaginary, and their acquisition of pride in being thus established as bell-cows of the larger share of the theatregoing public. The end-product of the attitude is the public's acceptance of critical guidance which is no guidance at all but simply an advance reassurance that its tastes are what they properly should be. It is, in brief, a leadership in reverse.

One of the fruits has been those tabulated critical scores, published by theatrical publications like *Variety* and *Billboard,* which lay unction to the vanity of reviewers who are nominated leaders by virtue of their having picked the greatest number of box-office successes regardless of merit. The pleased reviewers seemingly never stop to reflect that the box-office hits would scarcely have become hits had they themselves not helped them to become so. They do not pick the hits, as the scores appear to show; by their praise they make them hits. If their critical standards had been worthier, they would not have endorsed many of the plays and, lacking endorsement, the plays would in fair chance have been failures, and the reviewers, consequently, far from being cocks of the Broadway walk, would be very much sounder and more estimable critics, and the state of the drama improved and elevated.

The play that boasts authentic quality thus often has hard sledding, and the best that generally may be hoped for is that the play which rests halfway between real quality and compromise will get by. In the usual run, we find that plays which refuse compromise and, whatever their place in the sun, make an honest effort in the direction of dramatic worth, suffer at the hands of most of the reviewers and are doomed. I offer, in example, a few such in the last five or six seasons: *The Beautiful*

People, Walk into My Parlor, Our Lan', Magic, Hello Out There, Run, Little Chillun, Outrageous Fortune, The Innocent Voyage, South Pacific, A Highland Fling, Trio, The Overtons, Dark of the Moon, The Deep Mrs. Sykes, The Assassin, A Sound of Hunting, The Mermaids Singing, Lute Song, The Fatal Weakness, As We Forgive Our Debtors, and *The Old Lady Says "No!"*

An extension of the journalistic attitude toward the drama may further be observed in the supreme Pulitzer prize nonsense. The committee of newspaper editors who bestow the annual award allowed at their 1947 meeting that not only was O'Neill's *The Iceman Cometh* not to be considered as worthy of any mention, but that neither it nor any other play of the year was deserving of the great honor that in previous years had been heartily conferred upon such masterpieces of the dramatic art as *The Old Maid.*

The Third Horseman, alias Cynicism, is the prime critical mountebank of the quartet. His adopted fury is sentiment. By nature soft as a fresh egg, he has persuaded himself, with visible strain, that a stern opposition to sentiment of any kind, except possibly in musical shows, will mark him out as a tough and superior mentality, not to be tricked by that feminine thing called the heart. Give him a play, however charming, that does not at least once relieve its emotional and imaginative delicacy with the ejaculation of a "son-of-a-bitch" and he makes a critical muscle. He is hardboiled, like little Lord Fauntleroy's cuffs.

His hypocrisy works its damaging will on various plays that deserve better. For example, one such as van Druten's engaging comedy, *The Mermaids Singing.* The theme, you may remember, had to do with a middle-aged married playwright and an attractive young girl who admired him to the point of urging herself anatomically upon him. His reluctance to enter into an affair with her, despite strong temptation, because he well appreciated all the nuisance and trouble it would get him into, constituted the body of the play, which was thoroughly adult, sharply perceptive, and witty. The Third Horseman, however, rode into it lashing right and left on the ground that it was altogether too sentimental in moral tone. Just where it was too sentimental in any tone was difficult to make out. Though it may have seemed so superficially, it was the exact opposite. The hard sense and cold calculation of the man in avoiding the sex relationship had about as much sentiment as double entry bookkeeping. Yet the overwhelming fear of being considered sentimental led the reviewers to discern a moral tone in the man's abnegation.

What is here being written is plainly not intended as an argument for the sentimental in drama. Far from it. The argument is simply that where and when the sentiment is sound, the blanket indictment of it on the part of posturing critics becomes worse than ridiculous; and what is equally ridiculous is the confusion of sentimental values in these same critics. There is probably no play of any quality essentially more sentimental than Shaw's *The Doctor's Dilemma*, yet though Shaw is at no pains to conceal the fact, the play is digestible to the critics on its author's general reputation, scarcely well-founded, for cynicism. There is on the other hand probably no play of any quality essentially more unsentimental than Saroyan's short *Hello Out There*, yet, because Saroyan has the general reputation for crying into his beer, it is decried in various critical quarters for its alleged softness. Sentiment seems somehow curiously to be associated in such critics' minds with playwriting hacks or with spongy dramatists like Barrie. Nor is it always a question of good and bad writing, as those looking for an easy way out may contend. Where a more shamelessly sentimental play than the *Swanwhite* of the misanthrope Strindberg, than the *Hannele* of the realist Hauptmann, or than the *Peer Gynt* of the revolutionary Ibsen? Where, contrariwise, less sentimental and tougher plays than such hack works as *The Great Magoo, Maid in the Ozarks,* and *Catherine Was Great*?

The Fourth Horseman demands laughs above everything. He can conceive of nothing as entertainment if it does not succeed in causing him to open wide his mouth and emit noises of an hyena volume. The art of the drama to him is a succession of simiantics. He goes to the theatre, he says firmly, to be amused, and he is evidently not to be amused by anything that aims a bit higher than his belly. He is to be recognized in several ways. "The play"—whatever it is—"is sadly lacking in com-

edy," he writes. "The laughs are widely scattered," he deplores.
"The humor, so far as it exists, is hardly robust," he complains.
"There are a few chuckles here and there," he allows, "but otherwise a sad dearth of merriment." And so on. One of the few
occasions on which he permits himself an excursion into the
higher critical altitudes is in the instance of Shakespeare, whose
clowns, he pontificates, are no longer funny.

No one not completely an ass protests against laughter in
the theatre, but no one but a complete ass admires it to the ex-
clusion of almost everything else. The Fourth Horseman's admiration, furthermore, is critically indiscriminate. Anything, so
long as it unbuckles his cackles, is due for his congratulations.
There is small distinction between a *Born Yesterday* on the one
side and a *Volpone* on the other. He is at once the interlocutor
and end-man in his own critical minstrel show. Wit, he seems
to maintain, is for the culturally snobbish; belly laughter is the
ticket, and this belly laughter is chiefly the kind that follows the
miscegenation of Billy Watson and the drama. We thus get
from him, when duly gratified, such frequent and familiar testi-
monials as—I quote literally—"A laugh riot," "A comedy smash,"
"A wow," "It brought the house down," "The roars shook the
ceiling," "One long, grand guffaw," "An uproarious show," "A
hilarious ticket's worth," etc.

So far does the prejudice in favor of laughs go that there
have actually been plays which have succeeded largely on the
score of a single thunderous midriff reaction. This has been
true since the evening, years ago, of *Turn to the Right*, with its
"Has anyone in this town *got* a hundred and twenty-five dollars?", to *Dark Eyes*, with its Negro butler's "I wish to seize this
opportunity to thank you ladies for the beautiful necktie you
gave me," and beyond. It was the last minute insertion of the
line, "She comes from one of the first families of Pittsburgh—
as you enter the city," that partly saved the day for an old
Channing Pollock show. And in more recent years the old-time
Fourth Horseman's sons have indited extravagant praise of
such dramatic claptrap as *Brother Rat*, *What a Life!*, *Junior
Miss*, *Over 21* and the like simply, it is to be assumed, because
the shoddiness of the plays has been camouflaged with an occasional similarly pleasing joke. Moreover, quality or no qual-

ity, it is significant that a large proportion of the critically en-
dorsed successes in the last ten years have been the comedy
laugh shows: *You Can't Take It with You, Yes, My Darling
Daughter, Having Wonderful Time, Room Service, Susan and
God, Amphitryon 38, Bachelor Born, Kiss the Boys Goodbye,
The Primrose Path, Skylark, The Man Who Came to Dinner,
Life with Father, The Male Animal, George Washington Slept
Here*, the venerable *Charley's Aunt*, and *My Sister Eileen*.
Along with *Arsenic and Old Lace, Blithe Spirit, Janie, Kiss and
Tell, Harvey, Dear Ruth, O Mistress Mine, Born Yesterday,
Happy Birthday, Years Ago, John Loves Mary, Mister Roberts*,
the comedy revivals like *Burlesque*, the *Brother Rat, What a
Life!, Junior Miss* and *Over 21* earlier noted, etc., etc.

To repeat, unnecessarily: there is assuredly nothing to be
said against laughter as such. Even the slapstick and the bladder have their virtues. But one prefers generally to believe with
Victor Hugo that comedy, when mingled with the drama, is
better if it contains something of a lesson and has something
of a philosophy. If that be the highbrow attitude, it is still what
the critical attitude should painfully bear in mind. The comedy admired by the Fourth Horseman is a lesson in vaudeville
and its philosophy that of a circus clown.

[From *The Theatre Book of the Year, 1947–1948*, pp. 149–57.]

Propaganda Plays

MR. SHERWOOD once defined a playwright's requirements thus:
"He must be sensitive, imaginative, naïve, gullible, passionate;
he must be something of an imbecile, something of a poet, and
something of a damn fool." On the occasion of *The Rugged
Path*, Mr. Sherwood, though surely neither an imbecile nor a
damn fool, presents himself in the other less flattering lights,
with sensitivity, imagination, and poetry nowhere visible in his
equipment. His play is for the major part a carpentered job
which belatedly plows up ground already deeply furrowed,
and is without critical merit save possibly for those whom he
himself in one of his play's passages ridicules for esteem of
mere sincerity. What he offers is essentially an overly extended

and at all times exoteric rewriting of the rococo exhibit about the idealistic newspaper editor who, unable longer to tolerate the principles of the paper's executive and his henchmen, resigns and goes forth to make, in one way or another, a better world. The theme has occupied playwrights for the last half century, and only last season again appeared, decidedly for the worse, in a play called *A Place of Our Own*. Here, Mr. Sherwood has employed it propaganda-wise in connection with the last war, and orates it into unduteous theatre with incorporated speeches on the evils of a journalism which bows to rich advertisers, of a *laissez-faire* Americanism, and of an individual negligence in the matter of solidifying the peace. On none of these points is he particularly convincing, since conviction is hardly to be achieved through old, flat and stereotyped phraseology.

The routine nature of his processes of thought is plain from his own comment on his play, delivered with unconscious but very firm banality to an interviewer. "The first thing a writer can do," he asserted with a Moseslike inspiration, "is to take an interest in the peace. Then he must say over and over again that every individual American must develop an individual sense of obligation. The writer must point out that when the structure of a free democratic world breaks down, the individual bears a share in it. The writer must keep repeating, in every way, this sense of the responsibility of the individual. You see, where this country went wrong was when it began the deification of the doctrine of every man for himself. . . . It is the old concept that a factory owner can hire and fire anyone he pleases, that he can do anything he likes, regardless of any social responsibility. From this stems the Fascist idea that if a man is strong enough he is responsible to nobody but himself." True to his statement, Mr. Sherwood's play repeats all this "over and over again" at the expense not only of interesting drama but of audience patience. In it, there is no faintest trace of the former relieving wit and humor of its author's *Reunion in Vienna,* no symptom of the former poetry of his *Acropolis,* no suggestion of the former critical observation of his *The Road to Rome.* Literality minus all rules of the stage.

"Religiosity," Irwin Edman has written, "is the malaise that seems to assail many men of letters in middle life or later, a failure of nerve which they identify with the access of spiritual insight and vision." Mr. Sherwood's acquired religiosity takes the form of a delayed, amateur passion for political therapeutics and the brotherhood of man, which he identifies with the access of spiritual insight and vision. In this, he seems to be at one with his fellows who constitute the Playwrights' Company. It has come to be that most of their plays are basically so identical in theme, thought, and manner that when you have seen one you have seen all. In the case of this *The Rugged Path*, for example, one had difficulty in persuading one's self that what was being shown was not just another Maxwell Anderson *The Eve of St. Mark* or *Storm Operation,* just another Elmer Rice *American Landscape,* just another Behrman *The Talley Method,* and just another Sherwood *There Shall Be No Night.* The Playwrights' Company, at least up to this point, has suffered from a severe attack of Roosevelt religiosity.

In the role of the idealistic editor, Spencer Tracy, returned to the stage after fifteen years wasted, save financially, in Hollywood, indicated that his competences as an actor had not, as is often the case, been riddled by the picture medium and gave a performance that injected at least a superficial belief into the unbelievable materials provided him. Jo Mielziner's settings, except for the usual papier-mâché and canvas palms jungle scene, were well contrived; and Garson Kanin's direction, notably in the instance of the darkened, sound-filled stage shadowing forth the bombed and sinking destroyer, if hardly in the last curtain business with its illuminated American flag, was adequate to the play's fancied purposes.

The occasion gave renewed rise to the question of the critical merit of propaganda in drama, a question which increasingly climbs atop its own soapbox and lifts its dual voice with more and more of its customary eloquence, and still more and more of its customary vehemence. The arguments pro and con have now again mainly followed the established patterns. The pros have had at the cons with the familiar retort that most drama is propaganda of one sort or another, however the propaganda be concealed or unrecognized as such, and that there is no more sound reason against its presence than against the stage's electrical equipment's, which similarly sheds a valuable light on things. The cons in turn have had at the pros with the equally familiar thrust that propaganda, or what is theatrically defined as such, has no place in any play that pretends even faintly to dramatic art, and that its proper place is elsewhere, if indeed (*business of being loftily cynical*) anywhere at all.

While one is privileged to doubt whether there are two sides to every question, since a contrary belief would be hospitable to anyone who maintained that the earth was flat and that the Martini cocktail is a wonderful appetizer, there may be two to the question at issue, though it is to be suspected that one considerably outweighs the other.

When the talk is of propaganda, one takes it to mean not advocacy of those elements in private and personal life with which the pros seek cagily to camouflage their argument, but advocacy of elements in public, national, and international life. And by advocacy is meant in turn, very plainly, not soft persuasion, not insinuation, and not suggestion arising naturally out of the drama itself but rather independent insistence, exhortation, and even command. The difference is that between a playwright who proves his plea, whatever it may be, for his drama instead of permitting his drama to prove it for him. And the further difference is that between a green traffic light which automatically indicates progress and a traffic cop who accompanies it with a loud, peremptory "Go!" Propaganda as we get it in the contemporary drama is that traffic cop, usually further equipped with a shrill whistle.

More than anything else it is this traffic cop in drama that has undone many of our modern American playwrights and much of our modern American playwriting. It has undone the better men and women along with the poorer; the wet rain has fallen on the just and the unjust alike. It has taken its grim toll of a Behrman, who began as a meritorious writer of serious comedy and who has vitiated his plays by infusions of so much propaganda for one cause or another that they have become, like *The Talley Method* and, most lately, *Dunnigan's Daughter*, indistinguishable from stages peopled by companies composed entirely of Mike Golds and their girls, with their faces made up.

As Jay Carmody, critic for the Washington *Star,* aptly noted in regard to the latter play, "Behrman labors prodigiously to catapult the masses out of what is wrong with them; he whacks them with more words than thirty-six old-fashioned anarchists, but all he contrives to say is: 'People on the wrong side of the railroad track, unite!' Behrman's, sad to relate, is accordingly less likely to be the voice to lead the people out of soot and earshot of screeching locomotives than one to keep them out of the theatre." This, and properly, of a playwright who, before the spirochetes of flagrant propaganda poisoned his dramaturgy, wrote in *Rain from Heaven, et al.,* some of the most quietly intelligent and animating plays of our theatre.

The Sherwood under immediate discussion is another. More and more his plays seem to belong less on the stage of a theatre than on a radio political broadcast. And more and more his particular case indicates the personal and, in a manner of speaking, even artistic confusion into which his passion for propaganda has thrown him. He has, under its spell, been turned into a squirrel frantically dashing hither and thither in a rapidly rotating world cage and falling embarrassingly upon his tail. In *Idiot's Delight,* he heatedly argued the imbecility of wars, only a few years later to find himself with the turn of events just as heatedly arguing for the holy justice of wars. In *There Shall Be No Night,* he subsequently cursed the Russians as bloody knaves and villains for their invasion of innocent Finland, only a short time later with still another turn of events to hail them as glorious Allies on the score of an identical invasion. That even he himself is conscious of his identity with *genus Sciurus* is to be appreciated from his apologia in connection with this *The Rugged Path.* "It was," he states, "written as an immediate post-war play and the idea is this: in our moment of triumph don't let us forget how wrong we (*Ed. note:* "Where do you get that *we* stuff?" as the banana retorted while floating down the Mississippi) were at one stage of the game."

Lillian Hellman in *The Searching Wind,* which was partly foreshadowed by her *Watch on the Rhine,* became so confusedly involved in foreign relations propaganda that the play, what with its mechanically incorporated love element, gave the impression of Clare Boothe Luce and Helen Gahagan Douglas sitting hand-in-hand on the steps of the State Department patiently waiting for Philander C. Knox to come out. And most of Maxwell Anderson's later efforts, with their Democracy up-roar, have proved to be little more than Benjamin Harrison torchlight processions, in blank verse.

Propaganda wears a variety of literary shirts. In the plays of the John Howard Lawson-Clifford Odets-Edward Chodorov coterie, it wears one wide open at the neck ostentatiously to reveal the hair on the chest and one that matches the choler of its wearers' faces with its own shade of red. In the plays of the Sherwood-Anderson set, it wears one of the less violent shades tucked somewhat more fastidiously into the trousers, but pop-ping its buttons none the less under its wearers' heavy breath-ing. In the plays of others, it even affects a necktie and pa-rades the stage with an air of *sangfroid* but, unable presently to stand the modish strain, tugs open its collar and lets go, with its Adam's apple in the nude. And in all cases the shirt, under the contemporary dramatic dispensation, is studiously unlaundered in the interest of proletarian fashion.

There are, however, signs and tokens that this cowbell drama is slowly on the way out, which augurs well for the future. Though many of the older, established playwrights are still partial toward it, the more talented of the newer lot now and then seem to be willing to disregard it; and there are renegades, too, among even the older theatrical figures. Consider, for ex-ample, one like Harold Clurman, whose Group Theatre was the hotbed of such drama. Turning turtle, Clurman now expresses himself thus: "I, for one, am tired of hearing about plays of social significance, although heaven knows I've been associ-ated with them. I think the qualifying phrase should be 'human significance.' The word 'social' has come to have about it a cachet of obnoxious urgency. It puts a curse on a play now to have it known as 'socially significant.' A smart author nowadays keeps his significances under wraps and is more concerned that his play should be known as 'good theatre.' The stage, I think, must get away from dealing in tracts."

Dramaturgy must again, in short, if it would be successful with audiences, abandon the iron fist and return to diplomacy. Set, ringing speeches, the penchant of the propaganda dramatist, must further give way to insinuation and to a play's natural, easy flow. No longer does an audience respond to one like this, for example, in Irwin Shaw's late *The Assassin*:

"The essential thing is quality. The quality . . . of a man's soul. Politics change. We must trust the quality of a man rather than the color of his politics. Today that's our only hope. If you would only fight beside Communists, and I would only fight beside Left Republicans, and young de Mauny would only fight beside Monarchists, France would be dead once and for all. But I believe that, deep down, under all the differences, we are good men and that we can operate for good ends. That's why, in spite of Marcel Vespery (Admiral Darlan), I believe in the Americans. They are good people. That does not mean that I will not wrestle with them to change their politics and criticize you to change yours, but somehow we have a foundation I believe in. Somehow, we all believe in the human race, that it deserves to live on the earth, and that there is hope it will learn how to live on the earth. As for de Mauny, I find his politics unrealistic. But his quality magnificent!"

What persuades an audience more greatly is much of the same idea allowed casually, like the fragment of a tune hummed in the mind, to filter through a Saroyan's *The Time of Your Life*.

No longer, as well, is an audience receptive, in a Tennessee Williams' *You Touched Me!*, to an Army aviator's extended diatribe on the future of too placid mankind, as was duly discovered shortly after the play opened and resulted in the amputation of the harangue. An audience clearly demonstrates its preference for a Tennessee Williams in the less didactic mood of a *The Glass Menagerie* and for a drunk's simply integrated, "Yes, movies! Look at them—all those glamorous people having adventures, gobbling the whole thing up! You know what happens? People go to the movies instead of moving. Hollywood characters are supposed to have all the adventures for everybody in America, while everybody in America sits in a dark room and watches them have them. . . ."

The newer dramaturgical injunction seems to be that when propaganda-wise you call something a son-of-a-bitch you had best smile.

It may be true that, in other directions, a soft answer turneth away wrath, but in the propaganda theatre it rather induces it, and much more auspiciously than one couched, as the propaganda playwrights customarily couch it, in thunder claps. An audience's indignation, left dormant by an excess of the playwright's own, better responds to and flourishes on whispers, hints, and adumbrations. The wrath of a Holmes-Lawrence *If This Be Treason* thus exercises none of the anti-war appeal exercised by the sardonic humor of a *Lysistrata*, and all the propaganda fury of a Toller's *No More Peace!*, an Irwin Shaw's *Bury the Dead*, and a Sherwood's *Idiot's Delight* fails to achieve half the effect that a gently ironic *The Good Soldier Schweik* does. The pro-Semitic violence of a Rice's *Flight to the West* gets nowhere, while the mild persuasion of a Schnitzler's *Professor Bernhardi* or a Werfel's *Jacobowsky and the Colonel* measurably prospers.

And so with most propaganda plays. The yells and shouts against dictators in a Rice's *Judgment Day* deafen reaction, whereas the implications of a Capek's *Power and Glory* stimulate it. The screams and gesticulations against Fascism in an Odets' *Till the Day I Die* or a Reade's *The Shatter'd Lamp* are unavailing against the delicate innuendos of an early Behrman's *Rain from Heaven*. The howls and screeches on behalf of Labor in an Odets' *Waiting for Lefty* and a Sklar-Peters *Stevedore* die on the wind, but the calm of a Galsworthy's *Strife* blows warmth into the mind. And the *Deep Are the Roots* and the *Jebs* probably in the end are of less value to sympathetic consideration of the Negro problem than *The Green Pastures*.

The relatively most eloquent defense of Democracy is not to be found on the soap-boxes of the Sherwoods, the Andersons and the Rices, but in a pair of gay musical shows by George Kaufman and Co. called *Of Thee I Sing* and *I'd Rather Be Right*.

[From *The Theatre Book of the Year, 1945–1946*, pp. 167–75.]

Truth in the Theatre

THE ONE great defect in the equipment of the majority of the younger playwrights currently operating in the Anglo-American theatre is the belief, and the assiduous practice of it, that to make truth seem truthful in the theatre it is necessary first to filter it through the dubious hypocausts and shell-games of dramaturgy. What results is almost uniformly truth rid of all truth: truth so exaggerated as to be no more itself than the reflection of a man in a trick mirror is a reflection of himself. The result, like the reflection in the trick mirror, is sometimes startling and often amusing, but it is at the same time plainly ridiculous. A dramatist like Hauptmann, in a play like *The Weavers*, appreciating that true realism is, after all, but poetry without a shave, contrives an enormous effect by laying hold of truth and letting it find its way to the stage through the fancy of an artist rather than through the prestidigitation of a playwright. A dramatist like Gorki, in *Nachtasyl*, does the same. For such men know that all this talk of the necessary exaggeration of truth and realism in the theatre is nonsensical, and that the theatre simply takes life and the truth off their stilts and reduces them to pigmies that antic on a platform for a couple of hours and leave behind them a hint of that greater drama that is the world. Lesser men, and more vainglorious ones, seem to intensify life, and what they produce, accordingly, is merely cheap showship melodrama.

Some of the poorest plays known to us are truthful theatre; that is, plays which, by an artful employment of proscenium dodges, are made to seem plausible to the average person during the two hours he sits before them. George Kelly's *Daisy Mayme*, though it has some reportorial virtues, is such a play. It takes truth and so smears up its face with grease-paint that, when it is over, one has the impression of having looked out of a window onto life but, unfortunately, at a moment when a circus parade was passing by. For there is occasionally grease-paint in actual life, too; looking out upon the world, we as often see an organ grinder's monkey or a Knights of Pythias convention as we see a starving beggar or a mother burying her baby son. So many of our playwrights, in gazing out of the window, see the former and imagine that, because it adorns the sunlight of actuality, it is necessarily part and parcel of living, human truth. Thus we behold the countless Noel Cowards and Dion Titheradges and Shipmans and Willard Macks going down into the street to find humanity and fetching back up with them into the theatre little more than stray clowns out of one-ring circuses, sandwich men with false mustaches and policewomen disguised as honest street-walkers.

If plays that are truthful chiefly in terms of the theatre are so often bad plays, plays that are of so ingrained, uncompromising and unadorned a truth that they fail in the Anglo-American theatre are not less often found to be of noticeable merit. In this catalogue, we have plays like Brieux's *Les Hannetons*, Schönherr's *Kindertragödie* and, perhaps more legitimately to name some whose content is closer to the native sympathy and comprehension, such lesser exhibits as the Howard-Mizner *The Only Law*, Maugham's *Our Betters* and Rita Wellman's *The Gentile Wife*. Plays like these put the truth out close to the footlights and let it stand there disconcertingly while the dramatist is giving the necessary three-dollar show back of it, whereas plays of the other sort put the truth in the background and distract the audience's attention from it with the show going on down front. In the former plays, the play is secondary to the truth; in the latter, the truth is secondary to the play. The one dramatizes the truth; the other theatricalizes it— and between the two, all playing with words aside, there is the difference between the truth as we see it with our own eyes and the truth as we hear it somewhat dubiously related by a stranger.

[From the *American Mercury*, January 1927, pp. 124–5.]

First-Hand Drama

THE MODERN critical business of slighting a writer, however able he may be, because he has not engaged his materials at first-hand sometimes goes to undue and even ridiculous lengths. Henry James wrote of various things which were without his sphere of direct experience, yet wrote of them convincingly and very soundly. So did a variety of men like Balzac (*Adieu* and *El Verdugo*, for instance), Thomas Hardy (*The Hand of Ethelberta*), Zola (the remarkable *L'Assommoir*), and Joseph Conrad (the very frankly titled *Tales of Hearsay*), among many others. It is the same in the case of drama. Consider, for example, in the way of characters Strindberg's *Simoom*, provincial Henry Arthur Jones' excursions into high life, or, for a flippant chuckle, Shaw's Mrs. Warren.

Harry Brown's play, *A Sound of Hunting*, to call a halt to such fancy talk and return to the muttons, is his first dramatic effort and indicates a surprising feel for what is called theatre. From what would seem to be doubtful dramatic fuels, since their essence is watery from a stage viewpoint, he manages to derive a measure of suspense and evokes audience reaction to what in other hands might possibly be altogether static and dull. The weakness of his exhibit in the immediate theatrical sense lies, paradoxically enough, in that selfsame accurate reporting to which earlier reference has been made. Plays with characters not dissimilar have already covered much the same ground and also with accurate reporting, some of it at firsthand, and an audience feels that it is listening to a thrice-told tale. Its interest is consequently not all that critically it should be.

Like others who through force of circumstances or choice have been removed from the theatre for some years, Brown has not known what has been going on in it while he was away. Whether it has been the war or Hollywood that has been responsible, aspiring playwrights have thus come into the theatre with wares which have been anticipated by playwrights who have remained on the scene. These others accordingly find themselves in the position of salesmen who excitedly ring the theatre's front door bell and try to sell its audience something, otherwise meritorious or maybe only a dramatic vacuum cleaner, of which the latter already has a closet-full.

Brown's contribution to the war play catalogue has a story simple to the point of tenuousness. A squad of American soldiers, caught in a bomb-devastated house in Italy during the invasion, miss one of their number who has been caught in turn in a dugout between them and a German gun nest.

Though they are due to move on to another position, their corps spirit causes them to insist upon remaining until their colleague, whom none of them especially liked, is rescued. He is finally found dead, and they proceed to Naples. But simple as the narrative thread is, the playwright has woven it into a drama which, while intermittently and perhaps unavoidably a little monotonous, flowers with honest pathos and honest humor, and one which compared with its British all-male counterpart, *Journey's End,* is in its avoidance of sentimentality a relative masterpiece. Only once or twice, and then but briefly, as in the final scene wherein one of the soldiers lingers over a piece of fruit-cake reserved for his dead comrade and with a sad shake of the head leaves it undisturbed, does Brown skirt the edges of that mawkishness which made the Sherriff play rather sickening. And only in his caricatured war correspondent does his honesty fail him. He presents his other men forthrightly, and in all their physical, emotional, and conversational mud, and the picture is as untheatrical and as real a one as the stage can well offer. The result is probably the best American war play since *What Price Glory?*

Among the arguments levelled against the play were its lack of "action" and the general familiarity of its soldier talk. The arguments were more argumentative, so to speak, than soundly critical. The play has quite as much action as Gorki's *Night Refuge,* Shaw's *Getting Married* and *Misalliance,* and a dozen or more equally interesting plays. That its soldier talk is basically familiar may be perfectly true. We have heard before, and often, the profanity, the sex, the complaints over food, the despair, and the rest of it. But we have not heard it reorchestrated with such life, such deep feeling, such humor, and such simple honesty.

There has also been some talk, accompanied by various elegant definitions, as to whether, after all, any such play may be listed in the category of dramatic Art. If and when the government adds to its personnel a Secretary of Culture and I am delegated to the post through the instrumentality of the eloquence of nobody in particular, my first official act will be an order peremptorily calling for the burning of any and all books, essays, and critiques containing disquisitions on Art, including my own. My act will be based upon an increasing conviction that such disquisitions have done more to make Art a term of contempt among the great masses of the people than any ten thousand Shakespearean hams the world over, and that their cremation will do more to promote a widespread appreciation of and enthusiasm for Art than anything that the human mind has yet been able to think up.

By way of preparation for my future office and public service I have lately reread no less than five dozen treatises which have exerted themselves in what their authors have deemed the one and only true definition of Art and, as a sacrificial guinea pig, I wish to say that as a consequence I have been clinically infected with such a distaste for Art that it will, I fear, be some time before I recover.

The business of defining Art seems to have reached the proportions of the wholesale underwear business, and shows no signs of deteriorating. And since the definitions are as various and contradictory, and on the whole as dubious and confusing, as so many alleged cures for hay fever and Poland it is small wonder that most people are driven crazy by them and content themselves in saying to hell with the whole thing. The apostles of Art are, in short, its worst enemies. They have proudly explained it, in so far as the majority of persons are concerned, right into limbo.

No one esteems W. Somerset Maugham more highly than I do, but nevertheless one of the first books to go on the bonfire for its analysis of Art is his otherwise admirable *The Summing Up*. Thus, Maugham: "The value of Art, like the value of the Mystic Way, lies in its effects. If it can give only pleasure, however spiritual that pleasure may be, it is of no great consequence or at least of no more consequence than a dozen oysters and a pint of Montrachet. [Note. In *Cakes and Ale* it was Beauty that wasn't as satisfactory as a glass of cold beer. Willie is stealing from himself.] If it is a solace, that is well enough; the world is full of inevitable evils and it is good that man should have some hermitage to which from time to time he may withdraw himself; but not to escape them, rather to gather fresh strength to face them. For Art, if it is to be reckoned with as one of the great values of life, must teach man humility, tolerance, wisdom, and magnanimity. The value of Art is not beauty, but right action."

That our friend has here written some very pretty word music is not to be denied. But that he has not contributed further to the public befuddlement on the subject of what Art is and what it isn't is to be allowed, one fears, only by his one-eyed readers. The two-eyed will surely find themselves wildly chasing their tails trying to figure out, among other things, just how such hitherto recognized great Art as, say, the David of Michelangelo, the Ninth of Beethoven and half the painting of Rembrandt can possibly be reckoned with as one of the values of life in view of its failure to meet Maugham's demand that it teach man humility, tolerance, wisdom, and magnanimity, singly or in combination.

To the flames next will be conveyed, in the interests of the public weal, T. S. Eliot's *The Sacred Wood* for this example of prime double-talk: "In a peculiar sense he (the poet) will be aware also that he must inevitably be judged by the standards of the past. I say judged, not amputated, by them; not judged to be as good as, or worse or better than, the dead; and certainly not judged by the canons of dead critics. It is a judgment, a comparison, in which two things are measured by each other. To conform merely would be for the new work not really to conform at all; it would not be new, and would therefore not be a work of Art. And we do not quite say that the new is more valuable because it fits in; but its fitting in is a test of its value—a test, it is true, which can only be slowly and cautiously applied, for we are none of us infallible judges of conformity. We say: it appears to conform, and is perhaps individual, or it appears individual, and may conform; but we are hardly likely to find that it is one and not the other." If the innocent bystander is not driven to forsake Art and marry Mae West on the spot after vainly trying to make head or tail out of such literary dialect, I am the wrong candidate for Secretary of Culture and they had better start looking around for another man at once.

The more the public is dosed up with such highfalutin stuff, the farther off is the day when few people will disagree with the late Kin Hubbard's Abe Martin that "classical music is the kind that we keep hopin' will turn into a tune." Consider, for another example, Komisarjevsky, whose *The Theatre* goes on the bonfire without delay if I have my way about it. "The un-literary theatre is the only genuine form of theatrical Art," pontificates Komy, who gallops on to observe that "the Art of the theatre is an Art of actors and directors and not of writ-ers." Imagine the average man, hopeful of self-cultivation, not drooling at the mouth on being inoculated with such balder-dash. So the only genuine form of theatrical Art is not the lit-erary theatre of anyone like Shakespeare, Molière or Shaw but the theatre of Owen Davis, Anne Nichols or Phoebe and Henry Ephron! So the only real and true form of theatrical Art is a stageful of competent actors competently directed in some dish of illiterate garbage like *Make Yourself at Home* or *Marriage Is for Single People.*

Bang on the next pyre goes George Santayana's *Obiter Scripta* for sending the public further on its way to the lunatic asylum with things like this: "To attempt to abstract a so-called aesthetic interest from all other interests and a so-called work of Art from whatever work ministers, in one way or another, to all human good, is to make the aesthetic sphere contemptible. . . . When creative genius neglects to ally itself in this way to some public interest it hardly gives birth to works of wide or perennial interest. Imagination needs a soil in history, tradition or human institutions, else its random growths are not signifi-cant enough, and, like trivial melodies, go immediately out of fashion." If all this is so, the average culture seeker after vainly scratching his head to the bone very likely asks how comes it then that the fine old rules of form, style and manner no longer in and of themselves count for anything; how comes it that, de-spite the Santayana dictum, the plays of men like Strindberg still have a wide and perennial interest; how comes it that trivial melodies like *I've Been Working on the Railroad, The Sidewalks of New York, Melancholy Baby,* and many others such have not gone immediately out of fashion?

If for no other reason than that it contains the definition, "Art, even the most realistic in method, is confession and ab-breviation," Ludwig Lewisohn's *The Creative Life* will also be invited to visit the bonfire. The abbreviation end of the definition may pass muster. But the confession theory, that is, that the artist inevitably cannot help betraying his psychological self in his work however much he may exercise himself to conceal it, offers considerable challenge to the future sanity of anyone trying to get the hang of the whole Art business. The idea that such confession obtains in the case of numerous artists calls in the swallowing for a copious chaser of banana oil. Witness, for example, such exhibits as *The Cenci, Aïda, The Dark Flower, The Spectre's Bride* (Dvořák), and dozens of others.

Think of the disastrous effect upon the average man's mind when he reads such things as the Goncourts' "Art is eternization in a supreme force absolute and definite of the fugitivity of a creature or of a human being." Picture his bewilderment, upon his eventual recovery, when he then runs across something like Catulle Mendès' "In the Art of painting no painting is equivalent to the invisible reverse of the canvas." Imagine his doubled perplexity when a little later he reads Taine's "Arts of design require a soil not too highly cultivated," de la Roque's "All the arts the end of which is not immediate reproduction of nature, such as music, poetry and architecture, owe their processes to physical laws the exactitude of which is mathematical," and Henry James' "Art is nothing more than the shadow of humanity." That his aesthetic soul may be saved, onto the bonfire all of them. And with them onto the bonfire in the great cause of Art Alexander Bakshy's *The Theatre Unbound,* wherein this morsel: "The theatre, if its object is real Art, must free itself of illusionism." And Magnard for his "Individually the Arts have produced so many masterpieces that they seem to be exhausted," to say nothing of his "There is no dramatic expression in the Art of music." And Alfred Stevens for his remarkable "Flies respect the Art of good painting," not to forget his hardly less remarkable "A badly built man was never a master in the plastic Arts." And Houssaye for his matchless "In the literary Art it is only bad books that are good for anything." And Saint-Gaudens for his "What garlic is to salad, insanity is to Art." And all kinds of others.

The wise words of Buckle provide our conclusion. "To look upon an acquaintance with literature as one of the objects of education," he said, "is to mistake the order of events and to make the end subservient to the means. It is because this is done that we often find what are called highly educated men the progress of whose knowledge has been actually retarded by the activity of their education. We often find them burdened by prejudices, which their reading, instead of dissipating, has rendered more inveterate. For literature, being the depository of the thoughts of mankind, is full not only of wisdom but also of absurdities. The benefit, therefore, which is derived from literature will depend not so much upon the literature itself as upon the skill with which it is studied and the judgment with which it is selected."

[From *The Theatre Book of the Year, 1945–1946*, pp. 188–95.]

Nostalgia

NOSTALGIA, once so warmly acceptable to readers of writings on the theatre, seems to have gone out of fashion. The current style is for the writer not only cautiously to sidestep it and loudly to deny any trace of its existence in himself but even more emphatically to decry it in others, to dismiss them as feeble-minded and in all probability with one foot already in the grave, and to proclaim blanketwise that nothing in the older days was what it has been cracked up to be and is to be compared with the remarkable glories of the present. This is supposed to indicate several things: that the writer is an open-minded, sagacious, and independent fellow upon whom memory has been allowed to play no tricks; that he is still satisfactorily young enough to appreciate the miraculous fact that the world never fails enormously to advance and improve; and that he is sufficiently wise to realize that distance generally lends an unwarranted enchantment to the view. What it rather indicates, I daresay, is that the writer is simply up to the dodge of hiding what he does not know by airily dismissing the desirability of knowing it and reassuring those of his readers whose experience is as limited as his own that they have not missed what they have missed.

This is not to say, of course, that writers of a nostalgic bent are not just as often frauds. Trading in nostalgia is no better than boycotting it. It becomes a legitimate business, however, when memory is born partly of the mind and not wholly of the emotions, or at least when recollection has been filtered through a measure of critical perception. Too frequently, though, even when it is not arbitrary, it is the offspring of an emotionalism either soberly uncontrolled or the result of temporary indisposition or alcoholic liquor. Malaise has a way of turning the thoughts backward to other days, and the bottle, it need hardly be confided, induces an agreeable melancholia wherein one basks whimsically in the moonshine of the yesterdays.

The practising, professional school of nostalgia may be illustrated by some such selection as this from a recently published book on the Edwardian period in the London theatre, *Carriages at Eleven*, by one W. Macqueen-Pope:

> The great building (Covent Garden) is aglow, its gas cressets blow in the summer breeze above its high pediment, the odd little glasshouse perched on its portico is a pool of light, every window gleams, and a rich yellow flood pours out from under its covered carriage drive. One by one, in endless procession, the carriages roll up Long Acre or up Bow Street from the Strand, cockaded coachman with rug-covered knees, cockaded footman with arms folded and white buckskin legs, sitting stiffly to attention. Inside are handsome, moustached men in tails and white waistcoats; lovely ladies in their full array of trains, low necks, and silks and satins. And on their arms, their fingers, their corsages, around their necks, gleam a fortune of jewels—rubies, emeralds, sapphires, diamonds, pearls in rope and dog-collars. And on their elaborate coiffures glitter diamond tiaras, for every woman in those days was a queen and behaved accordingly . . .
>
> Champagne popped and fizzed, pretty mouths munched sandwiches of caviar or foie gras . . . Kisses were freely given, or stolen adventurously, vows were made, hearts beat and fluttered—and always the dance went on and laughter rang everywhere . . . And still the waltzers revolved, or the lancers made them scream with delight as the strong young males lifted the dainty girls off their feet. Who cared for to-

morrow? It would be as today, as yesterday. The world was
rich, secure, and prosperous . . . The youths went to work
unjaded, for the tonic of joy kept them alert—and there was
the night to look forward to again; the girls to sleep and
dream until the day failed and dusk came with the stars
and the gas lamps for another round of frolic in the eighties,
the nineties and the Edwardian nineteen-hundreds which
seem so far away but which are so near in terms of time.

The school is compounded of equal parts half-truth and re-
plete buncombe merchanted through a kind of travel-brochure
literature. It follows closely the pattern of perfume advertisements interlarded with references to past figures and institutions. And its net effect is to induce in all but the most sentimental reader a sensation akin to having partaken of a keg of
mush soaked in an apricot sauce. It isn't that its merchant is
sometimes not wholly honest according to his lights, if unfortunately still in the grip of an arrested juvenility. It is simply
that often what was actually a fifty-cent oil-painting is ped-
dled in a frame embellished by a thousand dollars' worth of
gilt.

But there is, as well, another kind of nostalgic writing, based
on times and things that were accurately observed and upon
which is impressed the bona fide romantic memory derived
from such accurate observation. Distance has been tried and
not found wanting; recollection is treated to doubt and skepticism and yet survives, with all its little silver bells still tinkling.
It is not, however, always thus buoyant; sometimes it is decidedly unwelcome and disturbing, since, while delusion may
make one happy, equally beautiful truth may depress one. Nostalgia is accordingly now and then much less agreeably wistful,
as most believe, then disagreeably incommodious. Far from
providing an escape from the present, it doubly stresses the
present. It is, in short, often as dangerous to your self-content-
ment and pleasure as thinking of the excellent dinners you got
twenty years ago for a dollar while presently paying a ten-
dollar check for a considerably less satisfactory one, or, I impertinently venture, of your yesterday's girl in the presence of
your venerable wife.

Revivals of drama do not much suffer from nostalgia, since drama frequently has a way of recreating itself whoever acts in it. It is the musical shows that are vassals to it; not the superior examples like *The Merry Widow* and the like, for they can stand largely on their own, but the lesser ones and the song-and-dance and girl shows. It is, of course, too much to say that one such of the past is impossible of entirely conciliating revival, though I have no statistics at hand to prove it. But it is not too much to say that the challenge is a severe one. I for one, indeed, cannot think of a single such revival in many years—and that includes relatively very good ones like *Show Boat*—which has wholly succeeded in exiling the original from blissful memory. Too many factors interpose themselves, realistic as well as purely sentimental. Such shows, in the first place, are primarily for men in their younger and gayer years. As the years go on and men grow older and are less given to superficial pleasures, they are subject to a closer analytical scrutiny, which is disastrous. When one looks back on them, any such analysis is somehow remitted, since one looks back not on the shows alone but coincidentally on one's self as one was in those other days, and such remembrance has a way of confusing one's then rosier self with the shows. One saw them through still relatively shining and untroubled eyes in what was, in Kipling's phrase, a cleaner, greener world, or at least one that, compared with the world of today, seemed to be so.

Nor is the nostalgia necessarily sentimental; a lot of hard fact supports it in various directions. The shows of the years gone, in the first place, were much more attractive in physical detail. With the enormously increased expenses—something like four or five times as great—it is next to impossible to put on a revival of one of them with anything approximating its original splendor. The enforced economy takes its toll of scenery and costumes, and the result is a stage that generally looks like a poor relation of the original production. The theatres in which the revivals are housed, furthermore, miss all the air and color and style of those that housed the same shows in the yesterdays. Aside from the still remaining Ziegfeld, where is there one to match the New Amsterdam and its golden *Frolics* roof, or Dillingham's Knickerbocker and Globe, or the Casino, or

the Broadway, or the Herald Square, or their like? The Shu-
bert, Imperial, and the Music Box are good enough in their
way, but what of the others? The Adelphi has all the gayety and
tone of a retired car-barn. The Century's interior looks like a
provincial stock company house of fifty years ago. The Majestic and Forty-sixth Street theatres, with their steep tiers of
seats back of the orchestra proper, seem more appropriate to
sports events than to musicals, and the Coronet, National, and
Broadhurst, along with the St. James and Martin Beck, which
now and then are given over to musicals, remain essentially
houses for drama. One enters them in a dramatic, not a musical
show mood; when musicals are in them they seem self-conscious and a bit embarrassed, like rural churches that have
been turned for the nonce into summer theatres playing such
things as *The Voice of the Turtle*.

It is thus when one sees a revue in the austere surroundings
of, say, the National, that one reflects on the intrinsic geniality
of a revue theatre of yesterday like the Weber and Fields Music Hall, warm with crimson and gaudy and with its cheery
downstairs bar where the pretty girls gathered when the show
was over and where Mock Weber, Joe's brother, held forth expansively as host and raconteur. It is thus when one braves the
gales that howl down dark Fifty-ninth Street and goes to the
Century that one harks back to the old New Amsterdam, its
façade as brilliantly lighted as a Gilbert and Sullivan battleship,
its promenade broad enough to contain Charles Belmont Davis,
Diamond Jim Brady, Captain Jim Churchill and Marie Dressler
walking abreast, and its auditorium deep enough to render
Donald Brian's singing voice fortunately inaudible. And it is
thus when one sits in one or another of the present incongru-
ous theatres that memory turns back to Daly's, the home of
The Geisha, San Toy, and all those other softly lovely things, to
the Moorish Casino and the George Lederer shows with all
their gorgeous girls, and to other such houses enveloped by the
feel and aspect and very fragrance of music and dance and
charming femininity.

The girls, the girls. It is always the girls that figure most
prominently in any such business of recollection. That there
are not just as many attractive ones today as there were then

is obviously nonsense. There are plenty of them. But they do not seem to be on the music show stage. A musical with even one or two pretty girls in it these days is almost a phenomenon. What the producers seem fanatically intent upon giving us instead are female ballet dancers with legs beside which gnarled oaks look like young birches and with faces that are recognizable as such solely on the score of a large ear on either side. And not only such ballet sights but grotesque female comics, singers apparently chosen for their leather lungs, altitudinous show-girls with all the physical appeal of giraffes, chorus girls who mostly look like the inspiration for aspirin, and, above all, leading women who would have set Ziegfeld in his day to howling like a wounded coyote. In all the shows of the last three seasons, in fact, there have been but two or three principal girls of any perceptible looks in face and figure, and one of them scarcely assisted the picture with her talent for emitting from time to time a whistle so shrill that it shattered the eardrums. As to the chorus and show-girls, my count numbered only a handful out of hundreds who might have stacked up with all the many who tickled the vision, to specify but one of the affectabilities, in the past.

If this strikes the present generation as rather far-fetched, let anyone who can remember back no more than twenty years compare girl with girl now and then. Or let anyone try to find today other girls like those when this same show was originally produced. Here, for any such comparison, are the names of just a very few on the musical stage in that 1921 period: Marilyn Miller, Adele Astaire, Louise Brown, Betty Compton, Irene Delroy, Bobby Perkins, Lily Damita, Marion Sunshine, Marion and Madeleine Fairbanks, Claire Luce, Dorothy Knapp, Constance Carpenter, Hilda Ferguson, Gladys Glad, Marion Davies, Justine Johnstone, Edna Leedom, Anastasia Reilly, Ruby Keeler, Hannah Williams, Mary Eaton, Kathryn Ray, and Beth Meakins. Or, to go back not more than ten or twelve years, Grace McDonald, June Havoc, Carmen Molina, Marcy Wescott, Ann Miller, Evelyn Laye, June Allyson, Beryl Wallace, Prudence Hayes, Della Lind, Joyce Beasley, Marissa Flores, June Clyde, Carmen Miranda, Joan Wetmore, Helena Bliss, and at least two dozen similar fragrant blossoms. Or, to go back only six or seven years or even less, Evelyn Wyckoff, Leila Ernst, Jane Ball, Sunnie O'Dea, Elaine Barry, Vera-Ellen, Marjorie Knapp, Sally Bond, Joyce Matthews, Mary Healy, Susan Miller, Irene Hilda, Diane Davis, Frances Mercer, Patricia Marshall, Ilona Massey, Mary Ganley, Mary Roche, Nan Wynn, Althea Elder, Eva Reyes, Kathleen Roche, Geraldine Stroock, Vera Zorina, Geraldine Speckels, etc., etc. Small wonder the eyes roll backward.

And what of the music? Aside perhaps from Richard Rodgers, where today is there anyone who consistently approaches the quality of Victor Herbert, Reginald De Koven, Franz Léhar, Emmerich Kalman, Jerome Kern, Edmund Eysler, Ivan Caryll, Sidney Jones, Lionel Monckton, Leslie Stuart, Gustave Kerker, Ludwig Englander, Paul Tietjens, Henry K. Hadley, Edward German, Paul Rubens, Ed Jacobowski, Alfred Robyn, André Messager, George Gershwin, Vincent Youmans, and men like them? Small wonder, as well, that ears turn backward. Even the Frimls do not seem to be composing any longer, if you want to bring that up.

And where nowadays is there anything like the lush, purple, moonlit scenery of Joseph Urban, or like the old Ziegfeld numbers with all the girls sailing over your head on Springtime swings laden with fresh flowers of the fields, or the orchestras of sixty and seventy musicians, or such whole choruses of beauties as one saw in *The Wild Rose, Havana,* and many other such shows, or comedians making their entrance with parachutes, or first-night audiences like those photographed on the covers of old Empire Theatre programs dressed to the hilt and magnificently devoid of moving picture scouts and similar contemporary vermin? Or the neighboring bars with their entr'-acte huge goblets of champagne, or the toasts of the town like Lillian Russell, Edna May, Lotta Faust, Helen Hale and suchlike, or the stage-doors choked with florist messengers, or the great, gala road theatres like Philadelphia's Broad and old Forrest, Pittsburgh's Nixon, Baltimore's Academy of Music and Cleveland's Euclid Avenue, or the dazzling openings that turned Atlantic City's Apollo into Manhattan on holiday, or stages with Sousa's whole brass band booming down the final curtain?

Sentimental, my eye! Facts, gentlemen, facts! And if facts are sentimental, make the most of it.

[From *The Theatre Book of the Year, 1948–1949,* pp. 15–25.]

Convictions about the Theatre

FEW other enterprises are ridden by more hollow convictions than the theatre. It argues, for example, that a play must never mix its moods, yet O'Casey's *Juno and the Paycock* does it very auspiciously. It still holds that the happy ending play is its best commercial bet, yet all kinds of plays like *Mourning Becomes Electra, Shadow and Substance, The Glass Menagerie, A Streetcar Named Desire, Mister Roberts,* and *Edward, My Son* have prospered as greatly. It believes there is no money in tragedy, yet *Medea, Anne of the Thousand Days, Death of a Salesman,* etc., have played to good business. It imagines that a musical show without a lot of dancing is a bad risk, yet *South Pacific* is one of the greatest successes in years. It maintains there is no large audience for wit and that only bellylaughs are the ticket, yet the revivals of *Lady Windermere's Fan, Caesar and Cleopatra, The Devil's Disciple, The Importance of Being Earnest, Man and Superman,* have attracted plenty folk.

It further believes that there is no box-office for a play in which the central character is unsympathetic, yet numerous plays like *Craig's Wife, The Little Foxes, Detective Story,* etc., have been very successful. It sneers at the mildew on Ibsen and then gives its prizes and box-office returns to a play like *All My Sons* which is identical in theme with one of Ibsen's plays. It prides itself on its increased sophistication, yet it revels in Oscar Hammerstein's innocent lyrics and Richard Rodgers' gentle tunes. It deplores the excessively increased cost of play production and points out dolefully that even a one-set play cannot be brought into New York for less than fifty or sixty thousand dollars, yet such successes as *The Glass Menagerie, The Silver Whistle,* etc., cost nowhere near any such fancy sum. The two-set *Clutterbuck,* furthermore, cost only thirty-three thousand.

It firmly believes that "a young woman can't play Juliet and when she gets older and can play it she is too old for the role," yet Mary Anderson played Juliet and caused a sensation when she was seventeen. Fanny Kemble did the same at nineteen, Julia Arthur was said to have been extremely able in the role even at fourteen, and Elisabeth Bergner was just twenty-five when she triumphed in the part. As to the older actresses, Jane Cowl made an admirable Juliet at thirty-six; Julia Marlowe, whose first appearance in the role was at twenty-three, was still lovely in it at forty; Helena Modjeska's Juliet began at thirty-three and continued to enchant audiences at forty; Florence Roberts was still effective at forty-one; and Eleanor Robson was in her very late thirties when her Juliet captivated audiences.

It insists that the title of a play which is not easily pronounceable or clearly understandable to the general public will inevitably spell ruin, yet innumerable plays and shows like *Amphitryon 38, Believe Me Xantippe, Déclassée, Chauve Souris, Winterset, Brigadoon, The Voice of the Turtle, Ah, Wilderness!, R.U.R., Tovarich, Liliom, Laburnum Grove*, etc., have paid no attention to the argument and have been successful. It reasons that college boys never turn out to be much good as actors and directors and that the best training for acting and directing is to be had in spending one's early life instead around the Broadway theatres and with the road troupes, yet José Ferrer is regarded as the best of the younger actors on the present stage and Joshua Logan as one of the very best newer directors, and both are Princeton men.

It additionally convinces itself that a play or show whose title begins with one of the first letters in the alphabet and which hence will occupy a top position in the newspaper theatrical advertising columns will stand a much better chance of attracting customers than one down at the bottom of the list, yet among the biggest popular successes of the last two seasons have been such tail-enders as *The Winslow Boy, Private Lives, Where's Charley?, The Member of the Wedding*, and *South Pacific*, to say nothing, in the middle advertising position, of *Mister Roberts, I Know My Love, Howdy, Mr. Ice, Kiss Me, Kate, Man and Superman, Medea, Make Mine Manhattan, Lost in the Stars, Lend an Ear*, etc. It insists that there is no money in literary or highbrow plays, yet such dramatists as Shaw, Giraudoux, Robinson Jeffers, Eliot, O'Neill, *et al.*, draw in the paying trade.

It still believes in the great drawing-power of name actors and actresses, yet in the last three seasons the following at times have been failures in that respect: Katharine Cornell, Ruth Chatterton, Paul Muni, Fay Bainter, Elisabeth Bergner, Burgess Meredith, Walter Hampden, Lee Tracy, Eva Le Gallienne, Ernest Truex, Canada Lee, Ruth Gordon, Martha Scott, Mady Christians, Emlyn Williams, Miriam Hopkins, Mary Boland, Raymond Massey, Margaret Wycherly, Melville Cooper, Leo G. Carroll, Jane Cowl, Maurice Evans, John Gielgud, Oscar Karlweis, Oscar Homolka, Gertrude Lawrence, Betty Field, June Walker, Flora Robson, Eddie Dowling, Jack Buchanan, Thomas Mitchell, Peggy Wood, *et al.* On the other hand, in the same period unknowns or novices like June Lockhart, Marlon Brando, Julie Harris, Meg Mundy, William Lanteau, Iris Mann, *et al.*, have helped to bring money into the box-office.

It cherishes the notion that a play that has a dog in it arbitrarily stands a good chance to win the public's favor and, to its credit, plays containing dogs from *Uncle Tom's Cabin* to *Peg o' My Heart* and on to *The Barretts of Wimpole Street* have seemed to support its conviction, yet there have been many plays, and some fair ones, with dogs in them that have got nowhere, among them *Young America, The Hound of the Baskervilles, Storm Over Patsy, A Case of Youth,* etc. It also persistently thinks that an insane character if treated humorously is objectionable to an audience, yet from the vaudeville days of Aaron Hoffman to plays like *The Misleading Lady* and in more recent years *Arsenic and Old Lace* such a character has entertained and amused audiences no end.

It believes that a play which consists mainly of talk and which is deficient in action does not stand a chance at the box-office, yet the recent revival of Shaw's *Man and Superman* has played to record business all over the nation, and Eliot's *The Cocktail Party* has played to standees. It contends that the public will not abide curtain-raisers, yet both *Hope Is the Thing with Feathers* and Wilder's *A Happy Journey* were successful as successive curtain-lifters to Sartre's *The Respectful Prostitute*. It believes that plays ending in suicides are a dangerous gamble, yet from the far days of Fitch's *The Climbers* to the present days of *All My Sons* and *Death of a Salesman* the belief has been proved senseless. It argues that a play without a plot and a more or less direct story line is doomed, yet one like *You Can't Take It with You* played to large profits. It holds that a musical comedy that does not bring down its final curtain on a rousing ensemble number is likely to send an audience out disappointed, yet *South Pacific*, the finale of which is nothing of the kind, has been an enormous success.

It fancies that what the mass public demands is novelty, yet the ice skating shows, which are largely and merely duplications of one another, have been attracting huge crowds for nine years now. It fears as non-commercial dialogue of a literary flavor, yet the dramatization of a Henry James novel titled *The Heiress* has been highly prosperous, as has the aforesaid *The Cocktail Party*. It was firm in its theory that the public had become fed up with war plays, yet *Command Decision* and *Mister Roberts* confounded it. It believes that a moving picture name is helpful to the box-office, yet in the last few seasons among the well-known film figures whose plays and shows failed have been Jean Pierre Aumont, Michael Redgrave, Claire Trevor, Philip Dorn, Melvyn Douglas, Charles Laughton, John Garfield, Anthony Quinn, Boris Karloff, Anne Jeffreys, Nancy Kelly, Jean Parker, Annabella, Helmut Dantine, Alexander Knox, James Mason, Peggy Ann Garner, *et al.*

It concludes that English actors are arbitrarily admired by American audiences who will pay out money to see them at the expense of the native product, yet that has been far from the case in recent seasons, as the failure of Donald Wolfit and Co., Cicely Courtneidge and Co., the *Power without Glory* company, and of various actors like John Gielgud, Jack Buchanan, Emlyn Williams, Graham Payn, Isabel Jeans, *et al.*, has attested. It thinks that present day audiences gag at smut, yet one of the heartiest, loudest laughs heard in the theatre in the last two seasons was at the tag of *Strange Bedfellows*, which would have brought a blush to the cheek of Minsky in his prime.

It believes that audiences that are tardy in returning to their seats are one of the curses of the theatre, yet it also believes that if bars were to be permitted in theatres it would help the theatre a great deal. It subscribes to the theory that the experimental theatres can be of real help to the Broadway theatre by uncovering fresh, new forms of entertainment, yet when one such experimental theatre discovers some such fresh, new form in the shape of the bill called *Ballet Ballads* and turns it over to the Broadway theatre the latter will have nothing to do with it. It contends that when business is bad on the road it is because the road will not accept second and third companies and demands the original New York article, yet the *Life with Father, Mister Roberts, Streetcar,* and the several *Oklahoma!* road troupes, among a dozen others in the last ten years, have reaped a harvest.

It places considerable emphasis on the quality of stage scenery and holds that Broadway audiences will not tolerate a noticeably skimpy production, yet *Harvey,* with stage settings that looked as if they had cost not more than fifty dollars, crowded the theatre for several years. It eloquently argues that the trouble with the theatre is a lack of good plays, yet when it produces good plays like *A Sound of Hunting, A Highland Fling, Outrageous Fortune, The Mermaids Singing,* etc., people do not go to see them. It also argues that cheap Tin Pan Alley tunes are responsible for the failure of various musical shows, yet when composers like Heitor Villa-Lobos and Benjamin Britten appear on the scene audiences similarly will have none of them.

It maintains that decentralization would accomplish wonders for the drama, which is allegedly hamstrung by Broadway, and that the independent tastes of non-New York audiences should be given a lot of kindly consideration, yet fully eight of the better plays which have been shown in the Broadway theatre in recent seasons have had thumbs turned down on them when they were tried out in the road theatres. It fondly weeps into its beer over what it sentimentally refers to as the Royal Family of the American Theatre, yet one member of that family has not been near a stage for thirty years and has consecrated his art to the films, which hail him as the Grand

Old Man of the movies; a second deserted the theatre in his early forties for the pictures and spent most of the rest of his life in them; and the third abandoned the stage for the screen some years ago and says she prefers to sit beside her comfortable Hollywood swimming pool to returning to the theatre.

And, finally, it believes that Gilbert and Sullivan, even if not too well done, cannot fail to draw money into the box-office and that this has been true since the time they were first produced here. No other of the local theatre's legends has enjoyed a greater longevity and none is more insecurely grounded on fact. Gilbert and Sullivan have intermittently come bad croppers and on occasion, as with one lavish production of *The Gondoliers,* have lost small fortunes.

[From *The Theatre Book of the Year. 1949–1950,* pp. 39–44.]

ON CRITICISM AND CRITICS

Critical Conclusions

To speak of impersonal criticism is as ridiculous as to speak of impersonal drama, impersonal music, impersonal painting, or impersonal reaction to alcoholic liquor. There is no such thing. There is only live criticism and dead criticism. To speak of even the latter as impersonal is to confuse criticism with its practising corpse.

The younger the critic, the more he is fetched by mere theme. If the theme, in his eyes, is an important one, that is, one that deals with matters of immediate public concern, treatment takes second or even third place with him. It is thus that any play, however otherwise defective, which treats of something in the popular consciousness of the moment usually receives his hearty endorsement not only as a play of weight but as one of considerable artistic merit as well.

Patriotism is the enemy of sound criticism. It is thus that three-quarters of the criticism generally written in wartime never survives the armistice.

What the actress as woman is off the stage reflects itself for better or worse, whatever the nature of the role, when she is on. This may sound nonsensical, but it somehow seems to be true.

What it proves critically I wouldn't know, but the fact remains that in fifty years of the American stage only one out of the many plays that have shown a small, illuminated railroad train moving by night across the backdrop has been a failure. That one was *Fulton of Oak Falls*, which achieved a run of but thirty-seven performances. The rest have made lots of money.

"A good play enacted by competent principals," one of my colleagues has written, "can easily survive an ineffective bit by an untalented bit player." Not always so easily. I have seen an otherwise very competently acted *The Weavers* go completely to pieces on the shoals of its child Mielchen.

The vogue of the short skirt is one of the severest trials that actresses have ever been made to suffer.

The notion, favorite of women and effeminate actors, that the critics, being for the most part not overly blessed by nature, are enviously contemptuous of handsome actors is far from the fact. Every handsome actor on the modern stage, with but one exception that I can think of, has been given a happy deal by the critics. The exception was Lou Tellegen, who was such a bad actor that the critics, for all the good will in the world, could not help themselves. Henry Dixey, Richard Bennett as a young man, George Alexander, William Faversham, James O'Neill, E. H. Sothern, Kyrle Bellew, James Carew, James K. Hackett, Charles Cherry, Hamilton Revelle, Harry Davenport, Vincent Serrano, Frederic De Belleville, Henry Miller, Herbert Standing, William Courtenay, Edgar Selwyn, Harry Woodruff, John Barrymore—these and others of the pictorially elect have literally been made by their friendly, ugly brothers, the critics.

There are actors, whatever their share of talent, who find audiences prejudiced against them from the start. Let an actor be too precise and glossy in his dress, like the late Robert Hilliard, or move about with a too severely erect posture, like the late Tellegen aforesaid, or steal a glance at the ladies out front so much as once, like the late Lowell Sherman, or be or do any such trivial thing and he is doomed.

I not long ago read this, from the pen of one of the colleagues: "He (the playwright) hasn't learned the most elementary principle of dramatic construction, which is that you cannot have a good person evilly put upon without making his persecutors pay for their crimes." Hardly elementary, my dear Watson, except in the case of box-office dramaturgy. Examples: Strindberg's *The Father,* Becque's *The Ravens,* Galsworthy's *Justice,* among many others.

Criticism as the adventures of a soul among masterpieces is an ideal. Criticism is most often bound to be the misadventures of a soul among gimcracks.

The critic who can remain absolutely honest in his appraisal of an exceptionally pretty actress is either a genius or a fool.

"There are," I once observed, "critics who are less interested in the impression a play makes upon them than in the impression they make upon the play." But do not jump to too sarcastic conclusions. Shaw was one such, and a better critic of the drama never lived.

Whatever the faults of much of contemporary drama, it at least has avoided one of the weaknesses of much of contemporary literature. The latter, especially where it is the product of the younger practitioners, seems often to be ridden by the notion that there is something strangely virile and impressive in sexual intercourse conducted *al fresco*. The drama, even when written by the younger playwrights, generally refrains from any such undergraduate nonsense and keeps it indoors, where it belongs. The anatomical romance hypothetically implicit in bramble-bush, hillside, sleeping-bag and other such extramural discomforts, however starlit, is considerably less the material for serious fiction or drama than for farce, good and loud. Nature, as the saying goes, may be wonderful, but—.

Acting is the world's only profession in which a person is loudly applauded at the end of his day's work for drawing down a higher financial reward than he often deserves.

What of the American playwriting gods of the drama critics of yesterday? What is their standing today? Augustus Thomas, Edward Sheldon, Charles Klein, Eugene Walter, George Broadhurst? Let us take time out for laughter.

It is a pity that so many valid dramatic ideas seem to fall into the hands of incompetent playwrights. The waste is sad to contemplate. The idea in *South Pacific*, which a few seasons ago ran for only five performances, for one example, was much too good to lose: the Negro's ironic position in the atmosphere of two different civilizations. And over the years there have been many others, light and serious, in such failures as *The Man Who Ate the Popomack*, treating of the influence of odors on human society; *The Upstart*, dealing with the final inefficacy of mere speech, however eloquent; etc., etc. A catalogue of all the tasty ideas that have been quickly buried in the storehouse for lack of skilful treatment would fill a book.

To critics who write praisefully of an actor having "felt" his role, let us commend Coquelin's retort to Madame Ristori's insistence that the actor cannot express on the stage an emotion which he does not really feel. "Yes, madame," observed Coquelin, "but you often die."

Thinking of illustrious French theatrical figures of the past, much of the wisdom which they otherwise contributed to the dramatic record is today found to be not only hollow but quite foolish. For example:

(a) "A meditative being may not enter into any dramatic combination."—Paul Bourget. *Hamlet, Brand,* and half a hundred others make mock of the criticism.

(b) "As romantic situations are always very special, the more you make use of them in plays the more you decrease general interest."—Brunetière. *Camille,* Cyrano de Bergerac, and half a hundred others are observed thumbing their noses.

(c) "It is permissible to make a mistake in the details of the execution of a play, but it is not permissible to make a mistake . . . in facts."—Alexandre Dumas, fils. *Vide* the drama of Shakespeare and Bernard Shaw.

(d) "A playwright must write many bad plays before he can make a good one."—Houssaye. Shakespeare, Strindberg, Ibsen, Björnson, Heijermans, Hofmannsthal, Pirandello, Hauptmann, O'Casey, O'Neill, among various others, didn't somehow seem to know it.

(e) "The dignity of tragedy demands some grand state interest, or some passion nobler than love."—Corneille. As, for example, *Romeo and Juliet.*

(f) "The tragic author admits atrocious crime, conspiracy, murder, parricide, regicide, and so on. Comedy, less audacious, never goes beyond the conventional, because its pictures are drawn from conventional manners."—Beaumarchais. *Arsenic and Old Lace,* for one example out of many.

The worst of all bores encountered by a dramatic critic is the one who approaches him after the first act and asks him what he thinks of the play. My own usual retort to any such jackass is to inquire of him in turn what he thinks of a dinner after the oysters.

In real life any woman who sought to express her rapt interest in a man's words by blinking her eyes throughout his conversation would be put down by him as a transparent idiot. On the stage she is customarily regarded by the reviewers as either a delightful ingénue with a very promising future or as an actress of more mature years who has remarkably retained her youthfulness and girlish charm.

The old schoolroom saying that genius is the capacity for taking infinite pains calls for revaluation. It is mere talent, rather, which demands that capacity. I have just looked up again the stories of some hundred acknowledged geniuses from Aristophanes to Shakespeare and Bernard Shaw, along with the sculptors, painters and composers, and much of the greatest of their work seems to have been the result of no particular over-assiduity or headaches.

So many of the well-made plays of the past, notably those of Pinero and his school, give one the impression of nothing so much as well prepared dinners served with paper napkins.

The majority of our popular playwrights seem to have as their worshipful credo the old German saying, "Beautiful is youth; it never comes again." Youth to their way of thinking and writing is the desideratum above all desiderata, and their plays are full of wistful elderly creatures who yearn for its recapture and blissful return. What, one meditates in one's later years, if it did return? Gradually, as one slid back over the years, one would lose the proud and secure place one had made for one's self in the world; one would lose the happy job that has gone hand in hand with it; one would lose all the good and trusted friends whom one had gathered in the fuller years of one's life; and, worse still and more awful to contemplate, if the metamorphosis were extreme, one would wind up again having to drink milk!

On that day when an audience, as in the theatre, interrupts the progress of a film with periodic applause and remains at the end to cheer the screen play and players I will be persuaded to believe that the moving pictures can approach the effectiveness of the living drama.

The word "charm" is usually as critically obnoxious to me as the words "glamour" and "authority," but I am afraid I shall have to fall back on it, since that is just what I am going to talk about. So: the one commodity lacking in the greater proportion of our current actresses is charm. And sadly, because most other things considered and duly allowed for, an actress without the attribute is much like a pickpocket with it. We have all kinds of actresses with talent; we have all kinds who can do their jobs well and some who can do them beautifully; we have expert technicians and very satisfactory minor players and all of that. But among the lot there are not in the present years more than a handful who have in them that rare quality which, like a prehensile mist, steals over the footlights and gathers men into its warm embrace. Without descending to the ungentlemanliness of mentioning the few actresses, young and not so young, who possess it and thus wounding the plurality who do not, I can at this moment think of only two older actresses who are blessed with the property, and only two in the middle bracket, and only two in the younger. Which amounts to just a paltry, if welcome, six out of many hundreds. Some of these others have what is known as sex appeal (a phrase also obnoxious to me—at least, I should say, literarily); some are endowed with looks; some are among the leaders in their acting age groups. But without charm they are, if the truth were told, even for a good half of the Critics' Circle little more than proficient hams.

The fact remains that there is not a single leading actor on the contemporary American stage with a speaking voice that one affectionately remembers. There is not one with the dry and wonderful impressive voice of a William Gillette, or one with the grand romantic tones of a William Faversham, or one with the smooth finish of a John Drew, or one with the warm gentleness of a Bruce McRea, or one with the crackle and fire of an Arnold Daly, or one with the halting charm of an early William Courtenay, or one with the winning inner smile of a Leo Ditrichstein, or one with the summer thunder of a Henry Miller, or one with the silken challenge of a Kyrle Bellew, or one with the quiet style of a Guy Standing, or one with the soft ease of a Frank Worthing or an E. S. Willard.

While plot as plot is the chief concern of our amateurs, box-office hacks and deficient literary and dramatic practitioners generally and while I myself am perfectly willing to leave it to admirers of detective stories, murder melodramas and other such diversions of the emotionally unwashed, it nevertheless paradoxically strikes me that the fear of it, instilled in them by literary and drama critics, has dulled the plays of a number of our younger and more ambitious playwrights. Afraid of plot lest they be superiorly relegated by these critics to the company of mere pulp writers, they hit it over the head, whenever it pops up in their plays, with wisecracks, satirical spoofs, heavy witticisms and similar self-criticism. The consequence is usually plays not only without sufficiently satisfactory stories, however slight, but without sufficiently satisfactory wit, humor or original viewpoint to make one remit the absence of plot.

The difference between an actress like Elisabeth Bergner and one like, say, Ethel Barrymore is the difference between a minute chemical analysis of a cocoanut pie and the cocoanut pie itself.

A novelist may introduce his hero in any manner whatsoever with no worry over his readers. A dramatist, on the other hand, must often arbitrarily take his audiences into concerned consideration. To give just one example out of many, it would be next to impossible for a playwright to introduce his hero by having him rush onto the stage with the words, "Quick! There's not a moment to lose!" Since his hero in all likelihood would be cast with a more or less prominent actor he would have to figure on the audience applause which would greet his first entrance and which would hold up the stage and make the speech ridiculous. The laugh which would inevitably follow would obviously ruin not only the moment but the action immediately following.

It is generally overlooked by historians of the theatre that variety theatres in their earlier day were shunned by respectable women as if they were so many houses of ill-fame. It was Tony Pastor who rid them of their prejudice, not by changing materially the form of stage entertainment but by bribing them into his theatre with prizes of half-barrels of flour, half-tons of coal, and fancy dress patterns. The erstwhile aloof girls flocked to his playhouse in droves and his theatre soon became so packed with them that he had to add extra chairs to accommodate the overflow.

It significantly remains that ninety-five per cent of the fifty straight plays which have achieved the longest runs in our modern American theatre have had so-called happy endings.

The American passion for short sentences has gone to such an extreme that any sentence containing more than ten or twelve words is regarded not only as a literary affectation but as so extraordinarily involved that it is almost impossible to disentangle it.

The spectacle of a college professor-critic trying to be one of the boys has always been one of the most diverting acts on the bill of our national vaudeville. But it has seldom since been so amusing as the performance of the late Prof. Brander Matthews. Not only did he come out on the critical stage in a red undershirt and baggy pants and proclaim the Irish comedian, Ned Harrigan, a blood-brother to Molière but, before the stomps and whistles ended, sprang this personal nifty: "An American professor of dramatic literature, whenever he came to discuss the lyrical burlesques of Aristophanes, was in the habit of sending his whole class to Weber and Fields that his students might see for themselves the nearest modern analogy to the robust fancies of the great Greek humorist."

The villains in the old-time melodramas were almost always identified as such on the score of their superior diction. There seldom was a dyed-in-the-wool scoundrel in those shows who didn't speak English impeccably—and whose trousers, incidentally, weren't just a shade too short.

There is much bosh about this or that Hamlet actor, whatever his other virtues, not looking like Hamlet. A number of the critics have recently been saying it again about Maurice Evans. Aside from one or two faint and debatable clues, Shakespeare gives us very little idea of what Hamlet really looked like, so who knows for certain? Hamlet's looks amount in the end very largely only to the particular prejudice of his beholder. Anyway, if the player is a good one, what matter? Where is the stage Juliet who ever looked fully like the Juliet of our imaginations? Or, God knows, the Cleopatra, Ariel, or Titania? Or even the Julius Caesar or Marc Antony? Few actors ever look exactly like the characters we are requested to imagine them to be. The only characters, indeed, who uniformly look like the actors playing them are Uncle Tom, Topsy, Charley's aunt, Mrs. Malaprop, and Cinderella's stepsisters.

Despite the common directorial belief, little is so ruinous to the effect of an actress' performance, save in farce and certain comedy, as too much vitality. The best actresses are those who silently and inwardly suggest it. The worst are those who physically demonstrate it. The great Eleonora Duse in all the thirty-odd years I beheld her in various roles in different corners of Europe and America never for a moment allowed her audiences to feel that she had just eaten a large Porterhouse steak and was rarin' to go. There was about her always, even in her earlier and more vigorous years, the faint suggestion that she was not physically quite up to snuff. The Katina Paxinous, on the other hand, habitually have at their customers with so much energy that, if Joe Louis were out front, he'd swoon.

It is said that the trouble with many of the newer playwrights is that they have not learned the business of sound play construction and that, as a consequence, their plays, even when possessed of intermittent merits, miss fire. This, in many instances, is sheer critical twaddle. The real trouble with the playwrights is not that they have not mastered the dramaturgical technique but that, even were they to be veritable hounds at it, their mental, spiritual, emotional and imaginative quotient is woefully deficient. It is, of course, perfectly true that a knowledge of technique is valuable, but that it is a prime essential is far from true. Genius, or merely an unusual talent, may be ignorant of it or may loftily wave it aside and nonetheless produce plays of worth. Gorki's admittedly best play is almost amateurish technically, at least in the sense that the critics understand the word. Most of Shaw's plays would have been marked G-minus by dramaturgical professors of the George Pierce Baker school. As a matter of record, Maurine Wakins' admirable satirical farce, *Chicago*, which subsequently proved a great success in the theatre, was so marked by Baker when the author, a member of his class, submitted it to him for his criticism. Wedekind's best play is a technical botch, and so, to the pundits of his day, was Georg Kaiser's. And Strindberg's *The Dream Play* originally had the critics yelling for mama. . . . Saroyan is a particular goat of the technical assayers. If only he obeyed the dramatic rules, they say, his plays would be what they should be. As Bobby Clark exclaimed in *All Men Are Alike,* Oh, bal——derdash! If Saroyan wrote his plays according to the stricter dramaturgical formula they would be unspeakably bad. One of their greatest virtues is their very neglect of that formula. Those who believe the opposite are those who insist that poetry is not poetry unless it rhymes. Some of the very worst plays in the theatre of the last ten years have been technically perfect. And some of the very best have been as technically imperfect as Shakespeare's *King Lear* and *A Midsummer Night's Dream.*

Whenever a musical show of the past is revived, the critics are pretty sure to write that one of its greatest assets is the evocation in an audience of the nostalgic mood. This, I believe, is only partly true. What is also evoked, particularly by the lovely old songs, is the antonym of nostalgia. Fond melody does not make one think tenderly alone of what has been and is gone. It also sometimes makes one think of what may come in one's life, of sentimental dream and hope, and of wished-for illusion and flowered horizon.

A final, horrible thought assails the critic. Maybe the very quality of such thoughts as these provide ample evidence that the rot-the-mind advocates may be right.

[From *The Theatre Book of the Year, 1946–1947,* pp. 177–88.]

Critical Observations

Instinct and Criticism.—Although there is inevitably something suspect—and intelligibly so—about any such *ex post facto* argument as I am herewith about to advance, it seems to me that one of the reasons for the poor theatrical business in certain quarters lies in the fact that, when it comes to judging plays in advance of their production, the average manager hasn't anything like the shrewdness of the average play reviewer. Show me a critic and a producer with an equal share of theatrical experience and, four times out of every five, I'll show you a critic who can spot the producer's dismal play some considerable time before the misguided producer lifts a curtain on it. There are plays that smell bad even before one knows a thing about them, and a sixth critical sense, combined with the obvious third, makes the critic aware of their approach long before they have come into sight. Sometimes it is nothing more than a matter of cheapness of title; sometimes it is the nature of the previous activity of the author; sometimes it is nothing more intelligent than a vague feeling; and sometimes it is what may, for want of a sounder phrase, be termed critical instinct. But whatever it is, for all the fond faith and trust of the producer who has picked the play, it predicts with a peculiar certainty the complete worthlessness of the imminent exhibition.

Why is it that, when two or three new plays open on the same evening, play reviewers pretty generally contrive to select the one to see that subsequently turns out, whatever its deficiencies, to be at least the best of the lot? This is found to be true even where no prejudice as to a particular producer or a particular theatre exists and where the two or three plays are the work of equally unknown playwrights and the effort of no particularly significant producers. And why is it that the so-called second- and third-string reviewers so regularly and foreseeingly are assigned to cover plays bound for the storehouse even before they show themselves? It isn't guesswork; it is presentiment and a species of foreknowledge; and it is also intuitive sense. In the last four years, I recall only one occasion when the reviewers dismissed a pretty good play in favor of some less worthy opening, that play being Hugh Stange's *Veneer*. But in the general run of things you will usually discover that when almost anything at all opens against plays like *Did I Say No?*, *Enemy Within*, *The Guest Room*, *Money in the Air* or *Divorce Me, Dear,* the latter are sagaciously left by the reviewers to their own successless devices.

Thousands upon thousands of dollars are wasted annually by producers upon plays that even a blind man can tell do not stand the ghost of a chance. That such plays are sad affairs even before their first curtain goes up is a fact so well appreciated by any intelligent reviewer whose acquaintance I enjoy that, a week ahead of time, you will hear him confidentially growling over the possibility that he may, willy-nilly, because of the requirements of his job, have to throw away an evening on them. As for myself, being luckily a somewhat more foot-free fellow, I seldom bother to go around to any of them and verify my advance opinion of them. That advance opinion, if I may be privileged to abandon modesty for the fraction of a moment, has gone back on me only twice in the last half dozen years, once when I went doubtfully to a play by Dorrance Davis called *A Lady in Love* and was surprised to find that my intuition had not been entirely up to its splendid standard, and again when I had persuaded myself that something called *Conflict*, by a gentleman named Lawrence, did not promise much and found upon looking at it that it was not without certain minor virtues. Both of these plays, incidentally, despite the share of critical satisfaction that I to my surprise discovered in them, lived up to my intuition otherwise by being quick failures.

Another puzzle that entertains the critic is the apparent inability of many producers to detect the inferiority of a play manuscript after a mere perusal of its first three or four typed pages. It is a well-known fact that a magazine editor of any ability at all can readily detect a poor piece of fiction by the time he has read the first two or three hundred words of the manuscript. If an author is a dud, he betrays himself, both as to style and cast of mind, in his opening paragraphs. In the theatre, any experienced critic can pretty well tell the character and quality of a play after the curtain has been up ten minutes. And, though it grantedly sometimes happens that a play without quality of any kind will turn out to be a box-office success, the occurrence is hardly frequent enough, the statistics of the last ten years prove, to warrant producers in taking any such big gambling chance.

Where money is lost in the theatre, and in such great sums, is in the thirty or forty worthless plays that fail, and whose failure is critically foretellable, as against the one critically worthless play that accidentally succeeds. The worthlessness of those thirty or forty plays, I somewhat bumptiously contend, might be detected as quickly by the producers after a reading of their first few pages as it is subsequently detected by the critics after a seeing of their first few minutes.

[From *The Intimate Notebooks of George Jean Nathan*, 1932, pp. 158–61.]

The Criticism of Inferior Works

IF, from time to time, I select for discussion trivial plays that reach the storehouse before the words on them reach my readers, it is because now and then I find in them certain elements that suggest the bases for general critical doctrines. The perfect play, after all, offers small ground for interesting critical exploration. One may write of it extensively; one may even write of it entertainingly, provided one exercises a care that one's commentary concern itself with sprightly subjects only indirectly associated with the matter directly in hand; one may praise, praise and praise yet again. But, after the fireworks are over, there is found to be little new in the way of contribution to critical knowledge, for all the things that may be said of perfect plays have already been said a hundred times and said better than anyone presently performing in the critical pulpit, myself surely included, can say them. Not one thing written of the drama of Shakespeare in the last twenty years, for instance, contains anything seriously to interest the student who knows the Shakespearean criticism of earlier years, and nothing has been said of the finest work produced in our time that has not been a mere parotting of what was written of the finest work of other times by the critics of other days.

The objection to this point of view is naturally the obvious one of protesting that, if it be valid, all criticism must henceforth concern itself chiefly with relatively inferior works. The objection is silly. The point is simply that, since we know what absolute worth is and since only the veriest numskulls among critics, due to their own shortcomings protest the contrary, the business of criticism has become the business not so much of arguing that what is excellent is excellent as arguing that what is not excellent should be excellent, and trying to indicate, as best it can, the ways and means gradually to make it so. Criticism otherwise is of small service and is converted into a mere parlor game of slap-hands, giving issue only to an automatic applause that turns the true artist's stomach. The critic who consistently devotes himself to announcing that what is good is good is in the position of the clergyman who consistently devotes himself to announcing the goodness of God and in the process bores his congregation, already presumably privy to the news, to death.

Read the criticisms of the classics written in the last two decades and try to find one thing new in them. One thing new, that is, of critical value. You will find a number of critical estimates that present the stale facts in a fresh manner; you will even find some, like certain of my own, if you will forgive me the presumption, that will seem to have a measure of new and vital bounce; but if you will look closely into any of these, my own in particular, you will discover to your chagrin that there is not a single new idea in them from nose to tail and that what you mistook for new ideas were simply so many tricks of the writing craft. It is very easy to lay hold of an idea so old that its beard trails the dust and make it seem as frisky as a colt with turpentine up it if one knows the persuading chicanery of the English language. And it is equally easy, by the exercise of crafty literary hocus-pocus, to convince the majority of readers. For it is a Polichinelle secret, known surely to men whose trade is the merchanting of opinions, that—contrary to the general belief in certain bemused quarters—a reader wishes above all things to be convinced by his writer; and not only does he wish to be convinced; he actually lends to the writer a volitional self-hypnosis.

I speak, of course, not of the occasional mountebank who reads criticism only for the satisfaction he may get from loudly disputing it, whether he believes it to be right or not, but of the average, quiet, intelligent and open-minded man who is seriously interested in the subject. Such a man does not seek substantiation of his own beliefs so much as he seeks the critic's susbtantiation of his own beliefs. Otherwise, why the tremendous popularity of the critical writings of Shaw and others who have taken the *contra mundum* attitude and, by the exercise of wily thinking and writing, given it an apparently substantial foundation of plausibility? The reader of Shaw, as the reader of Nietzsche before him and as the reader of Voltaire before *him,* comes to market not to refuse to buy, but to buy and fetch back home. A man with a sore throat does not go to a doctor to be told that he hasn't a sore throat; he knows damned well that he has a sore throat and he wants to get rid of it. In the same way, a man does not go to a critic to be told that his opinions are well; he goes to be told that many of them are sick, and what the cure is. The critic who simply echoes the opinions of his readers is either a sad newspaper dolt on a sadder newspaper, or one whose publisher loses money if he prints more than five hundred copies of his book. I am not saying—it should be plain—that the critic who arbitrarily postures an oppugnant point of view, and without the justification of a sound and workmanlike knowledge, can win his reader for long, even where the reader is a more or less willing victim. What I am saying is rather that the reader does not wish to go on hearing the same old argument that one and one makes two, advanced by a mathematician who doesn't know what two and two make, so much as he longs, and understandably, to hear from someone gifted in the art of subtraction as well as multiplication that one minus one—the former digit being platitude and the latter being common sense—leaves nothing.

Many of the most valuable contributions to dramatic criticism have been inspired by negligible dramatic and poetical works; many of the least valuable by modern critics who, laboring under the delusion of professional dignity, have sought to plough up already long ploughed-up classical ground. Thus, in the former category, we have a share of the critical wisdom of D'Aubignac taking flower from such things as the *Esther* of Du Ryer; of John Dennis from trivial comedies that passed quickly into limbo; of Dryden from the *Rollo* of Fletcher, Rowley and Massinger, to say nothing of from the very worst of Ben Jonson; of Thomas Rymer from Buckingham's *The Rehearsal;* of Addison from Otway's *The Orphan;* of Goethe from Raupach's *Erdennacht,* Klopstock's *Hermann's Schlact,* and the like; of the younger Dumas from the worst

of Scribe; of Brunetière from the collaborations of Paul Bocage
and Octave Feuillet; of Schlegel from the *pièces à tiroir* of
Boursault and the hollowness of Gottsched; of Coleridge from
negligible German tragedies; of Hazlitt from such things as
Mrs. Centlivre confected, to say nothing of Gay's *What-d'ye-
call it?*, Cibber's mediocrities, and the plays of Bickerstaff, Mrs.
Cowley, Murphy and company; and, to come closer to the
moment, of Shaw from the unspeakable trash produced in the
London theatres in the 1890's. . . . As for the latter side of
the critical picture, I need only refer the skeptic to any four
out of five present-day professorial tomes that he will find at
the nearest book-stall.

[From the *American Mercury*, January 1927, pp. 122–3.]

Advice to a Young Critic

THE GREATEST weakness of the average critic is his wish to be
more than critic. He somehow believes that, however capable
he may be as a critic, there is a call for him to demonstrate
his talent in fields removed from criticism if he would aug-
ment and solidify his standing in his profession. We thus find
critics as novelists, playwrights, producers, poets, biographers,
husbands and what not, striving to support their critical position by achievements in extrinsic directions. For they imagine
that they will be regarded as greater critics if they prove that
they can do something apart from criticism, however dubious
the quality of their performances. They shrink nervously from
the charge that they are merely critics and not what are known
as creative fellows. All this has led and leads to a deterioration
of criticism, for the simple reason that criticism worth its salt
is a job quite sufficient unto itself and calling upon its practitioner's fullest time and resources.

The art of criticism is too often looked upon as a mere prel-
ude and stepping-stone to a practice of one of the other arts,
when it should be regarded—as, of course, it is by those sufficiently familiar with it in its finest flower—as an art of itself
and a thing apart. The good critic has earned his right to reward by being a good critic. If he happens also to be some-

thing of a genius and succeeds as well in some other art, he deserves a doubled reward, of course. But, in the general run of things, he should be content to be what he is, a critic first and last, and leave to other men the jobs that they in turn should content themselves with.

2

If you have violent prejudices, do not be afraid of them. Give them a free course. Do not be disquieted because they seem to be at variance with the convictions of other critics. Few things are absolutely true in this world and you stand as good a chance of being right as the next man. Only exercise a caution never to be indignant and always to smile. In the event that it turns out that you have been wrong—even to the extent of being idiotic—you will thus be safe, for most persons will conclude that you were just fooling and will secretly be a bit abashed for having fallen into your trap.

3

If you are accused of arbitrarily adopting a *contra mundum* attitude, don't lose any sleep over it. Nine-tenths of the world's greatest men achieved greatness by arbitrarily opposing the convictions and beliefs of the majority. The criticism of you might just as aptly have been directed against Christ, Galileo, Columbus, Voltaire, Pasteur, Mergenthaler and the Wrights— if, after you have confected some ephemeral little destructive essay on John Drinkwater or the movies, that gives you any comfort.

4

Take your work seriously, but not yourself. Fifty years hence your work may prove to have amounted to something. Fifty years hence, on the other hand, you will have been eaten by the same indiscriminating worms that found Clement Scott and Acton Davies such appetizing delicatessen.

5

Don't be afraid to dissent from the opinions of the critically great. Remember that Nietzsche considered Kotzebue a more talented dramatist than Schiller, that Hazlitt placed Foote and

O'Keefe among the immortals and called the latter the English Molière, that Dryden declared that Fletcher came nearer to perfection in comedy than Shakespeare, that both Lessing and Diderot considered George Lillo a model dramatist, that George Bernard Shaw thinks Brieux the greatest living dramatist this side of Russia, and that William Archer once actually observed (*vide The Theatrical World of 1895*, p. 271) that he venerated Mr. Augustus Thomas' *Alabama* so highly that he wished it would be published in book form so that he might go around quoting it!

6

I need not tell you, obviously enough, that morals have no place in any consideration of art. But do not make a fool of yourself when the point comes to issue, as so many critics are in the habit of doing. The latter often make themselves as ridiculous in their way as the moralists do in theirs. If the question before the house is one of authentic art, that is, if the work criticized is of genuine artistic integrity and if the question of its morality is interposed by meddling smutsers, let fly at the dolts with full artillery. But if the work criticized has no artistic justification and integrity, don't make yourself silly by defending it with the same arguments used in the former case. There is such a thing as art, and it should be held sacred and inviolate from the assaults of dirty-minded morons; but there is also such a thing as cheap smut, and it should be frankly admitted to be just that and nothing more. Certain critics, however, having established themselves in full feather as tomahawkers of all moral interference with anything, lack all discrimination when moral issues are raised and rush to the defence of Cabell and Mae West with one and the same argument. They grow as excited over the moral assault upon out-and-out dung like *Sex* as they do over the moral assault upon a first-rate piece of work like *Jurgen*. And, in so doing, they weaken their case—a case that must be kept strong at all costs and one that needs the fighting brains of all intelligent critics—and give the enemy certain points of advantage in the minds of liberal and rational men. After all, there is a difference between *A Night in a Turkish Harem*

and even Brieux's *Damaged Goods,* and to defend the former
in terms of the latter is like having a drink with the colored
gentleman who has defiled your sister.

7

Do not confound an aphrodisiacal actress with a talented one.
The majority of critics do so, and, I regret to confess it, understandably and even a bit justifiably. If an actress stimulates
your libido, say so frankly and do not try to conceal the truth
in a lot of rigmarole about histrionic art. There is certainly
nothing wrong with an actress who has sex appeal; indeed,
it is five times more valuable to her and to a liberal portion
of her art than all the stock company training this side of
Cleveland and Rochester; and even if the professors object to
what you write, the girl herself, I venture to say, will be tickled
to death. . . . You will note, if you take the trouble to investigate, that all the more profound treatises on the art of acting
are and have been written by grandpas, valetudinarians or
favorites of the celebrated Dowager Empress Tsen Hi.

8

The better and more honest critic you are, the fewer friends
will eventually send flowers up to the funeral parlor. One by
one they will soon or late withdraw from fellowship and good
will. Even one's closest friend cannot abide criticism of himself with half the fortitude and amiability of one's worst
enemy. Show me a critic with a quorum of artists as bosom
comrades and I'll show you a critic who is a hypocrite and
a liar.

9

Pay no attention to what people say or write of you. A man
in the brick-throwing business must expect occasionally to be
hit by a brick.

10

To be a critic automatically implies a certain self-sufficiency
and vanity. Never mind. You will never find an artist among
the diffident and submissive. Genuine artistic expression, in

whatever field, calls for a forthright faith and confidence. It took more nerve and downright courage to write the "Essay on Morals" than it took to fight Waterloo.

11

Never fall into the error of believing that simply because a thing is unpopular it must have esoteric points of merit. Vastly more trash fails to win popular approval than wins it. If Rostand's *The Last Night of Don Juan* runs only a week in the American theatre, remember that John J. Hack's *One Glorious Hour* doesn't run even that long. And if *Abie's Irish Rose* runs for five years, stop and reflect that *Hamlet* will run for five thousand.

12

Don't be afraid of being labeled a destructive critic. You will be in good company. Where would you rather be: in Hell with Swift, Voltaire and Nietzsche or in the American Academy of Arts and Letters with Richard Burton, Clayton Hamilton and Hermann Hagedorn?

13

Since you are an American, write like an American. Do not try to become a member of the Charles Lamb's Club and ape the so-called literary manner of the English critical essayists. Express yourself in the pungent idiom of your time, your land and your people; there is no apology necessary; that idiom may produce sound literature as well as the language of the dons. Don't be afraid of slang if it will make your point better and more forcibly than literose expression. Much that was erstwhile slang has already been accepted into the dictionaries of formal English; much more will be accepted in the near future. The objection to slang, at least to the more valid slang, is snooty and snobbish. Where a more expressive word or phrase in the language than *to cuckoo* (in the sense of *to imitate*), *sap, to get away with, bonehead, wow, to razz, joy-juice* (for *gin*), *to vamp, hickpricker, joy-ride* or *hoopla*? But, on the other hand, don't make the mistake of believing that a mere imitation of Brook, Indiana, will get you any farther than an imitation of Cambridge, England.

14

It is as absurd to believe that the general public is interested in sound dramatic criticism as it is to believe that the general public is interested in sound drama. It is to the credit of the majority of newspaper editors that they appreciate the fact and take pains not to discommode their readers.

15

There is, at bottom, very little difference between dramatic criticism and literary criticism. What, after all, is a play but an underwritten novel and a novel but an overwritten play?

16

The chief fault with many critics is that they strive to divert to themselves the attention, if any, that their criticism should attract to itself.

17

One of the worst curses that American dramatic criticism has suffered is the Shaw influence. Twenty years ago, there wasn't a young critic, myself included, who didn't in one way or another reflect the Shaw attitude, viewpoint and manner. Since that time, the influence has faded somewhat, but it is still sufficiently in evidence to be immediately recognizable. Shaw, surely, was a stimulatingly excellent critic and worse deities might have been and might still be picked out to emulate. But one wonders if the young men who still regard him as their critical *beau idéal* really appreciate the gaping holes in his dramatic taste and judgment. If they will take the trouble to read carefully his two volumes of "Dramatic Opinions and Essays," they may be rather alarmed and flabbergasted to find out that among the plays and the dramatists he selected for a share of his admiration were the following: "The Prude's Progress," B. C. Stephenson, H. V. Esmond's "The Divided Way," W. Yardley, "The Strange Adventures of Miss Brown," W. D. Howells' "A Dangerous Ruffian," "Mrs. Ponderbury's Past," "The Romance of the Shop-Walker," Miss Clo Graves' "Mother of Three," and W. G. Wills' "Olivia." As for his judgment of actors, they will perhaps be equally flustered to observe that he ranked Joseph Jefferson with Coquelin and Salvini. As for his estimate of dramatic literature, they will be somewhat shocked to encounter this: "Nobody ever could, or did, or will improve on Dumas' . . . plays." And as for his style, they may be dismayed to find him resorting to such clichés of present-day Hearst critical writing as *Amurrican* and the *long-lost chee-yild*.

18

All criticism, after all, is a criticism of the critic himself before it is one of the criticized.

19

The reason why there are so few good farces written in America is that the farce form is sneered at, or at least treated with an air of condescension, by nine-tenths of the men who write about the native theatre. This is particularly true, strangely enough, of critics who are otherwise competent and discerning fellows. Yet these, like the general run of ignoramuses, indirectly discourage our more capable dramatists from essaying farce by treating it as something more or less negligible. When these writers think of farce, they think of such things as "Charley's Aunt," "The Man from Mexico," and "The Strawberry Blonde," but for some reason or other they seem never to stop and think of such others as "The Frogs," "Le Bourgeois Gentilhomme" and "The Comedy of Errors."

20

The bulk of American criticism is corrupted by a blind adherence to and championing of favorites. There is hardly a critic in practice amongst us who hasn't a pet artist who, in his estimation, can do no wrong. Having once set the artist in question atop a pedestal, the critic is determined by hook or crook to keep him there, even though the fellow's work be periodically anything but sound and meritorious. The critic seems to imagine that such slips on the part of his loved one are black marks against his own critical judgment and against his initial estimate of the man. And so he takes pains to gloss them over and to keep the news quiet by loudly denying it.

The result is a great monkey-show in which genuine talent is often made mock of by a persistent refusal to admit that it is never anything but topnotch.

21

Don't hesitate to indulge in personalities. The common notion that there is something *infra dignitatem* about too personal criticism is just as silly as most other commonly held notions about criticism. When you are met with this personality blather, quietly refer your counsellor to such unseemly critical dealers in personalities as the Messrs. Cervantes, Voltaire and Zola or, if your counsellor has never heard of them, to Walkley, Archer and Shaw.

22

Don't go too 'far with the idea that there are no rules in the case of drama. There happen, fortunately or unfortunately, to be a few. Bumptiously to deny the existence of all such rules is to make one's self out a ninny. There are certain rules. What there are not, are commandments.

23

There is such a thing as a too great receptivity and liberal-mindedness on the part of a critic. The eagerness to miss nothing potentially worthy, to welcome talent in new fields and forms and to keep just a little ahead of the critical procession periodically leads the too open-armed critic into deplorable errors of judgment. Receptiveness and hospitality are valuable qualities in a critic, but they must be watched as closely as so many unleashed dogs, that they may not get out of hand, bark up the wrong trees and mess up things generally. Many peculiar estimates have been confected by critics whose cordiality of attitude has for the moment got the better of their sense of sound discrimination. Need I point, for example, to George Moore, surely an otherwise even bitterly cautious critic, and his warm hugging of such playwrights as Léon Hennique, Oscar Méténier and Michael Field, to Edmund Gosse's blanket embrace of Strindberg as both dramatist and novelist, or to Huneker and his over-valuation of Maeterlinck, to say nothing of the half-dozen or more lesser and already forgotten geniuses whom he over-enthusiastically patted on the head?

24

I am not so sure about the criticism we hear against special pleading. Is it always so ruinous to drama as they say it is? Is it too much to refer these critics, for example, to Shakespeare?

25

You will be told never to sit down to write unless you have something to say beforehand. This is the veriest buncombe; pay no attention to it. Some of the best things that a man writes occur to him after he has seated himself at his desk without the vaguest preliminary notion of what he was going to write—even, indeed, when he has cursed God for ever having put a pencil in his hand. Many a writer has produced something excellent after staring blankly at his pad of paper for hours. Ideas frequently come out of one's dull pencil in time as clear water comes eventually out of a muddy tap.

26

A sound piece of criticism has never yet been spoiled by an injection of humor, let the professors yell all they want to. There is a place for apt humor in even the most serious work. If there is a place for it in "Hamlet," why shouldn't there be a place for it in a criticism of "Hamlet"?

27

What constitutes a good play? There is no definition that meets the case, save it be some such completely obvious and broadly empty one as is now and then dispensed by the writers of dramatic text books. Any other attempt precisely to pigeon-hole the problem must meet with failure, since the moment you think up an apparently sound and satisfactory definition along comes an artist who writes a good play that your definition fails to cover. Thus, the definition chefs, full of Aristotle's unities, were put to rout by Georg Kaiser. Thus, full of wisdom about dramatic action, they were set to chasing their tails by Sierra and Shaw. And thus, full of dramaturgic rules and regulations, they have been flouted by Strindberg, Wedekind, Schnitzler, Evreinoff, Synge, Dunsany, Gorki, Pirandello, Hasenclever and many others. A good play must have action? Then what of "Professor Bernhardi"? A good play must have love interest? Then what of "Pasteur"? A good play must be built around a single dominating character? Then what of "Night Refuge"? A good play must be fitted into the three-hour theatrical span? Then what of O'Neill's "Strange Interlude"? A good play must centre upon a conflict of wills? Then what of "The Cradle Song"? A good play must not mix its moods? Then what of "The Dream Play"? A good play must take its audience into its confidence and not deceive it? Then what of "Seven Keys to Baldpate"? And so on, and so on.

The futility of any attempt to define exactly a good play may be illustrated no better, I daresay, than by giving a glance at the gymnastics of my alliterative colleague, Dr. Clayton Hamilton, author of "The Theory of the Theatre," "Studies in Stagecraft" and "Problems of the Playwright," "Any work of art is good," announces the professor, "if it forces the spectator or auditor to imagine and to realize some truth of life, and any effort of art is bad if it fails of this endeavor. Here is the final test of efficiency." What, one may relevantly inquire of the professor, is the particular truth of life that the auditor or spectator is forced to imagine and to realize by, let us say, Shaw's "Fanny's First Play," or D'Annunzio's "More than Love," or Zoë Akins' "Pappa," or Ibsen's "The Wild Duck"? Proceeding, the professor observes: "Any play, regardless of the method of the author, is a good play if it awakens the audience to a realization of some important aspect of the infinitely various assertions of the human will." To the realization of what important aspect of the infinitely various assertions of the human will, may I ask the professor, does Aristophanes' good play—and surely he will not deny that it is a pretty good play—called "Birds" awaken its audience? But yet the professor continues: "The good play must impose upon the spectator the educative illusion of reality; it must, by this means, increase vicariously his experience of life. It must lead the public out of living into life." Again, may one inquire politely of the professor how this phase of his definition manages to fit itself to, say, such a good play as "Chantecler," or "The Lady from the Sea," or "Ariane and Barbe Bleue," or "The Laughter of the Gods," or "Pippa Dances," or "The Dead City," or "The Hour Glass," or "Erd-geist," or "The Winter's Tale"?

[From *Art of the Night*, 1928, pp. 1–20.]

The Critic as a Black Sheep

It need hardly again be recalled that many of our theatrical producers' pet, consoling explanation of unfavorable criticism of one of their exhibits is that it was composed by a critic suffering from dyspepsia. That the explanation long since has taken its place in the joke-books has not hindered its auto-activation. The belief that a critic beset by one malaise or another is bound to be influenced by his personal discomfort against a play which duty compels him willy-nilly to review is but one of a number of fallacies shared alike by producers, playwrights, and volunteer secular diagnosticians. The fact of the matter is that, instead of being influenced against what he has to review, the critic's indisposition influences him rather in its favor, and for a reason that even the amateur psychologist may determine.

When the critic for one cause or another finds his physical and mental vivacity not what it should be, he, like any other man, is inclined to be self-apologetic and in that mood far from contentious. He is induced by his enfeebled state to resign himself for the time being to the doctrine of *laissez-faire,* to let things slide, and to avoid anything in the way of discommoding argument. The mere consciousness of so little as a pimple on his nose has been known to humble a man's self-assurance in the presence of another man or, more particularly, woman whom otherwise he would flee as from the plague. Any critic who has been practising for any length of time knows that the less fit he feels the greater his disposition to be easy on what he reviews. He will not, of course, openly admit it—his *amour propre* is too considerable for that; but the truth remains that any such one depressed by anything short of smallpox is naturally reduced to a charitableness which under other circumstances would be wholly foreign to him.

It is not only theatre criticism that has been inflicted with the opposite conviction. Criticism in general has frequently been criticized in turn on the senseless ground of its practitioners' health and, in some cases, even looks, as may be amusingly noted in a recent study of the methods of modern literary criticism, *The Armed Vision,* by one Stanley Edgar Hyman, wherein Van Wyck Brooks is summarily dismissed with the observation that he has aged and has now a white mustache. "In what way hair on the lip, no matter what its color, can interfere with critical judgment," Joseph Wood Krutch has added, "Mr. Hyman does not make clear."

Drama criticism remains, however, the chief victim of such simious prejudices and confusions. Shaw's devastatingly accurate criticism of Henry Irving, it will be remembered, was attributed by numbskulls to his jealousy of a rival for the affections of the fair Ellen Terry, and his equally riddling criticism of sentimental Victorian twaddle to the fact that he did not eat meat. And Beerbohm's objection to some of the juvenile sentiment flooding the stage of his day was argued by his detractors to be predicated on the circumstance that he had a bald head. Unfavorable criticism, in short, is ever thought to have a dubious wellspring or motive. The clichés are numberless: the critic is a disappointed playwright; the critic employs criticism as a derrick for his little ego; the critic is a failure who seeks to vent his spleen on others who have succeeded; the critic is a homely creature who dislikes an actor who is handsome; the critic is against an actress because she has won a role coveted by an actress of whom personally he is fond; the critic is a drunkard on the score that he enjoys a Martini before his dinner; the critic has dined well before the show and a decent meal notoriously corrupts the brain; etc.

It is further sometimes charged against the critic that his reviews tend toward one extreme or the other, that they are either comprehensively laudatory or comprehensively detractory, and that seldom if ever do they allow anything to the middle ground. The charge is often true, but its truth is retroactively foolish. There are various plays that are completely bad, plays with no slightest redeeming qualities, and the only honest manner in which to review them is to say just that, flatly. There are, as well, plays that are wholly admirable and qualifications of their admirableness are simply the gesture of critics who wish to be arbitrarily different and thereby attract some attention to themselves. Qualifications in such cases are infinitely less symptoms of critical acumen and equity than of a desire to gain a reputation for those virtues at the expense of judgment and intelligence.

A still further charge is that the critic is prejudiced in favor of certain kinds of drama and just as prejudiced against other kinds. Again, true. But prejudice, if sound, is what gives the critic his standing. Every man, whatever his calling, acquires prejudices based on experience, so why not the critic? There are, obviously, silly prejudices as well as sound, but the former soon betray and defeat their merchants. Prejudices which are the consequence of critical education are among the most forceful weapons in the critic's arsenal. Show me a critic without prejudices and I'll show you an arrested cretin.

A third allegation is that the critic too often aims to be clever and witty instead of being straightforward and simple, and that this is deplorable. How and why it is deplorable is hard to make out. A review is intended to be read and if cleverness and wit will help it to be read, so much the better. The theory, moreover, that cleverness and wit may not be reconciled with forthright honesty is kin to one which would maintain that intelligence is best to be expressed dully and that judgment is most acceptable if recorded in glassy writing. The most valuable dramatic criticism of modern times, from Shaw to Palmer, from Montague to Howe, from Béraud to Kerr, has been that which has been percolated through wit, humor, and literary legerdemain; the least valuable that which has been purveyed like an austere frost. Opinions long and strongly stated have a way of becoming objectionable and even slightly offensive, however valid they may be. Best to serve, they should be coated with varied brightly colored dyes.

The dyes do not penetrate seriously into them; they are largely superficial; but, as with an Easter egg, they engage and tickle the attention of such children as would disdain the egg in its common, unadorned state.

We hear that the critic should efface himself in his criticism and not, as is the practice of some, employ it in part as a personal show-window. The contention is that of other critics who hope to make acceptable their own lack of any personality by decrying it in their betters. Anyone who uses criticism as a personal show-window must have the goods to display in it or soon go out of business. A good critic can no more keep his personality and all it stands for out of his criticism than he can keep it out of his speech, his politics, or his love-making. Impersonal criticism, if there can be such a thing, is like an impersonal fist fight or an impersonal marriage, and as successful.

To ask of a critic that he dismiss his personality and its various facets from his criticism is an affront both to him and to criticism itself. It is like asking the individual to convert himself into a blank and to allow the blank, like a whitewashed flat wall, to reflect what rays there may possibly be against another such wall which is the reader. Personality, far from deflecting the light, makes it seem relatively brighter and yet more comfortable on the eyes by embellishing it with shadow and color. What the objectors object to is really not any such factual personality but what is sanguinely passed off for it through the common journalistic over-use of the first person singular pronoun. The critic who dots his paragraphs with "I's" may conceivably enjoy a personality as striking as Napoleon's or General Coxey's but he does not know how to sell it. True personality does not work itself thus contrabandly into criticism; criticism naturally mirrors it.

It is also the habit to look askance at the critic who contradicts himself. Such contradiction is held to be the mark of an insecure and untrustworthy mind. It should rather be the habit to look askance at the critic who does not occasionally contradict himself. Contradiction may as well be the offspring of increased education, experience, and perception as it may be of the vacillation induced by ignorance. The critic who stubbornly adheres to original statement is sometimes like a bulldog who gluttonously clings to a rubber bone. There is a tide in the affairs of art as there is in the affairs of man and, while the basic principles may not be affected, there are ripples that glint with new lights and these new lights now and then dim the antecedent ones. The critic who vainly is unwilling to contradict himself is accordingly in the position of a man who has been unpleasantly punched in the eye, which thereupon turns black, but who stoutly denies to witnesses of the contretemps both that it took place and that his eye is not its normal color.

"Whenever either side of the scale is overweighted," writes Eric Bentley in a treatise called *Theory and Theatre,* "it is for the critic to try—by exhortation, invective, satire, or whatever— to weight the other side. In a sense the critic's job is not to be impartial but always *to weight the other side* (italics his), the side that needs it." This is an applaudably generous point of view and one that appeals to every man's impulse to help the underdog, but otherwise it would convert the critic into a mere propagandist. The critic who would arbitrarily weight the other side, whatever it might be, would be a suspect critic indeed. The temptation to do it is wholly understandable, and in moments of careless thinking I have not been the only one who has succumbed to it (Mr. Bentley seems to prove that he, among others, is like me in this regard), but such weighting surely is no part of criticism. It is part, rather, of critical politics. I agree that in at least one sense the critic's job, as Mr. Bentley puts it, is not to be impartial. He should fight for what he soberly deems right and best, and should pitch his lance come hell or high water; and if overweighting his stand will assist his purpose, let him overweight it to the limit. If another critic who, though agreeing with him, elects then to posture as playing fair by sophisticating the virtues of the other side and thus elevate himself as a square-shooter over the other, he is not only critically dishonest but, however cunning, a critical fraud.

There is, finally, it need scarcely be repeated, a distaste for any man who sets himself up as a critic of other men and their works. It is not for me to argue its justice or injustice. But the terms in which it customarily vents itself are too often questionable. There surely must be better arguments lying around somewhere; I myself, indeed, can think of some honeys, though I shall here wisely keep them to myself.

A critic, for example, will be derogated because he is a "dapper dresser," like Richard Brinsley Sheridan, Chopin, and Disraeli; because he is self-assured and hence "pompous," like Talleyrand, Botticelli, and Wagner; or because he does not go to a barber frequently enough, like Andrew Jackson, General Grant, and Walt Whitman. He is discountenanced by ill-natured playwrights like Moss Hart who take to the radio to observe, acidly, that but one modern dramatic critic has ever written a successful play, to wit, William Archer and *The Green Goddess,* only to be informed to their embarrassment that among the large assortment who have written successful plays have been Robert de Flers, Franklin Fyles, Charles Hoyt (whose satirical farces have clearly influenced some of Hart's plays), Herbert Farjeon, Channing Pollock, St. John Ervine, C. M. S. McLellan, Charles Frederic-Nirdlinger, Victor Mapes, Charles Henry Meltzer, H. Granville-Barker, Frederick Schrader, A. E. Thomas, Frederick Donaghey, Frederic Hatton, Harry B. Smith, Pérez Galdós, Charlton Andrews, André Obey, Thompson Buchanan, Augustin Daly, Paul Potter, Walter Browne, George Ade, Hermann Bahr, Ashley Dukes, Edmond See, Harold Brighouse, Bronson Howard and, along with a lot of others, G. B. Shaw.

If the critic pens sweet words about a pretty new young actress, even one of unmistakable talent, it will be said of him that he is a sentimental mark when it comes to the fair sex. If he has no taste for cheap, soapbox propaganda in drama, it will be claimed against him that he knows nothing of what is going on in the world and that his interests are confined to the world of Broadway. If he reviews a succession of miserable plays exactly for what they are, he will be accused by their producer of conducting a vendetta against him, inspired by unstated but darkly implied motives. And, if by any chance he rises to any eminence in his profession, the gossip columns will not let an opportunity pass to make him ridiculous in one way or another and to minimize what esteem people may conceivably have for him.

He is, in short, a black sheep—in a pack of jackasses.

[From *The Theatre Book of the Year, 1948–1949*, Foreword.]

Frivolity and Criticism

"IF Nature had not made us a little frivolous, we should be most wretched. It is because one can be frivolous that the majority do not hang themselves." Thus, Voltaire.

I keep the M. Voltaire's dictum pasted conspicuously on my office piano, directly next to the rack of Beethoven's scherzi, to comfort me and assuage my feelings when some nuisance invades my sanctum and deplores my occasional professional levity. What the aforesaid nuisance observes is always of a cut. "Why do you, fundamentally a serious critic, so often spoil your reputation by indulging in facetiousness and buffoonery? You ought to be damned ashamed of yourself!" After having the nuisance thrown out on his ear forthwith, I again peruse the placard, order up a couple of beers, and am once more at peace with myself and the world.

That humor in criticism, however penetrating and sound, is looked at askance by $1,200-a-year college professors, actors in barnstorming Shakespearean troupes, presidents of ladies' drama study clubs and other such intellectuals is too well known a fact for me to waste time repeating it. The critic who injects humor into a review of even a Mae West play is looked upon as a less mentally proficient fellow than the one who treats of it in the manner of Schlegel. Frivolity is denied the dramatic commentator who would relish some standing in the community, even though his critical frivolity be in conjunction with a Minsky burlesque show or a tragedy by Henri Kistemaekers. Humor is permitted to artists of all kinds, but the critic of even the artists who handsomely indulge in it must always wear a long face if he cherishes the respect of his public. The situation, as I look at it, is eminently silly. The critic who would wax facetious in a consideration of a work of art is not a critic at all and should promptly lay in a supply of flour and a set of cardboard ears and hire himself out to a circus. But the critic who approaches a piece of junk with the air of a profound philosopher should immediately run around and get a job with the first named critic. There are plays and plays, and there is criticism and criticism. One can no more properly criticize O'Neill's "Strange Interlude" and Philip Barry's "Tomorrow and Tomorrow" in the same terms, though they both deal largely with the same theme, than one can similarly criticize Cyrano de Bergerac and Jimmy Durante, despite the equal length of their noses.

There has seldom been a good critic who has not been deplored on the score of his frivolity. When Shaw, in his *Saturday Review* incumbency, seized the prevailing British drama by the tail and gayly swung it around his head, the staid old gentlemen at the Athenæum Club wagged their heads solemnly and dismissed him as a vulgar and empty clown. When Leigh Hunt had sport with various actors of his day who tried to play Falstaff, when George Henry Lewes groaned ribaldly out of the depths of his innards over "Don Carlos," "Kabale und Liebe" and certain other such exhibitions, when Hazlitt ridiculed the audiences who went to see Kean's Romeo, there was, we are told, considerable trepidation for the security of their critical careers. What people apparently want—and then will not read—is what they call "serious" criticism, *i.e.*, criticism that says nothing, but says it solemnly, like Mr. Hoover.

I often wonder what people must think of a critic like myself, who freely confesses, with a frivolity whose detonation must shake the pince-nez off the noses of all the professors this side of the Waxahachie, Texas, Dental College, that he would rather see Ed Wynn any night than Blanche Yurka in Ibsen's "The Vikings of Heligoland" and who has a much better time at something like Ring Lardner's "June Moon" than at all the sober dramas Fritz von Unruh ever wrote. Surely there cannot be a very high opinion of such a critic who says in the same breath that a play like "The Death of Tintagiles" is so much dull pretense and that one like "Once in a Lifetime" is eminently meritorious stuff. When I die I can foresee my obituary notice: "He was not without some talent as a critic, but he lowered his standing by an admiration for music show comedians, pretty dancing girls and low farces." They will add, in all probability, that this was simply an affectation and a pose, and all I can say is that if they do, my will has a clause leaving $10,000 to hire gunmen to go right around to the newspaper offices and shoot everybody in sight.

Mencken has said that next to being run over by a taxicab and having his hat smashed, going again to "Rosmersholm" is the worst punishment that he can think of. As I own two hats, it seems to me to be the worst. Other terrible punishments are revivals of at least one-half of Shaw's plays; productions of the Hindu classic drama in Hindu; dramas on the futility and meaninglessness of life by rich Harvard boys; art theatre productions of Björnsterne Björnson's "Limping Hulda"; Tolstoy's "The Living Corpse" with Max Reinhardt lighting effects and a Chauve Souris string quartette, together with a Ned Wayburn toe-dancer, in the gipsy dive scene; "The Merchant of Venice" with orthodox Jewish gentlemen playing Shylock; revivals of "The School for Scandal" with the Restoration elegants played by the Summer colony of Provincetown transported to a New York stage; Spanish drama cast with Broadway actors; and Romain Rolland *in toto*. There may be something wrong with any critic like myself who, on the nights such things open, prefers to go around and watch Harry Rosenthal play the piano in a farce about song-writers, or amuse himself listening to Bert Lahr's jokes about the alvine flux of a bull, or look at Bill Robinson dance. But I can't help being what I am. No more so, according to their confessions in a similar situation, could such frivolous fellows as Thomas Hardy, Anatole France, Georg Brandes and Maurice Maeterlinck.

[From *The Intimate Notebooks of George Jean Nathan*, 1932, pp. 165–8.]

The Audience Emotion

THE WORLD may grow more civilized as the centuries pass, but I doubt whether the emotion of the theatre audience in any period or over any stretch of time, however great, shares in the proportionate increase of civilization. The nature of that emotion and of its reactions may alter in detail, usually negligible, but I have a feeling that it is, in sum, pretty much today what it was in the beginning, and that its fundamental innocence will remain inviolate until the world returns to dust. This, of course, is like saying in different words that human nature does not change and that, in the mass, it responds always in much the same way to the various phenomena of life with which it is brought into contact. But there is a difference, and this is it. A theatre audience enters a theatre with the deliberate intention either of forgetting itself for a couple of hours or of being reminded of half-remembered phases of itself, of its life, and of its dreams and despairs. In the matter of the former of these two psychological businesses it tacitly requests of the dramatist that he render it other than it actually is, that, as the phrase goes, he take it out of itself—in short, that he treat it not as it really is, whether in habitual thought or feeling, but as it would like to be. In the direction of thought, it urges the dramatist to rid it of its stereotyped mental processes and, in the direction of feeling, of its conventional emotions and substitute for them new and more soothingly desirable ones. It comes to the theatre ready, willing and eager to be made, for the nonce, other than it is. At home or in the street it is in its divers elements content to be conventional, average, normal. In its reaction to the various affairs of the world it is even insistent upon this conventionality and this normality. But in the theatre, on the occasions I allude to, it pays out its money with the deliberate motive of constituting itself other than in its heart and mind it is. It wants a momentary spree, a night off. And yet, try as a dramatist will to give it what it wants, try itself as it will to make itself other than it is, it cannot. The so-called crowd psychology has nothing to do with the matter. The truth of the contention would hold were the theatre to be occupied by only two or four such persons, for the fact is that what is true of a thousand boobs is true of two boobs, and that what is true of two is equally true of the thousand.

Matthew Arnold may have been right about the world, but he was wrong about that part of it that is the theatre. The theatre, in so far as the emotional quality of its audiences is concerned, does not move; it stands still. The audience emotion follows always an absolutely cut-and-dried routine, varied only superficially, and any fine attempt to change its course must, by the very nature of God's magnificent images, come to grief. Across the centuries, the signal fires in Aeschylus's *Agamemnon* evoke the same emotional response as those in Bronson Howard's *Shenandoah;* the audience's tears for Sophocles's Antigone when she seeks to follow her unfortunate sister are the same tears that are spilled over the girl in *The Two Orphans* who would do likewise; the laughter that was vouchsafed the drunk Dikaiopolis twenty-three hundred years ago is the same as that which is today vouchsafed the drunk Old Soak. We are asked by gentlemen who write books to believe that, where Sixteenth and early Seventeenth Century audiences viewed insanity as a comic affliction, modern audiences view it as a tragic one, but the gentlemen who write books have evidently never been members of the audiences who have roared over a score of shows beginning with *The Belle of New York* and ending with *The Misleading Lady* and *Chicago.* And they certainly are not vaudeville goers or they would know about the laughing success that has followed the Sam Mann sketch for many years. We are also asked to believe that physical deformity, once regarded as extremely jocose, is no longer so regarded, and that, as a consequence, Mr. Glass's One-Eye Feigenbaum and Miss Loos's Spoffard *père* are instruments of profound grief, and that it is all that a modern sideshow audience can do to keep from crying out loud over the fat woman, the living skeleton and the bearded lady.

These general reflections occur to me in specific connection with the play called *Spread Eagle*, by the Messrs. Brooks and Lister. It was the intention of these novices in the business of playwriting to persuade their audiences to gag at jingoism and the wars it periodically leads the nation into by playing upon the emotions of those audiences with the various instruments of jingoism and then to make the audiences honorously self-critical, skeptical and ashamed of their own facile reaction. And what did the novices discover? They discovered that the aforesaid instruments for the furtherance of jingoism were so much more powerful in the audience's case than the latter's talent for self-criticism and skepticism that, far from making it catch on to its evergreen credulousness and suscepti- bility, they actually convinced it all over again. Though they suggested forcibly to the audience that they were playing "The Star Spangled Banner" with their tongues in their cheeks, and were showing it rousing movies of Our Boys going off to the front with their fingers crossed, and were making Liberty Loan speeches with a wink of the eye, the audience would have none of the derision and accepted the whole thing liter- ally, and at one gulp. And what degree of success their play has had or may have, accordingly, was and will be due not to what they put into it but what they tried and hoped and yet failed to keep out of it. What they endeavored to do was to show a theatre audience, in terms of sardonic melodrama, the chicanery, mountebankery and nonsense of unthinking and blind patriotism; what they succeeded in doing was only to make their boob customers' hearts beat with the same old boob emotion when the drums got busy and the orators began orat- ing and the flag was let loose. Their play, from any critical point of view, is a very bad play, but its badness has nothing to do with its failure to move an audience in the way they desired to move it. The same basic theme and the same cen- tral theatrical device are present in a good play by Galsworthy called *The Mob*, and *The Mob* fails with an audience quite as *Spread Eagle* fails. Genius and hack alike inevitably fall before a mere brass band.

The one thing that a dramatist, however gifted, apparently cannot monkey with is the fixed and changeless emotional credo of the masses of the people. It is for this reason that satire is so seldom financially prosperous at the popular box- office. Now and again, to be sure, a freak play that assails the popular heart-beat achieves a moderate, freak success, but as a rule the play that wins the public is the play that in some relatively novel manner merely restates the ancient and time- honored emotional principles of the public. From the time of Aristophanes and his *Knights* to that of *Spread Eagle*—there are points of similarity in the former's Cleon, promoter of war, and the latter's Martin Henderson, ditto—the public of the moment has been found to react left-handedly to the intention of dramatists who would whip its emotions in a direction that tradition opposes. A dramatist may play with superficially new ideas, new philosophies and new points of view, but down under them he must invariably cause to flow in a steady stream the old and tried emotions. Shaw is an excellent example of a dramatist who sagaciously appreciates the truth of this. Even a superficial glance at his plays from beginning to end reveals his wise timidity in offering his audiences any thing unusual or new in the way of emotional values. The Shaw dramatic canon is grounded upon a bedrock of grandma emotions tricked out, for the pleasurable deception of his customers, in the latest styles of philosophical and controversial millinery. Shaw simply asks his audience to feel the old feeling lightly instead of gravely; he never on a single occasion has asked it to alter the intrinsic nature of those feelings. There isn't an emotional note in any one of his plays that the lowliest doodle cannot respond to safely and very comfortably, however much the doodle may be horrified by the ironic counterpoint that Shaw synchronously plays.

[From the *American Mercury*, June 1927, pp. 245–7.]

Reviewers and Critics

THE GENERALLY maintained theory that play reviewers who have to rush their reviews into type immediately after a play is over haven't the necessary time in which to arrive at a sound estimate of the play is flim-flam. The reviewer who can't make up his mind accurately as to a play's worth immediately it's finished hasn't any mind to make up. As well say that the reader of a book must moon around for days afterward and refer back to it periodically during that time before he can tell whether it's really good or bad. A play reviewer is supposed, often unwarrantedly, true enough, to have some taste, experience and judgment, and if he doesn't know the value or lack of value of a play after being in its company for three hours his boss should promptly reassign him to cover fires. It's my belief that the notion in question has been set in motion by the reviewers themselves, by way of craftily letting themselves down easily and apologizing for their critical incompetence. If they were given a week longer to meditate a play and arrive at a sounder point of view regarding it, it'd avail them little and it'd find them harboring their initial deductions, a fact sufficiently proven by their Sunday recapitulations which are merely expansions and substantiations of their morning-after opinions.

The trouble with reviewing against time doesn't lie in this direction at all. Where it lies is in the direction of a smooth, effectively written and lifting promulgation of expressed opinion, whether sound or unsound. Some men can write quickly and clearly under pressure for a spell, but even such blessed bozos can't manage it for long. Writing takes thought, and quiet, and time. Some of the finest examples of critical writing that have come down to us from the past are as full of nonsense as some of the worst examples of the critical writing that we're getting hereabouts today. But they're nonetheless literature, and at least superficially admirable. They've got, for all their intrinsic dubiousness, a fine bounce and kick. They weren't written between eleven o'clock and twelve of a night; they were written leisurely. Criticism is, after all, or at least it should be, something more than a magistrate's court or a slot weighing-machine. It should be something of an art on its own. Who cares what a poem says, so long as it's beautiful? Who cares what music seeks to prove, or painting definitely to portray? Who gives a damn about the meaning of "Hamlet," so long as one can delight in the soft thunder of its language? Facts and logic alone have never made criticism a full-bodied thing. They are, God knows, valuable and all too rare to it, but even a cannon, in order best to discharge its projectile, has to be carefully—very carefully and scrupulously—oiled and polished.

[From *Monks Are Monks*, 1929, pp. 201–3.]

Prejudice

IT is unreasonable to ask of me that I approach each and every book or play with an open and unprejudiced mind. That is to be expected only of the critical amateur and dilettante. Behind every book or play there is an author or a playwright and behind the author or playwright there is, in many instances, a record of previous performance. Where a complete lack of merit has been observable in such antecedent performances, I find myself unable to approach the new work without a certain prejudice against it. This prejudice has not turned out to be ill-founded, I have discovered, for in a quarter of a century of reviewing I have never known a case where an author or a playwright already put down as talentless has suddenly and miraculously turned into a genius overnight. The possibility that he may produce something worthwhile is an argument of critical commentators who, were they race-track followers, would be of the kind who, fondly hoping against hope, would regularly and to their ultimate woe play 200 to 1 shots. If, as might by a wild flight of fancy happen, one such incompetent were actually one day to write a really good book or play, I should be only too glad to change my point of view and confess to my prejudicial error. But until that day comes, I shall continue to cherish my advance conviction that this or that author or playwright will present me with nothing that is worth my serious consideration and thought.

[From *Testament of a Critic*, 1931, pp. 27–8.]

ON CENSORSHIP

THE PLAIN trouble lies not with censorship, but with censors. There isn't one of us, once his loud talk has died down, but believes in censorship in one degree or another. I should like to inquire of the stoutest foe of all censorship just what his attitude would be were a French peepshow, to which minors were freely admitted, to be opened on either side of his home. I should, further, like to make a similar inquiry of the staunchest opponent of theatrical censorship in the event that, let us say, the curtain to the dramatization of Dreiser's *An American Tragedy* were at one point kept aloft a few moments longer and the seduction episode in which Clyde and Roberta figure pursued with a Zolaesque realism. And I should like to continue the inquiry in the case of the loudest howler against literary censorship in the event that copies of John Cleland's immortal tome were published at a nickel each and sold freely to school-children. The way to beat censorship is not to deny all sense to it and all justification, but to give ground where ground must be given and then, when the enemy oversteps its bounds, to let fly with the full artillery of calm intelligence. The last way in the world in which to win a battle is to try to convince one's self that the enemy has no guns. To contend that the cause of art is in danger because the censors edit or condemn and suppress a lot of dirty postcards, pornographic pamphlets, cheap moving pictures and equally cheap plays, to say nothing of a second-rate novel or so, is to make one's self and one's convictions ridiculous. Now and again, of course, a good piece of work suffers along with the contemptible because of the ignorance of the censors, but art is a poor and pitiable thing if it cannot survive such an occasional calamity. It has stood it in the past, and often enough. A relatively few years pass, the suppressed work duly comes into its own again, and all is as tranquil as before. True art simply can not be suppressed for long; history proves that much. If it can be suppressed and stay suppressed, you may rest assured that it isn't art. In all the centuries, not one genuinely fine piece of work has been suppressed by censorship for more than a little while. Art crushed to earth soon rises again. Only the spurious in art remains lying in the dirt.

I am against censorship not because it is censorship, but because it is generally ignorant. I am against censors because, all the time, they disgrace the theory of censorship in its soundest sense and make it objectionable even to men who may be willing to grant its periodic integrity. I have before me two documents in illustration. One is a copy of an address, made recently on the floor of the House of Representatives by a Congressman from a Southern State, advocating a general censorship of magazines. After denouncing a certain magazine as immoral and corruptive, this would-be censor quoted at length, in chief and eloquent support of his case, an article which I myself had written, carefully omitting the name of the magazine in which it had appeared. Who among his hearers was to know that the article was published in the very magazine that he was denouncing? What is one to say of such open-and-shut hypocrisy and double-dealing? A second illustration is to be had in a letter lying on my desk as I write this. It comes to me from a gentleman of God and one of the two leading champions of censorship in New York State. This holy gentleman, mistaking my attitude toward censors and censorship, observes that it is his opinion that the stage of New York City is unutterably filthy, that the law should promptly and forcibly be brought down upon it, and then asks me to supply him with the names of any plays that are dirty, confessing that he has not seen any of them himself! In other words, what we engage here is a censor who is certain that censorship is called for but who doesn't know what it is that should be censored. It is men like these—and they are typical of the tong—who bring censorship into vile disrepute and who cause all fair-minded and upright men and women to hold their noses. But let us get on our knees and thank God for them. It is they who are ruining irrevocably the cause of censorship amongst even censorship's more rational proponents.

[From the *American Mercury,* June 1927, pp. 243–4.]

ON TWO DRAMATISTS

Eugene O'Neill

WITH the appearance of *The Iceman Cometh,* our theatre has become dramatically alive again. It makes most of the plays of other American playwrights produced during the more than twelve-year period of O'Neill's absence look comparatively like so much damp tissue paper. In it there is an understanding of the deeper elements of human nature, a comprehension of the confused instincts that make up the life of mortals, and an evocation of pity for the tortured existence of dazed mankind that not merely most but all of those plays in combination have not faintly suggested. It is, in short, one of the best of its author's works and one that again firmly secures his position not only as the first of American dramatists but, with Shaw and O'Casey, one of the three really distinguished among the world's living.

These, I appreciate, are big words and probably contributive to the suspicion that their inditer has forgone his old Phyrronism. They are also doubtless obnoxious and challenging to such persons as either resent what seems to be extravagant praise at the expense of other playwrights or are constitutionally averse to superlatives of any kind and ready to throw off their coats if anyone has the gall to say even that Bach was the greatest composer who ever lived or that horseradish sauce is the best of all things to go with boiled beef. But the words, I believe, are none the less in good order. If they are not and if the play is not what I think it is, I am prepared to atone for my ignorance by presenting gratis to anyone who can offer convincing contrary evidence the complete bound works of all our American playwrights from Bronson Howard through Charles Klein, David Belasco and Augustus Thomas down to the geniuses responsible for *Joan of Lorraine, Another Part of the Forest, Dream Girl,* and *Maid in the Ozarks.*

Laying hold of an assortment of social outcasts quartered in a disreputable saloon on the fringe of New York in the year 1912 and introducing into their drunken semblance of content-ful hope an allergy in the shape of a Werlean traveling sales-man, O'Neill distils from them, slowly but inexorably, the trag-edy that is death in life. Superficially at times suggesting a cross between Gorki's *The Lower Depths* and Saroyan's *The Time of Your Life*, let alone Ibsen's *The Wild Duck*, the play with its author's uncommon dramaturgical skill gradually weaves its various vagrant threads into a solid thematic pattern and in the end achieves a purge and mood of compassion that mark it apart from the bulk of contemporary drama. There are repetitions in the middle sections which O'Neill has deemed necessary to the impact of the play but which in this opinion might be got rid of with no loss. There is also still an excess of profanity, for all the author's liberal cutting, that becomes dis-turbing to any ear that gags at such overemphasis. And since the uncut version of *Hamlet*, which is a good play too, can be played in its entirety in little more than three and a half hours, the longer running time of *The Iceman Cometh* may seem to some, and quite rightly, not only superfluous but a little pre-tentious. Yet small matter. In the whole history of drama there has been only one really perfect tragedy—incidentally, only one-third as long—and, while this of O'Neill's is scarcely to be compared with it, it still rises far above its possible errors.

With a few nimble strokes, O'Neill pictures vividly the in-nards of even the least of his variegated characters, from the one-time circus grifter to the one-time police lieutenant, from the quondam boss of a Negro gambling den to the erstwhile Boer War correspondent, and from the night and day bar-tenders and the wreck of a college graduate to the former edi-tor of Anarchist magazines and the old captain once in the British armed services. Only in the characters of his three street-walkers does he work rather obviously; truthfully, per-haps, but in a theatrically routine manner. Yet in his major figures, Slade, the one-time Syndicalist-Anarchist, Hickey, the hardware salesman, Hope, the proprietor of the saloon, etc., the hand is as steady and sure as ever.

The long monologue, only now and then momentarily interrupted, wherein toward the drama's conclusion the salesman relates the relief from himself secured by the murder of his wife, is one of the most impressive pieces of writing in contemporary dramatic literature: emotionally searching and definitely moving. The relations of Slade and the young man with memory of his betrayed mother on his agonized conscience are maneuvered with high suspensive dexterity, even if at one or two points to the hypercritical slightly overplanted. The dialogue throughout is driving; there is robust humor to alleviate the atmospheric sordidness; and out of the whole emerges in no small degree the profound essences of authentic tragedy.

In the author's own analysis of his play as he has confided it to me the dominant intention has been a study in the workings of strange friendship. That intention, it is not to be gainsaid, has been fully realized. But as I read the script and see it in stage action it seems to me that, far above and beyond it, there rises the theme of the tragedy which lies in bogus self-substantiation and the transient, pitiable satisfaction which it bequeaths. That, however, is the play's virtue: to different men it may convey different things. But to all with any emotional understanding and to all with any appreciation of the drama it must convey the satisfaction of a theatre that, if only for a short while, has again come into its rightful own.

In a setting by Robert Edmond Jones which catches perfectly the atmosphere of the play and with lighting that alternately gives the stage and groupings the effect of Daumier and George Bellows, Eddie Dowling, with many acceptable critical suggestions from the author, has accomplished an impressive example of direction. In only two or three details has he missed, and the fault in those cases was scarcely his. O'Neill's men's toilet to the far left of the stage with the "This Is It" sign is gratuitous, since it is strangely, even phenomenally, never once used by any of the hard-drinking denizens of the saloon and since it thus serves no purpose and is simply a gesture in juvenile waggery. Dowling's idea that it be given some small justification by installing Hugo Kalmar, the drooling Anarchist editor, in it at one point and having him declaim his parrot lines from its interior—an excellent comedy touch that would have suited the action with no slightest violation of the text—was ve-

toed by O'Neill. The play's ending, which presently goes a little flat, might also, as Dowling wished, have been inspirited if,
as counterpoint to Slade's final "Be God, I'm the only real convert to death Hickey made here; from the bottom of my coward's heart I mean that now!," the drunken singing and wild
pounding on the table by the assembled, happily unredeemed
bibuli had not been cut by the author and had been moved a
bit forward from its place in the original script. And if the director had been allowed to lend a greater touch of his familiar
"mood" staging to the play, which he was not, the spirit of the
drama would have been materially aided.

O'Neill is the only dramatist in the history of the American
theatre who has achieved real world status. His plays have been
produced in most of the civilized countries of the globe; he has
been awarded the Nobel prize for the body of his work; he has
been the subject of critical discussion in South America, England, Germany, France, Italy, Greece, Russia, the Scandinavian lands, the Balkans, Australia, Japan and China. Almost as
much has been written about him as about one-half all the
living playwrights rolled together. Only Shaw has consumed
more space.

In the United States, South America, France, Italy, Russia,
the Scandinavian countries, Rumania, Greece, Australia, Japan and China, the critical attitude toward him in the main has
been extremely favorable. In Germany, when criticism was operating freely, it was, with a few exceptions, highly appreciative. In England alone has there most often been either a
lukewarm or chilly attitude toward him.

Here in America his preëminence as the first dramatist of his
nation is taken by the great majority of the critics for granted.
Now and again a small voice from the sidelines lifts itself in
contradiction and puts in some peculiar nomination for the
honor, but in the aggregate his position is unchallenged. In
France, where his plays have had their chief hearing at the
hands of Pitoëff, all save one or two of the recognized critics
have been impressed. In Russia, praise of him has been pretty
uniform, and understandably, since his dramatic philosophy
and usual attitude toward his subject matter find a sympathetic
echo in the Slav temperament. In Italy, those of his plays that

have been shown have fared well at most critical hands; his *Days without End,* which strikes a Catholic note, has received the Church's imprimatur and has been produced under the auspices of the Vatican. South America has paid him homage. Sweden has acclaimed him, and so has the theatre of Norway. Various of his plays have proved successes, both popular and critical, in Rumania, and Hungary, though to a lesser degree, has received him with hospitality. German critics, save in the few instances noted, have in the past treated him with respect, and in Japan and China the younger element, which alone is interested dramatically in the outside world, regards him, along with Shaw, as the most important of the Western playwrights.

On the other hand, though he has intermittently been accepted in England and even treated with considerable esteem by men of letters like Spender, *et al.,* the general run of drama criticism has frequently shown misgivings about him. In some cases, indeed, the misgivings have been accompanied by lofty derision.

For an example of the English attitude, we may turn to Eric Bentley and his recent observations in *The Playwright as Thinker.* I quote four typical samples:

a. "Among the untragic tragedians the most spectacular is Eugene O'Neill. At everything in the theatre except being tragic and being comic he is a success. . . . Tragedy is transported to the intense inane. . . . The tension that is missing in his work is inner tension."

b. "O'Neill has not as yet been able adequately to represent the bourgeois world as the nightmare which in the twentieth century it became, though his portraits of neurosis and decay are a labored and overconscious striving in that direction. O'Neill's more powerful, *unconsciously* symbolic tendency was to try to flee the bourgeois world, not like Wedekind by standing it on its head, but by trying to deny its existence, by proclaiming exclusive reality for the eternal. It was O'Neill himself who stood on his head."

c. "T. S. Eliot's 'conception' (in *The Family Reunion*) is clear, noble, and mature. . . . O'Neill's 'conception' (in *Mourning Becomes Electra*) is rude, simple-minded, gaga."

d. "Where Wedekind seems silly and turns out on further inspection to be profound, O'Neill seems profound and turns out on further inspection to be silly. . . . O'Neill has yet to show us he has a mind. So far he has only been earnest after the fashion of the popular pulpit or of professors who write on the romance of reality. Precisely because he pretends to be too much, he attains too little. He is false, and he is false in a particularly unpleasant way. His art is *faux-bon.* The 'good clean fun' of a Hitchcock movie is better."

Since every critic has a right to his opinion, and in view of the differences thereof which have been O'Neill's portion, I now that he has reappeared with *The Iceman Cometh* as a produced dramatist venture my own on the plays which he has contributed to the stage since first he began to function. In chronological compositional order, herewith the plays and the present commentator's views on them *in piccolo:*

1913–14. *Thirst* and four other one-act plays. Wholly negligible and plainly the work of a novice.

1914. *Bound East for Cardiff.* The first of his sea plays and the first indication of a significant new dramatic talent. A striking performance containing the seed of its author's future mental cast.

1916. *Before Breakfast.* A trifle. Little in it to encourage the critical hopes found in *Bound East for Cardiff.*

1917. *In the Zone, Ile, The Long Voyage Home, The Moon of the Caribbees.* The hopes were here reinforced in this rounding out of the cycle of short sea plays. *In the Zone* is the weakest of the four, melodramatically effective but built around an all too obvious theatrical device. *Ile* and *The Long Voyage Home,* however, show an advance in character portrayal, thematic feel, and dramaturgical expertness. *The Moon of the Caribbees,* the best of the four plays, is remarkable for the dramatic capturing of a mood and its projection. It remains one of the few genuinely important one-act plays in American dramatic literature.

1918. *The Rope, Beyond the Horizon, The Dreamy Kid, Where the Cross Is Made. The Rope* is an only fair excursion into psychopathic melodrama. *Beyond the Horizon,* his first full-length play (there were two or three written in his nonage which he destroyed and of which no traces remain), may be said to have influenced perceptibly the course of American drama. Its honest realism filtered through a poetic impulse came as a revelation to a stage chiefly given over, at its serious best, to rhinestone imagination and, at its worst, to vacuity illuminated by Broadway lamplight. While here and there suggesting a certain infirmity in dramaturgy, it betokened clearly the more finished work that was to come. *The Dreamy Kid* was and is a distinctly minor effort, and of no consequence. *Where the Cross Is Made,* the germ of the later full-length play, *Gold,* was and remains a fabricated one-acter partly redeemed by a potentially serviceable thematic idea.

1919. *Chris, The Straw.* Produced briefly in Philadelphia and withdrawn, *Chris* was a crude attempt at the play, *Anna Christie,* into which it was subsequently developed. *The Straw,* in its treatment of tuberculosis, is an unusual achievement of a difficult dramatic problem. Its emotional orchestration is one of O'Neill's best accomplishments.

1920. *Gold, Anna Christie, The Emperor Jones, Diff'rent. Gold,* though possessing several unmistakable virtues, fails in its entirety because of intermittent aberrant planning and uncertain playwrighting. *Anna Christie* is a new and forceful handling of a familiar theme, deep in its characterizations, driving in its firm composition, and etched with real observation and understanding. *The Emperor Jones* is a masterpiece of its kind. Its cumulative dramatic effect is irresistible. The tom-toms starting, in Richard Dana Skinner's apt phrase, at the rate of the human pulse beat and rising bit by bit as a fevered pulse would rise and which are of the warp and woof of the drama itself, sweep one along and up into a mighty climax and leave one without breath. Into this study of the Negro's dream of release from bondage to the whites and, upon the dream's coming true, his defeat by the very tricks of the whites which in practise have brought him release, or what he images is release, O'Neill has introduced a symbolic fancy uncommon to American dramatic writing. The succeeding

Diff'rent, however, is of small moment, a feeble distillation of Strindberg further debilitated by its author's handling of its materials.

1921. *The First Man, The Hairy Ape.* The former, with the later *Welded,* is one of O'Neill's two worst full-length performances. Here again, in both cases, close imitation of Strindberg has brought its penalties. Aping the technic of Strindberg, as I observed at the time, O'Neill sets himself so to intensify and even hyperbolize a theme as to evoke the dramatic effect from its overtones rather than, as is the more general manner, from its undertones. His attempt is to duplicate the technic of such a drama as *The Father,* the power of which is derived not by suggestion and implication but from the sparks that fly upward from a prodigious and deafening pounding on the anvil. The attempt is a failure, for all that one gets in O'Neill's case is the prodigious and deafening pounding; the sparks simply will not come out. Now and again one discerns something that looks vaguely like a spark, but on closer inspection it turns out to be only an artificial theatrical firefly which has been cunningly concealed up the actors' sleeves. The author goes aground on the rocks of exaggeration and overemphasis. His philosophical melodrama is so full of psychological revolver shorts, jumps off the Brooklyn Bridge, incendiary Chinamen, galloping hose carts, forest fires, wild locomotives, sawmills, dynamite kegs, time fuses, infernal machines, battles under the sea, mine explosions, Italian blackhanders, sinking ocean liners, fights to the death on rafts, and last-minute pardons that the effect is akin to reading a treatise on the theme on a bump-the-bumps. He rolls up his sleeves and piles on the agony with the assiduity of a coalheaver. He here misjudges, it seems to me completely, the Strindberg method. O'Neill intensifies his theme from without. He piles psychological and physical situation on situation until the structure topples over with a burlesque clatter, Strindberg magnified the psychos of his characters. O'Neill here magnifies their actions.

The Hairy Ape is in a class apart. Partly expressionistic and written with greater restraint if with greatly increased and sounder dramatic intensity, the play dramatizes its theme of despairing humanity gazing blinded at the stars with a signal drive.

1922. *The Fountain.* A very uneven and not particularly successful fantasy dealing with the quest of Ponce de Leon. Some of the writing is eloquent, but more seems labored. The protagonist is described as "a romantic dreamer governed by the ambitious thinker in him." The protagonist's confusion is shared by the playwright.

1923. *Welded, All God's Chillun Got Wings.* As for the former, see the above comment on *The First Man.* *All God's Chillun Got Wings* is a study of miscegenation wrought with honesty, sympathetic comprehension, and proficient dramaturgy. Its basic idea, the tragic difficulty in man's acceptance of reality and truth, is boiled out of the theme with a steaming emotionalism and persuasion.

1924. *Desire under the Elms.* The Strindberg influence is here again clear, but in this instance O'Neill has exercised greater caution and selection and has not allowed himself so fully to be dominated. The result is a drama of passion and incest that does not get out of hand and that by and large amounts to a satisfactory realistic treatment of some of the elements in the classic Greek drama.

1925. *Marco Millions, The Great God Brown.* *Marco Millions* is a witty satire, crossed with the poetic mood, dealing with the exploits of that prototype of the American go-getter, Marco Polo. It is everything that *The Fountain* is not. Much of the writing is delightful and the sentiment in, for example, the little Princess Kukachin's eager search for the lost suggestion of her hero's soul has real body. *The Great God Brown,* with its employment of masks, is one of O'Neill's major efforts and in many respects comes off laudably despite the difficult problems it offers to stage presentation. The psychological essences of the drama are craftily distilled and, for all the complexities projected by the frequent mask-changing on the part of the characters, the play manages much of the impression designed by its author. What confusion there is is less inherent in the theme than in the mechanical adornments visited upon it.

1926. *Lazarus Laughed.* An unsuccessful attempt at what

seems to be operatic Biblical fantasy. Less a theatre play than a libretto.

1927. *Strange Interlude.* A notable contribution to the drama. On an unusually broad canvas, O'Neill has plumbed the psyche of a woman in relation to her men with a handsome understanding. His knowledge of character has never been better displayed by him. There are one or two moments when matters seem to evade him, but he thereafter recaptures his purpose and pushes ahead with entire comprehension. On the whole, a psychological drama again touched by the Strindberg philosophy which leaves its immediate subject matter convincingly exhausted.

1928. *Dynamo.* A conflict between the depths and surfaces of man resolved into a drama that is overwritten, overstuffed, and that does not come off. Isolated scenes are dramatically stimulating, but the drama in its entirety becomes lost in its own tortuous philosophical alleys and leaves one with the impression that less symbolism and more simplicity would have served the playwright's purpose infinitely better.

1931. *Mourning Becomes Electra.* A fine paraphrase of the classic Greek drama. Bringing the incestuous theme of revenge into modern recognition, O'Neill has fashioned a tragedy that stands largely on independent feet and that presents his dramaturgical gifts in full flower.

1932. *Ah, Wilderness!* Turning from tragedy to comedy, the author has here achieved the tenderest and most amusing comedy of boyhood in the American drama. It is an answer to those who believe that he is without humor, a belief held by such as have engaged some of his antecedent work with a predetermined lack of humor.

1933. *Days without End.* Rewriting has spoiled a play that in its original conception was not without some merit. As it stands, it is an anachronistic treatment of its single-standard sex theme wedded to psychic release through religious faith. The many revisions made by the author in his several earlier drafts weakened the play's directness and have botched it. A poor performance.

1939. *The Iceman Cometh.* One of O'Neill's top achievements. A drama of the submerged tenth which, as previously noted, vaguely suggests Gorki's *The Lower Depths* but which is not only an immeasurably better play but one that explores the confused and agonized souls of mankind with rare understanding and with powerful dramatic result.

Two additional plays have been completed during the last four years and are awaiting metropolitan production: *A Moon for the Misbegotten*, already tried out in the Mid-West, and *A Touch of the Poet*. Pending a view of them, what is O'Neill's critical status to date?

That he is the foremost dramatist in the American theatre is, as has been recorded, generally granted. His eminence is predicated on the fact that no other has anything like his ability to delve into and appraise character, his depth of knowledge of his fellow man, his sweep and pulse and high resolve, his command of a theatre stage and all its manifold workings, and his mastery of the intricacies of dramaturgy. His plays at their best have in them a real universality. His characters are not specific, individual, and isolated types but active symbols of mankind in general, with mankind's virtues and faults, gropings and findings, momentary triumphs and doomed defeats. He writes not for a single theatre but for all theatres of the world.

It is argued by some against him that he is no poet, and that his drama hence misses true stature. Specifically and in the conventional sense, he may not be, but he is nevertheless, as must be evident to the close student of his work, driven ever by the poetic spirit. His weakness, where and when it exists, lies in his excesses—the excesses of overlength, overemphasis, overembroidery and overmelodramatization of the psychological aspects of his drama and of that drama itself. At his worst, these qualities edge him close to brooding travesty.

He has worked expertly in the field of tragedy, nimbly in the field of comedy, and less happily in that of fantasy. His brutality in tragedy is a handmaiden of the truth as he sees it. He cannot compromise with himself, right or wrong. Uncommonly gifted in a knowledge of the theatre, it may seem to some that he resorts occasionally to critically invalid devices to further his dramatic ends. If he does so, he does so unconsciously, never with calculation and deliberately. He would be content, I am assured, to publish his plays and forego the profits of production. He has written muddled and poor plays along with the valid, some very muddled and very poor. But the great body of his work has a size and significance not remotely approached by any other American. In a broader sense, he is certainly in no remotest degree the mind that Shaw is—his is an emotional rather than an intellectual; he is not by far the poet that O'Casey is, for in O'Casey there is the true music of great wonder and beauty. But he has plumbed depths deeper than either; he is greatly the superior of both in dramaturgy; and he remains his nation's one important contribution to the art of the drama.

Before the presentation of *The Iceman Cometh,* it was exactly twelve years and nine months since O'Neill's last previous play, *Days without End,* had seen production, and in the long intervening spell the theatre had had small news of him. Now and then came vague and contradictory reports that he was working on a cycle of eight or nine plays to be named by the general and somewhat turgid title, *A Tale of Possessors Self-Dispossessed*; that he was very ill and no longer able to do any work; and that he had successively retired from the theatre to Sea Island, Georgia, and the Valley of the Moon in California, there to devote the rest of his life to nursing his health, raising Dalmatian dogs, and laughing at most of current English dramatic criticism. But from the man himself there issued not so much as a whisper. What, really, was he up to?

It happens that we have been close friends for going on thirty years now, and that I am in a position to tell. That in the period of his absence he completed *The Iceman Cometh,* along with the subsequently to be produced *A Moon for the Misbegotten* and the still later to be produced *A Touch of the Poet,* the public had been apprised. These three plays, however, were by no means all. During the twelve-odd years, he not only outlined in minute detail not eight or nine but all of eleven plays of the cycle referred to—the eleven were to be played, however, as eight with three combined into duplex units and presented, like *Strange Interlude,* on the same afternoons, evenings and nights—but further definitely completed seven of them, including the three double-length ones, and got pretty well into the eighth. In addition, he finished a separate and independent play of full length called *Long Day's Journey into Night,* production of which he will not allow, for reasons which I may not specify, for many years. Nor, yet again, was that all. Besides *Long Day's Journey into Night,* he also completed the first play of a much shorter and entirely different cycle of which no word has reached anyone. Its title, like that of the contemplated briefer series in its entirety, is *By Way of Obit.* It runs for forty-five or so minutes and involves, very successfully I think, an imaginative technical departure from O'Neill's previous work. It contains but two characters and is laid in New York in approximately the same period as *The Iceman Cometh.*

All of which, one will agree, is not such bad going for a sick man.

The plays, *The Iceman Cometh* and *A Moon for the Misbegotten,* as well as the two last named, are distinct and wholly apart from the cycle of eleven plays. *A Touch of the Poet,* however, was to be first play of that cycle in revision. As to the cycle itself, he gradually convinced himself, after he had got as far as he had with it, that his dramaturgical plan was faulty. Without further ado, he destroyed two of the double-length, or four, of the plays he had written, preserving only *A Touch of the Poet,* the third double-header (*More Stately Mansions*), and one scene in another to be called *The Calms of Capricorn.* As for *A Touch of the Poet,* it seems to him to be a unit in itself and may well, he thinks, stand apart and alone. When and if he will return to work on the cycle as he has newly planned it, he does not know. In his head at the moment is an exciting idea for another play which bears no relation to the cycle. It will probably be his next effort after he has finished the production supervision of the other two plays noted.

The reason he withheld the three plays for so long is that he has made up his mind never again to permit a play of his to be produced unless he can be present. His health was such that it did not allow him to come to New York earlier. There was also another reason. He did not believe that, while the war was on, the theatre was right for the plays, though none is in any way related to it. It was simply his feeling that wartime audiences would not be in a mood for such serious dramas. His deter-

mination to be present at all future productions of his plays
stems from his experience with his play *Dynamo,* which was
shown in 1929. He was unable to come to New York for the
casting and rehearsals of that one and learned all too late
that the Theatre Guild had cast in the leading female role the
fair young cute one, Claudette Colbert, famous for the symmetry of her legs, and not wholly unaware of the fact. Throughout the play, the young lady sought to extend her fame by placing the two reasons therefor on display whenever one of the
other characters seemed to her to be diverting the attention of
the audience, and the play as a consequence ran a bad second
to her extremities.

"Henceforth," O'Neill averred, "I myself cast not only actresses but legs!"

In addition to the projected plays specified, the playwright
has made copious notes on at least three or four others. Some
of these notes were begun even before he went into retirement;
others were made during that period. They include plans for,
among the others, an heroic drama of ancient Chinese locale.
This he has been mulling for fifteen years, though if he does it
at all, which is doubtful, it would not be put into experimental
preliminary writing until he finishes the one—with an American
locale—alluded to as likely his next.

The long cycle, when and if he returns to it, will concern a
single Irish-American family over a span of approximately one
hundred and thirty years and will indicate broadly through
its successive generations the changes in America and American life. Not the changes in the obvious theatrical sense, but
the changes as they influence the members of the family. It will
continue to be a study in character rather than a study in national progress. The latter will be held to a dramatic under-
tone. O'Neill's dissatisfaction with the work as far as it had
gone proceeded from his conviction that it should deal with
one family and not two, as it presently did. And also that, in
the form he had written it, it began at the wrong point and
overtold the story. Though he appreciated that he could rewrite
what he had already done, he preferred to do away with much
of it and to start afresh. The cycle, as he now envisages it, will
begin with the French and Indian wars period and will present

its first member of the family in the light of a deserter from the fighting forces.

O'Neill's attitude toward criticism of his work in particular and in general has not changed. However denunciatory and stinging it may be at times, he shows no indignation and maintains at least outwardly an appearance of smiling tolerance. Unlike a number of his playwrighting contemporaries, he never makes public reply to it, though now and again to a close friend he will privately express his amusement over certain of its more capricious aspects.

An English critic recently, for example, had at O'Neill with the old, familiar contention that, though he may think of himself as a poet, he is far from one. In proof whereof, the critic delightedly quoted this speech by Marsden in *Strange Interlude*:

"We'll be married in the afternoon, decidedly. I've already picked out the church, Nina—a gray ivied chapel, full of restful shadow, symbolical of the peace we have found. The crimsons and purples in the windows will stain our faces with faded passion. It must be in the hour before sunset when the earth dreams in afterthoughts and mystic premonitions of life's beauty," etc.

"Didn't he realize," chuckled O'Neill, "that the attempt there certainly wasn't poetry, but poetic travesty? Marsden, as anyone must easily see, is a sentimental throwback, a kind of *Yellow Book* period reversion, and I was deliberately using that 'crimsons and purples in the windows,' 'staining our faces with faded passion' and so on stuff to indicate it."

The notion that O'Neill entertains a profound satisfaction with everything he has written and resents any opposite opinion—a notion that pops up in various treatises on his work—is nonsensical. I give you several instances out of my own personal critical experience. When his *The First Man* was produced, I wrote acidly of it, even indulging in some ridicule. Reading the criticism, O'Neill grinned. "You let it down too easy," he observed. "It's no good." When subsequently I wrote in the same vein about *Welded*, which he seemed to have faith in when he gave me the script to read, he allowed, "I know now I was 'way off; the play is all wrong; it's no good." When, on the other hand, I found certain things to my liking in *Gold,* he took me to task. "You're wrong. It's a bad play. I'm telling you." He further believes that *The Fountain* is even more defective than I found it to be, and that *Dynamo,* though granting its lapses, is considerably less so. Only in the case of *Days without End,* which I could not critically stomach, has he vigorously opposed my opinion, and even in this case he allows that he now feels he must rewrite the play's ending for the definitive edition of his works. As originally conceived, this *Days without End* was, as I have said before, laid back in the year 1857 or thereabout. Bringing it up to the 1930's seemed to me, among others, to render its single-standard sex idea somewhat archaic and shopworn. O'Neill, however, was not to be persuaded. What he has persuaded himself, nevertheless, is that his hero's final gesture calls for alteration, though the alteration consists simply in reverting to the dramatic scheme as he first conceived it.

He is a stickler for casting and direction. As to the latter, his constant concern is any sentimentalization of his work. "Where sentiment exists," he says, "there is sufficient of it in the characters, and any directorial emphasis would throw it out of all proportion and make it objectionable." As to casting, he is generally opposed to so-called name actors. "They distract attention from the play to themselves," he argues. "My plays are not for stars but for simply good actors. Besides, you can never count on the idiosyncrasies of stars; they may not stick to a play and may so damage its chances on the road. I'm afraid of them, as I've had some experience with them. Also, they sometimes want you to change certain things in your play. Not for me!"

To return, finally, to *The Iceman Cometh,* I have already twice remarked that it may very roughly be described as a kind of American *The Lower Depths.* Like that play of Gorki's, though it in few other ways resembles it, it treats of a group of degenerate outcasts and the advent among them of a man with a philosophy of life new and disturbing to them. Its language is realistic, at times over-violently so; its cast of alcoholic down-and-outs includes gamblers, grafting cops, circus lot sharpers, whores, pimps, Anarchist riff-raff, military failures, college-educated wastrels, stool-pigeons, *et al.*; and it is written in four parts. It attests again to the fact, lost upon some of O'Neill's critics, that he is far from lacking a healthy sense of humor. Some of the comedy writing is irresistible. It also demonstrates again the most barbed appreciation of character known to any of his American playwriting contemporaries. And it embraces, among many other things, the most pitifully affecting picture of a woman—the unseen wife of the protagonist—that I, for one, have encountered in many years of playgoing.

Among the criticisms of the play is the argument that the characters "do not grow." That they do not grow is O'Neill's specific dramatic theme. Human beings sometimes change but change is not necessarily growth. Change is frequently impermanent and retrogressive rather than advancing as O'Neill indicates. Another argument is that Hickey, the salesman of Death, in the end "explains himself with a textbook clarity that robs him of a truly dramatic role in the play, or a really human complexity." What of Nina in *The Sea Gull*? And a third condescendingly observes, "As for O'Neill's 'thesis,' it would seem to be that men cannot live without illusions; hardly a new or very disputable idea." Hardly new, granted; but not very disputable? Come, come. What of the sufficient disputations on occasion of Ibsen, Strindberg, Zola, Hauptmann, Tolstoi, Wedekind, Shaw . . . ?

[From *The Theatre Book of the Year, 1946–1947*, pp. 93–111.]

George Bernard Shaw—Hail and Farewell!

MAY God in His infinite wisdom spare him to us for many another year but, since mathematics seem to be inexorable in the scheme of Divine Providence and since he is now within two and one-half years of ninety, the Great Bookkeeper may have other ideas. It is this unhappy thought that prompts, while he is still alive, this reckoning of what George Bernard Shaw has meant, among so many other things, to the world of drama.

When Shaw in his earlier day as a critic looked upon the English stage, what he found, in the plays of Pinero, was simply a romantic servant-girl's view of sex made palatable to her even more romantic employers by identifying it with persons of a somewhat fancier social class. What he found further, in the plays of Henry Arthur Jones, though he deemed him Pinero's superior, was a relationship of men and women predicated merely upon its availability for ready theatrical effect, and a philosophy of that relationship facilely concocted by placing a sliver of banana peel under Pinero's moral rectitude. What he found still further, despite the strong wind beginning to blow down from Norway, was a drama still artificialized out of all reality by French influences. What he found in sum and in short was an English stage that interpreted life largely in terms of the powdered mentalities and evening-dressed emotions of high-life puppets or in the even more laughable terms of paper-knife melodrama.

Since critic and crusader are generally one and the same, for all the critic's customary lofty disdain of the impeachment, the disgusted Shaw didn't wait long before exchanging his critical robes for playwriting armor and, his white plume flying behind him, riding forth to battle. With the earlier help of his fellow-critic Archer, he drew first blood, if but a dribble, from the heathen by heaving onto the stage of the Independent Theatre Company of London *Widowers' Houses* which, though paradoxically imitative of the very drama he was tilting against, dared to introduce sociology and economics into the drawing room. This was the start, modest enough, but the start nonetheless of the putsch that was to revolutionize not only the modern drama of England but to a considerable degree the drama of the rest of the civilized world.

It was not, however, too easy going. The English were still happily swooning over the pretty parlor woes of Mrs. Tanqueray and her sisters when Shaw had at them with the ironic whimsicalities of *Arms and the Man*, which they appreciated only as a stage Russian pretends to appreciate licorice-pellet caviar, and, unforgivably, with *Mrs. Warren's Profession* which, while essentially not altogether dissimilar to Mrs. Tanqueray's, nevertheless so outraged the British morality that its production was forbidden.

Chuckling in his beard, Shaw thereupon said to himself, very well, if the numskulls prefer sentimentality, I shall give it to them, but in such clever and witty wise that they will not recognize the deletion of the *ality*. *Candida*, that most delightful of sentimental comedies, was the result. And slowly, like a tortoise making for a lily pond, the English public began to respond. And slowly its esteem for Pinero's innocent young women whose reputations had been knavishly stained (*The Benefit of the Doubt*) and less innocent older women who melodramatically burned Bibles by way of justifying their illicit relations with politicians (*The Notorious Mrs. Ebbsmith*) proceeded faintly to fade. Nor did Jones' Michaels and their lost angels or Wilde's ideal husbands bring the color wholly back to its cheeks. For Shaw, not dismounting from his charger for a moment, kept prodding sardonically with lances like *The Devil's Disciple*, which invited audiences to bring with them fewer glands and more brains into the theatre and which pleasantly surprised them by being not at all as painful as they had anticipated but, on the contrary, surprisingly amusing.

II

From this point on, our hero's crusade was, as the vulgar Yankee expression has it, pretty well in the bag. It was not that the English, who steadfastly worship anything old, whether a philosophy, an actress or a bathroom, deserted the dramatic order of yesterday en masse. Very far from it. The Episcopalian indiscretions of lords and manicurists (*The Gay Lord Quex*), the Lake Como moonlit adventurings of elegant strumpets (*Iris*), the spectacles of cross-examined "good" women battling to preserve their honor (*Mrs. Dane's Defence*), the necklaces of Mrs. Gorringe, the amatory maneuvers of Jane, and the various princesses and butterflies still exercised their perfumed influence. But that influence was not exactly the puissant thing it once was. And gradually and surely it was to become less and less under the Shavian pressure. And where in several other and more progressive countries it had not been earlier recognized, it was now not long before St. George was hailed as the voice in the dramatic wilderness and the prophet of the new dramatic order.

Having already produced the beautifully witty *Caesar and Cleopatra* on a stage chronologically identified with the prettily cologned *The Gay Lord Quex,* Shaw forthwith pitched in in earnest. *Captain Brassbound's Conversion,* after a lapse in *The Admirable Bashville,* was followed by *John Bull's Other Island* and that by *Major Barbara, The Philanderer* and *Man and Superman,* the three last produced in a single year. Scarcely had audiences recaptured their wind than *The Doctor's Dilemma* was heaved at them. And then in quick succession *Getting Married* (*The Shewing-Up of Blanco Posnet* suffered a deferred production), *Misalliance* and *Fanny's First Play.* And, not so long afterward, *You Never Can Tell* and *Pygmalion* and *Androcles and the Lion* and, to the bewilderment of any possible remaining doubters, that most remarkable of modern historical fancies, *Saint Joan.*

Shaw's position as the greatest dramatist in the English-speaking theatre of his time was now secure. Nor could that security be minimized by his later and enfeebled work. Although his *The Apple Cart, The Simpleton of the Unexpected Isles, Too True To Be Good, Back to Methuselah, Geneva, In Good King Charles' Golden Days,* etc., marked a clearly visible and here and there sorry decline, there were still traces of the real Shaw detectable in them. And at their worst, save in the case of *Geneva,* they were better than the great majority of plays that emanated in the same period from the English theatre.

It was not, throughout his theatrical career, that Shaw was the revolutionary dramatic thinker he was esteemed to be by his critics and audiences given to a confounding of impudent intelligence with a quietly reasoned and profound philosophy. Much of what was accepted as daring had already been long tried and tested when Shaw offered it. It was rather that he had the great ability to restate platitudes in such a manner that their weariness left them and that they took on again the color of youth. He brought with him many of the old stage toys but he painted them up in such brilliant and dashing colors that they seemed new. He laughed at the old conventions of the drama, nevertheless kept them and, by playing his wit over them, gayly deceived his willing customers that they were right out of the bandbox. And, above all, he had the enormous theatrical skill to make cynicism a merry thing.

Gratuitously to analyze his plays too closely is to look the gift horse in the mouth, for they have given their recipients some of the happiest hours the stage has afforded since their earliest birthdays. *Caesar and Cleopatra* overdoes the business of criticizing the British? All right, but it nonetheless remains the best play of its kind written in Shaw's time. The epilogue of *Saint Joan* is greasepaint humbug? True. But the play remains the best play of its kind in that same time. *Fanny's First Play* is on the trivial side? Sure enough, but where a better and more hilarious trivial one? The Life Force business of *Man and Superman* and the pursuit of man by woman is out of Schopenhauer, with a bow to Nietzsche for the Superman business? So what? Maybe the play as a whole isn't plentifully superior to it?

III

I am not writing definitive criticism; I am writing definitive appreciation of dramatic and theatrical favors. Writing thus, I may possibly deplore with the more definitively critical and worthy P. P. Howe Shaw's admiration for confusing such a character's name as Mr. Redbrook with Mr. Kidbrook or Ftatateeta with Teetatota and, with Howe, condemn it equally with Wilde's having named a character Kelvil in order to be able later on to call him Kettle (or even equally with Shakespeare's bequeathal of the name Elbow for subsequent punning purposes), but since it occupies only eight seconds out of two otherwise amusing hours I shall not complain too loudly. I may also make a wry critical face over the old vaudeville funny business of a woman getting drunk, but *Candida* is *Candida* all the same. I may professionally yelp a little when the great Catherine rolls around on the floor like a couple of 1890 German and Irish comedians, but the short play is pretty entertaining in spite of it. I may groan a bit over such undergraduate pleasantries, so Howe terms them, as "No man is a match for a woman except with a poker and a pair of hobnailed boots," but there are a hundred such compensating lines as "Captain Bluntschli, I am very glad to see you; but you must leave this house at once" or as "Life does not cease to be funny when people die any more than it ceases to be serious when people laugh." And I may, as a critic who gets paid for it, frown gravely over any number of other obvious shortcomings in the great old boy's plays but, as a man who doesn't get paid for it, I smile and laugh and moisten at so much that is otherwise in them that I nevertheless kiss him on both cheeks.

There is that word moisten. It would take a pretty tough character, or a *Viola tricolor,* to resist Shaw at his sentimental best, for in that best there is a world of tender wisdom distilled into some of the most beautiful prose that the modern stage has known. Caesar's speech to Cleopatra . . . Candida's gentle philosophy . . . Dubedat's bequest to Jennifer—these and a dozen, two dozen, others confound the criticism that once, and then seemingly not without merit, held Shaw to have a heart compounded half of secondhand Butler and half, in Wells' phrase, of parthenogenetic eggs.

And so when it comes to sex. The Shaw who once said, "There is never any real sex in romance; what is more, there is very little, and that of a very crude kind, in ninety-nine hundredths of our married life"; the Shaw who observed "One man's poetry is another man's pruriency"; the Shaw who asked, "Is any treatment of sex in the interest of public morals?"; the Shaw who remarked, "The novel which says no more about sex than may be said in a lecture on the facts to a class of schoolgirls of fifteen can be enormously more entertaining than a novel wholly preoccupied with sexual symptoms"—the Shaw who has uttered such beliefs has trouble explaining himself to the Shaw who, albeit perhaps unwittingly, has created some of the most desirable heroines that the modern stage has revealed. It is his paradox that his own passivity has created warmth in other men. Although he often hopes to write brilliantly of women as if they were so many lamps without shades, the softening shades are nonetheless born of his prose. And of his own irrepressible, natural sentiment no less.

Dick Dudgeon in *The Devil's Disciple* pronounces the word *love* "with true Puritan scorn," Mrs. Bridgenorth in *Getting Married* comments on the "everyday vulgarities of earthly love," and so with many another of his mouthpieces. But, as Stevenson hinted long ago to William Archer, Shaw was nevertheless born a romantic and continues to be one to this day.

And, as I myself observed years ago, his romanticism is no more clearly to be detected than through such of his animadversions on love and sex. He pretends not to see the latter for what they are and for what, deep inside him, he knows them to be. But all the fine irony and humor which he has visited upon them cannot conceal the romanticist hiding behind that irony and humor and slyly seeking to protect himself from the charge through them. If the author of the rare and beautiful letters to Ellen Terry isn't one of the most deeply romantic natures of his time and if he was not then, psychologically speaking, one who cunningly dismissed sex only and simply because he wished to safeguard his pride and disappointment in the presence of his successful rival, Irving—if Shaw was not and is not all of that, these observations are those of a two-year-old, and a backward one.

IV

The great man is nearing the threshold of the hereafter. The theatre has not seen his like before, and may not see it soon again. He has brought to it a merry courage, a glorious wit, a musical tenderness, and a world of needed vitality. He has laughed at the old gods and, to give them their due, the old gods have enjoyed it. And outside and beyond the theatre he has let a wholesome breeze into more assorted kinds of national, international, private and public buncombe than has any other writer of his period. Therefore, hail, Shaw, hail and —I hope I shall wait long before saying it—farewell!

[From the *American Mercury*, February 1944, pp. 233–8.]

Shaw and Dramatic Style

It is the fate of the Whig in drama to be converted by time into the semblance of a Tory, and that is what has befallen Shaw, at least in the case of such of his plays as *Man and Superman*. Originally regarded as something quite philosophically saucy, despite its obvious ideational derivation from Schopenhauer, Nietzsche and Co., it presently with the passing of the years seems to be as respectably tame and conservative as an elderly ex-playboy who, though fond of recalling himself as a hell-raiser, has married and wryly settled down. Its wit, once shocking to the easily shockable, suggests now a frock coat at a wienie roast, and its theme of the pursuit of the male by the female, once viewed as boldly venturesome, seems as audacious as the Prince's wooing of Cinderella.

It is an old story, of course, that what has appeared dramatically insurgent to one generation frequently takes on the sound of whimsical popgunnery to a later one. Ibsen, who slammed a door to open it and who startled a dramatic world sitting prettily on the gift chairs of Pinero and his contemporary interior decorators, in due course thus came to be looked upon as a sedate, if less parochial, village schoolmaster. Wilde's epigrammatic derisions, regarded as exceptionally impertinent and unblushing, became the favorite quotations of precocious bobby-soxers. Sartre in a very much briefer space of time has already this soon found his Existentialism spelled without the first s. And so, in the instance of his plays like this one, with Shaw.

The great man's whip-cracking disquisition on the Life Force, socialism, free love, and the like, which in earlier days earned him a reputation for intellectual courage and impudence neck-and-neck with that of Brieux for his own against social disease, race suicide, and the defects in the system of criminal justice, present today, as do the latter's, the appearance of lame platitudes attempting a jig. Such of his nip-ups as "That's the devilish side of a woman's fascination: she makes you will your own destruction" and "It is the self-sacrificing women that sacrifice others most recklessly," once esteemed as themselves pretty devilish, are belatedly recognized, with a pang, as having been that long ago already belated paraphrases of Rochefoucault et Cie. Lines like "No man is a match for a woman, except with a poker and a pair of hobnailed boots; not always even then," of old thought very nifty, and others like "Marriage is to me apostasy, profanation of the sanctuary of my soul, etc.," earlier considered the height of iconoclasm, have acquired the ring of penny cynicism on the one hand and of Greenwich Village on the other. And all such cartwheels, originally generative of oh's and ah's, as "We live in an atmosphere of shame; we are ashamed of everything that is real about us, ashamed of ourselves, of our relatives, of our incomes, of our accents, of our opinions, of our experience, just as we are ashamed of our naked skins"—all such, and they fill the play, seem as dated as the bravado of Frank Wedekind or the moral philosophy of Henry Arthur Jones. It is, in sum, not what Shaw says that gives his play what remaining measure of interest it may have; it is how he says it. For his uncommon drive and force in the art of pure writing are still amply evident, and it is this quality that, like the propulsive reserve of wheels no longer driven by fuel, keeps the play in some motion. Platitude is momentarily refreshed by a swig of alcoholic ink, and staleness inspirited with a squirt of belletristic turpentine.

Listening to the admirable phrasing of the Shavian line, whatever its content, we are haplessly reminded how seriously the ability of most of our more conspicuous contemporary American playwrights is disabled by the infirmity of their literary style. With slight exception, any trace of distinction is lacking in even the case of the relatively better plays, and the result is a drama that, however commendable it may be in other directions, has about it an air either of spurious cultivation or of downright commonness. It isn't that the playwrights do not strive for style. The striving is often only too clammily obvious. It is that by and large they seem to be either incompetent to achieve it or mistake for it a prose which suggests rented white tie and tails or a poetic expression which weds a Tin Pan Alley lyricism with a hamburgered verse form. As examples of the one and the other we may take such figures as S. N. Behrman and Maxwell Anderson. Some years ago, Behrman's writing seemed to be on the point of developing a style both graceful and witty, and in one or two instances was even successful in realizing it. But presently what had borne tokens of some authenticity tended more and more toward the manufactured botanical variety and soon produced any number of such fancy little blossoms (I quote from *Dunnigan's Daughter*) as "I was thinking—a multitude of thoughts—little winds of thoughts, springing up and dying down," and "A slim golden column; you could be a caryatid holding up the roof of some exquisite Greek temple." Let alone such exalted titbits as "I sense in you tonight a singular mixture of allure and threat"; "The constant hazard rather piques me"; and "A heart-murmur, he said. I was enchanted with the phrase. A murmur. Sounds like a berceuse. Should be set to music, don't you think? By whom? Debussy, if he were alive . . ."

Worse still, what earlier was simple, fluid and unaffected becomes transmuted into such jerks and rattles as "The function of the platitude. Very useful. As useful as the coins in a shop. No matter how worn, they serve. If not for platitudes, we should have to bare our hearts. Would one care, in general conversation, for all that nudity?" Or into such starched phraseology as "Surely, Ferne—you are intelligent—surely you don't believe in this universal love-myth hypocritically promulgated by the vested religions." Or into bubble-gum like "The serpent in the garden of Eden—he is coiled around us. We have to throw him off, some way. Evil is mobilized. Goodness not. Goodness is like you, mixed up, not resolute. Yesterday, Ferne, I saw a chance to play God; everybody likes to play God a little bit; but that is dangerous. The other God has seized me. The blind God . . ."

Anderson's gestures toward lyric expression, as has come to be appreciated, have frequently led him into a style not less phony. Though now and again he may capture a pretty phrase, a telling line, the bulk of his later writing amounts to little more than a cotton fancy draped in imitation tulle. In illustration:

> "Nothing but just to be a bird, and fly,
> and then come down. Always the thing itself
> is less than when the seed of it in thought
> came to a flower within, but such a flower
> as never grows in gardens."

In even more touching further illustration:

"You should have asked the fish what would come of him
before the earth shrank and the land thrust up
between the oceans. You should have asked the fish
or asked me, or asked yourself, for at that time
we were the fish, you and I, or they were we—

and we, or they, would have known as much about it
as I know now—yet it somehow seems worth while
that the fish were not discouraged, and did keep on—
at least as far as we are."

Compare the pseudo-polished comedy style of a Behrman
with, for example, the simple, finished product of an English
comedy writer like Maugham. A speech or two from *The Circle* will do. "For some years," remarks Champion-Cheney, "I
was notoriously the prey of a secret sorrow. But I found so
many charming creatures who were anxious to console, that in
the end it grew rather fatiguing. Out of regard to my health I
ceased to frequent the drawing rooms of Mayfair." Or the same
character's "It's a matter of taste. I love old wine, old friends,
and old books, but I like young women. On their twenty-five
birthday I give them a diamond ring and tell them they must
no longer waste their youth and beauty on an old fogy like me.
We have a most affecting scene, my technique on these occasions is perfect, and then I start all over again." Or, finally,
Teddie's all too familiar, "But I wasn't offering you happiness.
I don't think my sort of love tends to happiness. I'm jealous.
I'm not a very easy man to get on with. I'm often out of temper and irritable. I should be fed to the teeth with you sometimes, and so would you be with me. I daresay we'd fight like
cat and dog, and sometimes we'd hate each other. Often you'd
be wretched and bored stiff and lonely, and often you'd be
frightfully homesick, and then you'd regret all you'd lost. Stupid women would be rude to you because we'd run away together. And some of them would cut you. I don't offer you
peace and quietness. I offer you unrest and anxiety. I don't offer you happiness. I offer you love."

Or contrast the synthetic poetic expression of an Anderson
with the true singing line of an Irish playwright like O'Casey.
"Ashamed I am," proclaims O'Killigain in *Purple Dust,* "of the
force that sent a hand to hit a girl of grace, fit to find herself
walkin' beside all the beauty that ever shone before the eyes o'
man since Helen herself unbound her tresses to dance her wild
an' willin' way through the streets o' Troy." Or, to choose from
half a hundred speeches at random, Avril's reply: "It's I that

know the truth is only in the shine o' the words you shower on me, as ready to you as the wild flowers a love-shaken, innocent girl would pick in a hurry outa the hedges, an' she on her way to Mass."

In the case of playwrights who elect to abjure the chichi rhetoric of a Behrman or the rhythmic calisthenics of an Anderson, any chance for style goes aground on their peculiar theory regarding the spoken word. It is apparently their conviction that the latter can under no circumstances bear any resemblance to the written or so-called literary word, and that, as a corollary, it can have verisimilitude only if it lacks grace. The consequence is dialogue which often not only bears small relation to human speech above the grade of that employed by the lower order of morons but which is ugly and painful to the critical ear.

The notion that the spoken word is dramatic only if it departs sharply from what may be called the literary word is responsible for night after night of such sore lingo as the following:

a. "Don't fling that at me, Mr. Caldwell—you'll get nowhere with that. That's my wife's attack. 'I didn't take a lover. You took a mistress.' Well, I don't consider that a virtue, see? But to hell with that now. Get this through your heads—all of you. It's not just because my wife's going to live in California that I'm fighting for Christopher—I wouldn't care if she was going to live on the next block. I want my son with me —all the time. I want him to live with me—to be part of my life. I want him." (*Christopher Blake*, Moss Hart.)

b. "I know! I know! Why bother to step outside and look at life, when it's so cozy indoors and there's always a shelfful of books handy? For God's sake, hasn't anything ever happened to you? Have you never been drunk? Or socked a guy for making a pass at you? Or lost your panties on Fifth Avenue?" (*Dream Girl*, Elmer Rice.)

c. "I once set up a travel booklet about them. I was a linotyper after I had to quit college. You learn a lot of crap setting up type. I learned about the balmy blue Pacific. Come to the Heavenly Isles! An orchid on every bazoom—and two bazooms on every babe. I'd like to find the gent who wrote that booklet. I'd like to find him now and make him come to his goddam Heavenly Isles!" (*Home of the Brave*, Arthur Laurents.)

The apology that such language is perfectly in key with the characters who merchant it does not entirely hold water. It may approximate the characters' speech to a degree, but only to a degree. It amounts merely to a fabricated approach to the exact speech. Among other things, it misses a fully accurate ear and is simply a paraphrase, and a poor one, of factual speech in terms of stage speech. It is, in short, no truer and infinitely less effective than so-called literary speech. Compare in this connection, whether for verisimilitude or dramatic effect—it need not, obviously, be added for beauty—such otomyces with dialogue like Carroll's for his Canon Skerritt:

"And since when has the Sacred Heart of our Redeemer, that kings and emperors and queens like Violante and Don John of Austria and the great Charles V and the soldier Ignatius walked barefooted for the love of—since when has it become a sort of snap door chamber where dolts and boobs come to —to kick ball and find themselves tripped up on an altar step instead of a goal post?"

Or like Shaw's for his Candida:

"Ask James' mother and his three sisters what it cost to save James the trouble of doing anything but be strong and clever and happy. Ask me what it costs to be James' mother and three sisters and wife and mother to his children all in one. Ask Prossy and Maria how troublesome the house is even when we have no visitors to help us slice the onions. Ask the tradesmen who want to worry James and spoil his beautiful sermon who it is that puts them off. When there is money to give, he gives it; when there is money to refuse, I refuse it. I build a castle of comfort and indulgence and love for him, and stand sentinel always to keep little vulgar cares out. I make him master here, though he does not know it, and could not tell you a moment ago how he came to be so . . ."

Or like Synge's for his Conchubor:

"There's one sorrow has no end surely—that's being old and lonesome. But you and I will have a little peace in Emain, with harps playing, and old men telling stories at the fall of night. I've let build rooms for our two selves, Deirdre, withered gold upon the walls and ceilings that are set with bronze. There was never a queen in the east had a house the like of your house, that's waiting for yourself in Emain."

Dramatic art in America for the greater part has become simply a playwriting business, and its practitioners are largely racketeers with a dramatic sales talk, devoid of anything remotely resembling literary taste, literary ability, and literary education. Most of them read and act like pulp writers crossed with telegraph key-men. Their style, so to speak, follows set tracks and is readily recognizable. It consists in the wholesale use of dashes, as in such dialogue as "Oh, God—if they don't come back—if they don't—come—back—." It hopes to conceal the obviousness of its content in such apologies as "What I've said—I know it's old hat and that you've heard it many times before—," etc. It relies upon crew-cut dialogue with its monosyllabic replies as a substitute for both suspense and humor, as, for example:

"Answer yes or no. You live downstairs, I take it?
"No.
"Oh, you don't live downstairs?
"Yes.
"Say, what the hell? Do you or don't you?
"Yes.
"Yes, what?"
"Yes, no.
"Wait, Sergeant. I think I understand her. You mean, yes, you do not live downstairs?
"Yes."

It further cuckoos its own style endlessly: "Everyone's a murderer at heart. The person who has never felt a passionate hankering to kill someone is without emotion, and do you think it's law or religion that stays the average person from

homicide? No—it's lack of courage—the fear of being caught, or
cursed with remorse. Our murderer is merely a rational animal
with the courage of his convictions." Profanity and obscenity
are regularly resorted to for a strength of expression that oth-
wise seems to be beyond the playwrights' competences, and
"Jesus!," "Christ!," "God damned," "bastard," and "son-of-a-
bitch" are scattered through dialogue like toadstools. "Yeah?"
is the mark of vulgar character; "Indeed?" of polite. "Wonderful" is the adjective common to most emotions, whether love
or a relish of kidney stew. And the habitual "I mean—" is the
refuge less of character than of playwright inarticulateness.

Passion is writ by rote: "But I need you. You know that! And
you need me. It's too late. We are helpless now—in the clutch
of forces more potent than our little selves—forces that brought
us into the world—forces that have made the world! Whether
you will it or not, this binding power is sweeping you and me
together. And you must yield!" The Pulitzer prize is given for
authentic Yankee speech to playwrights who confect such
lines as "Let a man get miserable and he is miserable; a woman
ain't really happy no other way," and as "It 'us then that the
scales dropped from my eyes! An' I seen the truth! An' when I
did, everything in the whole world 'us changed fer me! I loved
everybody an' everything! An' I 'us so happy I felt jist like I 'us
afloatin' away on a ocean o' joy!"

The "punch" style, miscellaneously indulged in, also has its
pattern: "The whole damn government's a gang of liver flukes
sucking the blood out of the body politic—and there you sit, an
honest liver fluke, arranging the graft for everybody else and
refusing to do any blood sucking on your own account! God, it
makes me sick!" Cousin to the punch style is the heroic-romantic style: "The important man, George, is the man who knows
how to live! I love Hocky, I think an awful lot of him. But, he's
like my father. They have no outside interests at all. They're
flat—they're colorless. They're not men—they're caricatures! Oh,
don't become like them, George! Don't be an important man
and crack up at forty-five. I want our lives together to be full
and rich and beautiful! I want it so much!" And cousin to the
heroic-romantic is also the heroic-scientific: "There is not a
man in medicine who has not said what you have said and

meant it for a minute—all of us, Dr. Nussbaum. And you are right, my friend. We are groping. We are guessing. But, at least our guesses today are closer to the truth than they were twenty years ago. And twenty years from now they will be still closer. That is what we are here for. Ah, there is so much to be done and so little time in which to do it that one life is never long enough . . . It's not easy for any of us. But in the end our reward is something richer than simply living . . . (*Sighs*) Come, Dr. Nussbaum, a little game of chess, maybe, or (*winks*) a glass of schnaps?"

The melodramatic style generally fits into a mold something like "For the love of God, listen to me! While you sit here quietly eating and drinking, tonight, enemy planes dropped seventy thousand kilos of bombs on Paris. God knows how many they killed! God knows how much of life and beauty is forever destroyed! And you sit here drinking and laughing! Are you worms? Are you lice? Get out of your soft chairs and off your soft tails and do something, *do* something! If you don't, you bastards, as God is my judge I'll bust the jaw of every God damned one of you!" And the "cultured" style, when not in self-protection crossed with a touch of banter, one something like this: "There is in your psychological composition, my dear, a touch of the chiaroscuro of Rembrandt, of the livid gauntness of El Greco, of the stark realism of Goya, of the springtime freshness of Botticelli. You are, my dear, in other words, an orchestration of that occasional color monotone in Brahms and that flowery ornamentation in Rossini."

The style is not only the man; the style is the play. And the style is *Man and Superman*. Give your ear, for example, to this: "Oh, they know it in their hearts, though they think themselves bound to blame you by their silly superstitions about morality and propriety and so forth. But I know, and the whole world really knows, though it does not say so, that you were right to follow your instinct; that vitality and bravery are the greatest qualities a woman can have, and motherhood her solemn initiation into womanhood; and that the fact of your not being legally married matters not one scrap either to your own worth or to our real regard for you."

Or to this: "I solemnly say that I am not a happy man. Ann

looks happy; but she is only triumphant, successful, victorious. That is not happiness, but the price for which the strong sell their happiness. What we have both done this afternoon is to renounce happiness, renounce freedom, renounce tranquillity, above all, renounce the romantic possibilities of an unknown future, for the cares of a household and a family. I beg that no man may seize the occasion to get half drunk and utter imbecile speeches and coarse pleasantries at my expense."

[From *The Theatre Book of the Year, 1947–1948*, pp. 84–94.]

Shaw and Sex

OBSERVES H. G. Wells in *The Way the World is Going:* "He [George Bernard Shaw] has made free use of the phrase, the Life Force, but what meaning he attaches to these magic words is unknown. . . . He has an aversion from sex . . . which may be either Butler or temperamental, and he seems to want mankind to try laying parthenogenetic eggs, and coming out of them full whiskered."

The notion thus somewhat facetiously expressed by the acute Wells restimulates a similar notion that for some time has been impertinently agitating my encephalon. That Shaw, as Wells says, appears not only to have an aversion to sex but also what amounts almost to a fear of it has not been lost upon those who have carefully pondered his writings. The reason for the peculiar aversion and for what seems to be even fear is difficult to make out, but the antipathy and distrust nevertheless remain clearly visible and often emphatic. Shaw's canon plainly betrays his dislike of sex and his evasion of it. In all his work from beginning to end I know of no instance where he has not deftly avoided self-commitment on the subject or has not indulged in equivoque of one sort or another in his treatment of it.

It is impossible, within the limits of the present chapter, to go fully into Shaw's writings and draw from them a comprehensive catalogue of illustrations. But one may suggest the color of his intrinsic and general attitude by skimming through them and extracting a few sufficiently pointed and revelatory examples. That, when he laid hold of the incalescent Cleopatra, he chose to contemplate her at the age of sixteen and, in spite of the fact that sixteen was maturity in that gala era, insisted upon comfortably regarding her as a species of pre-Mary Pickford flapper, that he presented the Caesar who had a baby by her as an historical Crocker Harrington, and that he once achieved the remarkable feat of writing sexlessly about the madam of a bordello, are phenomena familiar to everyone. That, also, in the series of interviews gathered by Archibald Henderson into *Table Talk of G. B. S.*, he orally betrayed an indifference, even antipathy, to sex is as readily recalled. I quote a few passages: (*a*) "It is admitted that alleged rejuvenations (*vide* Steinach) do not prolong life. And it is longevity which interests me and not the ghastly prospect of seeing all the moribund people bustling about and pretending to be gay young dogs"; (*b*) "There is never any real sex in romance. What is more, there is very little, and that of a very crude kind, in ninety-nine hundredths of our married life"; (*c*) "One man's poetry is another man's pruriency"; (*d*) "The novel which says no more about sex than may be said in a lecture on the facts to a class of schoolgirls of fifteen can be enormously more entertaining than a novel wholly preoccupied with sexual symptoms"; (*e*) "I could not write the words Mr. Joyce uses: my prudish hand would refuse to form the letters"; and (*f*) "Is any treatment of sex in the interest of public morals?" And where the interviewer shot embarrassingly direct questions on sex to the interviewed, the latter is remembered as having cleverly avoided direct answers in such circumlocutions as "A playwright has no patience with novels," or in disquisitions on economics, capitalism and what not.

Let us glance haphazardly through Shaw's work. Having presented us with a virginal Cleopatra and a Caesar whose amatory exercises are confined to lifting her upon his knee and playing horsie, he presents us with the inflammable Great Catherine as one of the Four Marx Brothers, and not Harpo either. He gives us a Pygmalion who will have none of his perfected Galatea and who, to use Shaw's own words, excuses his indifference to young women on the ground that they have an irresistible rival in his mother. "If an imaginative boy has a

. . . mother who has intelligence, personal grace, dignity of character without harshness, and a cultivated sense of the best art, . . . she sets a standard for him against which very few women can struggle, besides effecting for him a disengagement of his affections, his sense of beauty and his idealism from his specifically sexual impulses. This makes him a standing puzzle to the huge number of uncultivated people . . . to whom literature, painting, sculpture, music and affectionate personal relations come as modes of sex if they come at all." He gives us even a Don Juan who moralistically announces, "I tell you that as long as I can conceive something better than myself, I cannot be easy unless I am striving to bring it into existence or clearing the way for it. That is the law of my life!" His Larry, in *John Bull's Other Island*, prefers his friend Tom to the woman who implores his love. "I wish I could find a country to live in where the facts were not brutal and the dreams not unreal," is the character's oblique anatomical lament. His Dick Dudgeon, in *The Devil's Disciple*, pronounces the word *love*, "with true Puritan scorn." His Lady Britomart, in *Major Barbara*, "really cannot bear an immoral man." And his Eugene, in *Candida*, romanticizes his emotions out of sex.

"Moral passion is the only real passion," announces Tanner, in *Man and Superman*. "All the other passions were in me before; but they were idle and aimless—mere childish greediness and cruelties, curiosities and fancies, habits and superstitions, grotesque and ridiculous to the mature intelligence. When they suddenly began to shine like newly lit flames it was by no light of their own, but by the radiance of the dawning moral passion. That passion dignified them, gave them conscience and meaning, found them a mob of appetites and organized them into an army of purposes and principles." "Virtue," Shaw notes in *The Revolutionist's Handbook*, "consists not in abstaining from vice but in not desiring it." Charteris, in *The Philanderer*, accused of philandering, states that he is not guilty of any such low thing. "I hate it; it bores me to distraction!" Praed observes to Crofts of Mrs. Warren, apropos of a hint of sexual intimacy, "Your delicacy will tell you that a handsome woman needs some friends who are not—well, not on that footing with her." And Mrs. Warren repentantly thus: "Do you think I was brought up like you—able to pick and choose my own way of life? Do you think I did what I did because I liked it, or *thought it right*, or *wouldn't rather have gone to college* and been a lady if I'd had the chance?"

Speaking of the marriage contract in one of his prefaces, Shaw alludes to sex stimulation as "the most violent, most insane, most delusive and most transient of passion," expresses his disbelief that married people as a rule really live together, and says that "a man as intimate with his own wife as a magistrate is with his clerk . . . is a man in ten thousand." In response to the General's timid "But there are calls of nature—," in *Getting Married*, Shaw makes Lesbia reply, "Don't be ridiculous." And when the General is so much as allowed to venture on another occasion the word *assignation*, the Shavian get-out is accomplished thus: "Oh yes: she began the correspondence by making a very curious but very natural assignation. She wants me to meet her in Heaven"—the while Mrs. Bridgenorth comments on the "everyday vulgarities of earthly love." "I sinned in intention," says Juno in *Overruled*. "I'm as guilty as if I had actually sinned." Lina, in *Misalliance*, takes out her surplus energy on a flying trapeze and recommends the same diet to her adoring Tarleton. And in *Arms and the Man*, we find the Shavian protagonist not too proud for sexual dalliance, but too tired.

The point is not that Shaw's imaginative writing is sexless— that is a fact too well known to call for repetition; the point is that the body of his work as a whole reveals a man to whom sex, in the sense that the word is commonly used, is at once unpleasant, deplorable and disgusting. There are times, true enough, when he seems to advance the opposite point of view, but it will be found that, when he does so, he does so only subsequently to refute and demolish it. Nor is his argument of the other point of view even momentarily persuasive; it hasn't the ring of sincerity; it is a dummy set up merely for tackling purposes. Among conspicuous modern English men of letters and English critics of life, he alone is indefatigable in waving the white banner of biological asceticism. One of the cleverest dialecticians of our time, he is sometimes successful in concealing his true attitude for a moment, in masking his ferocious personal convictions and in giving a bland performance in the rôle of a hell of a fellow, but it fools no one. Chesterton once observed that it is the weak man who always, when taking a walk, most vigorously thwacks the bushes along the roadside with his cane. A mistrust of his own philosophical attitude toward sex may similarly account for Shaw's disputatious thwacking of it.

After reading *Cashel Byron's Profession,* Stevenson wrote to William Archer: "If Mr. Shaw is below five-and-twenty, let him go his path; if he is thirty, he had best be told that he is a romantic, and pursue romance with his eyes open. Perhaps he knows it." Shaw is still the romantic that he was when a boy. And his romanticism is no more clearly to be detected than in his animadversions on sex. He declines to see it for what it is; he cannot bring himself to regard it save in terms of sentiment, love, the Indian policy, Marxian socialism or the League of Nations. And all the fine irony and rich humor which he occasonally has visited upon the subject cannot conceal the romanticist hiding behind them and seeking to protect himself through them from the charge of romanticism. Shaw has always set up smoke-screens or avoidances of the issue to protect himself from himself. The hero of his early novel, *The Irrational Knot,* in answer to the query as to what he is going to do about his wife's elopement with a former lover, says, "Eat my supper. I am as hungry as a bear." His charming Szczymplica, in *Love Among the Artists,* is in her potentially most romantic moments restrained by the "soul commercial" that Shaw, with a cannily masked apprehensiveness, injects into her. Lydia Carew, whose "body is frail and brain morbidly active," is made to think coldly of the splendid Cashel Byron in terms of eugenical science. In *An Unsocial Socialist,* Shaw smears his inborn convictions with grease-paint and tries to make us believe that he believes the seven deadly sins, as Prof. Henderson notes them, are respectability, conventional virtue, filial affection, modesty, sentiment, devotion to women, and romance.

We have Shaw speaking of the wickedness and abandoned-ness of Offenbach's music and of the morals of Händel's. We find him waxing impatient with "the female figure free from the defect known to photographers as under-exposure" that he encounters on the statues and fountains in Paris. He writes, "What Hofmannsthal and Strauss have done is to take Clytemnestra and Aegistheus and by identifying them with everything that is evil . . . with the murderous rage in which the lust for a lifetime of orgiastic pleasure turns on its slaves in the torture of its disappointment and the sleepless horror and misery of its neurasthenia, to so rouse in us an overwhelming flood of wrath against it . . . that Elektra's vengeance becomes holy to us . . ." "In our sexual natures," he states in the preface to *Androcles and the Lion*, "we are torn by an irresistible attraction and an overwhelming repugnance and disgust." Again, "Marriage turns vagabonds into steady citizens; men and women will . . . practice virtues that unattached individuals are incapable of." In the preface to *Overruled*, thus: "That jealousy is independent of sex is shown by its intensity in children." Again, "Adultery is the dullest of themes on the stage, and from Francesca and Paolo down to the latest guilty couple . . . the romantic adulterers have been bores." Yet again, "It is ridiculous to say . . . that art has nothing to do with morality."

"If a young woman, in a mood of strong reaction . . . were to tell Mr. Herbert Spencer that she was determined not to murder her own instincts and throw away her life in obedience to a mouthful of empty phrases," he once said, "I suspect he would recommend the *Data of Ethics* to her as a trustworthy and conclusive guide to conduct. Under similar circumstances I should unhesitatingly say to the young woman: 'By all means do as you propose. Try how wicked you can be. . . . At worst, you will only find out the sort of person you really are. At best, you will find that your passions, if you really and honestly let them all loose impartially, will discipline you with a severity your conventional friends . . . could not stand for a day.'" In the preface to *Getting Married*, we come upon this: "The assumption that the specific relation which marriage authorizes between the parties is the most intimate and personal of human relations . . . is violently untrue." In "The Apple Cart," we engage the anatomically paradoxical spectacle of a King's platonic mistress. And, by way of a climax, we have a Garden of Eden in *Back to Methuselah* in which, when Shaw's Eve learns the secret of sex, "an expression of overwhelming repugnance" crosses her features and she "buries her face in her hands"!

[From *Testament of a Critic*, 1929, pp. 169–78.]

ON MUSICAL COMEDIES

BACK in the days when the world was younger and more salubrious and when Delmonico's at Fifth Avenue and Forty-fourth Street had not yet prosaically been supplanted by a railroad agency, Victor Herbert and I sat one gentle Spring evening over the wine and discoursed not only on it but on its two well-known and equally warming appendixes. A large and confiding soul, he brought himself finally to the third item in the evening's bill of particulars.

"When it comes to song," said the old boy, "success begins with a hum. A song that can be sung by people right after they have heard it for the first time is often doomed to failure. But if it eludes them for the time being and they can only vaguely hum it, one may be fairly sure that it is on the road to popularity. I should therefore rather compose one such hummer than any six songs that are more quickly and fully capturable."

It is the difference between the tunes of a talented musician and of a tin piano artificer that, while those of the former are frequently somewhat difficult of nabbing, those of the latter present no such problem. Politely refraining from naming names in the second catalogue, the tunes written by the parties for the Broadway shows are mostly of such an obviously derivative or elementary order that one can yodel them in their entirety after a first hearing, sometimes, indeed, after hearing only the first measure or two. Anyone gifted in even a one-finger playing of the piano may, given their opening bars, go on and play any number of them pretty accurately. But the songs of men like Herbert have a freshness, a compositional ingenuity, and an harmonic sleight that take a while to capture and, when captured, linger affectionately not only on the lips but in the memory.

It has been complained of Herbert that there is sometimes a slight excess of syrup in his songs. The criticism is partly true.

But it is true in such part mainly in the case of his love songs and is therefore not to be considered too nefarious. Love, I am informed by those of experience in the matter, induces in its victims a mood of a piece with uncrystallizable fluid separated from crystallized sugar in the refining process, and it is thus appropriate that songs of love recognize the fact. It is the worst kind of critical cynicism which forbids such purely romantic melodies as the "moonbeams and starbeams and stories" of Swinburne and that would have in their stead the sour flavors of something like "Sioux City Sue." Herbert was an Irishman trained and educated in Germany and when you have an Irishman trained and educated in Germany you are not likely to get from him love songs anything like "The Girl with the Three Blue Eyes." What you may expect is rather a good sentimental mixture of Cathleen ni Houlihan and Lorelei, and that is what you get from Victor. His songs are Rhine wine with sprigs of shamrock: mellow, melting, unashamed to weep a little, and with the shamrock handsomely bestowed upon the barmaid's coiffure.

.   .   .   .

Reviewing the musical comedies at the Gaiety all of thirty-seven years ago, the matchless Mr. Beerbohm had this to say:

"One reason why the place is irresistible is that nowhere else do we feel that we are so far away, and so harmlessly and elegantly far away, from the realities of life. We are translated into a sphere where the dwellers have nothing whatever to think about, and would be incapable of thought if there were need for it. All the people (except the ladies of the chorus, whose languor is part of the fun) are in the highest spirits, with no chance of a reaction. . . . Every one wants every one else to have a good time, and tries to make everything easy and simple all around. This good time, as I need hardly say, is of a wholly sexual order. And yet every one, from the highest to the lowest, is thoroughly 'good.' The most attractive of the men do no harm to the ladies who love them at first sight. Not less instantaneous than theirs are the conquests made by the most unattractive men. A homuncule, made up to look as ab-

surd as possible, has only to come by and wink at the bevy of
lovely ladies to whom he is a perfect stranger, when behold;
their arms are about his neck, their eyes devour him, they lan-
guish and coo over him. . . ."

The master's words are as apt now as they were when he
wrote them. And in them—which is the apology for quoting
them at length—is to be found the best answer to those present
critics who are forever deploring the books of musical comedies and urging upon them a greater measure of sense and
wisdom. If anything would ruin musical comedy it would be
such sensible books. Only a donkey would seek and demand intelligence on such occasions. Sense and intelligence are desiderata of drama. Musical comedy is best when it abjures them
and substitutes for them absurd fancy and all the wonderful
illogic of a wonderful world that never was. The best show of
the kind, in brief, is that one in which the people, like Topsy,
were not born but just grew, and whose growth, furthermore,
is stunted by mindlessness, giddiness, and irresponsibility.

That no one thinks in musical comedy and would be incapable of thought if there were need for it, as Beerbohm observed, is its prime asset. There can be no romance where
even one party to it brings his brain cells into action, and the
best musical comedy authors wisely appreciate the fact. Romance is a tacit agreement by both parties not for a moment
to analyze and think away their feelings. Even a touch of wit
is perilous. If you will forgive me for quoting from myself—"I
like to quote from myself," says Bernard Shaw; "it adds spice to
the conversation"—I repeat a few lines from a little book published some thirty years ago:

"It was moonlight in the courtyard where languished among
the flowers a lover and his mistress. The lover, presently, and
for the first time since he had known his fair lady, felt Wit flying close to his lips. The little god of Love who had dwelt with
the lovers in the courtyard since first they had come there,
sensing the flutter of the intruder's wings, took to his heels and
slid between the bars of the great bronze gate into a neighboring garden."

The critical insistence upon books that lean to some intelligence and realism has done much to debilitate musical comedy. Posturing a hostility to sentiment, the young critics currently in extensive practise have sought through manly sneers to exorcise it from the medium and to replace it with elements generally described as hard-boiled. One of their latest complaints is against even one of the best of all American musical comedies, *Show Boat*. It seems, as I observed at the time, that the love story of the wistful Magnolia and the handsome Ravenal is too full of the moonlight of the heart for them. What, I inquired, do they desire in shows whose very essence is necessarily sentimental romance: the story of a garbage collector and a female chiropodist? Such critics do not want musical comedy, but bastard drama embroidered with tunes. They do not want a beautiful stage world aglow with starlight and impossible dreams but one that theatrically resembles the yak, with the head of an ox, the tail of a horse, and the squeal of a pig. They want, in short, not a holiday from prosaicism but a return to it.

There is, of course, no accounting for tastes, as the man licking his chops over a frankfurter cynically observed of one eating a *châteaubriand papillote*. But, speaking for myself, when I go to a musical comedy I go in the hope of seeing something that will remove me from the gray world about me and not remind me of it with the spectacle of a black marketeer kicking a prostitute in the promontory the while her frowzy mother stands at the footlights and howls a song called "My Daughter Maybe Ain't No Lady, but, Oh Boy, She Brings Home the Dough." Somehow, eccentric as I am, I seem to prefer things like *The Merry Widow*, or *The Arcadians*, or *Music in the Air*.

It is not that I am sentimental. Very far from it. But I nevertheless will give you all the songs like "You Can't Get a Man with a Gun," in *Annie Get Your Gun*, with its allusions to the male behind, for one like "Egern on the Tegernsee" from the above mentioned *Music in the Air*, and all those like "Nuts," with their back-fence lyrics, in all the *Duchesses Misbehave* for even half a one like *Show Boat*'s "Make Believe" or *Gypsy Lady*'s "Springtide." Not that I don't relish lyric comedy; I am a mark for it, provided only it has the consideration to amuse me. But somehow I don't seem to find much amusement in vulgarity for vulgarity's sake. Nor is it, to continue the confidential autobiography, that I shrink, like a dollar shirt, from vulgarity. Honest vulgarity is also all right with me, but it has to be honest and not forcedly hot-house grown for huckster purposes. The simple vulgarity of some such song as "Dar's No Coon Warm Enough for Me" or "Shake That Thing" is down my alley. But the manufactured sort in such musical comedy numbers as "Katie Did in Madrid" and the like leaves me cold.

The best musical comedies and even comic operas and operettas, to return to our theme, are those in which sense is reduced to a minimum, the worst those which aim at some rationality. It is significant that, when *Arms and the Man* was converted into *The Chocolate Soldier,* the elimination of most of Shaw's most pointed observations and speeches helped it enormously. Imagine, if you can, a series of musical exhibits similarly derived from Shaw's plays in which the Shavian mind was permitted to exercise itself free from interference. Not even half a dozen Oscar Strauses operating on each simultaneously could triumph over them, save possibly in the case of music lovers with the virtuosity to fix their attention so completely on the music that they would not hear the words.

The charm of *Die Fledermaus,* aside from the Johann Strauss music, lies in the complete nonsensicality of its story, which invites the auditor to such a suspension of common sense that he sees nothing unusual in what is perhaps the most supremely idiotic ball scene plot ever shown on the stage. The delight of some such musical comedy as the current *Carousel,* apart from Rodgers' tunes, lies equally in a hero and heroine so devoid of the rudiments of intelligence and in subsidiary characters so ignorant that nothing interferes in the least with their persuasive communication of otherwise unbelievable emotions. The device of daftly transplanting Molnár's original characters from Hungary to Cape Cod, Massachusetts, further helps matters considerably. Since you thus do not believe anything to start with, whatever happens becomes paradoxically the more acceptable. If even one of the characters stopped sighing over love or revelling in clambakes for so long as a minute and offered evidence of a mentality developed to the point where he or she didn't believe that every one of June's thirty days had been gloriously sunny since the world began—if even one did any such thing, the show would miss a lot of its present pleasure and would probably make eight thousand dollars a week less, or maybe ten.

Topical and satirical musical shows like the meritorious *Of Thee I Sing* beside the argument, it accordingly holds that the most a good musical comedy may permissibly do is to hint occasionally at sense and then sensibly forget it. The bad one is most often found to be that one which tells or tries to tell its story with a reasonable approach to life and actuality. Life and actuality, unfortunately, are not veined with music, and music can only make their stage approximation that much more ridiculous.

The trouble, in short, is not, as the critics maintain, so much that musical comedy books are silly but rather that too frequently they are not silly enough. What we need in musical comedy is less the contemporary attempt to present us with fairly recognizable and slightly foolish characters than the wholly unrecognizable and completely foolish ones as in the gala old musical comedies and operettas, the sort that Beerbohm wrote about and that his father before him would doubtless also have written about if he had enjoyed his son's profession. What we need and crave are shows as handsomely preposterous as *Wang* and *Panjandrum* and the kind that George Edwardes used to put on at Max's Gaiety, not the current solemn species in which a man and woman who violently love each other decline to go to bed together and keep the audience out of it for three-quarters of an hour longer than is either desirable or necessary. What we want, despite the academic critics, is a return of the old-time enchanting absurdity, the old-time refusal to reflect life and reality in any degree, the old-time razzle and dazzle of the unreal and the incredible.

Close your eyes and think back and have yourself a time. Think back to the happy, innocent musical comedy days of *The Isle of Champagne* where all was Pol Roger instead of water and where Tom Seabrooke found half a dozen beautiful girls under every palm tree, all of them crazy about him. Or of *El Capitan* with Sousa's brass band in tons of gold braid gladdening the lovers' honeymoon no end by descending upon their love nest and booming out military marches before breakfast. Or *The Monks of Malabar* with Francis Wilson doomed to be executed at the stroke of twelve for the heinous crime of pinching the cheek of Hallen Mostyn's girl, Madge Lessing itchily waiting for the clock to strike, slowly counting off the strikes, and relieved to hear that they amounted to thirteen. Or *The Belle of New York* with the poor little Salvation Army lassie becoming overnight the social arbiter of the then tony and very exclusive Narragansett. Or *The Sunshine Girl* at Max's beloved Gaiety in which the parting of the lovers at the end of the second act was brought about by the horrible discovery by the hero that the beautiful heroine's millionaire father had odiously made his money out of soap.

And in the comic operas and operettas, permit yourself a wistful sigh over the nepenthe of a *The Queen's Lace Handkerchief* with the poet Cervantes becoming a brigand dressed as a waiter and persuading the King of Portugal, while serving His Highness an empty ale mug and while His Highness gurgled his satisfaction over the nonexistent beverage, that the Queen was innocent of any lascivious intentions toward him and loved the royal pot-hoister despite appearances. Or *The Fencing Master* (recall Marie Tempest, then so pert and frou-frou) with Marie brought up as a boy (and with that figure!) and completely deceiving the sporty Fortunio, rightful heir to the throne of Milan, the damn fool, as to her sex. Or *Martha*, with Lady Harriet, wearying of high life at the court of Queen Anne, disguising herself as a servant girl in search of a job and falling in love with a country bumpkin who turns out to be the only son of the Earl of Derby. Or *Madeleine* in which a slightly tired bachelor who has attained the age of one hundred years can lose twenty-five of them if one girl kisses him, another twenty-five if a second does, still another twenty-five if, without solicitation, a third does and, presumably, though the plot cruelly seemed to stop there, yet another ten, reducing his age to fifteen, if a fourth cutie were to deign to tickle his nose.

What nowadays do we most often get in place of such opium? In an *Are You With It?* an insurance actuary who makes a mistake in bookkeeping and in shame joins a sandlot carnival the romantic aspect of which is realistically registered by a fat colored woman, a brash stripteaser, and a couple of dwarfs, all given to the screeching of juke-box tunes. In a *Billion Dollar Baby* a gold-digger encouraged by her grafting mother to inflame the libido of a concupiscent old mug and get what money she can out of him. In a *The Duchess Misbehaves* a fashionable married female who poses in the nude for a department store janitor and who, when the painting is finished, spends the rest of the evening singing smutty songs the while she lifts her skirts above her navel. In a *Bloomer Girl* a boiler-house argument for women's rights. In a *Sadie Thompson* a prostitute who so overstimulates the lust of a quondam minister of the gospel that in remorse he commits suicide. In a *A Lady Says Yes* a hussy who goes on the miscellaneous make, and makes it. In a *Park Avenue* the spectacle of wholesale adultery. And so on.

Me, I'll take the old sentimental shows, however imbecile and lacking in sense.

[From *The Theatre Book of the Year, 1946–1947,* pp. 57–66.]

ON THE STRIP–TEASE

THE STRIP-TEASE art, which in the last five years has assumed a popularity previously not equalled even by virtuosi of the musical saw and professors of the Sawing a Woman in Two illusion, is hardly the latter-day phenomenon that most folk think it is. It was born forty-six years ago, and its mother— or rather grandmother—was a French baggage named Charmion. This Charmion subsequently toured the vaudeville houses throughout America for at least a dozen seasons and was during the period their star sensational attraction.

Although somewhat different from the act of her heirs and assigns, Charmion's performance was founded on the same general principle. That principle, as almost everyone now knows, is the gradual coy divestment of articles of feminine apparel to a sensuous musical accompaniment, and to the theoretical enormous stimulation of the masculine libido. But whereas the ladies presently do their divesting on a stage or some other such platform, Charmion did hers on a trapeze.

I remember her act well, child though I then was. (My father took me to see her no less than four times under the pretense that what interested him on the particular vaudeville bill was a trio of Swiss yodelers.) I say I remember her well, and if you think to insult me by allowing that a small boy's memory is not entirely to be trusted, I herewith prove it to your satisfaction, inch by inch.

A small dark hussy, Mlle. Charmion, clad in a long black satin cloak and with a large feathered black hat on her head, emerged elegantly from the wings. Bowing graciously and flashing her teeth in a provocative smile, she approached a lowered trapeze, deposited herself daintily upon it, and was raised aloft. The stage was darkened; a spotlight was centered on the beauty; and slowly the orchestra began to play.

Punctuating her process of déshabillé with many a cute

oo-la-la or winking tres-chic-n'est-çe-pas?, our siren now first took off her hat and dropped it to the stage below. Then followed her cloak, and our little pigeon was beheld in a dress of black silk, and with long black gloves. The gloves were discarded one by one, then off came the bodice of the dress, then off came the skirt. Mademoiselle was now in a long covering of pink petticoat, surmounted by an ample pink something or other. The latter was next in line for removal and was succeeded by the petticoat.

What one then observed was our Lorelei still in very sufficient black net underthings, black net stockings, and black satin slippers. The slippers were now the first to go, and after them came the net underthings—to the disappointment of the audience (doubtless including my father) revealing Mlle. Charmion in still more net underthings, albeit not quite so comprehensive.

By way of prolonging the terrible suspense, our temptress now maddeningly drew forth a small lace kerchief from her bodice and with a saucy gesture cast it aside. She thereupon added insult to injury by slowly adjusting a hairpin in her coiffure. But wait! One by one now off came the stockings, revealing a pink silk garter above each. Pause! And then, tantalizingly unfastening one of the garters, our Circe tossed it into the audience—and the lights went out and the act, with the person of our heroine still concealed in enough black net underwear to dress a whole present-day musical show chorus, was over.

Nevertheless, that was the birth of stripteasedom. True enough, any such evasion in strip-tease circles today would be sufficient to cause a mutiny in the United States navy, but we patriots need have no fear.

Since Charmion's day, the diaperphobe business has made great progress, and progress is the word. Not only have more and more remaining bodily concealments gradually been dispensed with in the name of the art, but the art itself has become a veritable industry. Despite the occasional interference by divers municipal authorities, by the police and by assorted moralists in mufti, the strip-tease has thrived in burlesque, which is its current chief home, in musical shows, in night clubs, in pleasure parks, honkytonks and carnivals, and, Will Hays or no Will Hays, even to a degree in the movies.

The most widely advertised of the later-day strippers is Gypsy Rose Lee (née Rose Louise Hovick), although Gypsy some time ago informed me she was, to quote her exactly, sick as all hell of the God damn business and rarin' to do something else. The daughter of a Pacific coast newspaper man, Gypsy invented what has come to be recognized as the modern strip-tease routine: the languorous removal seriatim of everything that the law allows, plus the suggested removal of that, too, just as the naturaliste undulates into the wings and out of sight of the audience. It was Gypsy also, who, if the records are accurate, first employed a purple spotlight to heighten the pseudo-Oriental atmosphere of her strip surroundings.

The other big shots in the exposing sorority are Ann Corio and Margie Hart. The former, whose name has erroneously been reported to have been derived from "anchor" as a tribute to the large burlesque sailor trade, is celebrated from coast to coast, has been at the game for a considerable time, was safely and respectably married to the same Irish husband for years, and draws the largest crowds in burlesque. Miss Hart, who is the best looker among the strippers, is of more recent vintage but has gained rapidly in popularity.

Less illustrious than any of these but familiar to addicts to the art are all kinds of other girls of all creeds, nationalities and color, including Chinese, Japanese, Irish, Danish, Swedish, French, Polynesian, Norwegian, Negro, and Bronx. There is, for example, the blonde Irish Della Carroll who for some years has dispayed her talent and epidermis not only in burlesque, but in night clubs both here and in London. There is Sen Lee, a Tahitian belle, known best to the night-club floor-show trade; and Noel Carter, English-American, who some months ago graduated directly from a Broadway burlesque stage to the fashionable Monte Carlo night club on New York's east side; and little Babette, family named Bernhardt, who bills herself as "The Tiniest Tease" and is something of an odzookens with the Middle Western connoisseurs; and Zorine, hardly to be confused with Zorina, who goes in for arty embellishments, calls her act *Sacrifice to the Sun God,* and duly and devoutly sacrifices to that deity everything but her G-string.

Also catering to the omnivorous trade are such artistes as Mary Blaine, a pert baggage who cracks funny jokes while baring her anatomy to the cognoscenti in Dave Rosen's *Stream-lined Follies* at the pleasure parks; the Latin Grace Carlos who features what she calls a teasing-tassel dance; the corpulent Margaret Gibson who kids Miss Carlos by doing much the same thing with a travesty slant; the blondissimo Alyn Payne who modestly permits herself to be billed as "The Versatile Venus" but whose versatility in song and monologue is considerably less impressive than her shape; and Peaches Strange, June St. Clair, Marcia Eloise and Linda Powers, genealogy unknown to this statistician and historian, who may be relied upon to pop the eyes of burlesque house Corinthians at least four times daily.

And I have skimmed only the surface. There are literally hundreds of other such houris with an allergy to clothing whom the strip industry has put more or less in the chips. Sherry Britton and the Chinese Noel Toy, for example, who pleasure the night-club trade; Maria Voe, who sheds a beaded costume bead by bead; Mariane Miller, who peels to the accompaniment of a hooch dance that knocks out the eyes of jack-tars even seated as far back in the burlesque theatres as row double-Z; Annette Cliff and Stella Miles, who substitute broad grins for the more usual faraway dreamy look while baring themselves to the breeze; Marie Cord, who lets go with a lusty soprano in the process of exfoliation; and the little Japanese Sue Loi, a newcomer to the sorority, who looks scared to death at the mere prospect of taking off even her hat. To say nothing of the experienced Georgia Sothern, who doesn't look at all scared of anything and goes to it on all cylinders; Elaine Park, erstwhile showgirl who won a recent strip contest at the National in Detroit and thus was graduated instanter into the professional ranks; and Trixie La Monte, Margie White, Florence Leeper, Donna Rogers, Doris Hudson, Sandra Lee and Rita Green, who even at the moment you are fascinatedly reading this are probably catching their deaths of cold by denuding themselves hourly somewhere or other in the Republic.

The highest salaried of all the burlesque strippers is Ann Corio, who draws down from seven hundred to eight hundred dollars a week. Miss Corio, however, is a girl with loftier ambitions and during the hot weather months periodically takes time off to appear in dramatic plays on the summer theatre circuit, courageously sacrificing her bank account and the applause of marines for her histrionic art and the applause of Connecticut and New Jersey society. Next to Miss Corio comes Margie Hart in the matter of reimbursement. Miss Hart, I am informed, rates as high as six hundred doughnuts weekly for revealing herself in *puris naturalibus,* and who am I to say she does not richly earn it?

While she was active in the industry, Gypsy Rose Lee topped both these ladies when it came to the mazuma, getting as high as two thousand a week, and sometimes more. But, as has been intimated, Miss Gypsy has latterly sought other means of expression, the cinema and belles lettres among them, and may no longer be considered strictly a member of the moulting aviary.

The weekly rewards of the other apostles of birthday clothes vary. Some of those who offer themselves to the pleasure-park trade get as little as twenty-five dollars for five shows daily, including Sunday; the night-club doffers draw anywhere from fifty dollars to two hundred; and some of the lesser burlesque baldies are lucky if they get fifty. In certain jitney burlesque joints and cabarets the star stripper is backed by a chorus line of six subsidiary strippers who get about twenty dollars a week for their exertions, when they get it.

Just what it is that makes one girl conspicuously successful in the strip-tease business and another not has baffled the experts, especially since both girls do exactly the same thing, that is, slowly take off their clothes. Yet the problem doesn't seem so difficult of solution. It isn't a matter of excellence of figure, as some maintain, since Gypsy Rose Lee herself once confided that her own figure was far from the kind adapted to the strip-tease. And some of the other girls who have triumphed at the box office similarly haven't enjoyed such shapes as have girls who have failed. Nor is it a variation of the strip-tease itself, as has been noted, since the strip-tease, wherever you find it, is much of a piece. And certainly it isn't beauty of face, as some of the most prosperous exponents of the art do not compare in looks with some of the least prosperous.

What it is, to judge from a punditical investigation over a considerable area, is manner pure and simple. One girl has it and another hasn't it. It consists in a relative delicacy of suggestion, in the trick of assumed modesty, in an appearance of disembodying the purely physical. I have seen dozens of strippers of the brazen school and not one of them, for all the applause of the hounds in the audience, has ever ultimately got much of anywhere. But those who have mastered the technique of sly innuendo, of factitious shyness, and of seeming to be publicly in the privacy of their own boudoirs, have gone places.

Toujours la femme.

[From *The Entertainment of a Nation,* 1942, pp. 218–24.]

ON THE BALLET

WHAT I am about to say will probably result in the denunciation of me as an obnoxious philistine, fit only for the company of halfwits and admirers of the art of Sir Walter Besant. However and nevertheless, I risk the indignation and say it. It is this. I offer you all but a relatively small portion of the modern art of the ballet for one American nickel. The remaining collop I'll keep for myself and, as for the considerable rest, if you haven't the nickel handy it is yours on the cuff.

I don't suppose this commercial transaction would be of any particular public interest if it were not for one fact. And that fact is the enormously increased American interest in the ballet during the last few years, not only in New York but in many other cities. Only in Australia, peculiarly enough, where a single ballet troupe not long ago enjoyed an unprecedented run of eight months in the three or four leading cities, has a greater increase in curiosity been manifested.

What leads me to my spuriously generous offer is the conviction that much of the modern ballet is a hybrid that is gradually getting to be less and less real ballet and more and more a freak form that vouchsafes all the beauty and grace of a one-armed Ubangi toying with a squab. There are exceptions, true enough, but the majority of the exhibits that I have honored with my attention impress me as being little more than very bad short plays, most of them with a minimum of sense, performed by mute actors suffering from incipient attacks of arthragra but doggedly determined that the show must go on.

In some instances, indeed, the nonsense has reached such a point that dancing in any genuine sense has been practically eliminated and has been supplanted by something that looks to any intelligent layman like a cross between an invisible doctor testing the cast's knee reflexes and the plebes' drill ground at the Culver Military Academy. William Saroyan's

The Great American Goof is a case in point. Not only is there no dancing in it worthy of the name, that is, outside a hospital ball for arteriosclerosis patients, but American speech has intermittently been provided the hoofers who, being foreigners, speak it like so many chipped Berlitz Russian and Swedish records. Supplement all this with scenery projected by colored magic-lantern slides which periodically act like jitterbugs and mingle an intended factory scene with a previous Ritz salon, or whatever it is meant to be, and you begin to get a faint idea that if you lay out that nickel I was talking about you will get the bad end of the bargain.

If, furthermore, you imagine that the aberrant Saroyan has been picked upon as a too easy horrible example your imagination needs looking into by a psychoveterinarian. There are a dozen boys and girls whose exhibits come pretty close to matching his, and another dozen who run him an even race.

Take a look, for instance, at something called *Mechanical Ballet*, by Adolph Bolm. Originally manufactured for the movies, it may be acceptable Hollywood but in any other place where bloom æsthetics on however modest a scale it is likely to impress the beholder as a paraphrase of Eugene O'Neill's *Dynamo* concocted by the Minsky family and performed by their uncles, cousins and nieces, in tights. It is possible that a stage full of characters called Dynamos, Gears, Pistons and Fly Wheels all jumping up and down to an accompaniment of bangs and clangs from the orchestra may be art in the minds of the more frenzied balletomaniacs, but to any slightly more realistic mind it seems to be merely a lot of obstreperous imbecility.

Or turn to the number called *Dark Elegies*. This one is the brain-child of Antony Tudor and consists in an effort to combine choreography with Gustav Mahler's song cycle, *Kindertotenlieder*. Inasmuch as Mahler composed his music after the death of a particularly beloved child and inasmuch, further, as it reflects his deep and intimate sorrow, the idea of accompanying it with a troupe of kickers and posturers comes about as close to the obscene and ridiculous as is humanly imaginable. The only analogous mixtures I can think of would be *Uncle Tom's Cabin* with whites in the Negro roles and Negroes in the white or a ballet founded on the *Internationale* and danced by a stageful of Republican senators.

Or, still again, for another example out of the humbug carload cast your eye upon something called *Hear Ye! Hear Ye!* Fabricated by a Miss Ruth Page with the connivance of Nicholas Remisov, this one seeks to dance a murder trial into a ballet. After flashing a number of tabloid scareheads on the curtain—"Murder in a Night Club," "Who Is Guilty?" etc.— we are vouchsafed a courtroom with judge on bench, jury in box, and a gross of wooden dummies representing the public in the spectators seats. Attorneys for the prosecution and defense get busy and then a series of flashbacks show seriatim the shooting of a male hoofer by a chorus girl, and the shooting of the selfsame hoofer by his male partner, each of the potshots being equally fatal. After each murder the jury proclaims the particular shooter guilty. At the conclusion, it turns out that a stray maniac did the dirty work, and the lawyers shake hands.

Now, gentlemen, I ask you! If such stuff, whatever the music and choreography, is appropriate ballet material, I resignedly await the day when we shall be treated to a ballet danced to the annual report of the Commissioner of Street Cleaning or choreography visited upon Jan Valtin's home life.

The more recent urge to Americanize the ballet has been responsible for some curios that outcurio almost anything this side of a believe-it-or-not museum. We have had everything from ballets showing roadside gas station operators imitating Nijinsky, as in the exhibit by the late American Lyric Theatre, to ballets displaying Russian dancers or their equivalents cavorting in far western ghost mining towns. Where the fatuity will stop, no one can tell. The time may not be distant when they will be laying the scene of *Scheherazade* in Columbus, Ohio, and when they will be having *Hommage aux Belles Viennoises* danced by the Four Inkspots.

The Messrs. Cole Porter and Gerald Murphy, otherwise honorable, have a lot to answer for. It was they who, nineteen years ago, inaugurated this sort of absurdity. Their job was called *Within the Quota* and was the first ballet with an American theme set to music by an American composer. I take the liberty of quoting the plot of the masterpiece as it has been succinctly recorded for posterity by that eminent antiquarian, Mr. Cyril W. Beaumont:

"An immigrant lands in America and before him pass, against a giant reproduction of an American daily newspaper, a cavalcade of American types—part real, part mythical—with which he is already familiar through visits to the cinema. His pleasures in these types is interrupted by a figure who assumes in turn the character of Social Reformer, Revenue Agent, Uplifter, and Sheriff. Finally the immigrant makes the acquaintance of the World's Sweetheart with the inevitable result, which brings the ballet to its conclusion."

That one is thrown in for extra good measure with the others, and all for the same nickel.

[From *The Entertainment of a Nation,* 1942, pp. 213–17.]

ON THE MOVIES

THE PROMISCUOUSLY voiced contention that absurd censorship
is responsible for the childish quality of the movies is sheer
flim-flam. Censorship has nothing to do with it. I have investigated carefully the deletions that have been ordered by the
various censorship bodies over a period of years and in not
a single case would any one of the pictures have been perceptibly better had it been allowed to remain intact. The
censors are idiotic, true enough; some of their recommendations are unbelievably asinine. But the pictures would have
been just as bad if they had not meddled with them. The
censors are the movie people's alibi. The latter groan that their
great masterpieces have been ruined because an overly damp
and prolonged smack or a Hun gouging out a doughboy's
eye has been snipped out of them, when, as a matter of fact,
the pictures have been given a modicum of gratifying subtlety,
albeit unintentional, and a relatively increased merit by these
very external interferences. Such pictures as the censors have
horned into more broadly I find to have been out-and-out rubbish in the first place: cheap-jack sensationalism about prosti-
tutes, social diseases and the like, on a par with the white-
slave pamphlets got out by the moralists ten or more years
ago, cheap-jack pornography and cheap-jack attempts at Continental sophistication. On such occasions as the movies have
tried to do anything even remotely endurable, it is to be noted
that the censors have very decently shut up. They didn't interfere with *The Last Laugh*; they not only let *The Big Parade*
and *What Price Glory?* alone, but even allowed them to do
and say things that, in the instance of the drama, would have
brought the police on at a gallop; they didn't harm *The Grand
Duchess and the Waiter* or any one of a dozen other such
attempts to lift the pictures out of the nursery book. All that
they cut out of the Russian picture, *Potemkin*, were a few
feet showing a wormy piece of meat and a baby having its

head mashed in, both of which were nauseating and unnecessary and rid of which the picture was better than before. And if they made *Variety* foolish in certain hinterland communities by converting the old fellow's inamorata into his wife, let us remember that they did nothing of the kind in the larger cities and that one can't judge the movies by Podunk any more than one can judge literature by Boston.

The movie censors have, contrary to what the movie press-agents have insinuated into print, actually done no damage to a single reputable picture that I can discover. They have even allowed the movies a wider latitude in the matter of morals than is presently allowed the drama. The suppressed plays, *Sex* and *The Virgin Man*, were baby fare compared with such freely circulated films as *Flesh and the Devil* or *A Night of Love.* If you tried to put on in the dramatic theatre such seduction scenes as you may see daily at any neighborhood movie parlor, you'd land in the cooler before you could say Malevinsky, Driscoll and O'Brien. All that the movie censors usually do is to change a few subtitles, awful garbage in the first place, cut out exaggerated gum-suckings and brassière-squeezings that any artistically intelligent director would never have put into the film, and object to elaborations of incidents that every writer with an ounce of dramatic ability would himself recognize at once as utterly nonsensical and entirely needless. If anyone can show me a single comparatively worthwhile movie that the censors have spoiled, I'll believe this gabble about censorship ruining the movie art. But until the news is brought to me, I decline to become a party to the movie people's howls.

Every act of vandalism that has been attributed to the censors will be found to have been confined to what, when it started out, was already unspeakable drivel. All that the censors have generally done is to make the drivel more drivelish. They have done some things that make one laugh at their ignorance, but the antecedent laughter at the movie people's ignorance in the case of the same picture has drowned out a considerable portion of laugh No. 2. If they have cut out scenes showing a woman going through the pangs of child-birth, so would any imaginative dramatist. If they have ordered out scenes showing a woman sewing sentimentally on baby clothes, they exhibit a critical sophistication highly to be commended. If they delete scenes showing gas-house ear-biting, they do no more than any half-way competent stage producer would do. The movie ignoramuses are simply up to their old trick of passing the buck. The only ones to blame for the abysmal stupidity of the movies are themselves. The circumstance that the censors have stolen some small coins out of their purse can't conceal the fact that the purse betrays an unmistakable resemblance to a sow's ear.

2

The movies will never be worth a hoot until the business end of the enterprise is absolutely and entirely separated from the actual producing department, and until nine-tenths of those presently in control of the latter are fired. Just as there never has been a magazine worth its salt that has got anywhere with a moneybags who meddled with its editorial content or one that has got anywhere when its financial, advertising and sales managers had anything to say about what went into its pages, so will there never be reputable movies until the money end of the business keeps its hands off. What few fairly worth-while pictures we have had will be observed to have been made by producers independent of the Zukors, Mayers, Foxes and other such financial padrones, by players or directors in command of their own destinies. I point, for example, to Chaplin's *The Kid,* Fairbanks' *Thief of Bagdad,* Griffith's *Broken Blossoms,* and to *Nanook of the North, Chang* and *Stark Love.* The other comparatively decent pictures that have come along from time to time have been the result of continuous fights with the money overlords on the part of directors and players, with the latter triumphing by hook or crook over the former's interposed hostility and objections.

To argue that the money men in the movies do not know their business is ridiculous. They do know it. The fact that almost every last one of them, before he went into pictures, was either a dinky fur salesman or an East Side push-cart vender and that now almost every last one of them is a millionaire, pretty well establishes the idea of business acumen.

What if they do waste money? It isn't their money but Wall Street's, and that makes not them bad business men but Wall Street. They have got and are getting all and more that is coming to them, you may be sure. The trouble with them, like the trouble with most successful business men, is that they aren't content to be simply successful business men, but wish to be something else besides. In the case of the movies, they want to be judges of dramatic literature, producers, artists. And as not a solitary one of them, on penalty of death, could tell you the difference between *The Two Gentlemen of Verona* and *The Gentleman from Indiana,* it is small wonder that their interference in the producing and acting end of the films has accomplished what it has.

3

The moving picture will never really find itself until it divorces itself from the drama. Some things, of course, the two are bound to have in common, but the pictures presently lean too heavily upon stage drama and too little upon their own possibilities and resources. Again, all contentions to the contrary on the part of champions of the movies are hollow. Many of the innovations attributed to the movies, rendering them distinct from the acted stage drama, have not been innovations at all, but simply borrowings from the theatre. Griffith's so-called inventions, hailed some years ago as marking a new era of originality and progress in filmdom, were actually mere bald steals from the theatre. His much-talked-of device of fade-outs was originated and used years before by William Gillette in the plays he wrote, staged and acted the leading parts in. His flashbacks were nothing more than the old Drury Lane and Hanlon transparent backdrop scrims wherein theatregoers of two generations ago used, while the hero or heroine was meditating in front of the grate-fire, to see scenes depicting the hero or heroine's childhood days and other such antecedent joys and aches. And his moving camera had its counterpart many years before in such stage productions as the Lilliputians' *Magic Doll,* with the steps of its walker through the forest followed, as some of you will recall, in exactly the same manner as in Griffith's photography. Griffith was an actor; he must have seen and remembered all these stage tricks; and when he became a director he took them over from the theatre with him.

But these are just tricks. The movie's real weakness lies in an attempt to cuckoo the drama's business and in the cuckooing to overlook and neglect what should be its own. The movie can never do the drama's work as effectively as the drama can, any more than dancing, even Pavlowa's, can, for all the trying, interpret music. The two are as intrinsically different as black and white. The movie must tell not the drama's stories in the drama's way, but its own stories in its own way. Now and again, it makes such an effort and the results point to what it may conceivably some day accomplish. *The Last Laugh* and *The Thief of Bagdad* are movie stories; the stage could not handle them; the movie can and does. So in the case of *The Big Parade*, at least that part of it that Stallings confected, though certainly not the cheap imitations of stage drama that the director inserted into the script. In the instance of *What Price Glory?*, those things in the drama that were finest on the stage are worst in the film, while those that could not, because of the limitations of the stage, be shown in the acted play, are the best.

The moving pictures, I need not say, are simply pantomime with a *compère* in the form of printed titles. Their limitations and possibilities are the limitations and possibilities of pantomime, plus only an elasticity in scenic environment and background and a gift for ocular legerdemain that stage pantomime cannot hope for. The best movie actors and actresses are expert pantomimists all cameras aside. Thus, Chaplin is a moving picture all by himself before a camera gets in front of him and starts grinding, as anyone is aware who has seen him do his confidential pantomimes of French farce and so on. The dramatic actor, off the stage, is a dog without a tail, without the dramatist he is nothing. But the competent movie actor is a competent movie actor with or without a camera. The camera should therefore be reserved chiefly—in the director's mind—for the externals of the movie story and the story itself be directed solely toward those players who are valuable pantomimic funnels. But what is generally the present system? It is to take the movie story away from the expert pantomimists and give it to the camera, in other words, to convert the camera into a dramatist. Well, the camera is not a dramatist and can never be one, and hence we get the current movie blobs. You can photograph pantomime and you can, further, photograph drama in so far as it is pantomime, but you can't photograph drama of any other kind, that is, and persuade anyone but a half-wit. You can't photograph, with the greatest camera ever invented, metaphysical drama, or the drama that lies in luscious, beautiful, moon-struck words, or the drama of wit, or the drama that emerges from the conflict of ideas. And that is what the movies, though they don't seem to be aware of it, often pathetically try in their simpleton way to do. They foolishly and vainly try to do such things as *Romeo and Juliet*, *A Woman of No Importance* and *Peer Gynt*, when all the while the world of honest pantomime stands knocking at their door.

If I were the captain of a movie lot, the first thing I'd do would be to tack up a sign with the word SILENCE on it in letters six feet high and not permit a single soul on the lot, directors, actors, camera men or what not, ever to utter a single word. Words get them into the habit of thinking and acting in terms of the speaking stage. They may not believe they do, but they do. It may sound foolish, but I'd make every one of them transact his share of the movie work in hand in pantomime, and I'd bank on the result. At its worst, it would at least be an improvement over the semi-callipygian stuff that the screen presently shows.

4

The movie as we see it by and large at the present time is simply a stage play, its unities corrupted, stripped of its words, and made to show all the scenes and episodes that the dramatist has, with artistic economy, laboriously succeeded either in deleting from his work or in keeping off stage.

5

If the motion picture ever hopes to be called an art by anyone besides the writers for the tabloid newspapers, it will first have to go into the back room, lock the door, sit down and take counsel with itself. And one of the first things it will have to persuade itself of will be this: that it will never get anywhere as an art simply by taking a generically static story and arbitrarily making it hop about, as it is presently doing. The mission of the motion picture is not to take what may be called a "still" story and give it legs that it doesn't need and that fit it grotesquely, but to take one full of movement and rid it of those static qualities that it might have, and unavoidably, as stage drama. However highly developed the movies may become, they will never be able to do such "still" plays as *The Lady from the Sea, Night Refuge, The Thunderbolt, Candida, The Father,* etc., one-thousandth so well as the theatre can do them. But, on the other hand, they may take galloping tales, aburst with fury and alarm, and do them in a manner that the stage cannot. Yet the movies seem to believe that everything is equally grist for their mill. They have utterly no sense of discrimination and the result is what amounts to nothing more than bastard drama. The movies can no more do the masterpieces of drama than the stage can do the masterpieces of prose literature, so let each concern itself with what it can do best. If the movies can't do *Hamlet,* neither can the stage do Conrad's *Youth* or *Heart of Darkness.* The difference between the drama and the movies is simply this: that the former knows it can't do such things and wisely refrains from an attempt to do them, whereas the movies ignorantly try to do everything and, as a consequence, cause a great nose-holding in the land.

6

That the moving pictures must be mindful that their job is different from that of the stage may be practicably indicated by observing a single phenomenon in connection with both of them. In the theatre, artificial scenery representing outdoor views is an accepted thing. Audiences accept it willingly for what it is supposed to be. They permit themselves illusion, as Coleridge pointed out, not by their minds' judging a forest scene, say, to be a forest but in a remission of the judgment

that it is not a forest. By all the rules, this should also be true
of the movies, but it happens that it isn't. It was true in the
beginning of the movies—when they were still a great novelty
—but it is true no longer, as anyone who has studied movie
audiences even superficially is aware. Show a movie audience
today an outdoor scene painted on canvas and shot within
studio walls and it will boo and snicker. It declines to remit
its judgment and properly, for it feels—yes, even a movie audience sniffs the fact—that the business of the movies is to be
absolutely realistic where the stage is artificial and (if I do
not give the movie audience credit for too much discernment)
on occasion artificial where the stage is sadly realistic. To put
it in plainer words, the movies are commanded to take advantage of their possibilities in the direction of realism, possibilities that are plainly beyond the stage's range, and of their
potentialities in the direction of artifice which, limited in the
case of the stage, cause the drama sometimes unfortunately
to be realistic against its will. Thus, in this latter regard, the
stage can never show a fairy tale so convincingly as the
movies, for the simple reason that, where the latter can achieve
the complete air of artificiality essential to such a story, the
stage at its best can only manage things half-way. On the
stage, there must always intrude a refractory note of realism
to dispel the illusion. The stage can evoke Cinderella's coach
only out of painfully realistic mick stagehands; the movies can
evoke it out of thin air. The stage can show a fairy princess
only in the disturbing Broadway flesh; the movies can show
her in misty intangibility. The stage, to speak of other than
tricks, for all its intention must remain visually realistic when
it tackles *Peter Pan,* whereas the movies may fully artificialize
the eye. That the movies, when they in turn tackle *Peter Pan,*
succeed in doing nothing of the kind simply proves that they
still so blindly follow the theatre that they botch what possibilities they have.

7

It is a trivial point, and one beneath the dignity of an old
professor, but I should like to inquire why those who have

wondered over the pull of the movies and the audiences they have drawn from the theatre haven't noticed how very much better-looking the girls are than those on the stage?

8

The extent to which the movies slavishly seek to emulate the drama, and in the act disembowel themselves, may be seen in their current practice of hiring playwrights right and left to work out scenarios for them. These playwrights, who, like everyone else, look on the movies merely as sucker-stuff to get easy money from, not only unload on the movies all the flap-doodle that they are too sensible even to suggest to the theatre, but have no more idea, however willing and eager they may be, of the real requirements of the movies than so many Holly-wood production managers. The number of fairly respectable movies that have been made since movies began are surely few and only one of these has been the result of a scenario prepared by a playwright. The rest have been made from scenarios manufactured by persons who were never near a theatre and who wrote for the camera purely in terms of the camera, even, in one case, where the idea was lifted over from a play that had been done on the stage.

Of all the playwrights, American and foreign, who have been imported to Hollywood, only one, Stallings, has shown the slightest sign of appreciating the difference between the screen and the stage and, by that mark, he is the only one of the lot who has been at all spectacularly successful—even from the movie-mongers' point of view. The rest have been misera-ble duds. There is no more reason why a playwright should make a good scenario writer than why a scenario writer should make a good playwright. Even more playwrights have come croppers in the movies than scenario writers like the authors of *Window Panes, The Jay Walker, The Woman Disputed,* etc., have come croppers as dramatists.

The movies are presently handicapped by the circumstance that they must all be fashioned with a single type of audience in mind, and that type the lowest. There are no different cir-cuits of movie houses, as there are in the case of theatres, and hence a single picture must be made to appeal to all kinds and conditions of movie-goers in the mass. In the theatre, things are different. There are the divisions in the so-called legitimate circuit, the big-time vaudeville circuit, the burlesque wheels, the little theatre chain, etc. Each of these can offer a specific fare, high or low, to appeal to the tastes of its own customers. In other days, there were the Syndicate circuit with its better grade of drama, the Stair and Havlin circuit with its second grade, the H. R. Jacobs and kindred 10-20-30 theatres with their knock-'em-down melodrama, and the stock company and other circuits. Theatrical entertainment was then, even to a greater degree than now, duly apportioned to the various strata of theatrical intelligence. But the movies never had such circuits or individualized playhouses and they haven't them yet. Consequently, a movie must be manufactured to meet the ten cent and two dollar trade on common ground. It succeeds in meeting the former.

The little theatre movement has begun to show faint signs of visiting itself upon the movie scene; already such playhouses catering to the minority taste are popping up here and there; and in them rests the artistic future of the films just as the artistic phase of the modern American drama found its birth in similar mangers.

It is difficult to understand why the moralists have failed to include in their uplift forays those quasi-religious spectacles which are periodically displayed in our midst. If anything in the world can succeed in ridding a people of its belief in God and Holy Writ, it is surely just such blasphemous and ridiculous exhibitions. It is doubtful that a hundred plays showing the carnalities of forty-five year old actresses and imitation Englishmen can persuade even a congenital imbecile of the romantic aspects of wenching, but I experience some travail in believing that the man who has just seen Jesus Christ in the person of a Lambs' Club actor in a Hepner wig will go around to church the following Sunday with much of his erstwhile gusto.

The visualization of divine and Biblical subjects by the drama and the moving pictures has undoubtedly done more to hasten the spread of agnosticism among the peasantry than all the engines of doubt and disbelief that have got up steam in the last two hundred years. The subjects of faith and the objects of religious worship may, save in a traditionally conventionalized manner, be pictured concretely only at the expense of a diminishing and sacrifice of such faith and worship. Time and custom have hallowed the symbol of the crucifix, whether in marble or ivory or oils, and fine art has brought its beauty and imagination to the establishment and furtherance of the spirit of the divine materials it has made its own. But when cheap playwrights and cheaper movie manufacturers, however lofty their purpose, lay hold of the same materials, they convert them into a species of pie theology and succeed magnificently in spreading a dangerous impiety and infidelity among a nation of dolts who must ever be kept in line by fear of the hereafter. It is pretty hard to believe that, after a journeyman electrician has seen Christ depicted in an exhibit like *Ben Hur* as a bunch of thirty-cent Mazda lamps, he will suffer quite the same humility that he did before. It is equally hard to believe that, after an advertising agent has beheld the Saviour in a show like *The Servant in the House* or *The Passing of the Third Floor Back* to be none other than a familiar endorser of Pelmanism, Muriel cigars and Lucky Strike cigarettes, he, in turn, will experience quite the feeling that he did previously. And it surely is no easy job to believe that, after thousands of morons have gone to such a moving picture as *The King of Kings* and seen the Son of God to be simply the actor who played the crook in *Alias Jimmy Valentine,* to say nothing of the fellow who fell so comically upon his stern in *The Ghost Breaker*—it is surely no easy job to believe that these morons will not come away rather more given to humanitarianism than they were when they went in. Herr Lang of Oberammergau has at least never cavorted in Broadway detective melodramas and farces, nor has he had photographs in the tabloids showing him playing golf in Hollywood.

But more important than all this, in the direction I have indicated, is the picturization by the movies of the Biblical miracles. It may, with a painful stretch of the imagination, be conceivable that a half-wit may be deeply impressed by the spectacle of a dozen fox-trotting habitués of the Cocoanut Grove in the rôles of the Twelve Apostles, but it must strain the imagination to the breaking point to believe that he longer regards the miracles taught to him in childhood as divinely inspired after he has seen them reproduced by film parlor-magic, the secrets of which he is made privy to by all the movie magazines. Reading of the miracles in the Bible, he is awed. But seeing them duplicated by a Los Angeles bald-headed man in puttees, he is simply made sniffish. He is like a child who regards his father as a great man when the latter pulls a rabbit out of a silk hat and whose faith in his parent's supernatural powers quickly vanishes when he later discovers that the hat contains a black velvet pocket in which the rabbit was concealed. Suckers no longer fall for the shell game after they know how it is done. And the movie devotee, being apprised of the fraudulent way in which the miracles are transferred to the screen, presently persuades himself that the miracles of old were negotiated in some equally fraudulent manner.

As I have hinted, the rank and file of the people must be kept in line by the police, whether mundane or celestial. A people that didn't believe in an Almighty God might constitute an intelligent nation, but it would prove a very tough customer to handle. At least one policeman would be needed to look after every single citizen, and the jails would have to be enlarged daily. The pseudo-holy plays and moving pictures are gradually converting former believers into skeptics, and skeptics, by a recognizably natural process, into criminals of one sort or another.

[From *Art of the Night*, 1928, pp. 1–119, 124–34.]

ON VAUDEVILLE

WHAT has killed vaudeville as much as anything else, I suppose, is the departure of what may be called the vaudeville
mood from life itself. The leisurely nonchalance, the caprice,
the happy irresolution that blessed living in the America of
another day have long since been drowned out by the loud
whirr of the machine that has got most of us in its grip. Even
among the rich, there is no leisure; there is only loafing. And
the difference is readily graspable. A gentleman has leisure;
a barbarian loafs. Taste, culture, experience and charm are
essential to an appreciation and execution of leisure; loafing
is the refuge of the unimaginative bounder. Vaudeville, like
the vanished hansom cab, the window tables at Delmonico's
and Sherry's, the four-hour lunches at Luchow's and checkers
at the Lafayette, has paid the price of modern speed, money-
grubbing and excited boredom. No longer is there time for
such things; no longer are ease and casualness part of our
lives; no longer are evenings to be sampled haphazardly.
"Dinner at 7:30 sharp; the theatre at 8:50 sharp; the motor at
11:05 sharp; supper at 11:20 sharp"—life has become sharp,
too sharp. Punctuality, once the privilege of princes, has become the command of stockbrokers. A cocktail, once a drink,
has become a drug; and a dinner, once an event, has become
an eventuality. Conversation has been supplanted by nervous
wisecracks fighting against time, and love is made in taxicabs.
Vaudeville was a symptom of the earlier dispensation, of a
time and a year when there was place for boyish fun and
simple nonsense and engaging unconcern. It was a kid game
for men in their kid moments. And men don't seem to have
such moments any more.

It is not that the old-time vaudeville show was a good show;
it often, certainly, was anything but that. It was rather that it
had an innocence and artlessness that made it appealing to

men who prefer to take their diversion in an easy-come-easy-go fashion instead of in the railroad-schedule manner imposed upon them by present-day theatrical managers and traffic cops. That is the trouble with amusement in America under existing conditions. It has become a business where once it was a pleasure—and that is true not only of the theatre but of drinking, under the strictures of Prohibition; of reading, under the strictures of book-of-the-month clubs; of dancing, under the boiled-shirt and boiled-collar strictures of gunmen-operated night clubs; of eating, under the protein and vitamin strictures of quack dietitians; and of almost everything else, including what the poets call love. Vaudeville, whatever its asininity, was at least to be taken casually and the worse it was the more jocular it seemed to fellows who didn't mind throwing away a dollar but who currently object to throwing away six to see the same *Schuhplättler* and acrobats performing in front of a diamond revue curtain instead of in front of the good old drop of Union Square peopled by Pepsin Gum, Moe the Tailor and Root Beer advertisements. No one complains about a drugstore sandwich, because a drugstore sandwich is taken for granted. But anyone has a right to complain if one gets a drugstore sandwich at Café de Paris prices.

[From *Testament of a Critic*, 1931, pp. 245–7.]

MARGINALIA

Thoughts During Intermission

I WONDER why it is that—

1. American actors with diction so slovenly that the mother tongue in their mouths sounds like the speech of an immigrant Polish barber nevertheless uniformly, when it comes to the two words "record" and "poem," articulate them with high-toned precision as "re-chord" and "poh-em"?

2. The characters in American plays representing young liberals usually wear suits that look as if two extra pairs of pants came gratis with them, are given to lipping innumerable unlighted cigarettes, and reserve their political and social ideals largely for the ears of the leading ladies?

3. Playwrights swoon with ecstasy at the sound of the word "Democracy" and would sooner die of cholera than define it in any such manner as being the theory that all men are born equal, notably in intelligence and wisdom, and that, even if they are not, they are bound to achieve those qualities if guaranteed complete independence from the influence of such as possess them?

4. The maids in middle-class American stage households seem never to wear garters?

5. The moment a second-rate playwright or song writer, hitherto a failure, has a Broadway box-office hit, he feels safe in constituting himself an authority on his art and becomes condescending to even the critics who have given him good notices?

6. A published poet may mention the moon sentimentally without criticism whereas even a first-rate musical comedy lyric writer will be derided if he does so?

7. Even the member of a theatre audience who thinks some such pun as referring to the Tennessee city noted for its imbecile censorship as *non compos Memphis* is amusing feels it

nevertheless incumbent upon him to shudder and dismiss it as beneath contempt?

8. Even very bad English actors never seem to be really as bad as they are?

9. Negro actresses, however otherwise beautiful, usually have feet that don't look right?

10. Middle-aged white actresses with henna'd hair, however immaculate they really may be, generally look a little soiled?

11. Whatever the nature of the stage lighting, even the smallest zipper on an actress' dress takes on the look of the Comstock lode?

12. Of all the various animals that have figured in plays, a horse has invariably looked to be the most uncomfortable and out of its element?

13. Though it was a rare season that at one time did not offer a play with a character designated as "Pablo, a peon," Pablo has not made an appearance even once in the last fifteen years?

14. The four-piece orchestras which are now and then hired to play entr'-acte music at the dramatic shows are seldom instructed in the nature of the play of the evening and regale the audience with such selections as "You're the Top," "Begin the Beguine," and "Dixie" for Euripides, Ibsen, and Chekhov?

15. Lady Percy's remark to Hotspur in *Henry IV* is generally believed to refer to one of the fingers on his hand?

16. One can usually much more readily foretell the resolution of good drama than bad and the ending of a fine drama is most often apparent whereas that of a pulp mystery play is relatively surprising?

17. More critics do not appreciate that one of the differences between a first-rate and second-rate dramatist is that the former thinks out his characters whereas the latter simply feels them out?

18. Though characters in plays have drunk champagne, brandy, Bourbon, Rhine wine, juleps, applejack, Montrachet, Chianti, cocktails, Madeira, sherry, ale, beer, punch, vodka, vermouth, rum, slivovitz, absinthe, gin, saki, and almost every other tipple known to Christendom, including most of the

liqueurs, there has never yet in the history of drama so far as I know been one who has drunk Scotch whisky straight?

19. Humor in criticism, however intelligent and searching, is generally looked at askance and privately deplored as corruptive of critical importance even by those who appreciate its appositeness and merit?

20. The better and worthier modern plays have seldom been those which have taken advantage of the latest developments and improvements in modern stagecraft?

21. The vanity of the average actor is so great that he has come to regard a critic's description of his performance as "adequate" as condescending and even a bit insulting, when "adequate," were he to look up its meaning in a dictionary, means "equal to the requirement or occasion" and "fully sufficient"?

22. No actor has ever failed to make an impression in the role of a drug addict or dope fiend, even when his performance has been a caricature of realistic characterization?

23. A cold in the head is always comical on the stage, and a sneeze downright hilarious?

24. In the plays dealing with the American Revolution no soldier has ever been shown as having carnal desires, much less demonstrating them?

25. Ibsen's *Rosmersholm* is customarily staged as if it had been lighted by Strindberg?

26. There is always one supernumerary in mob scenes who spoils everything by his seeming inability to restrain himself from staring out into the audience?

27. Negro servants in plays make their exits twice as slowly as white servants?

28. Many actresses can walk down a flight of stairs naturally but few can walk up without an air of self-consciousness?

29. A man and a woman character who declare their intention of making a new world for themselves never go about the business where they are but invariably depart for other quarters, usually indeterminate?

30. The proprietor of an Italian restaurant on the stage always comports himself as if he were afflicted with a benign St. Vitus dance?

31. However elaborate a stage dinner, there never seems to be any butter on the table?

32. A baby grand piano on the stage must always have a vase of flowers and at least one silver-framed photograph on it?

33. An actor who has few assets other than a deep voice and who reads his lines with great deliberation, even if they should not be read that way, is generally credited by the reviewers as being one of "authority"?

34. An actress known to be good-looking who plays a role which calls for her to indulge in a makeup that makes her look homely usually gets flattering notices from the reviewers, even if her performance isn't worth a nickel?

35. Audiences will always applaud a stage setting that contains a large crystal chandelier?

36. Music critics who on their nights off attend Broadway musical comedies sometimes praise scores which, if they were to hear them in a concert hall, would cause them to throw fits?

37. Actresses famous as great personalities are chiefly those who have had or have the manners of charwomen?

38. An actor has seldom if ever failed in the role of Napoleon Bonaparte?

39. A blonde actress is never fully satisfactory as a tragédienne?

40. One rarely if ever sees in the histories of the American theatre the name of Marc Lescarbot, who wrote its first acted play?

41. But one critic in England, David Garnett, and but one in America, your obedient servant, has even mentioned in the public prints the meaning of Hamlet's "country matters" speech to Ophelia and Malvolio's comments on the capital letters in the letter-reading scene, or has commented on the regular omission of one of the letters?

42. A reviewer who writes extravagant praise of a young playwright's first produced play will never confess his over-enthusiasm when the author's subsequent plays prove he was excessive in his view of the former's talents, but will elaborately qualify his doubts in order to persuade his readers that he was not a big fool in the first place?

43. In all the many plays in which a character has realis-

tically mixed Martini cocktails there has been only a single instance (*Town House*) where he has remembered to put an olive or onion into them?

44. Stage money never looks in the least like anything but stage money?

45. So few authorities on the American theatre seem to know that the first musical comedy written by a man of any American blood (he was part English) was *The Fashionable Lady* (1730) and that the author was one James Ralph?

46. A highly dramatic scene, however good, in a period play which involves an actor with trousers properly several inches above his shoe tops always waywardly seems just a bit comical?

47. Even those critics who write most rapturously about J. M. Barrie feel it necessary to do some apologizing for him?

48. The word "resin" has not been pronounced correctly by an American actor in the last forty years?

49. Actresses who act Shakespeare's inflammatory temptress, Cleopatra, customarily play her with such an imperious frigidity that it is a wonder Antony did not freeze to death in bed?

50. No actor, however incompetent, who has put a putty mole on his cheek and adorned himself with a seedy frock coat and stovepipe hat has failed completely in impressing the critics that he was a pretty good Lincoln?

51. It is usually overlooked in the treatises on the beginnings of realistic staging in the American theatre that a great sensation was caused simply by Mrs. John Drew's introduction of a carpet into one of the scenes in *London Assurance*?

52. It is not known that the only two four-letter words still believed never to have been spoken on the American stage were spoken by the late Richard Bennett during the New York run of *Jarnegan*?

53. No matter how bad the ad libbing of an actor when something goes wrong on the stage, it is sure to get a hand from the audience, which regards it not only as indicating remarkably quick thinking but as a pretty high grade of wit?

54. Heroic characters may be given to pipes or cigarettes but never to cigars?

55. I waste my time recording such trivial stuff as this and gaining a reputation for frivolity when I might be boring the

reader to death and earning a fine reputation by printing instead a dull essay on "The Relation of the Aristotelian Aesthetic to the Drama of Racine and Corneille"?

[From *The Theatre Book of the Year, 1948–1949*, pp. 70–6.]

Florenz Ziegfeld

THE DIFFERENCE between Florenz Ziegfeld and his imitators is illuminatingly revealed in a comparison of one of the Ziegfeld roof revues with such a show as John Murray Anderson's *What's in a Name?* This difference is not a matter of costumes —Anderson's are as beautiful as Ziegfeld's; it is not a matter of lighting—Anderson's lighting is, if anything, better than Ziegfeld's; it is not a matter of wit or humor or music—there is little if any wit or humor or music in the exhibitions of either the one or the other; it is not a matter of scenery—Anderson's is often as attractive as Ziegfeld's. It is, rather, that the touch of Ziegfeld is the touch of an artist, whereas the touch of such a man as Anderson is the touch of a showman. It is this touch of Ziegfeld's that takes a bag of canvas, costumes, lights and girls and converts the whole, with an unerring instinct for form, into something of fluid light, fluid color, and fluid beauty. It is this lack of touch that, in the instance of the Andersons, brings from the same bag a sometimes beautiful but always chaotic, and never fluid, vaudeville show.

It is only recently that Ziegfeld has been recognized for the man he is. In a theatre that holds David Belasco, Augustus Thomas and Nance O'Neil to be in their several ways great artists, it is not unnatural that a genuine theatrical artist, an artist of penetrating taste, fine feeling and delicate perception, should be overlooked. And not merely overlooked, but shouldered aside, at the mere thought of him, with breezy derision. And so it came about that this Ziegfeld, save for the clear vision of the few who observed in him the temperament and execution of the real craftsman of the theatre, was slow to be recognized for the fine skill that is his. It is, of course, as difficult for the average American theatregoer, who habitually confuses the Swiss cheese with the mustard, to persuade himself that an artist and a music show may in any way be related as it is for him to recognize the artist in a man who, like George Ade, writes in slang or in one who, like Montague Glass, writes mere magazine stories about the low-comedy creatures of the cloak-and-suit trade.

There is no producer in the world today who, in his field, in any degree approaches to this Ziegfeld. I have sat under them all. Out of the vulgar leg-show, Ziegfeld has fashioned a thing of grace and beauty, of loveliness and charm. He knows colors as a painter knows colors; he knows form; he knows quality and mood. He has lifted, with sensitive skill, a thing that was mere food for smirking baldheads and downy college boys out of its low estate and into a thing of symmetry and bloom. To appreciate what he has done, it is only necessary to have surveyed the efforts of such of his competitors as Butt and de Courville in England, Meinhard in Germany and Volterra in France. A man of manner in its nicest sense (rather than in its indiscriminate sense of tribute to any actor who doesn't pull up his trousers when he sits down), the fellow is. And those who see in his *Follies* and *Frolics* merely a number of young women running around the stage half-naked are the same yokels who believe that Brieus, the amiable satirist of *Les Hanneton,* is an inferior artist to Brieux, the indignant literalist of *La Robe Rogue.*

As to the claims of the others who, opposed to this Ziegfeld, are regarded as truer artists of the native theatre, Schopenhauer did away with such as Belasco when he observed that "It is essential to a work of art that it should give the form alone without the matter. . . . This is really the reason why wax figures produce no æsthetic impression and, therefore, are not, in the æsthetic sense, works of art at all; although if they were well made they produce an illusion a hundred times greater than the best picture or statue could effect; so that if deceptive imitation of reality were the object of art, they would have to take the first place." As for Thomas, recall Derely's "In an age when the struggle for life has become more exclusive than ever, is it not an empty anachronism to represent on the stage only the struggle for women?" And of such as O'Neill, her celebrated fellow-mime's, "The actor may mark with his imprint the parts that he interprets; but his imprint must be so well confounded with the reality of the personage as not to be realized by the spectator without reflection and comparison. . ." It took the American theatre ten years to realize that George M. Cohan had other talents than catarrh and hair that bobbed up and down. It has taken the American theatre quite as long to realize that Ziegfeld has other talents than Martha Mansfield and Lillian Lorraine.

[From *The Theatre, the Drama, the Girls*, 1921, pp. 145–8.]

The Dog as Actor

THERE was recently exhibited a motion picture named *The Eternal Triangle,* the story of which was enacted entirely by dogs. And not merely enacted—as the average Broadway play is enacted by the bipedal mime—but enacted intelligently, vividly and, in spots, almost brilliantly. I can, indeed, at the moment think of no more than *six* American actors who could have given a performance of the leading rôle any more effective than that vouchsafed it by the amazing Airedale who was engaged for the part. Here, plainly enough, we have a new light upon the actor and the business of acting. Those who are happy to regard acting as a high art, as an art calling for acumen, imagination, inventiveness and a lofty craftsmanship and fancy, must here surely find something slightly confounding. Imagine a dog taking Mozart's place!

That the dog may be the actor of the future is perhaps an even easier assumption than that maintained by such champions of the marionette as Gordon Craig and Anatole France. Whatever my misgivings personally, it is only fair to admit that there are many indications that point in this direction, and these indications are not lightly to be dismissed even by one like myself who finds some difficulty in accepting seriously an hypothesis that wears so absurd a mask. Yet, ridding oneself of prejudice and looking into the problem with as clear an eye as is possible under the apparently grotesque circumstances, one encounters a number of significant facts. In the first place, this dog performance of the story of the "eternal triangle"—regarded from the soundest level of criticism—is superior in almost every detail of dramatic projection to the recent local projection of any play dealing with the "eternal triangle" save alone Emmanuel Reicher's exposition of *Lonely Lives*. Compared with the recent acting of *When We Dead Awaken* in the Neighborhood Playhouse, it is a masterpiece. Compared with the amateur performance of *Aglavaine and Sélysette*, another triangle drama, revealed two seasons ago— a veritable histrionic gem.

That the dog is often an excellent actor hardly needs proof. The brilliant performance of the dog in Frederick Ballard's *Young America* is well remembered. The portrayal of a drunkard by the dog in Officer Vokes' familiar act is immeasurably superior to any American actor's portrayal of a drunken man in the last fifteen years—with perhaps the two exceptions of Edward Fielding in *Your Humble Servant* and Bruce McRae's admirable bit of work in *The Gold Diggers*. The astonishing *Dog Town* act in vaudeville with its company of practised Spitzes needs no citation. The incredibly fine performance of the dog in Alexandra Carlisle's company at the Empire some nine or ten years ago (I can't remember the name of the play; only the dog's performance remains vivid in my memory); the equally fine performance of a dog in a comedy called *The Young Clarissa*, enjoyed by trans-Atlantic voyagers in Milan in 1912; the world-famous performance of the lady dog Françine in the pantomime at the Concer Maillol; the marvellous dog Teddy in the Mack Sennett buffooneries; the human dogs of Alf Loyal; the compelling dog comedian who bears a remarkable resemblance to the late Weedon Grossmith and serves as the star of the Gaudsmith Brothers' act; the inimitable *Spare Ribs* who played with Claude and Fannie Usher for thirteen years; the amazing dachshund in Golman's famous Continental act; the Michael of Miss Laurette Taylor's original *Peg o' My Heart* troupe whose rôle, even the most prejudiced will grant, no actor could have played one-half so well—these provide further testimony to the dawning peril of the current pantaloon. Even as I write, indeed, one of the younger American producers is planning a dramatization of Ollivant's *Bob, Son of Battle*, with a well-known circus dog in the star rôle.

What has made *Uncle Tom's Cabin* one of the richest of American theatrical properties? The bloodhounds. For one person who goes to the theatre to see the play, there are two who—drawn by flamboyant posters—go to see the dogs. In the instance of tank-town companies where the rôles of the dogs have been played by actors (*vide* C. R. Miller's 1911 enterprise), the companies have quickly gone broke. George Bernard Shaw, so he has told Austin Harrison, had in mind, at the time just before he set to work on *Androcles and the Lion,* a Biblical play in which a dog figured conspicuously. He has told Harrison that he abandoned the play because he knew that the dog would, in the lingo of the theatre, run away with the play and would thus, irritating the vanity of his colleagues, bring Shaw a financial loss by breaking up the company in the middle of the engagement. Shaw therefore decided to write *Androcles,* let an actor play the spurious lion, and so insure a peaceful, harmonious acting company.

There are many reasons why the dog makes a good actor. Initially, unlike his bipedal rival, he belongs to no union and hence corrupts his work with no politics. Nor does he squander his time in clubs discussing the toothsomeness of this or that houri and the superiority of Cosmo Hamilton to Ibsen. He is faithful, respectful, eager to serve and to obey. If he does not obey he may be made to obey with a whip, whereas it is illegal to strike an actor in New York, Connecticut, Massachusetts, Idaho and South Carolina. Even in England, indeed, it is forbidden to hit an actor save with a vegetable. On the Continent, of course, . . .

More and more it becomes manifest that the old order giveth way to the new. In a day like the present, where literacy is no longer essential to the actor, where one of the best actors on our stage actually cannot read and has to learn his lines from a dictaphone, the human mime rapidly gives round to the canine. We have already seen Thackeray's *Rose and the Ring* enacted beautifully by wooden marionettes; we have already seen *Pomander Walk* done more brilliantly by babies of six and eight years than by its adult company; we have already seen *Othello* done well in the Lafayette Theatre by a company composed, aside from its Othello, Iago and Desdemona, of ignorant Negro elevator boys and unlettered black laundresses. We have seen that human intelligence may be no more necessary to the business of acting, however essential it may once have been, than it presently is to the become mechanical business of adding up a difficult column of figures and getting fine music out of a piano. The dog has already played an important part in Red Cross work and in the Police Department. And the time is perhaps not far off when his picture will be adorning the covers of the *Theatre Magazine, Variety,* and the *Dramatic Mirror.*

[From *The Theatre, the Drama, the Girls,* 1921, pp. 152–7.]

The Dramatized Novel

WHILE a cheap and commonplace novel may, I suppose, be dramatized and exhibited on the stage without damage either to the cheap, commonplace novel or to the cheaper and more commonplace customers of such theatrical stuffs, a reputable novel no more lends itself to completely satisfying drama than a reputable painting does to a completely satisfying lithograph. That, indeed, is what even the best novel dramatizations are: dramatic lithographs. They catch the external look and color of the original; they catch the scene and even some of the mood; but they fail to catch what never can be caught, to wit, that technical exactitude and precision of essence which makes a work of art what it is and which can no more be unblurringly duplicated in a secondhand copy than the clear, sharp outline of a typewriter's script can be caught by a carbon. Every art is a law unto itself and the borderlands between them are treacherous with difficult mountain passes and sinister gulleys. The occasional bridges joining one with another are at best rickety and dubious and result only in such triumphs of bastardy as talking moving pictures, grand opera and interpretive dancing. The dramatized novel thus takes its place alongside the novelized drama. Both are anomalies, freaks: robots in falseface, two distinct arts Siamesed with boloney skins.

[From *Testament of a Critic,* 1931, pp. 250–1.]

In the Matter of Criticism

IT is not criticism that the loudest yodelers against criticism object to, but the printing of criticism. Oral criticism, though it be exactly like the published criticism, you will find they don't in the least object to. It is criticism set down in black and white that disquiets them. The average man, called a *lausbub'* by another man, simply laughs it off with genial unconcern. But the moment the other man calls him a *lausbub'* in print, he gets hot under the collar.

[From the *American Mercury*, July 1925, p. 354.]

The Russian and the American Dramatist

THE RUSSIAN dramatist is one who, walking through a cemetery, does not see the flowers on the graves. The American dramatist is one who, walking through a cemetery, does not see the graves under the flowers.

[From *The Theatre, the Drama, the Girls*, 1921, p. 166.]

The Stage as a Profession

CHOOSING the stage as a profession, American women make a much better showing than American men for the same reason that Englishmen make a much better showing than American men. Women, and Englishmen, are actors by nature.

[From *The Theatre, the Drama, the Girls*, 1921, p. 92.]

Tragedy

TRAGEDY, as we know, can be the loftiest form of drama, but the promiscuous dogmatic identification of it as being *per se* superior to comedy on the score of its greater profundity is without sense or reason. Is *The Trojan Woman* anywhere near so profound as some of the comedies of Aristophanes? Is *The Cenci* as profound in its way as *The Way of the World* is in its? Are several of O'Neill's tragedies any more profound than several of Shaw's comedies? Let us be rid of ready-made definitions. The great purge quality of *Medea* is the talk of pundits; is there not as much so-called purge in the laughter of Congreve? Language can of course persuade, and beauty of writing exalt, but is not also such to be found in the finest comedies? Tradition, however, is tradition, and hard to down. Because the Greeks and Shakespeare have given us tragic masterpieces, tragedy has automatically and with no further inquiry been *ipso facto* accepted as the acme of dramatic art. The form has been confused with the performance. The venerating adjective "serious" has been miscellaneously pasted on the bottles without due regard to the worth of their contents. The defeat and downfall of man are more inspiring than his victories and triumphs. Crucifixion without Ressurrection has become the strange faith and ideal of drama criticism.

[From *The Theatre Book of the Year, 1949–1950*, pp. 232–3.]

An Actress' Charm

AN ACTRESS is charming on the stage in the degree that her audience imagines she is charming off the stage.

[From *The Theatre, the Drama, the Girls*, 1921, p. 43.]

Drama

WHAT literature does at night.

[From *Testament of a Critic*, 1931, p. 179.]

All really great drama is a form of scandal.

[From the *American Mercury*, September 1929, p. 122.]

The Actor as Gigolo

THE ACTOR is the gigolo of dramatic art.

[From the *American Mercury*, September 1929, p. 122.]

Great Drama

GREAT drama is the souvenir of the adventure of a master among the pieces of his own soul.

[From *The World in Falseface*, 1923, p. 3.]

Female Acting

IN the business of female acting, sentiment demands slenderness. The moment sentiment weighs 135 pounds, it becomes comedy; the moment it touches 136, it becomes farce; the moment it goes to 140, it becomes burlesque.

[From the *American Mercury*, September 1929, p. 117.]

The Child and the Actor

THERE never lived an actor so proficient in his craft that he could not learn something from watching a child. All children are natural actors—save nine-tenths of those on the stage.

[From the *American Mercury*, September 1929, p. 121.]

Abacus Britannicus

MUCH of the contemporary English polite comedy writing suggests a highly polished and very smooth billiard table with all the necessary brightly poised cues, but without balls.

[From *Encyclopædia of the Theatre*, 1940, p. 3.]

Melodrama

OF all forms of theatrical entertainment, melodrama possesses perhaps the greatest intrinsic integrity. As the stage is designed primarily to exaggerate and intensify life, so melodrama is similarly designed. Thus, more exactly than comedy, tragedy, farce or satire, does melodrama meet the demands of the stage. Comedy touches life too closely to come within the accurate, fundamental, unadorned principle of the theatre. Tragedy is but another form of comedy, a paraphrase, so to speak. Farce exaggerates life, but does not, by virtue of its humors, intensify it. And satire is, obviously, not a pure theatrical form. Melodrama alone meets the theatre's every law and by-law. It is the blood of the stage.

[From *The World in Falseface*, 1923, p. 37.]

Acting Success

IT has been said, foolishly, that no actor has ever failed as Hamlet. It might better be said, and wisely, that no actor has ever succeeded as Lear.

A ham is, simply, any actor who has not been successful in repressing his natural instincts.

[From the *American Mercury*, July 1942, p. 109.]

The Theatre

MEN go to the theatre to forget; women, to remember.

[From the *American Mercury*, July 1926, p. 376.]

The Hero in the Theatre

IN the popular theatre, a hero is one who believes that all women are ladies; a villain one who believes that all ladies are women.

[From the *American Mercury*, September 1929, p. 121.]

Drama as Literature

DRAMA is literature. But literature is not necessarily drama. That is why good literary critics often prove themselves poor dramatic critics.

[From *The World in Falseface*, 1923, p. 12.]

Actors' Aspirations

HAS there ever been an actor who did not aspire to be, at the same time, something else: a painter, a writer, a social favorite, a musician,—something to make him, in the eyes of the world, not merely an actor?

[From *The World in Falseface*, 1923, p. 17.]

Poetry in the Theatre

THE FALL of kings calls for a splendor of prose or poetry, otherwise it may be quite as unimpressive as the fall of little men. But the tragedy of the little man, to be as impressive as that of a king, calls as well for such treatment.

[From *The Theatre Book of the Year, 1948–1949*, p. 285.]

Hollywood

HOLLYWOOD is the worst of the dope peddlers because it sells its opium under a false label. Its customers pull at the pipe in the belief that it is harmless and, when finally they give it up, find that they are still helplessly dreaming the former delusions.

[From *The Theatre Book of the Year, 1948–1949*, pp. 300–1.]

Musical Show

THE MUSICAL show, in a word, is like the other fellow's wife or sweetheart. For one man who shares his taste, there are always those who wonder what he can see in her. Some of the wisest men I know relish such shows; some of the wisest men I know cannot abide them.

[From *The Theatre Book of the Year, 1948–1949*, p. 239.]

The Spectator's Imagination

IT is only the second-rate, third-rate or fourth-rate play that, deficient in imagination, encourages independent imagination in the spectator. It piques his disappointment into fanciful wings of his own. It stimulates imagination by virtue of imagination's very absence. As with a starved man's vision of a banquet, the auditor dreams and, dreaming, finds his imagination kindled. The poor play, as a matter of fact, imposes the necessity of so much imagination upon him that it often completely exhausts him.

[From *The Theatre Book of the Year, 1948–1949*, pp. 256–7.]

Musical Comedy

MUSICAL comedy is the pastry of the stage and sentiment is as inevitably a part of it as it is of patriotism, love, or old cuspidor heirlooms.

[From *The Theatre Book of the Year, 1948–1949*, p. 63.]

Jean-Paul Sartre

HE is his decade's foremost theatrical confidence man, which in view of the strong competition is no mean achievement. . . . His fecundity in such directions as philosophy, politics, sociology, the novel, the short story, the cinema and the drama is that of a rabbit, yet he seems to operate under the delusion that his reproductions are not rabbits but lions and tigers, whereas even the rabbits he factually delivers himself of are of the mechanical toy variety, stuffed with the sawdust of borrowed ideas.

[From *The Theatre Book of the Year, 1948–1949*, p. 223.]

Poets in the Theatre

POETS in the theatre, it appears, should be heard, not seen. And even if they are merely heard and not seen, the commercial results are not luxuriant, as Susan Glaspell found out with her play about Emily Dickinson, *Alison's House,* and as Martha Graham learned in another direction when she staged a talking ballet about the same poetess.

[From *The Theatre Book of the Year, 1947–1948*, p. 147.]

Negroes in the Theatre

WHENEVER the late Florenz Ziegfeld was at a loss what to do in one of his *Follies*, it was his wont to bring on the girls. Whenever a producer, whether of musicals or drama, is nowadays at a similar loss for an idea, he brings on the Negroes. It is thus that we have had them in everything from Aristophanes to Shakespeare, from Gilbert and Sullivan to Shaw, and from *The Show-Off* to *Arsenic And Old Lace*.

[From *The Theatre Book of the Year, 1947–1948*, p. 255.]

One-Day Drama

MANY of our current playwrights feel that they have contrived something extra-commendable if they contain the action of their plays within a single day. Most often the time economy is transparently arbitrary and fraudulent. Drama in *life* on only the rarest occasions confines its course to twenty-four hours. Much more often it ploughs slowly over days, months, and years before reaching its resolution.

[From *The Theatre Book of the Year, 1947–1948*, p. 269.]

Symbolism

WHAT often seems to impressionables to be symbolism in the plays of some contemporary playwrights is nothing but confusion of thought presented as deliberate intelligence.

[From *The Theatre Book of the Year, 1947–1948*, p. 269.]

Test of a Comedian

THE TEST of a real comedian is whether you laugh at him before he opens his mouth.

[From the *American Mercury*, September 1929, p. 122.]

Vaudeville

VAUDEVILLE is a species of entertainment derived from the dregs of drama and musical comedy assembled in such wise that they shall appeal to the dregs of drama and musical comedy audiences.

[From the *American Mercury*, September 1929, p. 117.]

French Sex Plays

IF the French, light wines and dancing of course aside, prefer anything above sex itself, it is plays that dissect it as if it were a cross between a peculiarly exotic disease and one of Torquemada's more complicated instruments of torture. Nothing is so paradoxical in the Gallic psychology. It isn't that the Frenchman does not find amusement in the farces and comedies which treat the subject instead as if the larger part of life consisted in hiding under beds or in clothes closets; it is rather that the amusement he gets in such instances does not compare with the rewarding agony he delightedly derives from the dramas in which love, whether sacred or profane, is diagnosed as comparable to a beautiful case of smallpox.

[From *The Theatre Book of the Year, 1949–1950*, p. 262.]

Emotion in the Theatre

WHAT the theatre saw and the movies do not see is that a popular audience, though it may react to the same old emotions, in due time will find its response diminishing unless the old emotions are filtered into it in some fresh and improved way. The theatre remains an undying institution because it educates its audience's emotions. The films have become increasingly moribund because they merely reflect and echo their audience's already experienced and set emotions, and because they reflect and echo them without any advance or let-up.

[From *The Theatre Book of the Year, 1949–1950*, p. 59.]

Sex and Dirty Words

HAROLD HOBSON, dramatic critic for the London *Sunday Times* . . . after a recent, brief visit here reached the annoyed conclusion that it is our theatre in particular that is obsessed by sex. I beg leave to amend his finding. It is not obsessed by sex nearly so much as it is by dirty words more or less related to sex.

[From *The Theatre Book of the Year, 1949–1950*, p. 119.]

English Actors

ASIDE from what talent they may or may not demonstrate, many of them have that carriage-trade air that makes a deep impression on our theatregoers, particularly such as are doomed to plebeian buses and subways. The unfortunate English player who hasn't it and can offer only professional ability in its stead has a rougher road in America, as the failure of Charles Laughton, Donald Wolfit, Valerie Taylor, and various others seem to indicate. But let one have the look and manner of a tubercular who is conscious of a mild stench in his vicinity yet who conceals his awareness of it in a painfully executed polite smile and the American will esteem him as a very high-toned and fashionable creature indeed.

[From *The Theatre Book of the Year, 1950–1951*, p. 34.]

The Playwright as Writer

THE THEORY that a playwright is necessarily and inevitably a writer is advanced by people with no education in etymology or, obviously, by those whose experience of the theatre is extremely limited. Anyone who goes to the theatre more or less regularly these days is made perfectly aware that any number of contrivers of plays—which is what the word playwright means—are writers merely and only in the sense that they put things down on paper, like composers of laundry lists or most blank verse.

[From *The Theatre Book of the Year, 1950–1951*, p. 54.]

Sex on Broadway

THE SUBJECT of sex, to be prosperous on Broadway, must generally be handled either sensationally or with the brand of sentiment that reflects more or less exactly the audience's own. Intelligence and sharp insight may not necessarily make it unpalatable, but they are likely to make it dull for the mass of theatregoers who, posture as they will, find satisfactory diversion not in a playwright's exercise of his mind but rather in his exercise of his characters' bodies.

[From *The Theatre Book of the Year, 1945–1946*, p. 211.]

Dramaturgy and Diplomacy

DRAMATURGY must again, in short, if it would be successful with audiences, abandon the iron fist and return to diplomacy. Set, ringing speeches, the penchant of the propaganda dramatist, must further give way to insinuation and to a play's natural, easy flow.

[From *The Theatre Book of the Year, 1945–1946*, p. 174.]

CHRONOLOGY AND BIBLIOGRAPHY

1882: Born on February 14 in Fort Wayne, Indiana

1904: Graduated from Cornell University

1905–6: On editorial staff of the New York *Herald*

1906–8: Dramatic critic and associate editor of the *Bohemian Magazine* and *Outing*

1908–10: Writer on the theatre for *Harper's Weekly*

1909–14: Writer on the theatre for *Associated Sunday Magazines*

1908–23: Dramatic critic of the *Smart Set*

1912–29: Dramatic critic for a national syndicate of newspapers

1915–16: Dramatic critic (with James Huneker) of *Puck*

1922–35: Dramatic critic of *Judge*

1935–6: Dramatic critic of *Life*

1914–23: Co-editor (with H. L. Mencken) of the *Smart Set*

1924–5: Co-founder and co-editor (with H. L. Mencken) of the *American Mercury*

1924–30: Dramatic critic of the *American Mercury*

1925–30: Contributing editor of the *American Mercury*

1930: Dramatic editor of the *New Freeman*

1924–34: Contributing editor of *Arts and Decoration*

1930: Editorial contributor and guest critic for the London *Daily Express*

1930–5: Dramatic critic of *Vanity Fair*

1932: Co-founder and co-editor (with Eugene O'Neill, Theodore Dreiser, James Branch Cabell, and Ernest Boyd) of the *American Spectator*

1937: Dramatic critic of the *Saturday Review of Literature*

1935–46: Dramatic critic of *Esquire*

1937–8: Dramatic critic of *Scribner's*

1937–40: Dramatic critic of *Newsweek*

1940–51: Dramatic critic of the *American Mercury*
1940–2: Dramatic critic of *Liberty*
1943– : Dramatic critic of the New York *Journal-American*
   and King Features national syndicate
1951– : Dramatic critic of *Theatre Arts*
1937–9: President of the New York Drama Critics Circle

❀   ❀   ❀

1913: *The Eternal Mystery*
1914: *Europe after 8:15* (with H. L. Mencken and Willard
   Huntington Wright)
1916: *Another Book on the Theatre*
1917: *Bottoms Up*
1917: *Mr. George Jean Nathan Presents*
1918: *A Book without a Title*
1919: *Comedians All*
1920: *Heliogabalus* (with H. L. Mencken)
1920: *The American Credo* (with H. L. Mencken)
1921: *The Theatre, the Drama, the Girls*
1922: *The Critic and the Drama*
1923: *The World in Falseface*
1924: *Materia Critica*
1925: *The Autobiography of an Attitude*
1926: *The House of Satan*
1927: *The New American Credo*
1927: *Land of the Pilgrim's Pride*
1928: *Art of the Night*
1929: *Monks Are Monks*
1931: *Testament of a Critic*
1932: *The Intimate Notebooks of George Jean Nathan*
1933: *Since Ibsen*
1934: *Passing Judgments*
1936: *The Theatre of the Moment*
1937: *The Avon Flows*
1938: *The Morning after the Night Before*
1940: *Encyclopædia of the Theatre*
1941: *The Bachelor Life*
1942: *The Entertainment of a Nation*
1943: *Beware of Parents*

1943, 1944, 1945, 1946, 1947, 1948, 1949, 1950, 1951: *The Theatre Book of the Year*

Mr. Nathan is contributor to the *Encyclopædia Britannica* and the *Britannica Book of the Year,* editor of the *Theatre Book of the Year* Dramatic Library, honorary member of the London Critics Circle, and American member of the Maximilian Society of London, England.

EPILOGUE

The World of George Jean Nathan is a faithful reprint of Nathan's publisher Alfred A. Knopf's personal tribute to the "Irreverent Dean of American Drama Critics." The book was published forty-five years ago as part of the seventieth birthday celebrations (mostly stag parties) for the co-founder and first president of the New York Drama Critics Circle. Nathan never wrote for the *New York Times*, yet he was the highest paid drama critic ever, the long acknowledged leader of the American critical fraternity and an internationally known literary figure. His epigrammatic prose style, full of linguistic foolery, dazzling exuberance, virtuoso verbal twists and paradox was never dull, always entertaining. The style's purpose: to keep readers talking and thinking about what Nathan loved most — the Theatre and its literary face, the Drama.

No less a critic and dramatist than George Bernard Shaw wrote him in the winter of 1950, "Attaboy! I hope you write a thousand more. I like your stuff, and rank you as Intelligent Reader and Playgoer Number One."

This volume's editor, the late Charles Angoff, was a younger contemporary who worked with Messrs. Nathan and partner H.L. Mencken in the 1920s on the staff of their legendary magazine, *The American Mercury*. Mr. Angoff liked Mr. Nathan and admired his way of life. His selections reflect his particular preference for Nathan's tongue-in cheek social commentary upon his contemporaries' mores and culture. Less than one-half of the anthology is devoted to dramatic and theatrical criticism, although Nathan was above all a drama critic. For example, Angoff chose to include the last chapter of *Beware of Parents*, but not a classic statement of George Jean

Nathan's aesthetic credo, the foreword to *The World in Falseface* (1923). The anthology editor was a man of his times. One should note that in 1952 readers were familiar with Nathan's vigorous, practical, in-the trenches criticism and it seems clear that Angoff delighted in his subject's amusing and intentionally provocative digressions on life. To George Jean Nathan all the world was, quite literally, a stage, upon which eventually appeared all that was human. Good writing with witty styling kept his readers rapt through arid theatrical seasons.

Indeed, the 1951-52 season was so abysmal that he refused to memorialize it with his usual annual volume, instead writing a new essay "On Monthly Magazines" for *The World of George Jean Nathan*, and waiting in the hope that a second season might bring more of dramatic value. He continued to attend the theatre an average of four times a week — at age seventy-one! A sample attendance record for the 1928-29 season: out of 225 productions on the boards, Nathan saw 208 shows and referred to 161 in print. He loved the Theatre and his service to the Drama was through his allegiance to Criticism as a companion art.

His last book, *The Theatre in the Fifties*, (1953), ranged widely over the State of the Theatre, Shaw, foreign imports, musicals, actors, critics and reviewers and of course, playwrights — both old and new. He speaks of Arthur Miller's *All My Sons* and *The Crucible*, *The King and I*, Lillian Hellman's *Little Foxes* and Horton Foote — all of current interest in the 1996-97 New York season! He corectly foresaw (and bemoaned) the development of "director's theatre," with playwrights and their plays as "little more than tools and toys of egotistical self and box-office masseurs." The issues Nathan discusses in his final volume are fresh today and ready for a new generation to consider.

The following year he was seriously ill. He had periodically been troubled with neuralgia for years, but this was ATH — arteriosclerosis. The disease was diagnosed as acute and he realized he was going to die. The longtime bachelor announced his engagement to the second love of his life (the first was Lillian Gish), the ethereal actress Julie Haydon. They had met in 1935 on the set of Hecht /MacArthur's film *The Scoundrel* with Noël Coward, and Miss Haydon had been a constant in his life since the late thirties. They were married at sea by the Captain of the Grace Lines' *S.S. Santa Rosa* on June 19, 1955. Nathan was seventy-three and Haydon just forty-five years old — the first and only marriage for both. The couple honeymooned in Curacao, visiting the Ernest Hemingways in Cuba en route.

Back in Manhattan, the Nathans maintained a Victorian marital living style. She moved from the Algonquin Hotel across the street with her terrier, Maxim, to quarters above his in the Royalton Hotel. He kept the same suite, lined from floor to ceiling with books, that had been home for fifty years. Mr. Nathan continued as much as possible his professional writing discipline, but by 1956 was no longer able to go regularly to the theatre. He gave up his position on *Theatre Arts* magazine and his nationally syndicated column for Hearst's King Features. (Never a newspaper man, he had taken on the column in 1943 at the dying wish of his friend, Bill Curley, who proceeded to make a full recovery, but held Nathan to his promise.) It was the end of an era. Henry Lewis Mencken, his fellow literary bad boy of the teens and twenties, died the same year. Together they had knocked out the old dual iron corsetry of American puritansim and sentimentality to make room for the best of European dramatists and new American writers, ushering in the new era of psychological realism. America had been dragged, kicking and screaming, into the literary twentieth century. He had long since done what he had set out to do.

In early 1957 Nathan, the old iconoclast, told his wife to telephone nearby St. Patrick's Cathedral and request instruction in the Roman Catholic faith. Father Charles MacManus was deputed to visit the caged lion. He found Nathan chair- and bed-bound, being cared for full time by Julie Haydon and a valet whose Christian name was Nathan. Over a period of months George Jean Nathan uniquely converted himself by a method of dialogue with the priest in a form of Medieval dialectic, which Nathan always initiated. He was received into the Church with Walter and Jean Kerr acting as "godparents." What had no doubt begun as an emotional attachment dating from his mother Ella Nirdlinger Nathan's Notre Dame Convent school friendship with Eugene O'Neill's mother, Ella Quinlan O'Neill, became intellectual commitment.

In January 1958, George Jean Nathan's preface to Ralph Ginzburg's *An Unhurried View of Erotica* appeared, beautifully presented, complete with slipcase.

> My friend Ralph Ginzburg has a mind alert to all the various idiosyncrasies of censorship and knows the different imbecile turns it has periodically taken. There are some shrewd pictures of the censorship mind psychologically illustrated by some strange delvings into the muddy waters of the Ganges. His book, I think, will go a long way to analyze and purify censorship of its muddy stink. It should add a valuable dose of history to the disgraceful general picture of the Bluenose as it has poked into and disturbed the American scene.

During the same period, Arnold Gingrich convinced him to write an essay for *Esquire*. Despite the fact that Nathan was paralyzed and the piece had to be dictated to his wife, "Memories of Fitzgerald, Lewis, and Dreiser" ran to seven oversized pages of prose containing all the excitement and writing muscle of a young man. It was published posthumously in the *Esquire* Silver Anniversary issue XXV in October 1958.

George Jean Nathan had died in his hotel home, his wife near him, the previous April 8 at age 76. His last will and testament designated half of his not inconsiderable estate to establish the richest prize in the American Theatre, and the only award of its kind then and now, the George Jean Nathan Award for Dramatic Criticism. Harold Clurman was the first recipient.

To his wife he left the remainder of the estate with the instruction "Go to the colleges and universities, there lies the future of the American Theatre."

Let me invite a new generation to begin an evaluation of George Jean Nathan and American dramatic criticism with a valediction from William Saroyan:

> George Jean Nathan never had anything "instructive" to say about the "writing" of plays, but he knew more about the Theatre than anybody else I've ever talked with. He . . . both invited and compelled participation . . .
>
> And all of a sudden he was sick, and it was terrible . . .
>
> And then he died and Broadway was diminished enough not to be thought of seriously again.
>
> Did he really do anything for Broadway, for New York, for America, for the Theatre, for Art, for Life?
>
> Yes he did. He dressed neatly and went out

among the thieves and assassins ... He ... berated and scorned frauds of all categories. And he wrote ... And everything he wrote had laughter in it. He was one of the most serious men in the living world, ... but he refused to burden his writing, or his readers, with the agony of his unconverted and apparently indestructible soul ... There can't ever be anybody like him again.*

Patricia Angelin

Literary Executrix,
The George Jean Nathan Estate

*Permission is granted by the trustees of the Leyland Stanford Junior University.

THE LIFE OF THE DRAMA

by ERIC BENTLEY

"The most adventurous critic in America."

—Kenneth Tynan

"Eric Bentley's radical new look at the grammar of theatre...is a work of exceptional virtue, and readers who find more in it to disagree with than I do will still, I think, want to call it CENTRAL, INDISPENSABLE...If you see any crucial interest in such topics as the death of Cordelia, Godot's non-arrival...THIS IS A BOOK TO BE READ AGAIN AND AGAIN."

—Frank Kermode, *The New York Review of Books*

"*The Life Of The Drama*...is a remarkable exploration of the roots and bases of dramatic art, THE MOST FAR REACHING AND REVELATORY WE HAVE HAD."

—Richard Gilman, *Book Week*

paper • ISBN: 1-55783-110-6

SLINGS AND ARROWS
THEATER IN MY LIFE

by Robert Lewis

"A decidedly good read. Breezy, intelligent, and chatty. A stylish, entertaining, and above all theatrical book."

—*The New York Times Book Review*

"He's a marvelous storyteller: gossipy, candid without being cruel, and very funny. This vivid, entertaining book is also one of the most penetrating works to be written about the theater."

—*Publishers Weekly*

"The most interesting book about the theater since Moss Hart's *Act One*."

—**Clifton Fadiman**

"A superior performance."

—*The Los Angeles Times*

paper•ISBN 1-55783-244-7

THE SMART SET:
GEORGE JEAN NATHAN
& H.L. MENCKEN

More than any other critic, George Jean Nathan was responsible for the emergence of Eugene O'Neill to the forefront of the American theatre. He blew the trumpets for him season after season, badgered the Broadway producers to do him, shamed the Theatre Guild into sponsoring him, and then watched the momentum of all these campaigns culminate in the Pulitzer, and eventually, the Nobel Prize. It was Nathan who discovered James Joyce's *Dubliners* and published it in *The Smart Set*. F. Scott Fitzgerald was first recognized by Nathan, who published Fitzgerald's first fiction in *The Smart Set*. And when Fitzgerald needed a model for a lively drama critic in his novel *The Beautiful and the Damned*, Nathan was immediately and perfectly cast.

Thomas Quinn Curtiss has reunited Nathan with his cohort, H.L. Mencken, together with the rest of their set. This is a biography of an era of men whose stories could only be written by an eyewitness.

ISBN 1-55783-312-5• HARDCOVER

THE COLLECTED WORKS OF HAROLD CLURMAN

Six Decades of Commentary on Theatre, Dance, Music, Film, Arts, Letters and Politics

edited by Marjorie Loggia and Glenn Young

"...RUSH OUT AND BUY *THE COLLECTED WORKS OF HAROLD CLURMAN*...Editors Marjorie Loggia and Glenn Young have assembled a monumental helping of his work...**THIS IS A BOOK TO LIVE WITH;** picking it up at random is like going to the theater with Clurman and then sitting down with him in a good bistro for some exhilarating talk. This is a very big book, but Clurman was a very big figure."

JACK KROLL, *Newsweek*

"**THE BOOK SWEEPS ACROSS THE 20TH CENTURY,** offering a panoply of theater in Clurman's time...**IT RESONATES WITH PASSION.**"

MEL GUSSOW, *The New York Times*

CLOTH •ISBN 1-55783-132-7 PAPER • ISBN 1-55783-264-1